NEW INTERNATIONAL BIBLICAL COMMENTARY

New Testament Editor,
W. Ward Gasque

2 CORINTHIANS

New Testament Series

NEW INTERNATIONAL BIBLICAL COMMENTARY

2 CORINTHIANS

JAMES M. SCOTT

Based on the New International Version

© 1998 Hendrickson Publishers, Inc.
P. O. Box 3473
Peabody, Massachusetts 01961–3473
U.S.A.

First published jointly 1998, in the United States by Hendrickson Publishers, and in the United Kingdom by the Paternoster Press,
P. O. Box 300, Carlisle, Cumbria CA3 0QS
All rights reserved.

Printed in the United States of America

ISBN 0–943575–98–2

First printing — August 1998

Library of Congress Cataloging-in-Publication Data

Scott, James M.
   2 Corinthians   /   James M. Scott.
     (New International biblical commentary. New Testament series; 8)
   Includes bibliographical references and indexes.
   ISBN 0–943575–98–2 (paper)
    1. Bible. N.T. Corinthians, 2nd—Commentaries. I. Title. II. Series: New International biblical commentary; 8.
BS2675.3.S36   1998
227'.3077 — dc21   98–22047
                                                                        CIP

British Library Cataloguing in Publication Data
A catalogue record for this book is available
from the British Library.

ISBN 0–85364–943–X

Scripture taken from the HOLY BIBLE, NEW INTERNATIONAL VERSION. Copyright © 1973, 1978, 1984 International Bible Society. Used by permission of Zondervan Bible Publishers.

Table of Contents

Foreword vii

Abbreviations xi

Introduction 1

   §1   Opening (2 Cor. 1:1–2) 17
   §2   Thanksgiving (2 Cor. 1:3–11) 23
   §3   Accusations (2 Cor. 1:12–2:13) 34
   §4   Glory (2 Cor. 2:14–4:6) 59
   §5   Body (2 Cor. 4:7–5:15) 102
   §6   Ambassador (2 Cor. 5:16–6:2) 133
   §7   Self-Commendation (2 Cor. 6:3–10) 147
   §8   Hearts (2 Cor. 6:11–7:4) 150
   §9   Repentance (2 Cor. 7:5–16) 165
   §10 Gift (2 Cor. 8:1–9:15) 173
   §11 Accusations (2 Cor. 10:1–18) 193
   §12 Boasting (2 Cor. 11:1–12:13) 203
   §13 Visit (2 Cor. 12:14–13:10) 242
   §14 Closing (2 Cor. 13:11–14) 260

For Further Reading 269

Subject Index 273

Scripture Index 280

Foreword
New International Biblical Commentary

Although it does not appear on the standard best-seller lists, the Bible continues to outsell all other books. And in spite of growing secularism in the West, there are no signs that interest in its message is abating. Quite to the contrary, more and more men and women are turning to its pages for insight and guidance in the midst of the ever-increasing complexity of modern life.

This renewed interest in Scripture is found both outside and inside the church. It is found among people in Asia and Africa as well as in Europe and North America; indeed, as one moves outside of the traditionally Christian countries, interest in the Bible seems to quicken. Believers associated with the traditional Catholic and Protestant churches manifest the same eagerness for the Word that is found in the newer evangelical churches and fellowships.

We wish to encourage and, indeed, strengthen this worldwide movement of lay Bible study by offering this new commentary series. Although we hope that pastors and teachers will find these volumes helpful in both understanding and communicating the Word of God, we do not write primarily for them. Our aim is to provide for the benefit of every Bible reader reliable guides to the books of the Bible—representing the best of contemporary scholarship presented in a form that does not require formal theological education to understand.

The conviction of editor and authors alike is that the Bible belongs to the people and not merely to the academy. The message of the Bible is too important to be locked up in erudite and esoteric essays and monographs written only for the eyes of theological specialists. Although exact scholarship has its place in the service of Christ, those who share in the teaching office of the church have a responsibility to make the results of their research accessible to the Christian community at large. Thus, the Bible scholars who join in the presentation of this series write with these broader concerns in view.

A wide range of modern translations is available to the contemporary Bible student. Most of them are very good and much to be preferred—for understanding, if not always for beauty—to the older King James Version (the so-called Authorized Version of the Bible). The Revised Standard Version has become the standard English translation in many seminaries and colleges and represents the best of modern Protestant scholarship. It is also available in a slightly altered "common Bible" edition with the Catholic imprimatur, and the New Revised Standard Version appeared in 1989. In addition, the New American Bible is a fresh translation that represents the best of post–Vatican II Roman Catholic biblical scholarship and is in a more contemporary idiom than that of the RSV.

The New Jerusalem Bible, based on the work of French Catholic scholars but vividly rendered into English by a team of British translators, is perhaps the most literary of the recent translations, while the New English Bible is a monument to modern British Protestant research. The Good News Bible is probably the most accessible translation for the person who has little exposure to the Christian tradition or who speaks and reads English as a second language. Each of these is, in its own way, excellent and will be consulted with profit by the serious student of Scripture. Perhaps most will wish to have several versions to read, both for variety and for clarity of understanding—though it should be pointed out that no one of them is by any means flawless or to be received as the last word on any given point. Otherwise, there would be no need for a commentary series like this one!

We have chosen to use the New International Version as the basis for this series, not because it is necessarily the best translation available but because it is becoming increasingly used by lay Bible students and pastors. It is the product of an international team of "evangelical" Bible scholars who have sought to translate the Hebrew and Greek documents of the original into "clear and natural English . . . idiomatic [and] . . . contemporary but not dated," suitable for "young and old, highly educated and less well educated, ministers and laymen [sic]." As the translators themselves confess in their preface, this version is not perfect. However, it is as good as any of the others mentioned above and more popular than most of them.

Each volume will contain an introductory chapter detailing the background of the book and its author, important themes, and other helpful information. Then, each section of the book will be expounded as a whole, accompanied by a series of notes on items in the text that need further clarification or more detailed explanation. Appended to the end of each volume will be a bibliographical guide for further study.

Our new series is offered with the prayer that it may be an instrument of authentic renewal and advancement in the worldwide Christian community and a means of commending the faith of the people who lived in biblical times and of those who seek to live by the Bible today.

W. WARD GASQUE

Abbreviations

Common abbreviations

A.D.	Anno Domini (in the year of our Lord)
B.C.	Before Christ
ch(s).	chapter(s)
lit.	literally
LXX	Septuagint
MT	Masoretic Text
NIV	New International Version
NRSV	New Revised Standard Version
NT	New Testament
OT	Old Testament
p(p).	page(s)
par.	parallel
sc.	namely
trans.	translator
v(v).	verse(s)
vol(s).	volume(s)

Pseudepigrapha

Apoc. Ab.	*Apocalypse of Abraham*
Apoc. Mos.	*Apocalypse of Moses*
Apoc. Zeph.	*Apocalypse of Zephaniah*
Ascen. Isa.	*Ascension of Isaiah*
2 Bar.	*2 Baruch*
1 En.	*1 Enoch*
2 En.	*2 Enoch*
Gk. Apoc. Ezra	*Greek Apocalypse of Ezra*
Jos. Asen.	*Joseph and Asenath*
Jub.	*Jubilees*
L. A. E.	*Life of Adam and Eve*
Mart. Isa.	*Martyrdom of Isaiah*
Ps.-Philo	*Pseudo-Philo, Biblical Antiquities*
Pss. Sol.	*Psalms of Solomon*
Sib. Or.	*Sibylline Oracles*
T. Ben.	*Testament of Benjamin*

T. Dan	*Testament of Dan*
T. Gad	*Testament of Gad*
T. Jud.	*Testament of Judah*
T. Job	*Testament of Job*
T. Jos.	*Testament of Joseph*
T. Levi	*Testament of Levi*
T. Mos.	*Testament of Moses*
T. Reu.	*Testament of Reuben*
T. Zeb.	*Testament of Zebulun*

Rabbinic literature

b.	Babylonian Talmud
B. Bat.	*Baba Bathra*
B. Meṣiʿa	*Baba Meṣiʿa*
Ber.	*Berakot*
Deut. Rab.	*Deuteronomy Rabbah*
Eccl. Rab.	*Ecclesiastes Rabbah*
ʿErub.	*ʿErubin*
Exod. Rab.	*Exodus Rabbah*
Gen. Rab.	*Genesis Rabbah*
Ḥag.	*Ḥagigah*
Ker.	*Kerithot*
Lev. Rab.	*Leviticus Rabbah*
m.	Mishnah
Mak.	*Makkot*
Meg.	*Megillah*
Menaḥ.	*Menaḥot*
Midr. Ps.	*Midrash Psalms*
Num. Rab.	*Numbers Rabbah*
Pesiq. Rab.	*Pesiqta Rabbati*
Pesiq. Rab Kah.	*Pesiqta de Rab Kahana*
Pirqe R. El.	*Pirqe Rabbi Eliezer*
Qidd.	*Qiddušin*
Qoh. Rab.	*Qohelet Rabbah*
Ruth Rab.	*Ruth Rabbah*
Sanh.	*Sanhedrin*
Šabb.	*Šabbat*
Šebu.	*Šebuʿot*
Song Rab.	*Song Rabbah*
Sukka	*Sukka*
Taʿan.	*Taʿanit*
Tg. Hos.	*Targum Hosea*
Tg. Isa.	*Targum Isaiah*
Tg. Onq.	*Targum Onqelos*
Tg. Ps.-J.	*Targum Pseudo-Jonathan*
Yebam.	*Yebamot*
Zebaḥ.	*Zebaḥim*

Josephus

Ant.	*Antiquities*
Life	*Life*
War	*Jewish War*
Ag. Ap.	*Against Apion*

Dead Sea Scrolls

CD	*Damascus Document*
1QH	*Thanksgiving Hymns*
1QM	*War Scroll*

Apostolic fathers

1 Clem.	*1 Clement*

Journals, series, and reference works

AB	Anchor Bible
ABD	*Anchor Bible Dictionary*
ABRL	Anchor Bible Reference Library
AGJU	Arbeiten zur Geschichte des antiken Judentums und des Urchristentums
AnBib	Analecta biblica
ANRW	*Aufstieg und Niedergang der Römischen Welt*
BAGD	Bauer, Arndt, Gingrich, and Danker, *Greek-English Lexicon of the New Testament and Other Early Christian Literature*
BETL	Bibliotheca ephermeridum theologicarum lovaniensium
BHT	Beiträge zur historischen Theologie
BJS	Brown Judaic Studies
BTB	*Biblical Theological Bulletin*
CBQ	*Catholic Biblical Quarterly*
CBQMS	Catholic Biblical Quarterly Monograph Series
CRINT	Compendia Rerum Iudaicarum ad Novum Testamentum
DJG	*Dictionary of Jesus and the Gospels*
DPL	*Dictionary of Paul and His Letters*
DSD	*Dead Sea Discoveries*
EvQ	*Evangelical Quarterly*
HTR	*Harvard Theological Review*
ICC	International Critical Commentary
IEJ	*Israel Exploration Journal*
JBL	*Journal of Biblical Literature*
JJS	*Journal of Jewish Studies*
JQR	*Jewish Quarterly Review*

JSJ	*Journal for the Study of Judaism in the Persian, Hellenistic, and Roman Period*
JSNT	*Journal for the Study of the New Testament*
JSNTSup	Journal for the Study of the New Testament: Supplement Series
JSOT	*Journal for the Study of the Old Testament*
JSOTSup	Journal for the Study of the Old Testament: Supplement Series
JSPSup	Journal for the Study of the Pseudepigrapha: Supplement Series
JTS	*Journal of Theological Studies*
NHC	Nag Hammadi Codices
NICNT	New International Commentary on the New Testament
NovT	*Novum Testamentum*
NovTSup	Novum Testamentum, Supplements
NTS	*New Testament Studies*
OTP	*Old Testament Pseudepigrapha*
RB	*Revue biblique*
RevExp	*Review and Expositor*
RevQ	*Revue de Qumran*
SBLDS	Society of Biblical Literature Dissertation Series
SBLSBS	Society of Biblical Literature Sources for Biblical Study
SBLRBS	Society of Biblical Literature Resources for Biblical Study
Schäfer	Schäfer, Peter. *Synopse zur Hekhalot-Literatur,* Texte und Studien zum antiken Judentum 2; Tübingen: Mohr Siebeck, 1981.
SJT	*Scottish Journal of Theology*
SNTSMS	Society for New Testament Studies: Monograph Series
SPB	Studia post-biblica
ST	*Studia theologica*
STDJ	Studies on the Texts of the Desert of Judah
TBei	*Theologische Beiträge*
TDNT	*Theological Dictionary of the New Testament*
TDOT	*Theological Dictionary of the Old Testament*
THAT	*Theologisches Handwörterbuch zum Alten Testament*
TLNT	*Theological Lexicon of the New Testament,* ed. C. Spicq
TSAJ	Texte und Studien zum Antiken Judentum
WBC	Word Biblical Commentary
WMANT	Wissenschaftliche Monographien zum Alten und Neuen Testament
WUNT	Wissenschaftliche Untersuchungen zum Neuen Testament
ZNW	*Zeitschrift für die neutestamentliche Wissenschaft*

Introduction

Second Corinthians is part of the lively correspondence between the Apostle Paul and the congregation he founded on the Peloponnesian coast of Greece in ca. A.D. 50–51. In all likelihood, 2 Corinthians is not the "second" letter of Paul to the Corinthians, for he mentions two other letters, which are probably no longer extant: one sent before the writing of 1 Corinthians (cf. 1 Cor. 5:9), and another sent between the writing of 1 and 2 Corinthians (cf. 2 Cor. 2:3–4). Hence, 2 Corinthians is at least the apostle's fourth letter to the Corinthians, written in ca. A.D. 55/56.

Second Corinthians reveals much about Paul's conception of himself, as he vigorously defends his apostolic claim in Corinth against internal dissension and external intrusion. However, since Paul gives us only his response to the developing situation in the Corinthian church, we must try to piece together a complete picture of the church from often sketchy evidence. Indeed, 2 Corinthians presents such an intractable complex of exegetical problems that Pauline scholarship has been unable to come to any consensus on them.[1] The following commentary represents merely one attempt to get at the meaning of the text within its original historical, literary, and theological context.[2]

1. Occasion and Purpose of the Letter

Between the writing of the letters we now call "First" and "Second" Corinthians, the situation in Corinth had changed dramatically. When Paul wrote 1 Corinthians, his apostleship was not yet under attack within the Corinthian church, though its significance was being diluted by the many other "guardians" who were gaining influence (cf. 1 Cor. 1:10–12; 4:15). In 1 Corinthians, Paul could therefore point to his apostolic weakness and suffering as a basis of authority and exhortation (cf. 1 Cor. 2:3–4; 4:8–17), for at the time of the writing of 1 Corinthians, the problem was largely *within* the church, not between the church and its apostle.[3]

When he wrote 2 Corinthians, however, Paul's legitimacy as an apostle was itself being called into question *because* of his weakness and suffering. Under the influence of the "false apostles" (cf. 2 Cor. 10:4, 13–15), some within the church were interpreting Paul's apostolic lifestyle of suffering and weakness as a sure sign that his claim to be a true apostle of Jesus Christ was fraudulent. The devastating effects of these sufferings on his mortal body were taken as proof positive that Paul was far from the God-appointed mediator of the life-giving Spirit that he claimed to be.

Obviously, Paul's foothold in Corinth was slipping, and he had to do something to secure his position before it was too late. Everything he had worked for during the eighteen-month founding visit (cf. Acts 18:1–18) was beginning to unravel. So when the crisis first began to develop shortly after the writing of 1 Corinthians, Paul changed his travel plans as originally announced in 1 Corinthians 16:5–9 and made an emergency trip to Corinth. It was now his intention, after visiting the church there and settling matters himself, to journey north into Macedonia and then return again to Corinth on his way to Jerusalem. By doing so, he hoped to give the Corinthians a "double pleasure" (2 Cor. 1:15–16).[4] When Paul arrived in Corinth, however, he found himself the object of a painful attack (2 Cor. 2:5; 7:12). A faction within the church, led by an unnamed member, evidently slandered Paul, while the congregation as a whole stood idly by, perhaps out of fear (cf. Gal. 2:12) or complicity. Paul does not mention what the nature of the offense was, but we may surmise that it had something to do with Paul's apostolic authority.[5]

Rather than trying to solve the problem right then and there and possibly precipitating a purge in the process (cf. 1:23; 13:10), the apostle decided to retreat temporarily from Corinth and allow a cooling-off period. Hence, instead of returning to Corinth after journeying to Macedonia, he changed his travel plans once again by making his way straight back to Ephesus (2 Cor. 1:23; 2:1). From there he shot off a scathing letter, written "out of great distress and anguish of heart and with many tears" (2:3–4). This "tearful letter," which is probably no longer extant,[6] called upon the Corinthians to demonstrate their solidarity with Paul and to punish the one who had offended him (2:3, 4; 7:8, 12).

The letter was presumably delivered by Titus, one of Paul's trusted coworkers. In any case, it was from Titus, returning from his visit to Corinth, that Paul expected news of the Corinthians' response to his letter, apparently confident of a positive outcome (2 Cor. 7:14–16). Paul planned to meet Titus in Troas, so he left Ephesus and made his way there. He found an excellent evangelistic opportunity in Troas, but because Titus had not yet come, and because he was so anxious to meet him and to find out how the Corinthians had responded, he left, traveling northward and crossing over into Macedonia in hope of intercepting Titus on his way to Troas (2 Cor. 2:12–13). When Paul reached Macedonia, he found himself embroiled in the bitter persecution that the churches of Macedonia themselves were experiencing (7:5; 8:1–2), and this only compounded his anxiety. When Titus finally arrived, Paul was greatly comforted at the news of the Corinthians' repentance and reconciliation (7:5–7, 13–16). Titus told Paul of the Corinthians' zeal to demonstrate their affection and loyalty by punishing the one who had slandered him.

Paul responded to this good news by writing another letter, our 2 Corinthians. Here he stated how glad he was that the Corinthians had acted so vigorously to clear themselves. He urged them now to forgive and restore the offender "in order that Satan might not outwit us" (2:5–11). The tone of this part of the letter is overall quite positive.

We must not get the impression, however, that all was well again in Corinth and that the apostle had no more cause for concern, for the situation that had prompted his emergency visit to the city was still festering. A careful reading of 2 Corinthians itself reveals that only an uneasy truce had been reached, and the final outcome had yet to be decided. While Paul had many supporters in Corinth, and "the majority" had willingly carried out his directives (cf. 2:6), some had lingering doubts about him, particularly about his erratic travel plans, his handling of collection funds, his bodily weakness, and his apostolic authority. Still others in the congregation were downright hostile. Furthermore, the "false apostles" remained, fueling dissension in the Corinthian house churches and trying to extend their own influence at Paul's expense.

Therefore, despite the precarious situation, Paul thought that the time was ripe to announce a third visit to Corinth. To wait any longer might mean losing the church completely, although, of course, coming at this time might also precipitate the purge he had hoped to avoid during the second, painful visit. Ever since writing 1 Corinthians, Paul had promised to come to Corinth for an extended visit (1 Cor. 16:5–9). Though circumstances in Corinth had hitherto caused him to change his travel plans several times, he now planned to make good on that promise. In preparation for the visit, Paul wrote 2 Corinthians with several purposes in mind. First, he wanted to shore up and extend the existing support he had in Corinth. Second, Paul wanted to bolster his sagging image both by answering charges and by defending his apostolic authority. Third, he wanted to warn any unrepentant rebels that there would be a showdown when he arrived. Finally, he wanted to resume the collection for Jerusalem initiated in 1 Corinthians (16:1–4).

2. Form and Structure of the Letter

Although many interpreters regard 2 Corinthians as a composite of several Pauline letter fragments that were arranged and pasted together by a later redactor, the canonical letter is the only form of the document that was ever transmitted in the textual tradition.[7] Therefore, we must try to make sense of the final form of the letter as we now have it.

Taken as a whole, the literary form of 2 Corinthians can be described as an appeal for concord,[8] which seeks to calm the outbreak of faction by dissuading from strife and exhorting to harmony. In 2 Corinthians 13:11, the apostle exhorts the Corinthians to "listen to my appeal, be of one mind, live in peace. . . ." As we have seen, the Corinthian church is wracked with dissension among factions in the congregation (cf. 2 Cor. 12:20; 1 Cor. 1:10). As we shall see later, Paul evidently views the situation in light of Korah's rebellion against Moses and Aaron in Numbers 16–17. Therefore, Paul calls the congregation back to harmony both with himself and with each other in order to avoid divine judgment.

The peace of which Paul speaks in 2 Corinthians 13:11 is not just a cessation from strife, but rather a state of mutual harmony based on genuine agreement in the truth of Paul's gospel (cf. v. 8), which Paul regards as ultimately inseparable from himself as an apostle. Since Paul is an apostle commissioned by God through Christ, whose missionary work itself was an embodiment and expression of his gospel, being of one mind necessarily includes accepting Paul and his apostleship (cf. 6:1–2). Throughout the letter, Paul emphasizes various aspects of the mutuality between himself and the Corinthians (cf., e.g., 1:1–2, 3–11, 14, 18–22, 24; 2:2; 3:18; 4:12, 14; 6:11–13; 7:2; 8:1, 16–17; 9:11; 12:14–15; 13:11). Speaking to his "brothers" in Christ, who are "sons" of the Father and who are being transformed into "the same image" of the resurrected Lord, Paul appeals to the Corinthians to reflect that transformation by "thinking the same thing."

Second Corinthians clearly consists of three main parts: chapters 1–7, 8–9, and 10–13. Each of these sections mentions and in some way makes preparation for Paul's imminent third visit to Corinth. By that time at the latest, the apostle expects the congregation to submit to his appeal for concord in all of its ramifications or else face the consequences. In the *first* section (chs. 1–7), Paul presents a defense of the legitimacy of his apostleship in the face of various accusations against him in Corinth, including his change of travel plans (cf. 1:12–2:13). His imminent third visit is considered in light of the debacle of his second visit and the subsequent repentance of the Corinthians. Paul encourages the Corinthians to dissociate themselves fully from his opponents in Corinth (e.g., 2:17; 5:12; 6:8; 6:14–7:1) and to evaluate his apostleship in light of a valid criterion ("the heart") rather than the criterion of the opponents ("the face"). Clearly, all was not completely resolved, despite Paul's statements of total confidence (cf. 7:4, 16). Although most of the church had repented (7:5–16), some were evidently still siding with Paul's opponents, whether actively or passively (cf. 2:6), and complete relapse was a distinct possibility.

In the *second* section of the letter (chs. 8–9), Paul builds on the confidence that he has in the Corinthians by reviving his plan for the Jerusalem collection. But he is still anxious lest some of the Corinthians not fully and willingly cooperate with the collection when he arrives. Perhaps he is worried that his opponents might finally succeed in causing the congregation to disaffect from him completely. Or perhaps he is concerned that a minority in the church at Corinth will disrupt the collection efforts.

Therefore, in the *third* section of the letter (chs. 10–13), Paul prepares for his imminent third visit to Corinth by handling the problem of the opponents in a more frontal way than he has in the previous sections of the letter. In the process, Paul reinforces the defense of his apostleship from 2:14–7:4, particularly in view of the opponents' attack against its legitimacy. He also warns that any unrepentant Corinthians will encounter the full power of his apostolic authority when he comes. Paul is determined that this third visit to Corinth will not be another debacle.

3. Integrity of the Letter

The foregoing summary of 2 Corinthians, which attempts to understand the letter as a unity, differs sharply from much of the current thinking about 2 Corinthians.[9] According to many interpreters, the breaks in thought found throughout the letter are evidence that it is really a composite of various Pauline letter fragments. These breaks in thought notwithstanding, most interpreters support the unity of at least chapters 1–9. It is chapters 10–13 that cause 2 Corinthians to be regarded as a composite letter. Since these chapters are written in a tone and about a subject so different from that of chapters 1–9, they are considered a fragment of a letter written either before or after chapters 1–9, for, suddenly, the collection is no longer a subject. Suddenly, Paul's "complete confidence" in the Corinthians dissipates (7:16). Paul begins abruptly in 10:1 with a fierce defense of his apostleship against the attacks of his opponents in the Corinth that differs sharply from his defense in 2:14–7:4.

Many interpreters regard chapters 10–13 as part of the "tearful letter" referred to in 2:3–9 and 7:8–12. In that case, chapters 10–13 would have been written *before* chapters 1–9. However, this view has several difficulties: Chapters 10–13 are missing the instructions to punish the one who offended Paul, and chapters 1–7 do not mention the elimination of the opponents referred to in chapters 10–13. Other interpreters regard the "tearful letter" as lost, and postulate that 2 Corinthians 10–13 were written sometime *after* chapters 1–7 (or 1–9). According to this scenario, the opponents evidently returned to Corinth (or came to Corinth for the first time) and caused the conflict between the church and Paul to flare up once again; hence, Paul goes against the opponents with guns blazing. The main difficulty with this view is that there is no explicit mention in chapters 10–13 that Paul had received fresh information about a relapse at Corinth.

The connection of 2 Corinthians 10–13 to the rest of the letter will remain controversial. It is largely a matter of judgment whether one considers the final section of 2 Corinthians sufficiently different in tone to conclude that it was written at a different time and under different circumstances from the rest. In principle, a historical reconstruction that can operate with the unity of 2 Corinthians has the advantage over partition theories, since it works with fewer unknowns. For the purposes of the present commentary, 2 Corinthians 10–13 is treated as an integral part of a letter to the Corinthians that originally comprised all thirteen chapters. This position not only coheres with the textual evidence but also makes sense of the complex and volatile situation that Paul faced in Corinth. The apostle had to contend not just with a repentant majority, which he realized could still be tipped against him, but also with a hostile minority still under the influence of the intruders. Seen in this light, the letter is trying to consolidate and extend any gains that have already been made, to correct what is still wrong, and to warn that the final showdown will come when the apostle arrives. This explains the apologetic tenor of the whole letter; the numerous expressions of Paul's anxiety over the developing situation in Corinth, including the role of the intruders; and the positive statements, even the final section, expressing affection (cf., e.g., 1:8; 8:1 and 13:11; 6:11–13 and 12:14–15; 7:1 and 12:20). Paul ultimately hopes that the situation will turn out for the best, if not for all, at least for the majority. But even on this point Paul is willing both in chapters 1–9 and in 10–13 to make positive statements about "all" the Corinthians (cf. 7:13, 15; 8:7; 13:14).

Many correspondences between 2 Corinthians 1–9 and 10–13 will be noted in the course of the commentary. For example, like the first section of the letter, the final section presupposes an ongoing Korah-like rebellion in Corinth that will be crushed by divine judgment when Paul arrives. Both sections refer to Paul's "coming again" and the possibility of another painful visit (cf. 2:1; 12:21). Moreover, like the first section of the letter, the final section presupposes that Paul has had experience with the *merkabah,* which makes him a mediator of divine revelation (note the link between 2:17 and 12:19).[10] While perhaps none of these correspondences is enough in itself to establish the unity of the letter, their cumulative effect is persuasive.

4. Corinth, Achaia, and Paul's Mission to the Nations

Who were the Corinthians from Paul's perspective? How did they fit into his overall missionary strategy as an "apostle to the nations"? How should we understand Paul's notion of apostolic territoriality, which comes to expression in 2 Corinthians 10:12–18? We will have a difficult time understanding the apostle in this letter if we fail to comprehend his geographical and ethnographic horizon. As we shall see, Paul, as a Diaspora Jew, is a traveler between two radically different "worlds," or rather conceptions of the world—the Greco-Roman and the Jewish.

On one level, Paul knows the Corinthians as residents of the Roman colony of Corinth, situated at the southwest end of the narrow isthmus connecting mainland Greece and Macedonia with the Peloponnesus. With this location, Corinth was uniquely important in ancient times as the junction of the only land route from the north to the south of Greece and as the shortest sea route from Asia Minor to Italy. The commentaries and Bible encyclopedias rehearse the details about how Corinth had been largely destroyed and depopulated in 146 B.C., how the city was refounded as a colony by Julius Caesar in 44 B.C., and how it was later made the capital of the senatorial province of Achaia. Paul himself explicitly identifies the Corinthians in a special way with Achaia (2 Cor. 1:1; 9:2) and pits them in friendly rivalry with Macedonia (8:1–5; 9:2; 11:9–10), another Roman province. He identifies Erastus, one of the members of the Corinthian church, as the "city treasurer" (Rom. 16:23). Certainly, there were many things about the Roman city of Corinth that would have attracted the apostle.

But Paul not only moves in a Roman world, he also travels in a Jewish one. The careful reader of Paul's letters will realize that his Jewish background shapes his perceptions and influences practically every aspect of his apostolic ministry, not least his view of the world. On the surface, Paul seems merely to appropriate the normal Greco-Roman terminology of his day. Upon closer inspection, however, we will find that Paul shares a fundamentally Jewish perspective on world geography and ethnography.

Paul is generally acknowledged to be the apostle to the nations (Rom. 11:13), tracing his gospel back to the Abrahamic promise (Gen. 12:3 [+ 18:18]): "In you shall all the nations be blessed" (Gal. 3:8). In the OT context of Paul's modified citation, "all the nations [of the earth]" refers back to the Table of Nations in Genesis 10. In developing his missionary strategy, the former Pharisee and Hebrew of Hebrews appropriated the OT and Jewish tradition of the Table of Nations (Gen. 10; 1 Chron. 1:1–2:2; Ezek. 27, 38–39; Dan. 11; Isa. 66:18–20). Briefly stated, the genealogy of Genesis 10 represents the fundamental view of the world that continues in subsequent OT and Jewish literature and that is timeless in its applicability.[11]

As regards the past, although several of the identifications in the list remain uncertain and the criteria by which the nations were distinguished are disputed, the main contours of the earth's division are relatively clear. The world is divided among the three sons of Noah: the nations of *Japheth* in the northern and western lands, including Asia Minor and Europe (Gen. 10:2–5); the nations of *Ham* in Egypt and North Africa (vv. 6–20); and the nations of *Shem* in Mesopotamia and Arabia (vv. 21–31). As Yohanan Aharoni observes, "All of the human family is divided into three main groups which *surrounded Palestine:* the sons of Shem to the east, the sons of Ham to the south and the sons of Japheth to the north and west. . . . The Table of Nations . . . gives a faithful sketch of Palestine's position among the peoples and kingdoms of the ancient Near East where the three spheres of Shem, Ham and Japheth intersected."[12] First Chronicles 1:1–2:2 describes the world and the relationship of nations to Israel as they were at the time of writing in the postexilic period. It lists the nations of the world "in a circle" that moves counterclockwise—from the north, to the west, to the south, and to the east—with Israel in the center.

The Table of Nations is not only valid as a description of the past, but is also reflected in texts about the eschatological future. In Ezekiel 38–39 nations from both the north and the south will converge on the center of the earth to destroy and plunder Israel of the restoration. Isaiah 66:18–20, however, contains a positive future expectation when the nations will see God's glory and participate in Israel's restoration. The Table of Nations is thus seen as the fundamental point of orientation for describing Israel's place among the nations of the world and the basis for envisioning world geography and ethnography in the eschatological future.

This fundamentally Jewish view of the world is evident in the decision of the so-called apostolic council in Galatians 2:7–9, that the apostles observe territorial jurisdictions in their respective missions, probably drawn along the lines of the respective territories of the sons of Noah in the Table of Nations. At the same time, the apostles agree that Paul will undertake a collection for the poor saints in Jerusalem (Gal. 2:10). The decisive impulse for the collection very likely came from Isaiah 66:18–20, mentioned above.

After the apostolic council, territoriality becomes an increasingly important factor for the Pauline mission. On the one hand, it focuses the scope and direction of Paul's mission on reaching Asia Minor and Europe, while maintaining his orientation on the center, Jerusalem. The apostle's mission encompasses the territory of the Japhethites, that is, of the descendants of the third son of Noah who settled in the region of Asia Minor and in Europe from Cilicia to Spain. Acts presents the scope and direction of Paul's mission in much the same light—a mission radiating out from Jerusalem "to the ends of the earth" (cf. Acts 1:8; 13:47), concentrating on Asia Minor and Europe, and complementing the missions to Shem (2:1–8:25) and Ham (8:26–40).

On the other hand, territoriality becomes increasingly important for the Pauline mission because Paul now has a strong sense of his own territorial jurisdiction vis-à-vis that of others (2 Cor. 10:13–16). Paul wants to do pioneering missionary work and not to build on another's foundation (2 Cor. 10:15; Rom. 15:20), although all churches in his jurisdiction, whether founded by him or not, stand under his authority (cf. Rom. 1:5–6). Paul does not infringe on the territory of the Jerusalem apostles, and he expects that they (and/or their emissaries) will not infringe on his. When intrusion does happen, however, Paul immediately responds either offensively (Gal. 2:11–14) or defensively (2 Cor. 10:13–16). For Paul, such actions are an attempt to undermine his apostolic authority and to usurp his God-given apostolic territory. Once we understand, then, the fundamentally Jewish nature of Paul's mission to the nations, we realize that when Paul refers to the Corinthians and to Achaia, he is not merely referring to the Roman colony or to the Roman province, but rather, on a deeper level, to descendants of Japheth to whom he has been especially called as apostle.

When Paul came to Corinth, he looked, from a Jewish geographical perspective, at a center of the Jewish Diaspora. He spent eighteen months in Corinth, preaching in the synagogue on the Sabbath, and through his influence Crispus and his family were baptized. The Jews of Corinth were embittered by Paul's activities; they brought him before Gallio, proconsul of Achaia. At this point, the Jewish world touches the Roman world. Paul chose Corinth as a base of operations in part because of its importance as a Jewish center, since the synagogue could be used as a basis for spreading the gospel among the Jews of Greece and their sympathizers, the God-fearers (Acts 18:1–18). His preaching in the synagogue threw the community into a great turmoil, pitting groups of members against each other. One group of Jews forbade Paul to continue preaching in the synagogue; however, many hellenized Jews and Gentile adherents of the synagogue (i.e., God-fearers) were favorably disposed toward Paul. It was the latter group, discipled in the rituals of the synagogue and leaning toward Judaism, who became the predominant medium through which Paul disseminated the gospel in the region.

5. Paul's Opponents in Corinth

Paul has two groups of opponents in Corinth who challenge his apostolic authority: (1) a minority within the church's own membership, which is probably splintered into several factions, and (2) certain outsiders who infiltrated the church. Together, these groups of insiders and outsiders form an opposition that, for Paul, is tantamount to Korah's rebellion against Moses and Aaron in the wilderness (Num. 16–17). For the moment we will focus on the intruders and their agenda, leaving the subject of the minority within the church to the commentary.

Who are these intruders? Where do they come from? With whose authority do they appear on the scene? What passages in 2 Corinthians refer to them? The secondary literature on these questions is enormous, and the range of scholarly opinion is astonishingly broad.[13] While we must confess with James D. G. Dunn, that "the character of the opposition (if that itself is a correct description) will never be more than tantalizingly obscure—shadowy figures which seem to emerge with some clarity at some points only to disappear at others behind the shifting mists of our knowledge of the historical context,"[14] we may offer a few salient observations on the subject.

First, we observe that Paul regularly had to deal with opponents who infiltrated the churches he had established, whether in Galatia, Philippi, or Corinth. This does not necessarily mean that all the opponents are the same in each instance, all part of a united counter-Pauline mission. Nevertheless, the possible connection between them—or at least their position—is worth considering, even if that position was modified to fit the Corinthian situation. Very clearly, the intruders in Corinth are Jewish Christians (cf. 2 Cor. 11:22), just as the opponents in Galatia are. Moreover, Paul accuses the interlopers of preaching a "different gospel" from the one he preached (2 Cor. 11:4), which recalls what Paul writes about a "different gospel" in Galatians 1:6–9. In fact, Paul uses essentially the same argument to combat the opponents in Corinth (cf. 2 Cor. 3:1–18) as he does against the opponents in Galatia (cf. Gal. 3:1–14; 4:1–7). From Paul's perspective, the intruders in Corinth who tout themselves as "servants of righteousness" (2 Cor. 11:15) are really promulgating a "ministry of condemnation" that brings "death" (cf. 3:6–7); hence, they deserve to be "anathema" for preaching a "different gospel" (cf. Gal. 1:6–9).

Second, we notice that the opponents have intruded into what Paul considers his own, God-given apostolic territory (cf. 2 Cor. 10:12–18; 11:4). The intruders' chief aim, from Paul's perspective, is to undermine his apostolic authority and to usurp his apostolic territory. As we have seen, Paul seems to understand the territory of the Japhethites as his exclusive apostolic prerogative. Indeed, the apostolic council acknowledged both Paul's gospel and his rightful claim to a particular territorial jurisdiction (cf. Gal. 2:1–10). Therefore, the apostle repels any attempt to intrude on his territory and to undermine his mission (cf. Gal. 2:11–14). When exactly the intruders arrived on the scene is uncertain; however, since there are references to the interlopers throughout the letter, even in chapters 1–9,[15] we may surmise that Paul's emergency second visit to Corinth was necessitated by the news of the arrival of the opponents in Corinth. In that case, these infiltrators may have influenced the one who offended Paul during the "painful visit" (2 Cor. 2:5; 7:12).

Third, we find that the intruders introduce themselves as "apostles," brandishing letters of recommendation (probably from the Jerusalem church) to authenticate their claim (cf. 2 Cor. 3:1)[16] and boasting that they excel Paul in every respect (cf. 11:22–23). They even have visions and revelations of the Lord (cf. 12:1). Paul had to rely on self-recommendation (cf. 3:1; 4:2; 5:12; 6:4–10; 10:12, 18), for the Corinthians did not stand up for him (cf. 12:11) as they should have done both in word and in deed (cf. 3:2–3). What makes the intruders' claims so deceitful is that they undeniably look and sound better than Paul (cf. 10:10; 11:6). Paul regards them as "false apostles" (11:1–4) and scornfully calls them "super-apostles" (11:5) because of their boast of superiority. From Paul's perspective, these men are nothing more than "false apostles . . . masquerading as apostles of Christ" and "servants [of Satan]" (11:13, 15). Paul tries to show that, as a servant of Christ, he is actually "superior" to the opponents (cf. 11:5, 23).

Fourth, we observe that the intruders were amazingly successful in the Corinthian church. The Corinthian house churches, which had already been wracked by strife and division (1 Cor. 1:10–12), were easy prey for the intruders, who were received with open arms (2 Cor. 11:4, 20) and quickly gained positions of prominence and influence. As a result, the interlopers were able to exact payment from the Corinthians for services rendered (cf. 2:17; 11:20), whereas Paul steadfastly refused to exercise his apostolic right to financial support in Corinth (cf. 1 Cor. 9:1–18). Not to be outdone, the opponents claimed that Paul's refusal was tantamount to admitting he was a fraud, and that in any case his refusal showed a lack of affection for the Corinthians. Caught in the crossfire of such perverse charges, the apostle was forced to defend his actions and to prove his apostolic credentials (cf. 11:5, 7–11; 12:11–15; 13:3, 6). Furthermore, when Paul did endeavor to raise money, not for himself but for Jerusalem (chs. 8–9), the opponents again cast aspersion on his motives, claiming that he was involved in a confidence game (12:16–18). So whatever Paul did—whether he refused money or raised money—the "spin doctors" in Corinth found a way to malign him while magnifying their own stature in the community.

Notes

1. For a recent bibliography of secondary literature on 2 Corinthians, see Victor Paul Furnish, "2 Corinthians," in *Pauline Theology, Vol. II: 1 & 2 Corinthians* (ed. David M. Hay; Minneapolis: Fortress, 1993), pp. 270–84.

2. On the textual evidence of 2 Corinthians, see the more detailed treatment in the larger exegetical commentaries and in Bruce M. Metzger, ed., *A Textual Commentary on the Greek New Testament* (2d ed.; Stuttgart: United Bible Societies, 1994), pp. 505–19. For a theological treatment of the letter, see Jerome Murphy-O'Connor, *The Theology of the Second Letter to the Corinthians* (New Testament Theology; Cambridge: Cambridge University Press, 1991).

3. For the view that already in 1 Corinthians Paul had to defend his apostleship, see Gordon D. Fee, *The First Epistle to the Corinthians*

(NICNT; Grand Rapids: Eerdmans, 1987), pp. 4–11; Karl A. Plank, *Paul and the Irony of Affliction* (SBLSS; Atlanta: Scholars Press, 1987), pp. 12–24.

4. On the issues relating to Paul's travel plans in 1 Cor. 16:5–7 and 2 Cor. 1:15–16, see Margaret E. Thrall, *A Critical and Exegetical Commentary on the Second Epistle to the Corinthians, Vol. 1: Introduction and Commentary on II Corinthians I–VII* (ICC; Edinburgh: T&T Clark, 1994), pp. 69–74.

5. On the various suggestions about the offender and his offence, see Thrall, *Second Corinthians*, vol. 1, pp. 61–69.

6. Cf. Thrall, *Second Corinthians*, vol. 1, pp. 57–61.

7. P^{46}, an Egyptian papyrus dating to ca. A.D. 200, contains all thirteen chapters of 2 Corinthians. As we shall see, *1 Clement* probably attests to the existence of 2 Corinthians already at the end of the first century A.D. Cf. Kurt Aland and Barbara Aland, *The Text of the New Testament: An Introduction to the Critical Editions and to the Theory and Practice of Modern Textual Criticism* (2d ed.; trans. Erroll F. Rhodes; Grand Rapids: Eerdmans, 1989), p. 296.

8. On the issue of genre in 2 Corinthians, see, e.g., John T. Fitzgerald, "Paul, the Ancient Epistolary Theorists, and 2 Corinthians 10–13: The Purpose and Literary Genre of a Pauline Letter," in *Greeks, Romans, and Christians: Festschrift for A. J. Malherbe* (ed. D. L. Balch, et al.; Minneapolis: Fortress, 1990), pp. 190–200.

9. Hans Dieter Betz goes so far as to state that "few scholars continue to defend the unity of 2 Corinthians . . ." ("Corinthians, Second Epistle to the," *ABD*, vol. 1, pp. 1148–54 [here p. 1149]). For a recent survey of the various literary-critical positions, see Thrall, *Second Corinthians*, vol. 1, pp. 3–49; N. H. Taylor, "The Composition and Chronology of Second Corinthians," *JSNT* 44 (1991), pp. 67–87.

10. We also may note a few other correspondences between chs. 1–9 and 10–13 that bind the letter together as a unity. First, certain key terms are used throughout the letter: e.g., "thought, mind" (*noēma*; cf. 2:11; 3:14; 4:14; 10:5; 11:3); "Satan" (2:11; 4:4; 6:15; 11:14; 12:7); Paul's alleged conduct "according to the flesh" (*kata sarka*; cf. 1:17; 10:3); "commend" (*synistanein*; cf. 3:1; 4:2; 5:12; 6:4; 7:11; 10:12, 18; 12:11). Second, the creation/fall tradition (Gen. 1–3) is woven into Paul's letter at various points (cf. 2 Cor. 4:4–6; 5:3, 17; 11:3; 12:4). Third, hyperbolic language is characteristic of 2 Corinthians as a whole (cf. 1:5, 8, 12; 2:4, 7; 3:9, 10; 4:7, 15, 17; 7:4, 13, 15; 8:2, 7, 14; 9:8, 12, 14; 10:8, 15; 12:7, 15). Fourth, Paul's reason for writing a letter rather than coming in person (1:23; 13:10) is stated.

11. The broad outlines given here are based on the detailed discussion in my book, *Paul and the Nations: The Old Testament and Jewish Background of Paul's Mission to the Nations with Special Reference to the Destination of Galatians* (WUNT 84; Tübingen: Mohr Siebeck, 1995). Cf. also my article, "The Geographical Horizon of Luke: A Confluence of Jewish and Greco-Roman Worlds," in *The Book of Acts in Its First Century*

Setting, Vol. 2: The Book of Acts in Its Graeco-Roman Setting (ed. David W. J. Gill and Conrad Gempf; Grand Rapids: Eerdmans, 1994), pp. 483-544.

12. Yohanan Aharoni, *The Land of the Bible: A Historical Geography* (London: Burns & Oates, 1979), pp. 6, 8. See also Yohanan Aharoni and Michael Avi-Yonah, *The Macmillan Bible Atlas* (3d ed.; New York: Macmillan, 1993), p. 21 (with a map showing the intersection of the three spheres).

13. For a concise summary, see P. W. Barnett, "Opponents of Paul," *DPL*, pp. 644-53. See further C. K. Barrett, *Paul: An Introduction to His Thought* (Louisville: Westminster John Knox, 1994), pp. 33-38.

14. James D. G. Dunn, "Prolegomena to a Theology of Paul," *NTS* 40 (1994), pp. 407-32 (here p. 417).

15. Despite the difference of tone in 2 Cor. 1-9 and 10-13, both sections of the letter repudiate opponents who commend themselves (3:1; 10:18; cf. 5:12) while maligning Paul as weak, vacillating, and deceitful (1:17; 4:2; 7:2; 10:2, 10; 12:11, 16-17). Hence, the two sections probably have in view the same opponents.

16. If Paul's opponents in Corinth do have letters from the Jerusalem church, then the situation in Corinth can be compared to the conflict in Antioch (Gal. 2:11-14; cf. Acts 15:24). In that case, however, it remains a profound mystery why the Jerusalem apostles repeatedly violated the agreed spheres of apostolic jurisdiction (Gal. 2:1-10) by sending emissaries into Paul's territory in order to gain control of his mission. Nevertheless, Paul seems to imply that the terms of the Jerusalem accord were indeed violated when the intruders overstepped the bounds of their authority (cf. 2 Cor. 10:12-18). Perhaps the answer lies in the possibility that the Jerusalem authorities did not know and could not control all that their emissaries were doing in the field (cf. Barrett, *Paul*, p. 36).

§1 Opening (2 Cor. 1:1–2)

In an ancient letter, the purpose of an opening, or prescript, is to establish a relationship between the sender and the addressees. Accordingly, in 2 Corinthians Paul and Timothy are named as the senders of the letter; "the church of God in Corinth, together with all the saints throughout Achaia" represents the recipients; and "grace and peace" is the expression of greeting and good will. Paul deviates somewhat from the established form by adding details about the senders, and by using the word "peace" in a new sense. The prescript here intends to establish Paul's position of apostolic authority over the Corinthians. In a situation in which the relationship between Paul and the Corinthians is strained to the limit, and Paul's apostleship has been called into question, the prescript thus becomes an important first step in Paul's defense.

1:1 / **Paul** introduces himself, according to his regular practice, as an **apostle,** i.e., one who has seen the resurrected Lord and has been commissioned by him to preach the gospel (cf. 1 Cor. 9:1; 15:8–11; Gal. 1:12, 15–16; Rom. 1:1–5). First Corinthians begins in much the same way: "Paul, called to be an apostle of Christ Jesus by the will of God" (1:1). Nevertheless, when Paul states in 2 Corinthians 1:1 that he is an apostle **by the will of God,** the statement takes on special significance in view of the polemical situation that has developed in Corinth since the writing of 1 Corinthians, for, after the arrival of the opponents in Corinth, the legitimacy of Paul's apostleship itself was called into question within the church. Therefore, Paul wants to stress from the beginning that he does not write as a private person who happened to choose a ministerial "profession," but rather in his official capacity as an apostle, a position to which God himself has appointed Paul. This shows that the apostle does not speak or act in his own authority, but in the commission and authority of the one who sent him. We may compare Korah's rebellion, in which the sending of

Moses was called into question, and Moses had to defend it (cf. Num. 16:28; see further on 2 Cor. 1:24; 2:6–7, 15).

In Galatians 1:15–16, Paul describes his call to apostleship as a sovereign act of God's grace (cf. 1 Cor. 15:9–10; Rom. 12:3; 15:15–16), predestined even before Paul was born. The resurrected Lord appeared to Paul on his way to Damascus, and Paul instantly became a servant of Jesus Christ. In the Corinthian correspondence, Paul bases his apostolic authority on having seen the resurrected Lord, who was revealed to him by God (cf. 1 Cor. 9:1–2; 2 Cor. 4:5–6). Therefore, the prescript of 2 Corinthians cuts to the heart of the controversy over the legitimacy of Paul's apostleship and prepares the way for his defense in the rest of the letter. Here he implies what he later explicitly states, i.e., that his opponents are not bona fide apostles, but rather "pseudo-apostles," "deceitful workmen," and "servants of Satan" (2 Cor. 11:13–15).

Paul names **Timothy** as the co-sender of the letter, which may at first seem surprising. Why would the apostle include Timothy, if he himself is the sole author of the letter, and if much of 2 Corinthians amounts to a defense of Paul's own apostolic authority? First of all, Timothy was present when the apostle founded the church at Corinth (cf. 2 Cor. 1:19). In a situation that now calls the apostle's authority into question, Paul subtly wants to remind the Corinthians that he was the one who founded the church at Corinth, a point that he repeats many times in the letter (e.g., 2 Cor. 3:3; 6:13; 12:14). Second, Timothy had recently visited the church at Corinth on Paul's behalf (cf. 1 Cor. 16:10). Third, Timothy represents a united front with Paul against the prevailing situation at Corinth. If Paul faces attack from a multiplicity of opponents in Corinth, as well as the disaffection of the Corinthians, then it only makes sense to show that he does not stand alone in his position. Furthermore, by generously mentioning Timothy as the co-sender of the letter, Paul is able demonstrate his solidarity with his faithful coworker.

Timothy was a native of Lystra in Lycaonia, the son of a mixed marriage, since his mother was Jewish and his father Greek (Acts 16:1). He was brought up in the Jewish faith but was not circumcised in infancy. During Barnabas's and Paul's first visit to his home town (Acts 14:8–20), he became a believer (cf. 16:1). When Paul passed that way again a year or two later, he became better acquainted with Timothy, who was highly regarded by the believers in Lystra and Iconium (cf. Acts 16:2). He decided to enlist Timothy as an associate in his apostolic ministry but circumcised him first as a practical matter in order to make his dealings with Jews easier (cf. Acts 16:3). Timothy proved himself to be a devoted servant with Paul in the work of the gospel and thus earned the apostle's deepest admiration and affection (cf. Phil. 2:20–22). He was entrusted with important missions, such as those to Thessalonica (1 Thess. 3:2) and Corinth (1 Cor. 4:17). When Paul was setting out on his last journey to Jerusalem, Timothy was in the party (Acts 20:4), and he was at his side during his Roman imprisonment. Indeed, Paul drew special comfort from his presence and planned to send him on a mission to the Philippian church (Phil. 2:19–24).

Paul calls Timothy **our brother.** There are two possible ways to interpret this expression. On the one hand, the first person plural (**our**) may include the Corinthians with Paul as brothers of Timothy. As adopted sons of God (cf. Gal. 4:6; Rom. 8:15), believers are united as "brothers" in Christ, who is the Son of God and "firstborn" brother into whose image all believers will be transformed at the Parousia (cf. Rom. 8:23, 29; 2 Cor. 3:18). In that case, Paul uses the reference to Timothy to point to the unique bond of kinship that all believers share. Despite the disaffection of the Corinthians from their founding apostle, Paul stresses that they remain brothers in Christ with himself and Timothy (cf. 2 Cor. 1:8). On the other hand, the "our" may refer to Paul alone, for he commonly uses the so-called apostolic (or literary) plural to refer to himself alone, especially in 2 Corinthians (see, e.g., 1:3–4; 5:18–21). In that case, Paul may be emphasizing a special sense of brotherhood that exists between Timothy and himself. Insofar as Paul sees himself as a Moses figure who is embroiled in a Korah-like rebellion in Corinth (see on 1:24; 2:6–7, 15, etc.), Paul may view Timothy as an Aaron figure (cf. 1:19; see also 1 Cor. 4:17; 16:10–11; Phil. 1:1; 2:19–24; Col. 1:1; 1 Thess. 1:1; 3:2, 6; Phlm. 1; 1 and 2 Timothy, esp. 2 Tim. 3:8–9). Aaron was Moses' "brother" (cf. Exod. 4:14; 6:20; 28:1; Num. 26:59; 27:12–13; Deut. 32:50; 1 Chron. 6:3; 23:13). The phrase "Paul and Timothy," which occurs often in Paul's letters (cf. 2 Cor. 1:19; Phil. 1:1; Col. 1:1; 1 Thess. 1:1; Phlm. 1:1), may imitate the word pair "Moses and Aaron," which occurs over sixty-five times in the OT.

With the mention of the addressees of the letter, we catch a glimpse of how Paul envisions his missionary enterprise geographically and ethnographically. **Corinth** is the capital of the Roman province of **Achaia** and also the place where Paul gained his first converts in Achaia (cf. 1 Cor. 16:15; 1:16). As we discussed in the Introduction, Paul, the "apostle to the nations" (Rom. 11:13), thinks in terms of the original nations, which, from a contemporary Jewish perspective, are approximately coextensive with the current Roman provinces. Once he has evangelized a representative number of people in a particular locality, Paul's job as evangelist is over, and he is eager to proceed to unreached territories (cf. Rom. 15:19–20, 23). He expects the gospel to radiate out from the established center(s) to the rest of the nation/province. Hence, although 2 Corinthians is particularly relevant to the church at Corinth, Paul addresses the letter also to the rest of the nation/province in which Corinth is included. In the apostle's endeavor to reach Spain with the gospel (cf. Rom. 15:24, 28), Corinth occupies a strategic position about halfway to the goal (see further on 2 Cor. 10:13–16; also Rom. 15:19).

By referring to the Corinthians as **the church of God**, Paul draws a direct comparison between his apostleship and the church at Corinth as works of God, for just as Paul is an apostle "by the will of God" (cf. v. 1), so also the church that he founded through God's competence (cf. 3:1–6) is "the church of God." In this way, the prescript doubly puts the Corinthians under the authority of God. Paul presents himself as God's apostle addressing God's church, for, as he goes on to say later in the letter, God makes his appeal to the world through him (5:20). Paul and his message are integrally linked; to reject one is to reject the other.

Paul reminds the Corinthians that, as **saints** (*hagioi*, lit., "holy ones"), they are the people of God called to be separate from the world and separated unto God. The OT roots of *hagios* lie in such passages as Exodus 19:3–6; 29:45; Leviticus 11:44–45; 19:2; Deuteronomy 7:6; 14:2, 21; 26:19; 28:9. As 2 Corinthians 6:14–7:1 makes clear, Isaiah 52:11 ("Therefore come out from [them] and be separate") is especially significant in this regard. The reality of the Corinthians' faith is demonstrated in their putting into practice the implications of the new covenant situation, which includes personal "sanctification" (*hagiōsynē*, 2 Cor. 7:1) and, in the current situation, separating themselves from the false apostles (cf. 5:12; 6:14–16; Num. 16:26). If the Corinthians are truly the holy people of God, then their faith will manifest itself in obedience from the heart to the Pauline gospel. If not, then the warnings of judgment found in 13:1–10 will come upon them. Ultimately, it is allegiance to Paul himself that will determine whether the Corinthians' faith is genuine or not (cf. 6:1; 13:5).

1:2 / After establishing his authority over the Corinthian church, Paul greets the Corinthians in a rather formulaic manner adapted from the ancient oriental letter form. He uses exactly the same greeting in other letters (cf. 1 Cor. 1:3; Rom. 1:7); therefore, we should probably not read too much into the wording for the particular situation in Corinth. In one brief wish of **grace and peace,** Paul is able not only to demonstrate his goodwill toward the Corinthians but also to capture the essence of the gospel and its effect. At the beginning of the greeting, Paul innovatively uses the term "grace," one of the fundamental tenets of his theology, which summarizes the whole salvific act of God accomplished in Christ for believers. Yet, as Paul warns in 2 Corinthians 6:1, the Corinthians are in danger of forfeiting the grace of God because of their stance toward him as their founding apostle.

Peace here refers not merely to inner contentment and serenity, but rather to wholeness and well-being that encompass the whole person, the whole household, or even the whole nation. In the OT, it is considered a gift of God (cf. Lev. 26:6; 1 Kgs. 2:33; Pss. 29:11; 85:8; Isa. 26:12).

Both grace and peace come from **God our Father and the Lord Jesus Christ.** As we shall see, one of the central features of Paul's theology is the concept that God and Christ act together (cf., e.g., 2 Cor. 5:19). God has exalted the crucified and resurrected Christ to his right hand (cf. 1 Cor. 15:25; Rom. 8:34) and given him the name that is above every name (Phil. 2:9). Hence, both God and Christ are now co-occupants of the divine throne and perform activities either together or interchangeably (cf. 2 Cor. 5:10; Rom. 14:10). God is the Father not only of the Son but also of all believers in Christ (see above on "our brother" in v. 1).

Additional Notes §1

1:1 / Ancient epistolography is a subject on which much has been written in recent times. See the overview of Hebrew, Aramaic, and Greco-Roman letters in *ABD* vol. 4, pp. 282–93; also James M. Lindenberger, *Ancient Aramaic and Hebrew Letters* (Atlanta: Scholars Press, 1994).

Elsewhere, too, Paul introduces himself as an **apostle** (cf. Rom. 1:1; 1 Cor. 1:1; Gal. 1:1; Col. 1:1; Eph. 1:1). This is his regular practice, although he sometimes deviates from it (cf. Philippians, 1 Thessalonians, and Philemon). On Paul's use of the term, see P. W. Barnett, "Apostle," *DPL*, pp. 45–51. Strangely enough, this is the only occasion in the entire letter when Paul refers to himself as "apostle" (cf., however, 12:12), even though much of the letter is concerned with defending his apostolic claim and authority. Otherwise, he attributes the term only ironically or polemically to his opponents (cf. 11:5, 13; 12:11).

By characterizing himself as an apostle of **Christ Jesus**, Paul evidently emphasizes his position of service under the messianic kingship of Jesus, as the forward position of the term "Christ" possibly shows (cf. Martin Hengel, " 'Christos' in Paul," in *Between Jesus and Paul* [Philadelphia: Fortress, 1983], pp. 65–77). In 2 Cor. 5:20, the apostle calls himself an ambassador for Christ.

When Paul considers himself called to be an apostle by the **will of God**, he seems to have the concept of the OT prophet in mind. Like a true prophet, Paul did not have anything to do with his commission; this was the sovereign will of God, foreordained before Paul's birth (Gal. 1:15; cf. Isa. 49:1; Jer. 1:5). According to Paul's own testimony, he was pressed into service by divine necessity (1 Cor. 9:16).

On **the church of God** in Paul, see further Thrall, *Second Corinthians*, vol. 1, pp. 89–93.

If we are correct that Paul portrays his opponents in Corinth as rebels like Korah and his followers, who challenged Moses' authority in the wilderness (Num. 16–17; see, e.g., on 2 Cor. 1:24; 2:6–7), then Paul's use of **saints** *(hagioi)* may have special significance in this polemical situation, for Korah revolted against Moses' authority on the ground that the whole congregation were *hagioi* (Num. 16:3; cf. Exod. 19:6).

By the time of the writing of the Corinthian correspondence, **Achaia** had converts not only in Corinth, but also in Cenchrae (Rom. 16:1) and Athens (Acts 17:34).

1:2 / In Ezekiel, to which Paul alludes several times in 2 Corinthians (cf. 3:3; 6:16), the eternal "covenant of peace" is a future blessing that involves the reestablishment of the relationship between God and his people, the restoration of the Davidic kingship, and the reinstatement of God's sanctuary among them (cf. Ezek. 34:25; 37:26). This is precisely what 2 Cor. 6:16–18 has in view (cf. also 3:1ff. on the restoration of God's glory among his people)! Furthermore, 2 Cor. 5:18–19 envisions peace or reconciliation for the whole world.

§2 Thanksgiving (2 Cor. 1:3–11)

Usually the opening of a Pauline letter is followed by a thanksgiving for the church to which the apostle is writing. In 1 Corinthians, for example, Paul begins with the following thanksgiving: "I always thank God for you because of his grace given to you in Christ Jesus" (1:4). In Galatians and 2 Corinthians, however, Paul deviates from his normal practice. Is it a coincidence that in both cases the apostle was writing to a church that was in the process of defecting from him and his gospel, or that in both cases the situation required Paul to offer a defense? Galatians omits the thanksgiving completely and proceeds after the opening directly to reproof. Second Corinthians avoids giving thanks for the church at Corinth by beginning with praise for the way that God rescued Paul from mortal danger in Asia.

Nevertheless, this opening praise does relate to the Corinthians in at least two important ways. First, the comfort that Paul received during that very trying experience in Asia now indirectly supplies "comfort" through Paul to the church at Corinth: God has comforted Paul in his tribulation *so that* Paul will be able to comfort others in their tribulation (1:4). Paul thereby emphasizes his mediatory role between God and the Corinthians, a subject to which he will return in the body of the letter. Hence, Paul's emphasis is not so much on the suffering itself but on its beneficial results for others. Second, in the process of praising God, Paul shares intimately of his tribulation and deliverance in order to regain the sympathetic affections of the Corinthians (cf. 2 Cor. 6:11), hoping that the church at Corinth will join him both in praising God for his deliverance and in praying for future deliverance. Whereas usually it is Paul who gives thanks for his addressees, here his addressees are supposed to give thanks for him. One reason for this is that Paul needs the Corinthians' support to advance his mission, thus he must win them back to his side. Therefore, Paul tries to move the Corinthians to solidarity and partnership with him in his sufferings. Second Corinthians will have much to say about Paul's sufferings and weakness, since they are a hallmark of his apostleship and one of the reasons for which Paul is being criticized in Corinth.

Employing the eulogy, a particular form of praise common in OT and Jewish liturgy, Paul blesses God for his deliverance from a nearly fatal situation in Asia (cf. vv. 8–11). Structurally, the eulogy proper is found in verses 3–7. The following passage (vv. 8–11) then explains and supports the reason for Paul's praise in verses 3–7. In that the section begins (v. 3) and ends (v. 11) on the note of praise, the whole composition becomes unified by an *inclusio* (note the similar *inclusio* in the thanksgiving of Eph. 1:3–14).

1:3 / The apostle introduces his thanksgiving with a wish. Here, Paul expands the normal OT and Jewish liturgical formula "Blessed [is/be] God" (cf. J. Scharbert) by adding the words, "and Father of our Lord Jesus Christ." This reference to the **Father** recalls the greeting in verse 2, where God is called "our Father." For the third time in the first three verses of the letter, Paul is pointing out the divine kinship that he and the Corinthians share together in Christ, the firstborn Son of God (cf. Rom. 8:29). Later, Paul will return to this notion of divine adoptive kinship to argue that the Corinthians should dissociate themselves from his opponents, who stand outside the sphere of Christ (cf. 2 Cor. 6:18 in the context of 6:11–7:4).

Paul then elaborates on the words "God" and "Father" in chiastic order: **the Father of compassion** (cf. *Lev. Rab.* 17:4 to 14:34) and **the God of all comfort** (Rom. 15:5). For Paul, God is the one "who comforts the downcast" (2 Cor. 7:6). What exactly does this comfort include here? Is Paul speaking here of an inner feeling of relief or consolation? Or should we think rather of concrete help and assistance that God brings to the apostle in a dire circumstance? Or both? The following verses help us see more clearly.

1:4 / The descriptions of God continue in verse 4, giving the reason for which God is blessed. Starting in this verse, however, Paul suddenly shifts from using **us/our** in an inclusive sense to using it to refer to himself alone. Verse 6 highlights the explicit contrast between "we" (Paul) and "you" (Corinthians). Yet Paul's train of thought helps us realize that the change most probably took place already in verse 4. Paul's point at this juncture is not that God comforts **us** believers in general in all **our**

troubles, but rather that God comforts Paul in particular in all his troubles; his comfort, in turn, overflows to the Corinthians (cf. vv. 5–6). The comfort that Paul receives belongs fundamentally to his apostolic ministry.

What does it mean that God "comforts" Paul in all his troubles? The word **trouble** *(thlipsis)* is used in Paul almost exclusively in the sense of the "oppression" or "tribulation" that is caused by outward circumstances or events (e.g., Rom. 2:9; 5:3; 8:35; 12:12; 1 Cor. 7:28; 2 Cor. 1:8; 4:17; 6:4; 7:4–5; 8:2; Phil. 4:14; 1 Thess. 1:6; 3:3, 7; 2 Thess. 1:4, 6). The other use of the word, in the sense of an inner "distress" or "anguish," occurs only in 2 Corinthians 2:4 and Philippians 1:17. That the former use of the term is intended here is shown by the fact that *thlipsis* in verse 4a (and the verb *thlibesthai* in v. 6a) corresponds to "the sufferings of Christ" in verse 5a (see below). When Paul speaks comprehensively of **all our troubles,** he has in view especially the tribulation portrayed in 1:8–11, for the introductory eulogy in verses 3–7 is explained and substantiated in verses 8–11. There Paul speaks of the "tribulation" *(thlipsis)* that he experienced in the Roman province of Asia (v. 8a) and describes it as an extremely dangerous situation that almost cost him his life (see further below).

If verses 8–11 make it clear that "troubles" refers to a dangerous situation caused by outside circumstances, then **comfort** refers primarily not to an inner feeling of encouragement or consolation, but to divine intervention in the perilous situation and deliverance from it (cf. v. 10). Hence the expression "the God of all comfort" (v. 3b) corresponds to the "God, who raises the dead" (v. 9b), and the phrase "who comforts us in all our troubles" (v. 4a) relates to "who has delivered us from such a deadly peril and will deliver us" (v. 10a). The language from Israel's hymnal, the Psalms, bears a close resemblance to Paul's description here (see Additional Notes below).

The purpose for which Paul is comforted in all his troubles is given in verse 4b. The divine comfort (= deliverance) that Paul receives as an apostle is thus mediated to others through Paul. Far from disrupting his apostolic ministry, Paul's trials actually contribute to its efficacy. In being comforted (delivered) from adversity, Paul is able to spread that comfort to others.

1:5 / The word **For** *(hoti)* introduces an explanation of verse 4b, how it is that Paul's comfort can comfort others. Paul draws a comparison here (**just as . . . so also**) between two kinds of overflowing: the overflow of Christ's sufferings to Paul, and the overflow of Paul's comfort through Christ to others. Paul emphasizes thereby how his own comfort comes to his readers. Just as Paul shares in the sufferings of Christ, so also the Corinthians share in Paul's comfort. As an apostle, Paul is a mediator, an agent for the transmission of the comfort (= deliverance). No matter how much Paul has suffered, God's deliverance has always been greater, and the overflow of that comfort in turn comforts others.

In this instance, the **sufferings of Christ** are those that Paul specifically takes upon himself for the sake of both the crucified Christ and the message about the crucified Christ (cf. 4:11). Paul gives abundant examples of the sufferings that he endures in 2 Corinthians 4:7–18; 6:4–10; 11:23–33; and 12:10 (cf. 1 Cor. 4:9–13). He understands the suffering that he must endure in his apostolic ministry and role as revelatory mediator as participation in the suffering of Christ (cf. Gal. 3:1; 6:17). He experiences both "the sharing of his sufferings" and "the power of his resurrection" (Phil. 3:10). By comparing his own sufferings to those of Christ, Paul is able both to begin deflecting criticism of his apostleship, which his sufferings drew from his opponents, and to regain the sympathies of the Corinthians.

When Paul characterizes the comfort (= deliverance) he has received from God as a comfort that **overflows through Christ**, this is based on the idea that God reveals himself in the resurrection of Jesus Christ as the "God who raises the dead" (v. 9b; cf. Rom. 4:17, 24; 1 Cor. 15). In that God saves the apostle of Jesus Christ from a deadly tribulation, he shows the same resurrection power that was revealed in the resurrection of Christ (cf. 2 Cor. 4:7–18; 13:4).

1:6 / Paul now applies the idea developed in verses 4–5 directly to the Corinthians. This verse refers first and foremost to the proclamation of the apostle. The word **salvation** is to be understood in the normal, comprehensive sense of the term in Paul. The preaching of Paul is attended by his being **distressed** and **comforted.** His life is a visual portrayal of Jesus Christ as crucified (cf. Gal. 3:1; 2 Cor. 4:10–12). Yet Paul's gospel is the medium that effectively promises and makes available God's comfort and salvation. Insofar as Paul can proclaim this gospel as one who is distressed and comforted, then his situation serves to enable people to understand the gospel and thus to experience the divine promise of comfort and salvation for themselves. Furthermore, if Paul is comforted, he himself in his apostolic existence witnesses to the saving resurrection power of the one whom he proclaims as the "God of all comfort." Paul is, in effect, *living proof* of the gospel in action; namely, that the "God and Father of our Lord Jesus Christ" and "the Father of compassion and the God of all comfort" does not abandon his own in the midst of tribulation.

Because Paul comforts with divine "comfort," those who are in tribulation can bear their suffering with **patient endurance**, while trusting the God "who raises the dead" (v. 9b). For Paul, sharing in the sonship of Christ and in his kingdom as heirs requires that believers suffer with Christ here and now (cf. Rom. 8:17). This is quite normal for the time before the Parousia, although the Corinthians in particular have not always understood that sharing in the final glory is inseparable from sharing in Christ's sufferings (cf. 1 Cor. 4:8–17). The comfort, understood as salvation, is not fully complete until the future, when all things will be rectified entirely and finally. For now, the Corinthians are partners with Paul in the same sufferings that he suffers. Rather than rejecting Paul for his weakness and suffering, the Corinthians ought to view Paul's apostolic experience as a vivid display of God's ability to sustain and deliver his people from trial, for they too participate in that deliverance. Paul's life thus becomes an object lesson of God's faithfulness as portrayed in the death and resurrection of Christ.

1:7 / Paul underscores what he has said in verse 6 about the Corinthians' participation in his comfort. Paul and the Corinthians are partners both in suffering and in comfort, that is, in (ultimate) deliverance. Paul is obviously trying to bring the Corinthians into alliance with him by pointing out what they have in common.

Paul's **hope** is firm and unwavering, even if its object is yet future (cf. 1:14). As he states in Romans 8:24, "We were saved in hope." Because God himself imparts what he pledges and accomplishes what he promises, the church will also experience God's comfort as his saving and preserving intervention. The promised comfort that the apostle expresses as a mediator of divine **comfort** is a performative word, which in the form of the gospel actually imparts deliverance from tribulation and death. In this sense, Paul's message is very much like the oracle of the prophet that announces the end of the people's tribulation in exile: "Comfort, comfort my people, says your God" (Isa. 40:1). Likewise, Sirach 49:10 says of the Twelve (minor) Prophets: "they comforted Jacob and delivered them [sc. the Israelites] with confident hope."

1:8–11 / In this section, Paul concretizes what he has said about suffering and deliverance in verses 3–7 by means of a recent personal example.

1:8 / Paul begins the example solemnly by not wanting the Corinthians to be **uninformed.** Evidently, they had not yet heard what had happened to Paul, perhaps because it had happened so recently. Paul addresses the Corinthians as **brothers,** a term of endearment that includes the whole congregation and not just males. Paul is again pointing to the unique bond of kinship that unites believers in Christ, the firstborn brother (see on 1:1, 2, 3). The apostle shares very intimately about a severe persecution that he experienced in **Asia,** i.e., the Roman province in western Asia Minor, whose capital is Ephesus.

It is impossible to ascertain from the rather sketchy description in verses 8–10 exactly what kind of tribulation Paul suffered. He is sometimes indefinite when recounting profoundly personal experiences (cf. 12:2–4). The event described in 1 Corinthians 15:32 ("If I fought wild beasts in Ephesus") is probably not referred to here, for the Corinthians had already heard about that in a previous letter. Many interpreters adduce the riot in Ephesus (Acts 19:23–20:1) to explain the background of Paul's remarks, although Acts does not record that Paul was harmed on that occasion. In any case, the tribulation was undoubtedly some kind of external circumstance that came upon Paul in Ephesus or perhaps on the way to Troas (cf. 11:26), perhaps even during an otherwise unknown Ephesian imprisonment.

The danger was evidently so great that Paul thought he would perish: **we despaired even of life** (cf. v. 9a). Paul's hyperbolic language here stresses the severity of the affliction. Probably we are to think of a life-threatening physical assault rather than of severe depression bordering on suicide. Paul gives ample evidence in his tribulation catalogues of the kind of persecutions and other dangers he commonly experienced (cf. 4:8–9; 6:4–10; 11:23–33; 12:10), including mortal dangers (11:23).

1:9 / Paul further describes how he felt during the mortal danger described in verse 8. By stating twice in rapid succession that he thought he was going to die, Paul conveys the intensity of the situation. In fact, Paul had already pronounced a **sentence of death** (or "verdict of death") on himself, accepting his imminent demise as the providence of God (cf. 1 Cor. 4:9). He saw in the situation the divine purpose that he should trust solely in the God who raises the dead and not in himself. Paul expresses the same kind of resolution to life or death in Philippians 2:19–26.

Paul employs the perfect participle of *peithein* to mean "have confidence in, trust in" (cf. 2:3; 10:7; Phil. 3:3). Is there a question that the apostle would **rely** on himself rather than on God? Paul describes another, unrelated experience in 12:7 when God gave him a "thorn in the flesh" so that he would not be conceited about his revelatory experience. It seems that at one time Paul had a problem with humility and self-reliance. Likewise in 1:9, God's purpose in subjecting Paul to the Asian tribulation was not to kill him; rather, Paul received this "sentence" or "verdict of death" *in order that (hina)* he would trust not in himself, but in the God who raises the dead (v. 9b). Paul is called in a life-threatening situation to trust in the **God who raises the dead,** indeed the God who already raised Christ "from the dead" by means of the Spirit (cf. Rom. 1:4). Because Christ, in whose sufferings and death sentence Paul shares, was raised from the dead, so also Paul can hope to participate in his resurrection of the death. Paul will come back to this point in 2 Corinthians 4:7ff.

1:10 / Paul's confidence in the "God who raises the dead" was not misplaced, for God intervened on the apostle's behalf with his marvelous power by delivering Paul from the danger of death in Asia. The expression **deliver from a deadly peril** (another textual reading has "from the dead") occurs frequently in the OT (cf. Pss. 33:19; 55:14; 116:8; Job 5:20; 33:30; Prov. 10:2; 23:14). Normally, the expression is used of deliverance from the danger of death rather than from death itself. In the present context, however, Paul may also intend the latter meaning as well, especially as it is applied to the future in the second half of the verse.

The help that Paul has received in the past gives him the hope of further deliverance in the future. This does not necessarily mean that he will be rescued from all near-death situations, for he realizes that he is in the process of dying (cf. 4:10–12) and that he could be destroyed at any time (5:1, 8). Ultimately, Paul is confident only of the deliverance that will take place in the future resurrection (cf. Rom. 8:28–39).

1:11 / Paul has set his hope on God for continued deliverance from death (v. 10b). In verse 11a, Paul indirectly requests the Corinthians to pray for him in his ongoing apostolic ministry. The Corinthians' **prayers** function not only as entreaty on behalf of the apostle for deliverance from death but also as a sign of solidarity with him in the face of opposition (see also Rom. 15:30–31; Phil. 1:19). Prayer is just one way to achieve unity (cf. also 1 Thess. 5:25; Phlm. 22).

In verse 11b the ultimate purpose (*hina*, lit., "in order that") of the Corinthians' prayers on behalf of the apostle is doxological, that is, praise to God for Paul's ministry. By intervening and saving Paul from death, God enabled him to continue ministering. Therefore, when they meet together for worship, many believers should give thanks to God for Paul's deliverance, which is here called a **gracious favor** (*charisma*; cf. 12:9). Even Paul's most severe crisis must contribute to the praise of God. Certainly Paul's approach to his own apostolic experience of suffering and dying differs sharply from that of his opponents in Corinth, who believe that these things demonstrate that Paul is an apostolic pretender, a fraud (cf. 5:16).

Second Corinthians 1:3–11 ends as it began on a note of praise and thanksgiving to God, thus giving closure to the whole section. For Paul, the universal praise of God is not just a religious duty or an incidental nicety; it is the goal of history (cf. Rom. 15:9–11). He hopes that "the grace that is reaching more and more people may cause thanksgiving to overflow to the glory of God" (2 Cor. 4:15). Paul's divine deliverance from death through the prayers of the Corinthians is accomplishing just that.

Additional Notes §2

1:3–11 / An opening praise, or eulogy, begins with the word "blessed" (Greek *eulogētos*, Hebrew *bārûk*) followed, often without a verb, by the name of God, in order to express the wish "Blessed [be] God." This thanksgiving formula frequently introduces **praise** for Yahweh's salvation from a specific peril in the past (cf., e.g., Pss. 28:6; 31:21;

66:20; 124:6; Gen. 14:20; Exod. 18:10; 2 Sam. 18:28; Luke 1:68–79; 1QM 14.4–5). Typically, the psalmist gives praise in the assembly that, in response to his cry for help, God delivered him from the clutches of death or from some other danger.

1:3 / The use of **Father** in the thanksgiving does not merely represent a "Christianization" of the Jewish formula, for the eulogy in 1 Chron. 29:10 already refers to God as "our Father." Jesus taught his disciples to pray to God as Father (see the Lord's Prayer in Matt. 5:9–13; Luke 11:2–4), and through Christ believers are adopted as children of God who cry *Abba!* to the Father, using Jesus' own Aramaic address to God (Gal. 4:6; Rom. 8:15).

Peter O'Brien argues that Paul's introductory thanksgivings have an epistolary, didactic, and parenetic function (*Introductory Thanksgivings in the Letters of Paul* [NovTSup 49; Leiden: Brill, 1977], pp. 233–40). Thus 2 Cor. 1:3–11 introduces one of the main themes of the letter; it expresses Paul's perspective on that theme; and it appeals to the addressees to join with the apostle in that perspective. Cf. Scott Hafemann, "The Comfort and Power of the Gospel: The Argument of 2 Corinthians 1–3," *RevExp* 86 (1989), pp. 325–44 (here esp. pp. 327–30).

Because Paul does not supply the verb here, the traditional eulogy form that Paul employs at this point can be seen either as a wish (e.g., 1 Kgs. 10:9 LXX) or as a statement of fact (e.g., 1 Chron. 29:10). See the similar situation in 2 Cor. 13:13.

The grammar of v. 3 suggests that Paul views God as **the God ... of our Lord Jesus Christ**, since the article governs both "God" and "Father." Cf. Eph. 1:17, "the God of our Lord Jesus Christ." Jesus himself subscribes to monotheism when he gives the *Shema* ("one Lord") as the greatest commandment (Mark 12:29; cf. Deut. 6:4).

Note that in the eulogy of 1 Chron. 29:10 **Father** stands in apposition to **God** in a way similar to that in 2 Cor. 1:3. Moreover, in 4Q372 1.16, God is addressed as "my Father and my God" in the context of the psalmist's plea for deliverance from oppression. Cf. Eileen M. Schuller, "The Psalm of 4Q372 1 within the Context of Second Temple Prayer," *CBQ* 54 (1992), pp. 67–79.

The predication of God as **the God of all comfort** can be compared to other descriptions of God in Paul's letters: "the God of endurance and comfort" (Rom. 15:5), "the God of peace" (Rom. 15:33; Phil. 4:9; 1 Thess. 5:23), "the God of love and peace" (2 Cor. 13:11).

The NIV uses **compassion** to translate the plural term *oiktirmōn* ("mercies"). Paul's expression, "the Father of mercies," is paralleled by the similar expression, "God of mercies," in 1QH 10.14; 11.29.

1:4 / On Paul's use of first person plural pronouns (**we, us**) to refer to himself in 2 Cor. 1–3, see Scott Hafemann, *Suffering and the Spirit: An Exegetical Study of II Cor. 2:14–3:3 within the Context of the Corinthian Correspondence* (WUNT 2/19; Tübingen: Mohr Siebeck, 1986), pp. 12–17; also C. E. B. Cranfield, "Changes of Person and Number in Paul's Epistles," in *Paul and Paulinism: Essays in Honour of C. K. Barrett* (ed. M. D. Hooker and S. G. Wilson; London: SPCK, 1982), pp. 280–89; Thrall, *Second Corinthians*, vol. 1, pp. 105–7.

Paul derives the idea of God's **comfort** (= deliverance) from OT and Jewish tradition. In Isa. 51, for example, the defeated and humiliated people of Israel, who fear continually because of the fury of the oppressor (v. 13 [*thlibōn* in the LXX]), call upon Yahweh to intervene in the situation with strength (v. 9), to which Yahweh answers: "I, even I, am he who comforts *(parakalōn)* you!" (v. 12). This promise is then explicated by a statement of hope and confidence (v. 14). Likewise in Isa. 52:9 ("the Lord has comforted his people, he has redeemed Jerusalem"), the verb "comfort" stands in parallel to "redeem." In some Jewish traditions, this comfort for Israel includes the resurrection of the dead (cf. *Tg. Hos.* 6:2). The Psalms refer to the comfort (= deliverance) of individuals who are in dire circumstances (cf. Pss. 71:20–24; 86:1–2, 7, 12–17; 94:16–22; 23:4–6). These circumstances are often called "tribulation" (LXX *thlipsis*; cf. 70:20; 85:7; 22:5). In these situations, the psalmist experiences the comfort from Yahweh, his God. The parallelism of the word "comfort" with terms of helping and saving makes it clear that the actual intervention of God in the situation is meant. Some psalms link comfort, preservation from death, and the granting of new life in communion with God (cf. Pss. 71:20; 86:13; 94:17). The psalmists characterize themselves as those who place their "trust" and "hope" in Yahweh (cf. Pss. 71:1, 5, 14; 86:2; 94:22). The praise of those who have been comforted by God proclaims his "comfort" (cf. Pss. 71:22–24; 86:12).

1:5 / Throughout the letter (e.g., 1:8; 3:9, 10; 4:7, 15, 17; 8:2, 7; 9:8, 12, 14; 11:23; 12:7), Paul emphasizes the superabundance of various things.

For other interpretations of the **sufferings of Christ** and Paul's relationship to them, see Thrall, *Second Corinthians*, vol. 1, pp. 107–10. Paul often parallels his own sufferings to those of Christ. Even the opposition that Paul experiences in Corinth has a parallel in the sufferings of Christ (see on 5:16). Paul is confident that, even if he must suffer a martyr's death, God's resurrection power will finally prevail (cf. 2 Cor. 4:14).

1:6 / It is no longer possible to ascertain what kind of tribulations the Corinthian church may have had to endure. Perhaps the young believers were oppressed by both Jews and non-Jews, for different reasons. Perhaps Paul is not thinking of any specific situation at all, but rather the suffering with Christ that is the common lot of all children of God and part of the sufferings of the present age (cf. Rom. 8:17–18). On Paul's concept of endurance, see Judith M. Gundry Volf, *Paul and Perseverance: Staying In and Falling Away* (WUNT 2/37; Tübingen: Mohr Siebeck, 1990).

1:8 / The NIV supplies the words **the province of.** While Paul might be thinking of the Roman province, his conception of geography and ethnography seems to be rooted firmly in conceptions drawn from the OT and Judaism (see Introduction). From a Jewish perspective, the heart of the Roman province of Asia was originally the Shemite territory of Lud, whereas Ephesus in Ionia belonged to the Japhethite territory of Javan, along with mainland Greece. Perhaps that is a contributing reason why Paul chooses to tell the Corinthians about this particular episode. We must always think on multiple levels when we read Paul's writings.

It is also possible that Paul experienced a severe illness, such as the one he describes as a "thorn in the flesh" in 2 Cor. 12:9, alluding to Ps. 32:4[31:4 LXX].

Whereas here Paul states that he **despaired even of life,** in 4:8 he writes that he is perplexed, "but not in despair."

1:9 / The **sentence of death** occurs nowhere else in biblical Greek, but the term translated "sentence" *(apokrima)* was used by other ancient writers as a technical term for any official decree that, in response to a petition or inquiry, settled a case. Insofar as Paul shares in the sufferings of Christ (v. 5), perhaps his sentence of death is analogous to that which Christ received when he was crucified. If so, Paul's death sentence strongly implies also the resurrection of Christ. Here we may also compare Hos. 13:14 LXX (cited in 1 Cor. 15:55), "Where is your verdict/sentence, O death?"

The NIV translation of v. 9b **(But this happened that we might not rely on ourselves)** makes it sound as though Paul came to the realization of the divine purpose of his travail only after the situation was over. In the Greek text, however, the second half of the verse is a purpose clause directly dependent on the first half. There is no break in the sentence.

1:10 / In the Greek text, v. 10 begins with a relative pronoun ("who") whose antecedent is "God." Hence, v. 10 follows on v. 9 without a major break. On the three difficult textual problems in this verse, see Thrall, *Second Corinthians,* vol. 1, pp. 120–22.

Like the suffering righteous in the OT and the suffering Christ, Paul is being led into situations of suffering in order that God may display his resurrection power of deliverance through Paul.

1:11 / **Many will give thanks** resembles the conclusion to an individual lament such as Ps. 22, in which the psalmist, after expressing steadfast hope in God for deliverance (vv. 4–5, 9–11), predicts that his testimony of deliverance in the great assembly will cause praise to redound to God, even in generations to come (vv. 25–31).

§3 Accusations (2 Cor. 1:12–2:13)

After the thanksgiving in 1:3–11, the body of the letter begins with a lengthy section in which Paul seeks to deal with various accusations the Corinthians have made against his character and conduct (1:12–2:13). By the writing of 2 Corinthians, Paul has heard the good report from Titus that most of the Corinthians have been reconciled to Paul (cf. 7:6–7). Yet, because of the discrepancy between Paul's written word and his actions, the Corinthians have become suspicious of Paul's motives, accusing him of duplicity and double-mindedness, especially in regard to his travel plans. Why, for example, did he delay his third visit? Why, instead of coming to Corinth, did he write a "tearful letter" after his painful second visit? And why did he then go to Macedonia first, instead of coming directly to Corinth? The Corinthians' suspicions against Paul stand in the way of a full and final reconciliation. Therefore, before his third visit to Corinth can take place with confidence, Paul needs to handle the accusations and clear up any misunderstandings, for he certainly does not want a repetition of the catastrophe that occurred during the painful second visit, which resulted in a Korah-like rebellion against Paul's authority.

1:12 / Paul begins this section quite directly with a general declaration of his innocence. But it seems strange that the apostle would start off with a **boast** in a section dominated by accusations that have been leveled against him. Perhaps this is already a hint of the bitter irony that characterizes Paul's boastful defense in the "Fool's Speech" later in the letter (11:1–12:13). As verse 13 makes clear, the issue here is the apparent duplicity of Paul's prior correspondence with the Corinthians, but the Jerusalem collection could also have been under attack. Certainly 1 Corinthians left Paul open to the charge of planning to embezzle the collection, for after refusing support from the Corinthians (1 Cor. 9:15–18), despite the fact that he accepted it from the

Macedonians (2 Cor. 11:7–11), he goes on to instruct them to take a collection ostensibly for Jerusalem (1 Cor. 16:1–4). The opponents probably targeted this apparent inconsistency, and Paul had to affirm his **sincerity** repeatedly (cf. 2:17; 7:2; 10:2; 12:14–18). Perhaps Paul also has in mind here the Corinthians' accusation that he had failed to carry through with his promise to make an extended stay in Corinth (1 Cor. 15:5–7). We will come back to the nature of these charges below.

Paul refutes such charges by appealing to the witness of his **conscience**, the inner tribunal that determines whether one's behavior agrees with the moral norms and requirements affirmed by the mind (cf. Rom. 9:1; 2 Cor. 4:2; 5:11; also 1 Cor. 10:25, 27). Since it acts as an independent judge over a person's behavior, it can also be called in to testify. The conscience, however, may not function properly, and each person's conscience may indicate a different correspondence between behavior and norms (cf. 1 Cor. 10:29b). Hence, Paul distinguishes the verdict of this personal tribunal from God's own judgment and the judgment seat of Christ, before which everyone must appear (cf. 2 Cor. 5:10). As Paul states in 1 Corinthians 4:4–5, "My conscience is clear, but that does not make me innocent. It is the Lord who judges me. . . . He will bring to light what is hidden in darkness and will expose the motives of men's hearts."

When Paul appeals to the testimony, or "witness" of his conscience, he is fully aware that, according to the law of Moses, "Every matter must be established by the testimony of two or three witnesses" (Deut. 19:15; cf. 2 Cor. 13:1). The apostle would like the Corinthian church itself, which he founded, to be tangible evidence of the legitimacy of his apostolic office (cf. 3:2). But if they, who know him best, have sincere doubts about his veracity, he can appeal only to God or the Holy Spirit (cf. Rom. 9:1 ["I speak the truth in Christ—I am not lying, my conscience confirms it in the Holy Spirit"]; 2 Cor. 1:18, 23; 11:31). Paul may solicit the witness of the Corinthians' conscience concerning what they already know about him (4:2; 5:11), but ultimately, because he is an apostle, Paul can be judged only by the Lord (cf. 1 Cor. 4:3–5; 2 Cor. 5:10). As we shall discuss on 13:1, the revelatory mediator stands in a unique position in having to testify to his own veracity.

When Paul boasts in his clear conscience, does he contradict his later dictum, "I will not boast about myself, except about my weakness" (12:5)? Boasting is a sensitive issue for the apostle, especially since he had received a thorn in the flesh to keep him from it in the past (12:7). Paul is aware here, however, that his conduct toward the Corinthians in accordance with the will of God comes from the **grace** of God, and not from his own ability. As he states in 1 Corinthians 15:9, "by the grace of God I am what I am," which summarizes his whole apostleship. Therefore, his boast is not self-praise, but rather a boast in the Lord (cf. 1 Cor. 1:31; 2 Cor. 10:17).

1:13a / Having affirmed his sincerity in verse 12, Paul proceeds in verse 13a to substantiate (**For,** *gar*) what he has said by addressing the specific grievance against his letter-writing. Evidently, the Corinthians charge Paul with having a hidden agenda in his letters: He writes one thing and does another. The problem is not that Paul's letters are sometimes inadvertently difficult to understand or ambiguous (cf. 1 Cor. 5:9; 2 Pet. 3:16), but that they are intentionally duplicitous and deliberately deceptive. Paul categorically denies this charge, claiming that his true motives are transparent for all to **read** and **understand**.

1:13b–14 / Paul hopes that the Corinthians' grievances against him and their misunderstandings about his intentions will eventually be removed. The Corinthians have already understood him **in part**. Does this mean that the Corinthians' understanding is partial or rather that part of the Corinthian congregation understands? The placement of the prepositional phrase after the pronoun **you** suggests the latter possibility. This interpretation is further confirmed by the fact that, throughout 2 Corinthians, Paul reckons with a majority that has favorably received the "tearful letter" and is now more or less reconciled to him (cf. 2:6), and with a minority that is still unrepentant and hostile toward him (cf. 10:2; 12:21; 13:2).

Paul can already **boast** in the Corinthians (cf. 7:4; 8:24; 9:2), and he expects to continue to be able to do so until the **day of the Lord** (cf. Phil. 2:16; 1 Thess. 2:19). Paul expects that by the day of the Lord at the latest, when he and all other believers will stand before the judgment seat of Christ/God (2 Cor. 5:10; Rom. 14:10), the Corinthians will completely understand what the apostle says and does and will thus be able to boast in him, and particularly in his heart (cf. 5:12), for at the Parousia, the Lord will reveal the purposes of the heart (cf. 1 Cor. 4:5; 13:12).

1:15–2:4 / Paul refutes the accusation that he is unreliable in his travel plans with two points. First, he shows that his evangelistic ministry is grounded in his apostolic commission (vv. 17–22). Second, he declares that he was faithful to this commission when he changed his plans in a situation that itself had changed (1:23–2:4).

1:15–16 / **Confident** that the Corinthians will understand him fully at the Parousia, if not before, Paul begins to explain his change in travel plans. Initially, Paul planned to visit **Macedonia** first and then go on to Corinth for a more extended stay (1 Cor. 16:5–7). In his itinerary in 2 Corinthians 1:15–16, however, Paul outlines *two* visits to Corinth: one directly after sailing from Ephesus, and the other following a visit to Macedonia. In this way, the Corinthians could send him finally on his way to **Judea** with the collection. Is the original plan for an extended stay in Corinth thereby scrapped? If so, this would have been interpreted as a gesture of contempt, since there had been so much conflict between Paul and the Corinthians.

In the revised plan that Paul gives in verse 15, the much-discussed expression, **so that you might benefit twice** (v. 15), probably refers not to the apostle's second visit to Corinth in relation to the founding visit, but rather to the two stopovers he planned to make in Corinth in accordance with his revised travel plans. In that case, the Corinthians would have had a double benefit (or rather, "gift") because Paul would have made Corinth both the starting and the finishing point of his collection for Jerusalem in the region, and the Corinthians would have had two opportunities to contribute to it. (We might even say a "double grace" to contribute, in view of all the trouble the Corinthians had been.) In the Corinthian correspondence, the term *charis* (most often translated "grace") is frequently used in the sense of "gift" for the collection for Jerusalem (cf. 1 Cor. 16:3; 2 Cor. 8:4, 6–7, 19). Now, as before, Paul wants the Corinthians to outgive the Macedonians who have given sacrificially (cf. 2 Cor. 8:6–7).

Paul must have changed his travel plans sometime between the writing of 1 Corinthians and the aftermath of the "painful visit" mentioned in 2 Corinthians 2:1, for, as of the writing of 2 Corinthians, the relationship between Paul and the church at Corinth was still disturbed over the issue. And Paul evidently thought that he would have to make one visit to correct the situation in the congregation and another on his way back from Macedonia to finish the collection. Furthermore, unlike 1 Corinthians 16:3–4, where he expressed some ambivalence,

Paul was now determined to deliver the collection personally (cf. 2 Cor. 9:5).

When and in what form Paul told the Corinthians of his change in plans can no longer be ascertained. Several possibilities have been suggested: (1) the announcement was delivered by Titus either during his first visit to Corinth to see about the collection (cf. 2 Cor. 12:18) or during his stay in Corinth to handle the conflict between Paul and the church; (2) it was written in the so-called tearful letter, which Paul sent to the Corinthians after his "painful visit" (cf. 2:3–4); or (3) it was detailed for the first time in 2 Corinthians. There is no evidence that Paul sent another letter to Corinth between the writing of 1 Corinthians and the painful visit. The Corinthians' accusation presupposes that Paul had broken his promise to visit them. At the time of the writing of the tearful letter, however, Paul was already determined not to travel to Corinth but to send Titus instead. Therefore, it is most probable that, as Paul left Corinth during the painful visit, he promised the Corinthians that he would return to them. Paul explains in 2:1–4 why he did not keep this promise. When Paul later departed from Ephesus (or Troas at the latest), he resorted to his first plan, i.e., to visit Macedonia first and then Corinth (cf. 1 Cor. 16:5–7; Acts 20:1–3).

1:17 / In the form of two rhetorical questions, Paul draws a conclusion from what he has said about his changed travel plans in verses 15–16, a conclusion that reflects the charges leveled against him in Corinth. The rhetorical questions obviously expect negative answers. First, when Paul revised his itinerary, he did not do so **lightly** (i.e., capriciously or double-mindedly). He had a definite purpose in changing his itinerary: to give the Corinthians a double opportunity to participate in the collection (cf. v. 16). Second, Paul is not the kind of person who makes his plans **in a worldly manner** (literally, "according to the flesh"). In 2 Corinthians 10:2, Paul explicitly refers to people in Corinth who think that he walks "according to the flesh," meaning that he is two-faced (i.e., timid in person but bold when away). Similarly, 2 Corinthians 1:17b reflects the accusation that the apostle speaks with a forked tongue, so that no one knows whether he is saying **yes** or **no** to a matter. The words **in the same breath** are not in the Greek text, but are added by the NIV translators to try to make sense of the difficult formulation. Yet, as L. L. Welborn has now shown, the double affirmation **(yes, yes)** and the double negation (**no, no**) substitute for an oath formula, which expresses the ambiguity of the situation in which Paul finds himself as a result of the Corinthians' suspicions about him. In effect, Paul answers the charge of vacillating in his travel plans by stating that the Corinthians have forced him into establishing the truth of his statements with an oath. It is interesting to note that Paul is forced to use oath formulas both elsewhere in 2 Corinthians (2 Cor. 1:18, 23; 11:10, 31) and in other letters with apologetic contexts (Gal. 1:20; Rom. 9:1).

1:18 / To further substantiate his claim that he is not double-minded, Paul adduces both God (v. 18) and his apostolic message (v. 19). First, Paul invokes God as his witness that he is speaking the truth when he states that he has not been double-minded in his travel plans. In other words, Paul's word to the Corinthians is unequivocal and dependable. The statement, **God is faithful** (cf. 1 Cor. 1:9; 10:13; 1 Thess. 5:24), functions here as another oath formula. Paul thereby bases the trustworthiness of his own statements on the trustworthiness of God, and there can be no doubt from the OT that God is faithful (cf. Deut. 7:9; Pss. 19:7; 145:13). But how can Paul so glibly connect his own veracity with God's faithfulness? In all likelihood, the apostle presupposes that he is the spokesman of God. Like Moses, who claims that his message is a word from the Lord, and that "God is faithful" (Deut. 32:1b–4), Paul claims that his **message** depends on God, and that God is faithful. Paul thereby emphasizes his mediatory apostolic role, a subject that he develops in detail in 2:14–4:6.

1:19 / As a second argument to substantiate his claim that he is not double-minded, Paul adduces his unequivocal apostolic message to the Corinthians. When Paul first preached to the Corinthians during his founding visit to Corinth, the content of his message was **the Son of God, Jesus Christ** (cf. 1 Cor. 2:1–2). After God commissioned Paul to apostleship by revealing his Son in or to Paul, that he might preach the gospel to the nations (cf. Gal. 1:15–16), the apostle began to preach Jesus Christ as the messianic Son of God (cf. Acts 9:20), and this became the normal content of his gospel (1 Thess. 1:10). Paul pins his apostleship on this message. **Silas** and **Timothy,** Paul's faithful coworkers who are known and trusted by the Corinthians, were with him during the founding visit (cf. Acts 18:5) and preached the same message. Paul reminds the Corinthians of the straightforwardness of his original message to them at that time. This was a message that the Corinthians obviously embraced, and their continuing faith attests to the character of the original message. Ultimately, the Corinthians cannot deny Paul's original message to them and his mediatory role in bringing it to them without at the same time denying their own Christian existence (Paul uses a similar argument in 3:1–6). Their own faith and salvation are the tangible evidence that Paul's preaching did not vacillate in either its intention or its outcome. The message that Paul preached to the Corinthians was unequivocally confirmed (**Yes**) to them in Christ: God revealed the message to Paul; Paul preached it; the Corinthians received it; and now they have it in Christ. The message was never retracted or amended (**No**) in any way.

1:20 / In verse 20a Paul explains (**For,** *gar*) why his message of Jesus Christ as Son of God was unequivocally confirmed to the Corinthians. Just as in verse 18 the faithfulness of God substantiates the veracity of Paul's general apostolic "word" (including statements about his travel plans), so also here divine **promises** substantiate Paul's more specific apostolic message of the gospel.

As Paul has mentioned repeatedly and in various ways in the previous context, the Corinthians are sons of God and thus brothers with Paul (cf. vv. 1, 2, 3). Hence, when Paul refers here to the "promises" that have already been confirmed to the Corinthians, he may have in view particularly the divine adoption of sons (cf. 2 Cor. 6:18, quoting 2 Sam. 7:14) that the Corinthians enjoy in Christ, the messianic Son of God promised beforehand through the OT prophets (Rom. 1:2–4). The only other use of the term in the letter comes at 2 Corinthians 7:1 and refers to an OT messianic adoption text (2 Sam. 7:14) as among the **promises** that Paul and the Corinthians already have. This does not, of course, exclude other promises from resonating with the text, especially since divine adoptive sonship includes Abrahamic heirship (cf. Gal. 3:26, 29; 4:1–7; Rom. 8:15, 17). Paul's message of Jesus Christ as Son of God was unequivocally confirmed to the Corinthians, for the latter participate in the sonship of the Son of God, in whom the promises are affirmed by their fulfillment ("**Yes**").

In verse 20b Paul draws an inference (**And so,** *dio kai*) from the fact that in Christ the Corinthians participate in the promises through Paul's preaching. Whatever this line may mean in particular, it seems clear that Paul portrays himself as a revelatory mediator. **Amen** is a transliteration of a Hebrew word that serves to confirm what has been said before. The Corinthians were familiar with this use of Amen (cf. 1 Cor. 14:16). Here, the Amen is spoken by Christ (**through him**) in that the promises spoken beforehand are fulfilled in him. That affirmation is, in turn, communicated by Paul (**by us**) to others, including the Corinthians. All of this has a doxological purpose (**to the glory of God**).

1:21–22 / Paul further explains how God is faithful (and thus that Paul's own message is unequivocal), emphasizing his activity in the whole process of incorporating believers into the promises. A more literal translation than the one given in the NIV seems preferable here, and could preserve both the parallelism and the word play from the Greek: "Now it is God who establishes us with you in the anointed one and has anointed us." Just as in verses 19–20 Paul draws attention to the comparison between the messianic Son and the sons of God, so also here he makes a comparison between the anointed one (Christ) and the anointed ones. Hence, the second **us** most likely includes both Paul and the Corinthians, rather than referring to Paul alone. We see once again how suddenly Paul can change the referent of the first person plural pronoun (see on 1:4). God establishes (cf. 1 Cor. 1:8–9) the union of believers **in Christ** through baptism by the Holy Spirit (cf. 1 Cor. 12:12–13). We may compare the teaching from Luke that Jesus was anointed with the Spirit for his messianic mission (cf. Luke 4:18, citing Isa. 61:1–2; cf. *4Q521* 1.2.1–14; 1 Sam. 16:13). In that case, just as God "anointed" Christ with the Spirit at baptism as the messianic son of God (cf. Luke 4:18 with 3:22), so also he "anoints" believers with the Spirit at baptism to become sons of God (cf. Gal. 4:4–6; Rom. 8:15).

In verse 22 Paul continues his description of God. God has everything to do with the security of the present relationship that believers enjoy in Christ and with its future culmination. He has put the **Spirit** in their hearts, a theme to which Paul will shortly return in defense of his apostleship (cf. 3:3). The Spirit is here described as a **deposit,** i.e., "down payment," or "first installment" (cf. 5:5; Eph. 1:14). Elsewhere the Spirit is described as "firstfruits" (Rom. 8:23). These metaphors suggest a connection between the present possession of the Spirit and the final redemption of the body at the resurrection, when the sons of God by adoption will be conformed to the image of the Son, their firstborn brother (cf. Rom. 8:23, 29; 2 Cor. 5:4–5), and share in the messianic inheritance (cf. Rom. 4:13; 8:17, 32).

Paul's point in 1:18–22 is to show that God is faithful, and that he is God's spokesman; therefore, the apostle's unequivocal message, which mediated the promises to the Corinthians, is not susceptible to the charge of double-mindedness. Even if Paul's travel plans have changed according to the changing circumstances, God's message spoken through him to the Corinthians—the basis of his whole apostolic ministry—has not changed and is still in effect. Indeed, it establishes the Corinthians in Christ until the consummation.

1:23–2:4 / In 1:23–2:4 Paul gives the real reason that he changed his travel plans: to spare the Corinthians from judgment (1:23–2:2) and to write a letter that would promote reconciliation between the Corinthians and himself (2:3–4). The vocabulary recalls a trial scene, perhaps one much like that which Moses conducted against Korah, who led his followers in rebellion against Moses and Aaron over the issue of power and control (Num. 16–17).

1:23 / Paul begins the section by again calling upon God as his witness in yet another oath, this time in regard to the specific matter of his changed travel plans. Strangely, the NIV does not represent *epi tēn emēn psychēn*, which should be translated "against my life." Paul puts his life on the line in calling God as **witness** against him if he is not telling the truth. Although in the face of opposition Paul must frequently avow that he is not lying (e.g., Rom. 9:1), and even calls upon God as a witness of his actions and speech (Rom. 1:9; 2 Cor. 5:11; Phil. 1:8; 1 Thess. 2:5, 10), he seldom stakes his own life on the truth of his claims. Here we can perhaps glimpse the magnitude of the ongoing opposition that Paul must have felt in Corinth. Despite the possible allusion to Matthew 5:33–37 in 2 Corinthians 1:17, Jesus' teaching against taking oaths seems to be unknown to Paul.

By making this strong oath, Paul wants to assure the Corinthians in no uncertain terms that the real reason he changed his travel plans and refrained from returning to them as promised was not his alleged double-mindedness, but **in order to spare you.** The changes in Paul's travel plans were an act of mercy on his part, as was his tearful letter (2:4). Paul was attempting to restore the Corinthians' allegiance to him (cf. 2 Cor. 7:8ff.) and to delay judgment coming upon the congregation. At the end of the letter Paul warns the Corinthians that, when he returns to Corinth this next time, he will not "spare" them (13:2). Evidently, he had warned them during his second, painful visit of possible punishment for the church when he returned. The term used in each case is *pheidesthai,* which Paul uses, for example, in the sense of God's not sparing his own Son but giving him up to death (Rom. 8:32). Hence, just as Paul calls upon God to take his life if he is not telling the truth to the Corinthians, so also the Corinthians' very lives are at stake (cf. 1 Cor. 11:30) when the apostle comes to visit them. As the situation stood in the time between the painful visit and the news from Titus, Paul did not want to return to Corinth for fear that he would have to use his awesome apostolic authority, which the Lord gave him really for building the Corinthians up and not for destroying them (2 Cor. 10:8; 12:19–21). Already in 1 Corinthians Paul had warned the church that he might have to come to them "with a stick" (1 Cor. 4:21).

1:24 / Since Paul's stated desire to spare the Corinthians from judgment (v. 23) strongly implies his apostolic authority to judge the Corinthians, Paul tries to avoid appearing too authoritarian and to reassure the Corinthians. When Paul states that **we** do not **lord** it over the Corinthians in the context of judgment, he may be alluding to Korah's rebellion, which challenged the authority of Moses and Aaron by accusing them of exalting themselves over the Israelites (Num. 16:3, 13) and by arguing for equality. If Paul is alluding to this OT incident, then the **we** might include Timothy (cf. 2 Cor. 1:19), the co-sender of the letter (1:1), who would then be seen as an Aaron figure.

The apostle tries further to defuse the situation by appealing to the mutuality between himself and the Corinthians, a theme begun in the opening (vv. 1–2) and thanksgiving (vv. 3–11). Despite his similarity to Moses, who had the divine authority to judge the congregation, Paul chose to spare the Corinthians. Unlike Moses, he is not in a ruler-subject relationship with the Corinthians. On the contrary, both Paul and the Corinthians are fellow workers, a description that Paul later uses of Titus, his trusted traveling companion and co-laborer (8:23). Furthermore, Paul and the Corinthians are working together for the benefit and **joy** of the latter, as manifested by the fact that the Corinthians stand firm in faith. The relationship between Paul and the Corinthians is therefore fundamentally positive (cf. 10:8; 13:10).

2:1–2 / Paul resumes his point from verse 23, that he did not return to Corinth too quickly after the painful (second) visit in order to spare the Corinthians from judgment (lit., "not to come to you again in sorrow"). If Paul had come to Corinth as promised, it would have meant more pain and sorrow for Paul himself (v. 2), but, more significantly, also for the Corinthians (v. 3). Instead of forcing the issue too quickly, Paul wanted to wait until there was some sign from the church of at least partial repentance and reconciliation before he would contemplate another visit, so he sent the tearful letter instead. Since Titus had recently brought him a positive report of the Corinthians' improved attitude (7:6–7), Paul could now write 2 Corinthians in order further to prepare for his long-awaited third visit (cf. 13:1–2). As the accusations against Paul in the present section make clear, Paul is, however, still struggling to win the Corinthians' total confidence and support.

2:3 / In verses 3–4 and verse 9, Paul gives three reasons why he wrote the tearful letter instead of coming to the Corinthians as promised after the painful visit. First, he wanted to prepare the way for his coming; for by changing his travel plans and writing a corrective letter instead (cf. 2:9; 7:8), Paul was merely delaying his trip to Corinth, not abandoning it altogether. He wanted to wait until the Corinthians were more receptive to him, so that his reunion with them would be an occasion for **joy** rather than sorrow. Remarkably, Paul expresses his **confidence in all** of the Corinthians, even the ones who are currently defecting from him and siding with the opponents. Such is his confidence in the transforming work of the Holy Spirit in the hearts of this congregation (cf. 3:1–18). Paul's hope for the Corinthians is firm (1:7) and his confidence in them is complete (7:4, 16). Of course, this is also grounded in the fact that Paul has already received evidence of the Corinthians' willingness to be reconciled with him.

2:4 / The second reason Paul wrote the tearful letter was to show his love for the Corinthians. This verse informs us that the letter Paul wrote after his painful second visit to Corinth was indeed a tearful letter. Many interpreters consider 2 Corinthians 10–13 part of that tearful letter, although very little sorrow is expressed there, and the problem is caused by false apostles (11:5, 13) rather than by a member of the Corinthian church (see the Introduction). Some interpreters, therefore, have associated the phrase **I wrote you out of great distress** with 1 Corinthians, especially chapter 5, although the immoral brother there did not grieve Paul personally. More probably, the tearful letter is one of the lost letters of Paul, along with the one mentioned in 1 Corinthians 5:9.

The **distress** *(thlipsis)* that Paul experienced over the situation at Corinth is different from the life-threatening "hardships" he suffered at the same time in the province of Asia (1:8), although the same Greek word is used of both. Perhaps the term is used in the present context so that the Corinthians will realize that the anguish of soul they caused Paul at that time added internal grief to external affliction. This interpretation of *thlipsis* correlates with 7:5, where Paul uses a related term *(thlibomenoi)* to suggest that the tribulations that he suffered during the period before he heard from Titus included an external and an internal component ("conflicts on the outside, fears within"). We may also compare 11:28, which includes external dangers alongside the daily pressure on the apostle because his concern for all the churches.

If the use of *thlipsis* in 2:4 is thus designed to recall Paul's tribulation as described in the thanksgiving (1:3–11), then it is interesting to note that his suffering in Asia happened for the sake of the Corinthians (1:6). Thus, both forms of *thlipsis* become expressions of Paul's **love** and concern for the church. Paul explicitly states that he did not write the tearful letter to grieve the Corinthians, although he is aware that it did temporarily grieve them (cf. 7:8–9); rather, he wrote in order to show his love for them (cf. also 6:6; 11:11; 12:15). Paul cared enough to confront them by letter, but he cared too much for them to visit them personally at that time (cf. 1:23; 2:1). Evidently, Paul considers his apostolic presence even more powerful and more potentially injurious to the unrepentant Corinthians than his apostolic letters (cf. 10:11; 12:19–21; 13:1–2, 10), despite claims to the contrary in Corinth (cf. 10:10).

2:5–11 / In this section, Paul explicitly mentions the person who was chiefly responsible for making his second visit to Corinth so painful and who evoked the writing of the tearful letter (v. 5). Like Moses, Paul wanted to give the rebel(s) a chance to repent before executing great judgment among the people. Since the church had now dealt with this offender, he discusses how the church should forgive him and restore him to fellowship (vv. 6–11).

2:5 / The offender is introduced in verse 5 for the first time in the letter. Neither here nor in 7:8–13 does Paul go into any detail about what this unnamed person did to **grieve** him. Evidently, a member of the Corinthian church insulted Paul personally, while the church stood by passively (cf. 2 Cor. 12:11). Very likely, the offender acted under the influence of Paul's opponents, who had recently come to Corinth, although nothing is said here about that connection. The insult must have been damaging to Paul's apostleship, for it caused him to retreat from Corinth. Perhaps the offender was the leader of a group who questioned Paul's divine sending and exalted position in the church, much as Korah led a rebellion against Moses for similar reasons (cf. Num. 16:3, 13, 28–29; see above on 1:23 and below on 2 Cor. 2:6–7). This might explain why Paul believed that the offender had **grieved** the whole Corinthian church, for in the case of Korah's rebellion the whole congregation was threatened with divine judgment because of the sin of one person (cf. Num. 16:20–22, 26). Alternatively, the offender may have grieved just a subgroup of the congregation, for the phrase **to some extent** may be understood as meaning "in part," that is, part of the congregation, as in 1:14 (see further on 2:6).

The malefactor's insult may also have included one or more of the accusations that Paul handles in the present section (1:12–2:4). For example, the accusation of untrustworthiness and double-mindedness leveled against Paul for his change of travel plans (1:15–2:4) could have been the cause of his grief. The malefactor may also have accused Paul of either unholiness (v. 12), insincerity (v. 12), or deception (v. 13). Perhaps the collection that Paul ordered the Corinthians to take on a weekly basis until he came (cf. 1 Cor. 16:1–4) became the basis for the malefactor's accusations against the apostle, for almost immediately after referring again to the man (7:12), Paul launches into an extended discussion of the collection that he wants the Corinthians to continue assembling (chs. 8–9). Ultimately, however, we do not know what the offender did to cause Paul grief, and we are groping in the dark. In 2:5 Paul is concerned merely to adumbrate an incident that the Corinthians know all too well. In any case, the offender's attack on Paul exceeded the bounds of acceptable controversy from the apostle's perspective.

From verse 5b it is clear that the actions of the malefactor had an impact on the whole church. But in what sense did he grieve the Corinthians even more than he **grieved** Paul? Perhaps he challenged the legitimacy of Paul's apostleship and thus called the whole church that Paul founded into question. Perhaps the judgment that this person experienced in particular was felt to some degree by the whole congregation. More probably, the offender grieved the church by causing Paul to send the tearful letter, which in turn brought grief to the recipients (7:8–11). The Corinthians were somehow implicated in the offense, even if they were merely passive during the assault.

2:6 / Paul announces that the offender's punishment is now sufficient and that the Corinthians should restore him to fellowship. By the writing of 2 Corinthians, **the majority** of the church at Corinth seems to have carried out the discipline of the malefactor that Paul had apparently ordered in the tearful letter (cf. 7:12). The term "the majority" probably indicates most of the members of the Corinthian church, with dissenters or abstainers still in existence. On the other hand, it may reflect a Hebrew technical term meaning the congregation as a whole (so, e.g., J. C. VanderKam). The interpretation of this expression is crucial to the question of the unity of 2 Corinthians, for if there are two (or more) factions within the Corinthian church, that might explain why Paul would vary his approach in different sections of the letter: first conciliatory and positive (2 Cor. 1–9) and then sarcastic and harsh (chs. 10–13). On the other hand, if Paul makes no distinction between groups within the church, then we are compelled to assume not only that he addresses the church as a whole but that the various sections of 2 Corinthians were written in very different situations. As we have seen on 1:13–14 and 2:5, however, Paul seems to divide the congregation into at least two subgroups: the part that has already understood him and the other that he hopes will eventually understand (1:13–14); or the part that carried out Paul's directive to punish the offender and the other that was grieved by this punitive action (2:5). Paul explicitly mentions "factions" in the latter section of the letter (12:20; cf. 10:2).

We do not know what form the punishment may have taken, but 1 Corinthians 5:1–13 indicates handing an immoral man over to Satan "for the destruction of the flesh" (v. 5) and exclusion of the individual from the fellowship. Are we to assume in our passage that Titus brought Paul word that the offender had repented of his misdeed, or that Paul absolved him unilaterally? Did the Corinthians appeal to Paul on behalf of the man? These questions are not directly answered in the text, but we find clues to their answer from the traditional background and from the subsequent context.

As far as the traditional background is concerned, an interesting parallel to the idea that the offender's punishment was **sufficient** *(hikanos)* is found in Wisdom 18:20–25, which describes the plague that struck Israel in the desert when they rebelled against Moses and Aaron after Korah's rebellion (Num. 16:41–50). During that judgment, Aaron is said to have intervened on behalf of the people by an intercessory prayer (Wis. 18:22, 23), so that the destroyer yielded: "for merely the trial [or, experience] of the wrath was enough *(hikanos)*" (v. 25). In other words, it was deemed sufficient that the community suffered the plague without being completely consumed (see also Isa. 40:2). Likewise in 2 Corinthians 2:6, the punishment of the malefactor who rebelled against Paul is deemed "sufficient." If Paul has Numbers 16:41ff. in mind as he writes (see Additional Notes below on 2 Cor. 2:15), perhaps our passage implies that Paul interceded on behalf of the offender (cf. 2:10), so that his punishment (and that of the church) would abate. The fact that Paul may be alluding to this OT tradition is supported by the following verse.

2:7 / As a result *(hōste)* of the offender's punishment being enough, the Corinthians should pardon the offender. The verb translated here **be overwhelmed** is *katapothē* (from *katapinein*), meaning "be swallowed up" with total extinction as a result (cf. 1 Cor. 15:54; 2 Cor. 5:4). Paul may have chosen this verb because, in the context of the offender's punishment being "enough" (2 Cor. 2:6; cf. Wis. 18:25), it would recall that those involved in Korah's rebellion were "swallowed up" *(katapinein)* by the earth (cf. Num. 16:30, 32, 34). In that case, the punishment to which the offender was exposed could have resulted in his demise (cf. 1 Cor. 5:5), for to be swallowed up in **sorrow** leads to death (2 Cor. 7:10).

The Corinthians are instructed to **forgive** the malefactor (cf. Gal. 6:1). The errant brother is not irrevocably condemned. Even one who commits the most heinous offense can be saved at least on the day of the Lord (cf. 1 Cor. 5:5). The church is also instructed to **comfort** *(parakalein)* the offender. If this person is thereby delivered from being "swallowed up" in a divine judgment similar to that experienced as a result of Korah's rebellion, perhaps the term should here be translated "deliver" (see on 1:3–11).

2:8 / Because the offender was in danger of being swallowed up in death, Paul forcibly repeats his exhortation to the Corinthians: **I urge you, therefore, to reaffirm your love for him.**

2:9 / The third reason, in addition to those given in verses 3–4, that Paul wrote to the Corinthians instead of visiting them as promised is given in verse 9. When Paul wrote the tearful letter he could not have known whether the Corinthians would be **obedient** in punishing the offender. As Paul explains in 7:12, he wrote to them so "that before God you could see for yourselves how devoted to us you are." Since that time, Paul has learned from Titus that the church has indeed complied. As an apostle, Paul has the authority and goal of making the Corinthians obedient (10:5–6). Indeed, the reason for which Paul received apostleship was to bring about obedience of faith among the nations (cf. Rom. 1:5).

The NIV translates verse 9b **to see if you would stand the test.** A more literal translation would be "in order that I might know your character" (cf. Phil. 2:22). Paul was subjecting the Corinthians' character to examination and approval, by seeing whether they would comply with his directive to punish the offender and thereby reaffirm Paul's apostolic authority. Whereas in the previous context Paul has been handling accusations leveled against his own character by the Corinthians, Paul now turns the tables by stating that he was examining the Corinthians' character (see the similar reversal in 12:19–21).

2:10 / Just as Paul has already urged the Corinthians to forgive the malefactor (vv. 7–8), Paul now reaffirms his willingness to forgive him for the sake of the Corinthians **in the sight of Christ** or "in the presence of Christ." The phrase "in the presence" (lit., "in the face") is used in the LXX of being in close physical proximity to another person (cf. Jer. 52:25; 2 Macc. 14:24; Prov. 4:3; 25:7). In light of Paul's whole train of thought in 2:14–4:6, however, the idea of "in the presence of Christ" is at least latent, for Paul argues in that passage that he is a Moses-like revelatory mediator who has direct access to the very presence of God in

Christ, that is, the throne of God and Christ in heaven (see below on 2:14, 17; 12:2–4).

When Paul states that he has forgiven the malefactor for the sake of the Corinthians "in the presence of Christ," he probably means this quite literally. The image is possibly that of Moses making intercession for the Israelites in the presence of God (see the allusion to Num. 16:1ff. above and Additional Notes on 2:17 [the allusion to LXX Exod. 32:11A] below). If Paul's forgiveness of the malefactor was **for your sake,** then the whole Corinthian church may have been somehow adversely affected by the offender's punishment, for the offender caused the church more sorrow than he did Paul himself (cf. 2 Cor. 2:5). In that case, Paul's intercession would actually have been for the whole church. The reason Paul cautiously puts in the clause, **if there was anything to forgive** (better: "if I have forgiven anything"), is perhaps a realization that, just as the offense was ultimately against Christ, insofar as it was his apostle who was slandered, so also the forgiveness must ultimately come from Christ and not merely from the apostle.

2:11 / The purpose for which Paul forgave the malefactor in the presence of Christ is so that Satan would not gain the advantage in the situation. There is little doubt that the name **Satan** *(ho Satanas)* is related to the Hebrew verb *satan* meaning "to slander, accuse" (cf. Pss. 38:21; 71:13; 109:4, 20, 29; Zech. 3:1). In later Jewish tradition, Satan is responsible for many of the sins mentioned in the OT. For example, it was Satan who was responsible for the Israelites worshipping the golden calf, because he deceitfully declared that Moses would not return from Mount Sinai (*b. Šabb.* 89a).

In 2 Corinthians 2:11 Paul may be playing on the meaning of "Satan" as "Slanderer," just as in 6:15 he seems to play on the popular etymology of Belial ("yokeless"), another of the many names for the "devil." Paul has been slandered by the malefactor, who is perhaps conceived as an agent of the "Slanderer" (cf. 12:7). Furthermore, if Paul has sought the forgiveness of the man "in the presence of Christ" in heaven (2:10), perhaps the apostle's familiarity with Satan and his ways (cf., e.g., Rom. 16:20; 1 Cor. 5:5; 7:5; 2 Cor. 11:14; 12:7; 1 Thess. 2:18; also 2 Thess. 2:9; 1 Tim. 1:20; 5:15) stems not merely from his acquaintance with the Jewish tradition (cf. 2 Cor. 11:14 with *Apoc. Mos.* 17:1), but also from personal encounters with Satan in heaven (cf. 2 Cor. 12:7).

For Paul, Satan is a conquered, yet still dangerous, foe. Although "the God of peace will soon crush Satan under your feet" (Rom. 16:20), Satan is still "the god of this age," who blinds the minds of unbelievers from seeing the light of the gospel of the glory of Christ (2 Cor. 4:4), and he is "the ruler of the kingdom of the air, the spirit who is now at work in those who are disobedient" (Eph. 2:2). There can be no fellowship between the realm of Belial and unbelievers, on the one hand, and the realm of Christ and believers, on the other; for they are as mutually exclusive as darkness and light (2 Cor. 6:14–16). Nevertheless, Satan tries to thwart believers at every point, either by leading them astray to "another gospel" (11:3–4) or by tempting them (1 Thess. 3:5; 1 Cor. 7:5). Likewise, Satan tries to thwart the apostle, whether by afflicting him (2 Cor. 12:7), by preventing him from going to certain places at certain times (1 Thess. 2:18; cf. Rom. 1:13), or by rendering his apostolic work useless (1 Thess. 3:5). Paul is aware that Satan has **schemes** by which he can gain the upper hand (cf. Eph. 6:11; 4QMMT C 29, referring to "the plans of evil and the scheme of Belial"). Therefore, in this spiritual warfare against a formidable adversary, believers need to be properly equipped with the armor of God, so that they may be able to withstand the onslaught (1 Thess. 5:8; Rom. 13:12; Eph. 6:10–18).

Because he does not want Satan to triumph in this struggle, Paul has forgiven the offending brother for the Corinthians' sake. Evidently, the apostle wants to present a united front against the adversary, for otherwise the enemy would **outwit** Paul. If Satan can divide the Corinthian church even more deeply than it already is (cf. 1:10; 3:1–4; 4:14; 6:1, 4, 6; 12:14–31), then he will have succeeded in completely neutralizing its witness, its role in attesting to the legitimacy of Paul's apostleship, its contribution to the collection, and its partnership with the apostle in the westward expansion of the gospel. If we can see 2 Corinthians as an appeal for concord (see Introduction; also on 13:11), then the readmission of the offender serves the purpose for writing the letter.

2:12–13 / Having discussed the issue of the one who slandered him during his painful second visit (vv. 5–11), Paul abruptly resumes his train of thought from verse 4, where he mentioned that his tearful letter was written as a reaction, under great distress and anguish. In verses 12–13 Paul goes on to state that, while waiting to hear of the Corinthians' response to his letter, he himself was overwhelmed with concern over the situation, and that he actually changed his travel plans because of that concern. Hence Paul is able to show that, far from being double-minded, his single-mindedness toward the Corinthians resulted in the change of plans that brought him to Macedonia. The apologetic tone of verses 12–13 is palpable once it is seen in the context of the foregoing section on accusations against Paul.

2:12 / Paul begins by explaining what he was doing in the period after sending the tearful letter. After his traumatic second visit to Corinth, he stayed in Ephesus for a while and then traveled to **Troas** (or to "the Troad," i.e., the whole region in which the city was situated) in northwest Asia Minor in order to do some missionary work. When Paul went is uncertain, but it was probably after the nearly fatal tribulation mentioned in 1:8–11. Why Paul went is also uncertain, other than that he seems to have made prior arrangements with Titus to meet him there (see v. 13). But why did Paul choose to meet Titus in Troas and not somewhere else? In the port city of Troas there was probably already a small number of believers to whom Paul had preached the gospel on his second missionary journey (cf. Acts 16:8–10; 20:7). Now he evidently wanted to continue the work that he had started there. The metaphor of an **opened door** indicates that the Lord had given him a good opportunity to preach the gospel (cf. 1 Cor. 16:9; Col. 4:3; Acts 14:27).

2:13 / Having mentioned the successful missionary work in which he was engaged in the period after sending the tearful letter, Paul then describes how his concern for the situation in Corinth overwhelmed him. Despite the good opportunity for spreading the gospel in Troas, Paul did not wait there for the arrival of **Titus.** Paul wanted to hear as soon as possible from Titus how the letter had been received in Corinth (cf. 7:6–15). When he did not meet Titus in Troas, Paul became so anxious that he traveled to **Macedonia** in order to try to find Titus, in effect reverting to his original plan of going to Macedonia before coming to Corinth (cf. 1 Cor. 16:5). Paul evidently knew that after delivering the tearful letter to the Corinthians and hearing their response, Titus would have taken a northerly route, making his way back to Paul in Troas via Macedonia. Here again we notice that, in describing his travels, Paul thinks in terms of Roman provinces like Achaia (1:1; 9:2; 11:10), Asia (1:8), and Macedonia

(1:16; 2:13; 7:5; 8:1; 11:9). He obviously has at least a mental map in view.

If Paul was willing to relinquish a golden opportunity to preach the gospel in Troas, an opportunity that the Lord himself had opened for Paul (v. 12), that shows how much the church at Corinth meant to him, and how concerned he was over the outcome of the situation. Whereas formerly the Corinthians, Stephanas, Fortunatus, and Achaicus, had given Paul's spirit rest, probably at the time they delivered the Corinthians' letter to Paul (1 Cor. 16:17–18; cf. 7:1), Paul now had **no peace of mind** (lit., "no rest for my spirit"; cf. 7:13b). Only Titus's report of a positive reply from the church at Corinth could do that. And much was riding on that response for Paul's entire enterprise: the success of his collection for Jerusalem, the advance of his mission to Spain, and the spiritual lives of the Corinthians themselves. No wonder Paul was uneasy! This anxiety is part of Paul's regular apostolic suffering on behalf his churches (cf. 7:5; 11:28).

At this point, Paul interrupts his travelogue and delays telling us how he met Titus in Macedonia and what Titus told him; he continues that story in 7:5–16. By delaying the narrative, Paul heightens the suspense in the letter and puts greater emphasis on the intervening section (2:14–7:4), in which he defends the legitimacy of his apostleship and appeals to the Corinthians to reconcile themselves to him. Actually, Paul has already begun both his defense and his appeal for reconciliation in the thanksgiving (1:3–11) and in the section on accusations (1:12–2:4).

Additional Notes §3

1:12 / Since 1:12–2:13 is a separate section, the *gar* (**Now**) that introduces v. 12 probably expresses continuation rather than having causative force.

Here the first person plurals (**our, we**) are, once again, literary plurals that refer only to Paul himself.

Paul appeals here to the witness of his conscience, a thoroughly private matter that no one else can test. In vv. 18–19, however, the apostle does mention Timothy and Silas in order to give credence to his oath-bound statement. See Additional Note on 1:23 on the oath formulas in 1:17, 18.

On **conscience**, see Judith M. Gundry-Volf, "Conscience," *DPL*, pp. 153–56.

The NIV evidently reads *en hagiotēti* ("in holiness") rather than *en haplotēti* ("with integrity"). On the textual problem, see Thrall, *Second Corinthians*, vol. 1, pp. 130–31, 132–33.

1:13b–14 / The **day of the Lord** is a standard feature in OT prophetic literature, one that Paul takes over and expands in his letters. For most prophets, the great and terrible day of the Lord meant that time in the relatively near future when Yahweh would judge not only his people's enemies but also his people themselves for breaking the covenant. Then, either through a new Davidic king or by acting directly, Yahweh would establish his own rule or kingdom over the earth (cf. Joel 1–3; Zechariah 12–14). Paul takes over the Jewish concept of the day of the Lord, including the twin themes of eschatological salvation and future judgment (cf. 1 Thess. 5:2; 1 Cor. 1:8; 5:5; 2 Cor. 1:14). However, he creatively integrates this OT hope with his own Christology, effectively transforming the **day of the Lord** (*kyrios* = Yahweh) into the **day of the Lord Jesus** (e.g., Phil. 1:6; 2:16). This corresponds with Paul's concept that the resurrected and exalted Christ, who has now sat down at the right hand in God's own throne-chariot (cf. 1 Cor. 15:25; Rom. 8:34, citing Ps. 110:1; see further on 2 Cor. 2:14; 3:16), has received "the name that is above every name" (Phil. 2:9), that is, the Tetragrammaton itself, which the Septuagint translates "Lord" *(kyrios)*.

On the **day of the Lord**, see Richard H. Hiers, "Day of Christ," *ABD* vol. 2, pp. 76–79; idem, "Day of the Lord," pp. 82–83. On Paul's use of **Lord** (Yahweh) with reference to Jesus, see L. W. Hurtado, "Lord," *DPL*, pp. 560–69 (esp. pp. 563–64).

1:15–16 / Note that in vv. 15–17 Paul changes to the first person singular (I). In v. 18 he switches back again to the plural, while still referring to himself.

On the various exegetical options for interpreting the double **benefit**, see Thrall, *Second Corinthians*, vol. 1, pp. 137–39.

1:18 / While Paul does use the term **message** *(logos)* when referring to his missionary preaching (cf. 1 Cor. 1:18; 2:4; 1 Thess. 1:6; 2:13), the connection between vv. 17 and 18 shows that he is dealing more generally with the trustworthiness of his speech.

Sometimes God himself changes Paul's travel plans (cf. the divine passive in Rom. 1:13); at other times Satan hinders Paul from going where he would like (1 Thess. 2:18).

Since Paul did not have divine authority for everything he said (cf. 1 Cor. 7:10, 25), he could not always vouch for its veracity based on the faithfulness of God.

1:19 / On **Son of God** as a messianic title, see, for example, 4Q174 1.10; 4Q246 1.9; Luke 1:32; 1 Cor. 15:25–28; Rom. 1:3–4. See further L. W. Hurtado, "Son of God," *DPL*, pp. 900–906.

On **Timothy**, who is named as the co-sender of 2 Corinthians, see on 1:1. There is a possibility that Timothy appears in this letter because he has come under criticism in Corinth (see on 1:24; 12:16–18). **Silas**, who is actually called Silvanus in the Greek text of 2 Cor. 1:19, is undoubtedly to be identified with the Silas of Acts, one of the leading men in the Jerusalem church (Acts 15:22). After he had broken up with Barnabas following the so-called first missionary journey, Paul needed another coworker who was well respected in the Jerusalem church. Hence, Paul chose Silas to accompany him on the second missionary journey.

M. Thrall (*Second Corinthians*, vol. 1, pp. 147–48) quite rightly points out that Paul's argument in v. 19 does not logically follow unless the readers accept Paul's own understanding of himself as Christ's ambassador, through whom God himself speaks (5:20) and Christ speaks (13:3); however, this is precisely the point of Paul's argument: The Corinthians had accepted Paul as a revelatory mediator; they had received his message of the gospel; and they had thereby received the promises of God.

1:20 / In Jewish tradition, the adoption formula of 2 Sam. 7:14 ("I will be his Father, and he will be my son"), which was interpreted messianically both in Qumran (4QFlor 1.10) and in *T. Jud.* 24:3, is applied to the eschatological people of God (cf. *Jub.* 1:24; *T. Jud.* 24:3). Cf. my *Adoption as Sons of God: An Exegetical Investigation into the Background of* ΥΙΟΘΕΣΙΑ *in the Pauline Corpus* (WUNT 2/48; Tübingen: Mohr Siebeck, 1992).

Elsewhere, Paul uses the plural **promises** in Rom. 9:4; 15:8; 2 Cor. 7:1; Gal. 3:16, 21.

1:21 / On Paul's use of **Christ**, see esp. Martin Hengel, *Studies in Early Christology* (Edinburgh: T&T Clark, 1995). The meaning and importance of the term *māšîaḥ/christos* in Second Temple Judaism has become extremely controversial in recent years. See, for example, James H. Charlesworth, ed., *The Messiah: Developments in Earliest Judaism and Christianity. The First Princeton Symposium on Judaism and Christian Origins* (Minneapolis: Fortress, 1992).

1:22 / Paul's concept of sealing *(sphragizein)* has an extensive background (cf. Thrall, *Second Corinthians*, vol. 1, pp. 156–58). The Greek *arrabōn* is a Hebrew loanword denoting "deposit." In keeping with the following metaphor of **deposit**, the NIV translates the participle *sphragisamenos* **set his seal of ownership.** In light of the foregoing imagery of (messianic) anointing, we might think here of a royal seal on a letter (cf. 1 Kgs. 21:8; Esth. 8:8–10). Later, the Corinthians are described as a letter from Christ delivered by Paul and written with the Spirit (2 Cor. 3:3). On the Spirit in general, see further Gordon D. Fee, *God's Empowering Presence: The Holy Spirit in the Letters of Paul* (Peabody, Mass.: Hendrickson, 1994).

1:23 / There is considerable OT precedent for Paul's calling upon **God as my witness.** The Lord refers to himself as a "witness" (cf. Isa. 43:10, 12). In Jer. 36(29):23, for example, the Lord calls himself a "witness" against Ahab and Zedekiah, that they "spoke a word in my name, which I did not command them to speak." The Lord threatens quickly to be a witness "against those who swear falsely by my name"

(Mal. 3:5). More importantly for our purposes, Yahweh is often invoked as a witness (cf. Job 16:20; 1 Kgs. 17:20), particularly in covenants and agreements (cf. Jer. 42:5). For example, in the boundary covenant between Laban and Jacob (Gen. 31:44–55), Yahweh is invoked as a witness, for there were no other witnesses available (vv. 44, 50). In the solemn agreement between friends, Jonathan vows, "As for the word which you and I have spoken, see, the Lord is witness between me and you forever" (1 Sam. 20:23), and David makes the same vow to Jonathan (v. 42). In his farewell speech (1 Sam. 12:1–25), Samuel challenges the people to bear witness against him of any wrongdoing that he may have done as judge of Israel (vv. 1–3). When the people agree that they can find nothing incriminating in his conduct (v. 4), Samuel invokes the Lord as "witness among you" of these findings (v. 5); indeed, "The Lord who appointed Moses and Aaron is witness, who brought our fathers up out of Egypt" (v. 6). God is a witness of a person's innermost thoughts (Wis. 1:6). In light of this tradition, Paul's invocation of God as his witness before the Corinthians was certainly a momentous matter, for it had grave consequences for the apostle if he was lying.

We may note that Moses is said to have called upon God as witness in order to vindicate himself during Korah's rebellion (cf. Josephus, *Ant.* 4.41, 46; *Ps.-Philo*, 57:1–3; Philo, *On the Life of Moses* 2.284).

1:24 / Since Paul obviously thinks of himself typologically as a Moses figure in 2 Corinthians (cf. 2:14–4:6), it only makes sense to ask whether he thought of the opposition in Corinth in terms of the wilderness rebellions, and particularly Korah's rebellion. Already in 1 Cor. 9:13–14, Paul justifies apostolic support by analogy of the support due the Aaronic priesthood (cf. Num. 18:8, 28; Lev. 6:16, 26). The orthographic similarity between the Greek names *Kore* ("Korah") and *Korinthoi* ("Corinthians") may have facilitated Paul's association of Korah's rebellion with the situation in the Corinthian church. Moreover, 1 Cor. 10:10 may allude to Num. 16:41, where the people grumbled against Moses over God's judgment of Korah and his followers (cf. also 2 Tim. 2:19a, citing Num. 16:5). In any case, 1 Cor. 10:1–13 uses the narratives about the exodus from Egypt and the wilderness wanderings in Exodus and Numbers as typological examples so that the Corinthians will not fall into the same sins.

In the OT, Korah is the central figure in the story of the rebellion against the authority and status of Moses at the time of the wilderness wanderings (cf. Num. 16:22: "If one man should sin"). The assembly is spoken of as his assembly (Num. 16:11, 40), and those who were swallowed up as "all the men that belonged to Korah" (v. 32). It is under Korah's name that the rebellion is subsequently mentioned (Num. 26:9; 27:3; Jude 11; but not Deut. 11:6; Ps. 106:16–18). Behind the uprising were Korah's complaint against the religious authority of Moses and Aaron, and the complaint of Dathan and Abiram against the leadership of Moses in general, charging that he had brought Israel out of Egypt to lord it over them and to have them die in the wilderness. Korah and his followers challenged the unique system represented by Moses and Aaron and denied that the supremacy claimed by them was valid in

Additional Notes: 2 Corinthians 1:24–2:6

view of the fact that the whole congregation was "holy." This was obviously a power struggle. The very fact that Num. 16 speaks of two rebel groups—one led by Korah and another led by Dathan and Abiram—that presented a united front against Moses and Aaron may have further facilitated Paul's appropriation of the tradition, for also in Corinth there are at least two groups of opponents—the outsiders (cf. Sir. 45:18), who infiltrated Corinth possibly from Jerusalem, and the insiders, who sided with the offender mentioned in 2:1ff. If Korah and his followers can claim that Moses and Aaron are superfluous as mediators, how much more can Paul's opponents claim in the new covenant situation that there is no need for mediators (cf. Jer. 31:34). According to Moses, however, Korah conspired not against himself, nor even against Aaron (v. 11), but against God (vv. 11, 28; 26:9; cf. Exod. 16:8), whose prophet he was (Exod. 19:9).

In 1 Cor. 3:9, Paul uses the concept of fellow workers for himself and Apollos; the Corinthians, in turn, are called "God's field" and "God's building." In 2 Corinthians, however, Paul includes the Corinthians with himself in various ways, often using "with-" *(syn-)* language (cf. 1:11, 21; 4:14; 7:3).

2:1 / For various reasons, some scholars deny that Paul ever made a second, **painful visit** to Corinth between the writing of 1 and 2 Corinthians. Cf. Thrall, *Second Corinthians*, vol. 1, pp. 54, 164–65.

Paul wants to spare the Corinthians his apostolic presence and writes them a letter instead. This implies that despite appearances to the contrary (cf. 10:10), Paul's presence can be quite intimidating. Since the apostle later compares himself to Moses (cf. 2:14–3:18), perhaps he has in mind here the fearful presence of Moses among the Israelites, which required the Lawgiver to wear a veil.

2:5 / On the exegetical options for identifying the offender in v. 5, see Thrall, *Second Corinthians*, vol. 1, pp. 61–69; Colin G. Kruse, "The Offender and the Offence in 2 Corinthians 2:5 and 7:12," *EvQ* 88 (1988), pp. 129–39.

In order to understand how the apostle was **grieved** by the Corinthian offender, we may compare the prayer in the Qumran *Thanksgiving Hymns* that expresses how the Teacher of Righteousness was severely grieved when his followers in the community slandered him and defected from him (1QH 13.20–15.5). 1QpHab 5.8–12 denounces the silent majority who stood idly by when the Teacher's authority was openly challenged in the midst of their whole community by an individual called the "Man of Lies." The similarity between the Teacher's situation and Paul's experience in Corinth is obvious.

2:6 / If we are correct in seeing an allusion to Korah's rebellion in this text, then we gain insight into the magnitude of the situation in Corinth from Paul's perspective. Cf. Rom. 9:3, where Paul implicitly compares himself to Moses as one who intercedes on behalf of those under judgment (cf. Exod. 32:32).

Later Jewish tradition explains the survival of Korah's sons by claiming that they repented of their sin (cf. Frederick J. Murphy,

"Korah's Rebellion in Pseudo-Philo 16," in *Of Scribes and Scrolls: Studies on the Hebrew Bible, Intertestamental Judaism, and Christian Origins Presented to John Strugnell* [ed. Harold W. Attridge, et al.; College Theology Society Resources in Religion 5; Lanham, Md.: University Press of America, 1990], pp. 111–20, here p. 117).

The *Rule of the Community* in Qumran deals with both the expulsion of disaffected members (1QS 7.15–18, 24–25) and their readmission (7.18–24). In the case of a person who has been a member for less than two years, the *Rule* grants readmission on certain rigorous conditions.

Cf. James C. VanderKam, *The Dead Sea Scrolls Today* (Grand Rapids: Eerdmans, 1994), pp. 164–65: "At Qumran the full membership is designated by the Hebrew word that lies behind Paul's 'the many/majority.' The Manual of Discipline lays down rules regarding who may speak and when during general meetings of the entire group: 'And in an Assembly of the Congregation [*ha-rabbim* = the many] no man shall speak without the consent of the Congregation [*ha-rabbim*], nor indeed of the Guardian of the Congregation [*ha-rabbim*]' (6.11–12; p. 69). The word appears in this sense twenty-six times in columns 6–8, once in column 9, and three times in the Damascus Document. In some of these instances 'the many' clearly had judicial functions, just as they do in 2 Corinthians: 'And furthermore, let no man accuse his companion before the Congregation [*ha-rabbim*] without having first admonished him in the presence of witnesses' (6.1)." We may note, however, that in describing the Essenes, Josephus uses the same term as Paul does *(tois pleiosin)* in order to refer to a true "majority" of the congregation (*War* 2.146–147).

On "the destroyer" in Jewish tradition, see S. A. Meier, "Destroyer," *Dictionary of Deities and Demons in the Bible* (ed. Karel van der Toorn, et al.; Leiden: Brill, 1995), pp. 456–64.

2:7 / On the verb **overwhelmed** *(katapinein)*, see L. Goppelt, "*katapinō*," *TDNT*, vol. 6, pp. 158–59. Interpreters have had difficulty in making sense of Paul's use of this term in our passage (cf. Thrall, *Second Corinthians*, vol. 1, p. 177).

2:11 / On **Satan**, cf. 2 Cor. 11:14; 12:7; also C. Breytenbach and P. L. Day, "Satan," *Dictionary of Deities and Demons in the Bible*, pp. 1369–80; D. G. Reid, "Satan, Devil," *DPL*, pp. 862–67.

2:12–13 / In Isa. 45:1, the Lord would open doors for Cyrus, his anointed, in the sense of military conquest.

2:13 / **Titus** was a Gentile by birth, and Paul strongly opposed circumcising him during the time of the apostolic council (cf. Gal. 2:3). Titus was not involved in the founding of the church at Corinth. Nevertheless, he was able to deliver the tearful letter and to assist in reconciling the church with Paul. Titus is bringing the collection in Corinth to a conclusion (2 Cor. 8:6). According to the Pastoral Epistles, Titus later worked as a church leader on Crete (Tit. 1:5).

Paul refers to his **peace of mind** (or "spirit") and its function in several other contexts as well (cf. Rom. 1:9; 1 Cor. 14:14).

§4 Glory (2 Cor. 2:14–4:6)

After 2:13 ("So I . . . went to Macedonia"), Paul suddenly interrupts his travelogue and begins a new section on his apostolic ministry, only to resume the travelogue in 7:5 ("For when we came to Macedonia"), recounting the arrival of Titus in Macedonia and the comforting news of the Corinthians' repentance. Hence, the intervening material on Paul's defense of the legitimacy of his apostleship (2:14–7:4) may seem digressive or even extraneous. In fact, some scholars think that 2 Corinthians 2:14–7:4 was not part of Paul's original composition.

Nevertheless, there are important reasons for considering 2:14–7:4 as part of 2 Corinthians 1–8 (cf. M. Thrall). In the previous context, Paul had been trying to counter the Corinthians' accusations against him, particularly in regard to his change of travel plans (1:12–2:13). In the process of defending himself and wooing the Corinthians back to his side, Paul appeals to his own straightforward, unequivocal apostolic commission and ministry. Like Moses, he is a spokesman of God who mediates the divine promises to the Corinthians (1:18–22). Even as Moses endured Korah's rebellion (Num. 16–17), Paul has also endured a rebellion against his own authority in Corinth (cf. 1:24; 2:6–7). The present section develops the comparison between Paul and Moses in more explicit detail by showing that the apostle is a revelatory mediator. Through Paul, the minister of the new covenant, the Corinthians have received the Spirit and thus have access to the glory of God. The Corinthians cannot reject Paul and his apostleship without denying their own participation in the promises he originally mediated to them during the founding visit. Thus, the very existence of the Corinthian church is tangible evidence of the legitimacy of Paul's apostleship (cf. 1 Cor. 9:2, "For you are the seal of my apostleship in the Lord").

This explanation of the general connection between 1:12–2:13 and the present section does not account for specific placement of the section in the middle of Paul's description of his trip to Macedonia to find Titus. Here we can only speculate as to Paul's motives. Since it was in Macedonia that the apostle heard the encouraging news from Titus, Paul may have inserted 2:14–7:4 into the travelogue in order to encourage more of the same repentance already shown by the Corinthians since the writing of the tearful letter. Indeed, Paul does conclude his defense with an appeal to the Corinthians to open their hearts to him (6:12–13; 7:2). Furthermore, if the purpose of the tearful letter had been to rebuke the Corinthians, then Paul's defense of his apostleship in 2:14–7:4 would fit in with the account of the anxiety he felt while waiting for their reaction to the letter.

2:14–17 / Paul begins the defense of his apostleship with a thanksgiving to God, whom he has personally encountered and who has made him a mediator of divine revelation. This encounter with God not only establishes Paul's legitimacy as an apostle, but it also distinguishes Paul from his opponents. Hence, the very first verses of the apology provide Paul's essential answer to the charges against him. The rest of the section (3:1–4:6) elaborates in one way or another on 2:14–17. As we shall see, already in 2:14–17 Paul begins the crucial comparison between himself and Moses, using it to highlight the superiority of his ministry of the new covenant over Moses' ministry of the Sinaitic covenant. Although the revelation that Moses received was glorious, the revelation that Paul has received is even more glorious. Hence, Paul defends himself first and foremost on the basis of his position as the revelatory mediator par excellence.

2:14 / Paul's defense commences with a thanksgiving to God for his apostolic ministry as revelatory mediator. We note here again Paul's use of the so-called apostolic/literary plural **(us)** with reference to himself, since Paul's apostleship is the main issue in this section. This verse is so pivotal to Paul's argument and yet so difficult to interpret that we will need to give it special attention.

The main problem is the interpretation of *thriambeuein*, which is correctly translated **leads in triumphal procession**. For some interpreters, this usage of the term conjures up an image of the apostle that seems quite unlikely, coming as it does as part of a thanksgiving at the very beginning of his defense for the legitimacy for his apostolic ministry. Further, Paul would thus seem to be portraying himself as a complete disgrace, a prisoner of war who is led by the conquering general (God!) in a triumphal procession that culminates in the apostle's death. Many scholars have sought to avoid this interpretation either by proposing an idiosyncratic usage of *thriambeuein* (e.g., "make known" [G. Dautzenberg]) or by assuming the use of a rhetorical strategy whereby the meaning of verse 14 is ultimately positive. More recently, however, the trend has been to recognize the unequivocal usage of *thriambeuein*, with its negative implications for Paul, and then to correlate the passage with Paul's apostolic self-conception as expressed elsewhere, particularly in his admissions of personal weakness and suffering in the Corinthian correspondence (cf. 1 Cor. 4:9; 2 Cor. 4:10–11).

Whereas most interpretations of 2 Corinthians 2:14 consider the metaphor of triumphal procession only with respect to Paul, no interpretation so far has examined the metaphor with respect to God as the acting subject. In order to grasp this we will first recall a basic motif of the Roman triumphal procession, with its focus on the triumphant general and his chariot. Then we will investigate how Paul uses this imagery metaphorically in our text.

The Roman triumphal procession was originally led by the victorious general appearing symbolically as the living image of Jupiter. By the time of the empire, however, the procession was celebrated to honor the gods in thanksgiving for the victory. The Roman magistrates, the Senate, people carrying booty from the campaign, the priests leading the bulls for sacrifice, and enemy captives (who were executed at the end of the ceremony) entered the city, followed by the victorious general on a chariot leading his army. Normally, the chariot was a quadriga, that is, a two-wheeled chariot drawn by four horses harnessed abreast, although four elephants were sometimes used instead (cf. Plutarch, *Pompeius*, 14.4; Pliny, *Natural History* 8.4). Since Roman imperial coins frequently included images of the emperor in a triumphal chariot, the concept of triumphal procession was familiar throughout the Roman Empire. What do these findings imply for our text? If, by using *thriambeuein*, Paul portrays himself as being led by God in a Roman triumphal procession, then the image is one of God riding in a quadriga.

The metaphor in 2 Corinthians 2:14, as with all metaphors, presents us with two thoughts of different things—tenor and vehicle—active together and supported by a single word or phrase, whose meaning is a result of their interaction ("two ideas for one"). The "tenor" is the underlying subject of the metaphor, and the "vehicle" is the means by which the tenor is presented. In our passage, the vehicle is the idea of a Roman triumphal procession in which a conquering general rides a quadriga. However, the underlying subject is different. Paul merely uses the idea of the Roman triumphal procession in order to convey another set of associations—the thought that God on his throne-chariot leads the apostle captive.

The divine throne-chariot is found in both the OT and Jewish tradition. Quite commonly, the "chariotry/chariot of God" in Psalm 68:17–18 is taken to refer to the *merkabah* in which God descended to Mount Sinai. Ezekiel's prophetic call-vision by the river Chebar (Ezek. 1:4–28; cf. 10:1–22; 43:1–4) gives us a cryptic picture of what later came to be known as the throne-chariot of God. In Jewish tradition, Ezekiel's vision is interpreted as a reference to a *merkabah* or "chariot," drawn by the four living creatures/beasts. This comes out most explicitly in a midrash (*Exod. Rab.* 43:8) focusing on the golden calf incident, which refers to the chariot of God as a "four-mule chariot." Also, in Habakkuk 3:8 Yahweh is said to drive a horse-drawn *merkabah* (cf. M. Haran).

In sum, we have seen that by using *thriambeuein,* Paul evoked the image of a triumphal procession in which the triumphant leader rode in a four-horse chariot. This, in turn, suggested the familiar idea of the *merkabah*, which was commonly viewed as a chariot drawn by the four living creatures/beasts of Ezekiel 1. We should not be surprised that Paul would use Roman imagery to suggest an OT idea. Paul, who does not like to discuss his visions and does so only under compulsion (cf. 2 Cor. 12:1ff.), uses a metaphor in order make his point without being overly explicit about ineffable matters.

Furthermore, it is possible that in 2 Corinthians 2:14 Paul is alluding specifically to Psalm 68:17–18. According the LXX version of this psalm, when God in his chariot ascended from Sinai into his holy sanctuary on high, he led captivity captive and received gifts among humanity. Ephesians 4:8 actually applies Psalm 68:18 [LXX 67:19] to the ascension of Christ and the spiritual gifts, including apostles (v. 11), which he gave to the church (cf. G. B. Caird). This kind of interpretation of the psalm would, of course, be very congenial at the beginning of Paul's defense of his apostolic office in 2 Corinthians 2:14–7:4. The use of Psalm 68:18–19 in Jewish tradition provides further evidence that Paul may have had this passage in mind when he wrote 2 Corinthians 2:14.

In Jewish tradition Psalm 68:18 refers not to God's ascent on high, corresponding to his *merkabah* descent to Mount Sinai in verse 18, but to the ascent of Moses, who took captive the Torah and gave the gift of Torah to humanity. Thus, for example, the Targum interprets Psalm 68:18 as a reference to Moses, who ascended into heaven, received the Torah there, and brought the Torah to the people (cf. *Exod. Rab.* 28:1). According to *Midr. Ps.* 68:18, Moses ascended to the divine beings and there received the Torah as a "gift" for Israel. In the Jewish tradition, therefore, Psalm 68:17–18 refers to Moses' *merkabah* encounter with God on Sinai and the revelation that he mediated to humanity.

Paul might be making the same connection between *merkabah* encounter and revelation in 2 Corinthians 2:14, for here also God both leads him in triumphal procession and "reveals" (*phanerounti*, **spreads**) through him the fragrance of the knowledge of God. In other words, Paul is presenting himself here as a mediator of divine revelation on par with Moses, summarizing the whole basis for his apostleship in this one verse. Hence, if metaphor is speaking about one thing in terms suggestive of another, then by speaking of a Roman triumphal procession in connection with divine revelation, Paul evidently suggests the throne-chariot of God and the powerfully complex tradition of Psalm 68:17–18. According to this tradition, God descended to Sinai in his *merkabah* and revealed himself to Moses and all Israel. Moses, in turn, ascended on high, took the Torah captive, and gave it as a gift to humanity. Although Paul's image turns this tradition on its head by making the apostle a captive rather than the triumphant one (cf. 2 Cor. 11:30; 12:5), it nevertheless preserves the idea that an encounter with the *merkabah* effects a revelation to humanity through a mediator. Paul's claim is especially crucial in the situation at Corinth, where his opponents evidently claim to have numerous visions and revelations (cf. 12:1).

Paul's thanksgiving in 2:14 **(But thanks be to God)** fits well in the context of *merkabah* tradition. The visionary often observed and sometimes participated in the angelic hymns before the throne of God, the praises of the heavenly beings being viewed as the model and example for heavenly worship (cf. *1 En.* 71:11–12; *Apoc. Ab.* 17:4–18:1; K. Grözinger). How much more, then, is Paul's praise warranted and justified, since his encounter with the *merkabah* rivals even that of Moses.

If God is said to be leading the apostle in triumphal procession **in Christ,** then we will do well to recall Martin Hengel's idea of the conjoint activity between the Father and the Son. As a result of being seated at the right hand of God at the resurrection, the Son now sits in the divine throne-chariot with the Father, and both together, occupying the same throne, now carry out activities together (cf. Mark 14:62). Hence, just as "God was in Christ reconciling the world to himself" (2 Cor. 5:19), so also here God "in Christ" leads the apostle in triumphal procession.

Once we recognize the traditional background of our text, it is not difficult to suggest why Paul would refer to his revelation as the **fragrance** of the knowledge of God. Jewish tradition associates wonderful aromas with the *merkabah* vision. For example, in the third heaven (= Paradise), where Paul encountered the *merkabah* (cf. 2 Cor. 12:2–4), the fruit trees are said to be ripe and fragrant, abundant crops give off a sweet smell, and the tree of life itself is indescribable for pleasantness and fine fragrance (*2 En.* 8:1–3). In sum, 2 Corinthians 2:14 presents God as revealing the knowledge of himself to the world through Paul. In connection with his ongoing encounter with the *merkabah*, Paul, as minister of the new covenant (cf. 3:6), becomes a revelatory mediator who infuses the world with an aromatic, Torah-like knowledge of God through the Spirit.

2:15–16a / Having presented himself as a revelatory mediator like Moses, i.e., one who mediates the revelation of the fragrance of the knowledge of God, Paul now substantiates (*hoti*, **For**) what he has said in verse 14 by identifying himself as the fragrance **(aroma)** of Christ, which brings either life or death. In keeping with the identification of the God and Christ who share the *merkabah*, the two fragrances are one and the same. Paul's knowledge of the glory of God in the face of Christ (2 Cor. 4:6) is life-giving knowledge. Like Moses, Paul sets before people life and death (cf. Deut. 30:15, 19).

At the outset of his defense, Paul divides humanity into two mutually exclusive groups, according to how each responds to his message: **those who are being saved** and **those who are perishing.** Paul's opponents, who reject his apostolic authority, obviously fall into the latter category, for Paul's message is inseparable from his person and commission (cf. 5:18–20). It is no coincidence that in 1 Corinthians 10:9–10 Paul uses the same verb of the Israelite rebels who spoke against God and against Moses and therefore "were destroyed" in the desert (cf. Num. 21:5–6). The apostle will come back to this dualism at the end of his defense, where he emphasizes the contrast between the two groups in terms of a series of antithetical pairs (cf. 2 Cor. 6:14–16a). For Paul, there are only two kinds of people: those who stand on the side of Christ and his apostle and those who stand on the side of Satan and his pseudo-apostles.

2:16b / Having stated in effect that he has had a *merkabah* encounter with God like that which Moses experienced on Sinai, that he has a role as a unique, revelatory mediator similar to that of Moses, and, furthermore, that his ministry is a matter of life and death just as Moses' was, Paul stops to ask a sobering rhetorical question: "And who is sufficient for these things?" ("And who is **equal to such a task?**"). Paul's question recalls the only parallel use of the term sufficient/competent *(hikanos)* in the LXX, i.e., the self-effacing words of Moses in Exodus 4:10 at the burning bush. There Moses expresses his inadequacy to lead God's people out of bondage in Egypt: "And Moses said to the Lord, 'I pray, Lord, I am insufficient *(ouk hikanos eimi)*. . . . I am weak-voiced and slow-tongued.' " Thereupon, God reassures Moses, "I will open your mouth and I will instruct you as to what you will say" (v. 12). Paul's sufficiency for his commission is the same as that of Moses, that is, God himself and the revelation of God through him. As Paul explicitly states in 2 Corinthians 3:5, his "sufficiency" *(hikanotēs)* comes from God. Hence, the expected answer to Paul's question would apparently be this: "By God's grace, I am" (cf. 1 Cor. 15:9–10). What follows in 2:17 shows unequivocally that a positive answer is expected here.

2:17 / The substantiation *(gar)* for Paul's sufficiency, particularly as a revelatory mediator like Moses (cf. v. 14b), is given in verse 17. The fact that Paul speaks **before God,** or better "in the presence of God" *(katenanti theou)*, is tantamount to saying that Paul speaks to God face to face, just as Moses did (Exod. 19:9; 20:19; 24:1–2; cf. *T. Mos.* 1:14). There is thus a unique, heavenly dimension to Paul's apostolic role, which sets him well apart from his opponents who peddle the word of God for profit. In this way Paul shows that he is sufficient as a revelatory mediator because, like Moses, he speaks "in the presence of God." In 12:19 Paul repeats his assertion that "we speak in Christ in the presence of God," thus providing a key indication of the structural unity of the letter.

Paul denies that he has any concern for personal profit from the divine revelation that he mediates. This is in contrast to Paul's opponents, to whom he refers as **so many** *(hoi polloi)*. If 2 Corinthians can be seen as a unity, as the repetition of 2:17 in 12:19 supports, then we can assume that the apostle is referring here to the same opponents as in chapters 10–13. Unlike the opponents who have come into the Corinthian church from the outside, Paul does not **peddle** the word of God. These "false apostles" have preached a different gospel (11:4) and have exploited the church (11:20). Paul, on the other hand, refuses financial support from the Corinthians, insisting instead on preaching the gospel free of charge (11:7–11; 12:14–18). The apostle does not want to be open to the charge of extortion, against which Moses himself had to defend himself during Korah's rebellion (cf. Num. 16:3, 15).

Like the profit-seeking false prophets in the OT (cf., e.g., Num. 22:7; Mic. 3:5), Paul's opponents evidently claimed visions and revelations (cf. 2 Cor. 12:1) and pretended to communicate **the word of God** itself (cf. Ezek. 13:1–16; Jer. 23:9–40). Unlike such self-styled prophets who lead others astray, Paul speaks the word of God with **sincerity** (cf. 1:12) and **like men sent from God** ("men sent" supplied by the translators). Paul is claiming not just to have been commissioned and sent from God, but rather more specifically to speak "from God," that is, God is the source of his message (see also 2 Cor. 5:20). In other words, Paul is a mediator of divine revelation (cf. 2:14), casting himself in the mold of the true prophet (cf. K. O. Sandnes). Paul is not a prophet for profit; he has even put aside his apostolic prerogative in this regard (cf. 1 Cor. 9:12, 15, 18). And when the false apostles use this to accuse Paul (2 Cor. 11:7ff. and 12:12ff.), Paul turns the tables on them by recalling the OT tradition of the false prophets and their sordid gain. Paul, on the other hand, is a prophet like Moses.

3:1–6 / Realizing both that his daring comparisons of himself to Moses in the opening lines of his defense might sound like self-commendation and that the Corinthians were seeking proof of Christ's speaking through Paul (cf. 13.3), Paul proceeds to adduce tangible evidence for his sufficiency and legitimacy as an apostolic revelatory mediator (cf. 2:16b), evidence that the Corinthians could not dispute without simultaneously denying their own faith and pneumatic experience. They had received the Spirit through Paul's apostolic ministry! Hence, the Corinthians themselves are revealed as Paul's letter of recommendation, written with the Spirit of the living God on tablets of fleshly hearts, attesting to Paul's apostleship for all who read it (vv. 2–3). If the opponents used or needed letters of recommendation either from or to the Corinthians, Paul needs only the results of his ministry among the Corinthians in order to demonstrate the veracity of his apostleship, for he founded the church. Furthermore, Paul goes on to identify himself—in direct contrast to Moses—as a minister of the *new* covenant (vv. 4–6). Paul's mediatory work among the Corinthians demonstrates that the eschatological new age of the Spirit foretold in Ezekiel 11:19 and 36:26 had now arrived. All of this goes to show that Paul's ministry is not merely an exercise in self-recommendation; it is the work of God in and through him that makes him competent to minister.

3:1 / Paul begins the new paragraph with rhetorical questions expecting a negative answer. The purpose of these rhetorical questions is to prevent the addressees from drawing a wrong conclusion from the argument in 2:14–17. By rejoicing in his *merkabah* experience in the very presence of God and in his role as mediator of divine revelation, Paul does not thereby **commend** himself to the Corinthians. The word **again** suggests that Paul had been accused of this in the past, that is, he presented himself without an introduction from a recognized and authoritative third party (see on 13:1). But Paul does not tell the Corinthians anything they do not already know (and believe) about him. His defensive strategy is merely to remind them of his apostolic qualifications and thereby to appeal to their conscience (cf. 4:2; 5:12; 6:4).

Paul continues to use the literary plural (**we**) in reference to himself. **Letters of recommendation** were given to a traveler so that he might find a good reception with the writers' relatives or friends abroad. Paul himself routinely included in his letters recommendations for his associates (cf. 1 Cor. 16:10–11; 2 Cor. 8:22–24; Rom. 16:1–2; Col. 4:7–9, 10; Philemon).

Whereas in 2:17 Paul refers to his opponents as the "many," here he refers to them as **some**. These opponents were evidently able to produce letters of recommendation in order to establish their legitimacy. Perhaps they even had letters from the Corinthians in order to find an open door in other Pauline churches; that would explain the reference to letters **from you**. The letters to the Corinthians (**to you**) would presumably be from an ecclesiastical body that the congregation would respect, perhaps even from the mother church in Jerusalem itself or from one of its leading apostles.

3:2–3 / Paul gives the reason he is not trying to commend himself to the Corinthians: he relies on the Corinthians as his letter of recommendation! If the Corinthians, who know him best and witness to his apostolic ministry, have sincere doubts about Paul's legitimacy, how can he appeal to anyone else for a testimonial, except perhaps God or the Holy Spirit? The Corinthians have already accepted Paul's apostolic message and have already experienced the Spirit in their midst mediated by Paul. Therefore, if the Corinthians were to deny Paul's apostolic ministry, they would actually be denying their own existence as believers, for he founded the church at Corinth. By this very clever metaphor (**You yourselves are our letter**), Paul effectively shifts the burden of proof for his apostleship away from himself and onto the Corinthians. In other words, Paul is no longer on the defensive, but rather now on the offensive (cf. 12:19).

The Corinthians are Paul's letter of recommendation, **written on our hearts.** This seems to recall the founding visit of Paul to Corinth, when the Corinthians first believed Paul's apostolic message and came to faith. At that time, Paul inscribed them on his heart in several senses, including his fatherly affection for them as their founding apostle. Besides this, however, Paul's whole defense is purposely framed by the term "heart" (cf. 3:2, 3; 6:11; 7:3). What Paul probably means in 3:2 is that the Corinthians are the visible manifestation of the legitimacy of his apostleship. In this sense, the Corinthians are a letter **known and read by everybody** (note the paronomasia between the two participles *ginōskomenē* and *anaginōskomenē*). Hence, wherever he goes, the apostle can present the Corinthians as evidence to authenticate his identity as a true apostle.

Paul shifts his image from the Corinthians as a letter of recommendation written on his heart (v. 2) to the Corinthians as a letter from Christ (see also 6:11–7:4). The Corinthians owe their existence as believers to the work of the **Spirit** that they received through Paul's ministry (cf. 2 Cor. 11:4; 1 Cor. 2:4–5); hence, their Spirit-led lives **show** (better: "reveal") the reality and legitimacy of Paul's apostleship (cf. 6:14–7:1). In keeping with his use of the language of revelation (cf. 2:14; 4:2; 5:11), Paul defends his apostleship by adducing the revelation of the Spirit from Christ, through himself (**the result of our ministry** [lit., "ministered, served by us"]), to the Corinthians. Hence, the authentication of Paul's apostolic ministry is not merely subjective (written on Paul's heart), but is also objective (known and read by everybody). Paul is, in effect, appealing to an argument that the Corinthians could not deny without at the same time denying their own faith and pneumatic experience.

In the process of emphasizing his mediatorial role in delivering the letter of Christ, Paul also contrasts in verse 3 the letter of Christ with the law in two ways: first, in terms of the *medium* with which the letter of Christ was written, and, second, in terms of the *material* on which it was written. In the second contrast, **tablets of human** [lit., "fleshly"] **hearts** clearly alludes to Ezekiel 11:19 and 36:26 (cf. Jer. 31:33), where God promises to give the exiled nation of Israel a new heart and a new Spirit, that is, a "fleshly heart" *(kardia sarkinē)* to replace their "heart of stone" *(kardia lithinē)*. Whereas before the exile the nation had not kept the law because of its continual hard-heartedness, after the exile the people would be gathered back to the land, restored to fellowship with God, and divinely enabled in the heart to keep the law. Paul's point in 2 Corinthians 3:3, and indeed in much of the rest of the context, cannot be understood without recognizing Paul's fundamental, underlying assumption, which was common to much of Second Temple Judaism: The nation of Israel had come under the judgment of God in 587/6 B.C. and would remain under judgment until God intervened in the eschatological restoration of Israel from exile. By stating that the Corinthians had received the Spirit in their fleshly hearts, Paul unequivocally expresses the conviction that the eschatological promise of Ezekiel 11:19 and 36:26–27 (cf. Jer. 31:31–34) was now being fulfilled through his own apostolic ministry.

3:4–6 / In this section, Paul continues his defense of his sufficiency and legitimacy as an apostle in conscious comparison with Moses (cf. 2:14, 16b). Whereas in verses 1–3 Paul adduces the Corinthians themselves as tangible evidence that he mediates the eschatological gift of the Spirit just as Moses once mediated the law, in verses 3–6 he emphasizes the divine origin of his sufficiency as the basis of his confidence, a confidence that testifies that Paul has been made sufficient to be a minister of the new covenant.

3:4 / Paul begins with an assertion that summarizes what he has been projecting about himself in the previous context. **Such confidence** as Paul has as revelatory mediator is not merely an exercise in self-commendation. Paul's confidence is objectively verifiable. It comes through Christ **before God** (see 2:17: "in the presence of God"). Thus, Paul alludes here again to his Moses-like *merkabah* experience in order to validate his apostleship. The revelation that Paul has received through this experience has mediated the Spirit to the Corinthians, so that they, in turn, become a verification of his true apostleship and a source of his God-given confidence. Such confidence is not self-confidence, therefore, since it comes only **through Christ,** the author of the apostle's letter of recommendation (cf. 3:3).

3:5–6 / Paul goes on to explain the divine origin of his confidence. Here the apostle explicitly reintroduces the term **competent**/sufficient from the previous context. Recalling verse 12, alluding to Moses' inadequacy (Exod. 4:10), Paul reiterates that God himself, "the sufficient One" (Ruth 1:20; Job 21:15; 31:2; 40:2), supplies his confidence. In himself, Paul is not "sufficient" to be an apostle, especially in view of his former persecution of the church (1 Cor. 15:9–10); however, because his "sufficiency" is now **from God,** Paul is "sufficient" to be an apostle (2:16; 3:4–5). During Korah's rebellion, Moses found himself in a similar situation, in which he needed to defend his sending as something not from himself but from God (cf. Num. 16:28).

The fact that the term **ministers** or "servant" *(diakonos)* in verse 6a emphasizes Paul's role as the mediator of the Spirit is substantiated by two observations. First, the term "minister" recalls the idea of "ministered/served through us" in verse 3, which clearly links Paul's apostolic role with mediating the "Spirit of the living God." Second, verse 8 explicitly refers to Paul's "ministry of the Spirit." Hence, by calling himself a "minister of the new covenant," Paul has in mind particularly his part in mediating the Spirit to the Corinthians through his gospel message. "Minister of the **new covenant**" *(kainē diathēkē)* alludes to Jeremiah 31(38):31, the only explicit occurrence of the term in the OT. According to Jeremiah 31:31–34, the nation of Israel and Judah had broken the Sinaitic covenant (and had therefore gone into exile); hence, God promises to make a new covenant that will involve forgiving their sins, writing the law on their hearts, and reestablishing the covenantal relationship with them. From

Paul's perspective, the promise of Jeremiah 31:31–34 was being fulfilled through his own ministry (cf. 1 Cor. 11:25; 2 Cor. 6:16–18).

When we understand the OT background of Paul's reference to the "new covenant," we realize the inner logic that holds 2 Corinthians 3:3b and 6 together, for both verses refer to conceptually related aspects of the restoration of Israel as found in Ezekiel and Jeremiah. On the one hand, Paul's ministry mediates the Spirit expected on the basis of Ezekiel 11:19 and 36:26–27. On the other hand, Paul's ministry mediates the new covenant expected in Jeremiah 31:31–34 when he "serves" the "letter of Christ" by means of the Spirit. In both cases we are dealing with allusions to OT passages that expect God to transform the people's "hearts" when he delivers them from exile and reestablishes them in covenantal relationship with himself. Hence, Paul's ministry of the "new covenant" implies that those who are in the church have now had their "hearts" transformed by God, so that their response to his will as revealed in the law ought to be one of willful obedience, instead of the stubborn disobedience so characteristic of preexilic Israel.

If Paul alludes in 2 Corinthians 3:6a to the "new covenant" in Jeremiah 31:31–34 (cf. Ezek. 36:25–26), then the meaning of the phrase **not of the letter but of the Spirit** in 2 Corinthians 3:6b becomes clear. Since Paul is a servant of the new covenant, he has been made sufficient to be a revelatory mediator of the Spirit through whom people are placed into the new covenant and obey the law by means of the Spirit with transformed hearts (cf. v. 3). Under the Sinaitic covenant, the people were unable to keep the law (here called **the letter,** i.e., the written expression of God's will without the empowering work of the Spirit) because of the hardness of their hearts. However, under the new covenant inaugurated by Christ and mediated through Paul's ministry, all that has changed for the better by means of **the Spirit,** who writes the will of God on the heart (cf. v. 3) and enables obedience (cf. Rom. 8:2–4; *Jub.* 1:22–24).

In 2 Corinthians 3:6c, Paul gives the reason (**for,** *gar*) God has made him sufficient to be a minister of the Spirit under the new covenant, rather than merely to serve the law without God's transforming power: **for the letter kills, but the Spirit gives life.** The law of Moses promised both blessings and curses, depending on whether the nation of Israel remained faithful to the covenant or apostacized. Among the curses of the law that would come upon the people for disobedience, the worst were exile and death for the whole nation (cf. Lev. 26:14–39; Deut. 28:15–68). Therefore, when Paul states that **the letter kills,** he refers to the fact, commonly acknowledged in Second Temple Judaism, that the curse of the law had indeed come upon the nation and had caused national death (cf. Deut. 30:15–20; Ps. 115:5; Jer. 8:3; Dan. 9:11–13; Hos. 7:13; *Exod. Rab.* 42:3; see also Gal. 3:10).

In contrast to the death that the law brings because of the people's inability to obey, Paul affirms that **the Spirit gives life.** According to Ezekiel, the life-giving Spirit is the central feature of the prophetic expectation of the restoration from exile. After the people have been punished and purged and brought again through the wilderness in a "new exodus," they will be given a new Spirit that will reanimate the nation dead in its trespasses and sins (cf. Ezek. 11:19; 18:36; 36:26). The Vision of the Valley of Dry Bones in Ezekiel 37:1–14 portrays the exiles as bones into which God breathes his Spirit in order to reconstitute the nation of Israel on a new basis in the land (cf. 37:15–28). Hence, as S. Hafemann correctly observes, "The startling implication of 2 Cor. 3:6 is that this promised restoration from the exile, never fully experienced by Israel at her 'return,' is now said to be taking place in and through Paul's new covenant ministry." Eventually, the Spirit will also be the means of bodily resurrection (Rom. 8:11, 23).

3:7–18 / Up to this point in context of his defense, Paul has alluded only to the similarities between his own apostolic ministry and the ministry of Moses (cf. 2:14, 16, 17; 3:4–5). In light of his assertion that "the letter kills, but the Spirit gives life" (3:6), Paul goes on in 3:7–18 to explain the essential difference between the two ministries. The apostle bases his argument on the biblical tradition of the glory and the veil of Moses from Exodus 34:29–35. Basically, Paul's argument is that Moses' ministry of the Sinaitic covenant did not provide for Israel the immediate and constant access to the presence and "glory" of God in the way that Paul's ministry of the new covenant does for the church. Indeed, the exile removed Israel from the presence of God altogether (cf. LXX 4 Kgdms. 17:18, 20, 23; 23:27; 24:3; Jer. 7:15). In effect, therefore, verses 7–18 give further evidence of the thesis in verse 6, that God made Paul competent to be a minister of the glorious new covenant.

Paul's argument is divided into two parts: In verses 7–11, the apostle compares the "glory" of the two ministries. Then, in verses 12–18, Paul draws a conclusion based on verses 7–11, including the implications of Moses' veil.

3:7–8 / This section contains the first of Paul's three comparisons in 3:7–11 between the ministries of Moses and Paul. The argument here, as in the other two comparisons, is from the lesser to the greater *(a fortiori* or *qal wahomer)*. Paul assumes that both his own ministry and the ministry of Moses have in common the **glory** that attends (or attended) them. For the apostle, there is nothing inherently wrong with the law (cf. Rom. 7:12). The difference between the two ministries is their respective effects (antithetical typology): Moses' ministry of the written law resulted in **death**, whereas Paul's ministry of the Spirit gives life. In a sense, verses 7–8 are really a restatement both of the letter/Spirit contrast of verse 6c and, reaching farther back in context, of the possible typological comparison in 2:15–16a.

As a result of the "glory" that attended the ministry of the law, the Israelites (lit., "sons of Israel") were not able to gaze at **the face of Moses** because of the "glory" of his face. Already in Exodus 32–34 LXX, the glory on Moses' face is clearly a mediation of the glory of God, manifesting Yahweh's presence (cf. the "glory" of the Lord in Exod. 33:18–23).

The people are afraid of Moses' descent (Exod. 34:30) and cannot gaze at his face because Yahweh had earlier warned them that the Lord's presence among them would cause their destruction as a result of their sin with the golden calf (Exod. 33:3, 5). Hence, Moses, who mediates the glory of God, must put on a veil after speaking to the people. Yahweh's glory could be in their midst, but only briefly (cf. Exod. 34:30–32; 34:34–35). From its inception, therefore, the law under the Sinaitic covenant brought judgment and death on the nation (cf. Exod. 32:27–29, 35), which is exactly Paul's point in 2 Corinthians 3:6c. It was Moses' mediation of the glory of God on his face that brought with it the judgment of God upon a rebellious people. When "the glory of the Lord appeared" in the assembly, judgment often followed, as in case of Korah's rebellion (cf. Num. 16:19, 42).

If this interpretation is correct, then the participle *(tēn katargoumenēn)* that modifies the word "glory" in verse 7c probably does not mean **fading though it was,** for indeed the verb *katargein* is never found in this sense. Furthermore, in Jewish tradition, the glory on Moses' face remained unchanged until his death (cf., e.g., *Tg. Onq.* Deut. 34:7). Elsewhere in Paul's writings the passive verb is used in the sense of "to be made ineffective, powerless, idle," "to be nullified," or "to be abolished, brought to an end." Hence, S. Hafemann plausibly suggests that Paul is referring in 2 Corinthians 3:7 to the fact that the veil of Moses brought the glory of God to an end in terms of its effect if not veiled, that is, the judgment and destruction of Israel.

In sum, Paul presents in verses 7–8 the distinction between his ministry and Moses' ministry in antithetical typology: If Moses' ministry of the Sinaitic covenant that consequently brought death came in glory, so that Israel could not endure it but had to have it repeatedly veiled, how much more does Paul's ministry of the Spirit exist in glory, since it brings life (and unveiled, constant mediation of God's glory). This argument goes to show that Paul is competent to be a minister of the new covenant (v. 6), for the Corinthians cannot deny either that, historically, Moses' ministry brought death or that, experientially, Paul's ministry has been instrumental in mediating the Spirit and the glory of God to them.

3:9–11 / With Paul's having established that the ministry of the Spirit exists in glory (v. 8), the purpose of verses 9–11 is to support this conclusion by explaining Israel's experience of the Sinaitic covenant (v. 7). Moses' ministry of death (vv. 6, 7) is further described as a **ministry that condemns** (v. 9) that is brought to an end (vv. 10–11). In contrast, Paul's ministry of the new covenant and of the Spirit, which gives life (vv. 6, 8), is further described as a **ministry that brings righteousness** (v. 9), of **surpassing glory** (v. 10), and as **that which lasts** (lit., "remains," v. 11).

3:9 / Here Paul introduces the second of his three *a fortiori* arguments that both compare the glory of Moses' ministry to that of Paul's ministry and also point to the differences between the two. The **ministry that condemns men** (lit., "the ministry of condemnation") refers to the effects of Moses' ministry on the nation of Israel after the golden calf incident. From then on, and throughout the long history of Israel, the Mosaic law worked to pronounce judgment on the nation for its hard-heartedness and apostasy. The story of Korah's rebellion (Num. 16–17) provides a forceful example. As Moses himself repeatedly foretold in the Torah, the curses of the law would come upon the nation in a full and final way (cf. Lev. 26:14–38; Deut. 11:26–28; 27:14–26; 28:15–68; 30:15–20; 31:16–32:47), as indeed they did in 722 and 587/6 B.C., when Israel and Judah were led into their respective exiles.

In contrast to Moses' "ministry of condemnation," Paul's ministry is described as **the ministry that brings righteousness.** The fact that Paul's new covenant ministry of the Spirit **brings righteousness** stems from the OT and Jewish expectation of what the Spirit would effect at the time of Israel's restoration (cf., e.g., Isa. 32:15–17; 59:21; Ezek. 11:19–20; 36:24–29; 1QS 4.20–22; Rom. 8:3–4). Furthermore, in comparison with the ministry of condemnation, the ministry of righteousness "abounds in glory."

3:10 / The reason (**For,** *gar*) is given for why the ministry of righteousness abounds in glory in comparison with the ministry of condemnation. When the divergent results of the two covenants are compared (i.e., death and life, respectively), Moses' ministry of the Sinaitic covenant **has no glory now.** The very fact that life, righteousness, and the glory of God come through Paul's ministry shows that God now reveals his glory through the new covenant rather than through the old Sinaitic covenant.

3:11 / The third of three *a fortiori* arguments on the comparison of the two ministries gives the reason (NIV misses the force of the Greek *gar*) Paul's ministry is a vehicle through which the surpassing glory of the new covenant is now being revealed. As in verse 7, the verb *katargein* should be rendered "bring to an end" (rather than **fading away**). As S. Hafemann explains, "The Sinai covenant's mediation of the glory of God, which due to the hard hearts of Israel had to be continually rendered inoperative by the veil . . . , is now *itself* described as that which 'was continually being rendered inoperative.' " We have seen that the whole history of Israel, beginning with the golden calf incident and extending throughout the preexilic period, is characterized by the hard-heartedness and sinfulness of the nation. The continual efforts of the prophets to call the people to repentance did not succeed. Hence, according to Jeremiah 31:31–34, the people irreparably "broke" (LXX: "they did not persevere in") the Sinaitic covenant (v. 32). Either the Sinaitic covenant had to be done away with or else the curse of the law would have remained on the people.

In contrast to the Sinaitic covenant, which was being rendered inoperative from its inception, the new covenant is described in 2 Corinthians 3:11b as **that which lasts** or "remains" in glory. The inauguration of the new covenant signals the beginning of the eschatological fulfillment of God's salvation-historical plan for his people and indeed for the world. This is the new and permanent vehicle for mediating God's glory. According to Ezekiel, to which the present context repeatedly alludes, God would establish an "eternal covenant" with his people (cf. Ezek. 16:60; 37:26).

3:12–18 / The apologetic contrast between the ministries of Paul and Moses begun in verses 7–11 becomes sharpest in verses 12–18. Unlike Moses' ministry, which mercifully blocked the glory of God, Paul's ministry mediates the glory of God to believers. The whole section can be seen as an extensive commentary on Exodus 34:29–35 in light of Jeremiah 31:31–34 and Ezekiel 36:26–27. In a stunning way, Paul continues to build an argument for the legitimacy of his apostleship by placing the goal of his ministry over against the consequence of Moses' ministry. In effect, the greatest man in the history of Israel is put beneath the itinerant tentmaker in an effort to get the Corinthian church to submit to the latter's apostolic authority.

3:12–13 / The section begins with a conclusion (**Therefore,** *oun*) drawn from the previous discussion in verses 7–11. Paul refers to the **hope** drawn from the fact that his ministry mediates a covenant that "exists in glory" (v. 8) and that lasts (v. 11). Because of his hope in the mode and permanence of the new covenant, Paul **(we)** is **very bold.** The term can refer to boldness before God or before others, depending on the context. In Philo, for example, Moses is said to have spoken "with boldness, candor" before God about his rhetorical inability (*On the Sacrifices of Cain and Abel* 12; cf. 2 Cor. 2:16b; 10:10). Paul has already spoken of the "confidence" he has before God (v. 4), as he speaks face-to-face with the divine occupant of the throne of glory (cf. 2:14a, 17). Now, however, he refers to the "boldness" with which he proclaims the apostolic message before others, based on his encounter with the *merkabah* and the revelation from it of which Paul is a mediator (cf. 2:14).

In 3:13 Paul contrasts his own boldness in mediating the glory of God through the proclamation of the gospel to Moses' repeated veiling of himself in Exodus 34:29–35. Most often, Paul has been understood to argue that Moses hid his face from Israel because the glory on it was fading *(tou katargoumenou)* and coming to an end *(to telos)*. On this interpretation, Moses comes off as being rather disingenuous, whereas Paul is forthright and honest. But the point here is that Paul does not minister as Moses did, with a **veil** *(kalymma)* on his face. After the incident with the golden calf, Moses continually placed a veil over his face, so that the obstinate Israelites might not gaze into "the consequence" *(to telos)*—i.e., the judgment—of that which was being rendered ineffective by the veil, that is, the Sinaitic covenant itself (cf. 3:7). In the words of S. Hafemann, "Far from duplicity, Moses' merciful *intention* was to keep Israel from being judged by the glory on his face, which was the *telos* of that glory in response to the hardened nature of the people." In contrast to Moses, Paul proclaims the gospel with boldness because he knows that the glory of God that is now revealed through his ministry need not be veiled, since by means of the Spirit of the new covenant, it produces life rather than judgment and death.

3:14–18 / In this section, Paul broadens his apologetic for his apostleship from a contrast between himself and Moses to a contrast between unbelieving Jews and believers. Jewish unbelief in Paul's message is not evidence against his apostleship, but rather an indication of the people's historic recalcitrance; however, those who do accept his message behold the glory of the Lord and are being transformed into his likeness.

3:14 / In contrast **(But)** to Paul's boldness in proclaiming his message (vv. 12–13a), Israel is described as hardened and closed to it. Here, the NIV translates the Greek verb *pōroun* as **made dull** instead of "were hardened." The former is an unfortunate translation, for it completely obscures the OT and Jewish tradition of Israel's obduracy (cf. C. A. Evans) that is brought to expression here. As we have seen, OT and Jewish tradition commonly views Israel on a historical continuum of sin and guilt due to the nation's hard-heartedness. Therefore, in verse 14 Paul can jump without strain from Israel in the time of Moses to Israel in his own day (cf. Deut. 29:4; Jer. 7:25–26; 11:7–8; Philo, *On the Life of Moses* 2.271; *Exod. Rab.* 42:9 on Exod. 32:9: "To this very day Israelites in the Diaspora are called the stiffnecked people"; 1 Thess. 2:14–16). We might say that God hardened them in their hardness. Hence, the legitimacy of Paul's apostleship is no more disproved by Israel's rejection of his authority and message than Moses' legitimacy was refuted when Israel rejected his authority and message.

In 2 Corinthians 3:14b, the tradition of Israel's obduracy is signaled by the important biblical formula, **to this day**. Paul is saying that from the time of Moses—and particularly the golden calf incident—to his own day, Israel has been blinded and unresponsive (cf. Ezra 9:7; Dan. 9:4–19; Bar. 1:19–20; Rom. 11:8). Just as Israel was hardened to the law in Moses' day (Deut. 29:3–4) and in the days of the prophets (Isa. 6:9–10), Israel continues to remain so under the old covenant in Paul's day as well (cf. Rom. 11:25; also Acts 28:26–27). As I have tried to show elsewhere, Deuteronomic tradition is crucial to understanding the apostle's view of Israel in relationship to the law. Paul's exilic perspective is similar to that found in *Hekhalot Rabbati*, which considers that Israel's "heart has been closed since the exiles, and the words of the Torah were hard like copper and iron" all the way through to the contemporary period (Schäfer, §293; cf. §§283, 331).

In shifting from Israel's past to its present, Paul continues to use the idea of the **veil** *(kalymma)* in order to show the historical continuity. Paul is saying that although Moses is read weekly in the synagogue, Israel is separated "to this day" from the revelation of the glory of God because of its rebellion. The original reason for the veil has not changed in all those centuries. The veil thus becomes a metonymy of effect (veiling) for cause (rebellious and unrepentant disposition).

Paul states that the veil remains to this day at the reading of the **old covenant** *(palaia diathēkē)*. In referring to the Sinaitic covenant as "old," the apostle obviously presupposes that the new covenant of which he is a minister has been inaugurated (cf. 2 Cor. 3:6). Those who are **in Christ** are now freed from the curse of the law and have the veil symbolizing their hard-heartedness removed by the Spirit of the new covenant. Without Christ, the majority of Jews remain hardened and cursed until the consummation, when "all Israel will be saved" (cf. Rom. 9–11). The negative effects of the **old covenant** persist, although they are in the process of being rendered inoperative (cf. 2 Cor. 3:11). It is Paul's ministry that is instrumental in taking away the veil of hard-heartedness by means of the Spirit. As S. Hafemann aptly observes, "The designation 'old covenant' is Paul's description of the Sinai covenant ministered by Moses *in view of the 'new covenant' inaugurated by Christ and ministered by Paul.*"

If, as we have suggested, Paul compares the Corinthian opposition to his apostleship with Israel's rebellion (and especially, Korah's rebellion), then the idea of a historical continuity becomes a powerful polemic against the apostle's Jewish opponents in Corinth. The implication is thus that Paul's opponents have not yet had the veil of hard-heartedness removed because they are yet not "in Christ" and do not have the Spirit. This corresponds to the way that Paul views the opponents elsewhere in the letter (cf. 6:14–16; 11:13–15). Hence, the apostle's "defense" in 2:14–7:4 begins to turn the tables on his critics and bring their own salvation into question.

3:15 / Having stated that the veil (a metonymy for Israel's obduracy) remains when the old covenant is read (v. 14), Paul restates this point in verse 15 and explicitly applies it to Israel's heart when she reads Moses. The NIV does not translate the adversative conjunction *(alla)* with which the verse begins. In beginning the verse in this way, Paul wants to stress that, although Christ is the one who removes the hard heart of Israel (v. 14), "nevertheless *(alla),* to this day, whenever Moses is read, a veil is being laid upon their heart." As the parallelism between verses 14 and 15 shows, the expression **when Moses is read** is synonymous with the expression "when the old covenant is read" in the previous line (cf. Acts 15:21: "Moses" is "read in the synagogues every Sabbath," i.e., the law or the Sinaitic covenant is read), for it was Moses who mediated the Sinaitic covenant and wrote it (cf. Rom. 10:5, 19). The condition of the Israelites' **hearts** is the problem, not the law itself. Just as the hardened hearts of the wilderness generation led them to oppose both Moses and the covenant that he mediated, so also the Jews in Paul's day remain unchanged. The veil of the people's hard-heartedness continues to render them incapable of properly responding to the law, as well as to the gospel message.

3:16 / Having mentioned in verse 14 that only in Christ is the veil taken away, Paul elaborates on this point in verse 16, explaining more about the process by which the veil is taken away. The text alludes to Exodus 34:34a, where Moses is said to remove the veil whenever he speaks with the Lord. Hence, the understood subject of the verb in our text is not **anyone** but rather "he," that is, Moses. Whereas a veil continues to be laid upon Israel's heart whenever Moses is read in the synagogue (2 Cor. 3:15), whenever "he" (namely, Moses) returns to the Lord, the veil is being taken away (v. 16). Yet, if Moses is the implied subject of the verb, he stands paradigmatically for any Israelite who returns to the Lord. The text is purposely ambiguous at this point so that it resonates with Exodus 34:34 while adding the idea of repentance. Turning **to the Lord** in this sense is more than returning to the presence of the Lord as Moses did in the tent of meeting (although that is implied here, too), but rather a process of repentance whereby Israel's hardened heart undergoes a fundamental change. Throughout the history of Israel, God had sent prophets to turn Israel to the Lord (1 Sam. 7:3; Hos. 5:4; 6:1; 2 Chron. 24:19; cf. 1 Thess. 1:9), albeit mostly without success. The prophetic call to repentance is a fixed motif of the Deuteronomic view of Israel's history that goes hand in hand with the theme of obduracy (cf. O. H. Steck). Hence, before the restoration could be inaugurated and the new covenant established, Israel would need to return to the Lord in wholehearted repentance; then God would bestow his Spirit on them, so that their hearts of stone would be taken away, and they would be able to keep his commandments in perpetuity (cf. Tob. 13:6; *Jub.* 1:15, 23; 2 Cor. 3:6). Once again, Paul is arguing here from the perspective that the exile and curse of the law are brought to an end in Christ (cf. 2 Cor. 3:14).

Whether **Lord** *(kyrios)* refers here to God (cf. 1 Thess. 1:9) or Christ seems superfluous, since as we have seen (cf. on 2:14), God and Christ work together or even interchangeably, and Christ reflects the glory of God (4:6; see also 1:14). Of course, in keeping with the allusion to Exodus 34:34, *kyrios* in our text refers primarily to Yahweh. From Paul's perspective, the veil that is now being removed when one returns to the Lord is the same one originally applied in Exodus 34:33. Paul hopes that through his own ministry some Jews will come to faith (Rom. 11:14; cf. 1 Cor. 9:19–20). Eventually, he expects that "all Israel will be saved" (Rom. 11:25–26), perhaps through a direct encounter with the resurrected Christ at the time of the Parousia (cf. Phil. 2:9–11). Similarly, Paul came to faith when he encountered the resurrected Christ on the way to Damascus and perceived him as the "Lord" seated at the right hand of God in accordance with Psalm 110:1.

As S. Hafemann correctly observes, Paul's idea of the removal of the veil corresponds to the Isaiah Apocalypse (Isa. 24–27), where the universal revelation of the glory of God on Zion is portrayed as an eschatological counterpart to the theophany at Sinai. According to that apocalyptic text, universal judgment would be followed by the reign of the Lord of hosts on

Mount Zion, when God would manifest his glory both before his elders (Isa. 24:1–23; cf. Exod. 24:9–16) and before all nations, thus reversing the veiling that took place in Exodus 34:29ff. (Isa. 25:6–8). The inclusion of the nations in this salvation would have been especially significant to Paul as the apostle to the nations (Rom. 11:13).

3:17 / Paul proceeds to explain (**Now,** *de*) the removal of the veil as providing access to the presence of the Lord through the Spirit. This extremely obscure and controversial statement seems to equate the **Lord** with the **Spirit** (cf. John 4:24). As we have seen, **Lord** can refer either to God or to Christ in Paul's writings, for they act together or interchangeably. Hence, the **Spirit** is closely identified with both God and Christ (cf. 13:14). On the one hand, it is called "the Spirit of God" (Rom. 8:9, 14; 1 Cor. 2:11, 14; 3:16; 6:11; 7:40; 12:3; Phil. 3:3), "the Spirit of the living God" (2 Cor. 3:3), or "the Spirit which is from God" (1 Cor. 2:12); and on the other hand, it is called "the Spirit of (Jesus) Christ" (Rom. 8:9; Phil. 1:19) or "the Spirit of his Son" (Gal. 4:6; cf. Rom. 8:14). In fact, Romans 8:9 uses "the Spirit of God" interchangeably with "the Spirit of Christ." The fact that 2 Corinthians 3:17a refers to the same close identification of the Spirit with God and/or Christ is signaled by the expression **the Spirit of the Lord** in verse 17b. In emphasizing the identification between the Lord and the Spirit, Paul shows the historical continuity between Moses' encounter with the Lord in the tent of meeting and believers' experience of the presence of the Lord through the Spirit of God.

The presence of the Spirit of the Lord spells **freedom** as a result of the new covenant situation in Christ. Upon returning to the Lord and receiving a new heart through the Spirit of the Lord, those who have been enslaved in exile receive freedom. The proclamation of liberty to captives is at the very core of the OT's "good news" for Israel (cf. Isa. 52:2–10; 61:1–2). Of particular interest is Isaiah 61:1, where the "Spirit of the Lord" *(pneuma kyriou)* who comes upon the prophet, sends him "to preach good news" *(euangelisasthai)* to the poor and to proclaim "release" *(aphesin;* MT, *derôr,* "liberty, freedom") to the captives. We find the same idea developed elsewhere in Paul (cf., e.g., Gal. 3:10–14; 4:1–7, 21–31; Rom. 8:14–16, 21).

3:18 / The apostle goes on to explain another effect of the removal of the veil and its similarity to Moses' experience in the tent of meeting. In the previous context, Paul has consistently used the first person plural **(we)**—the so-called apostolic/literary plural—with reference to himself alone. Since verse 16, however, Paul has begun to refer more generally to all those who return to the Lord. Therefore, "**we** all" (*pantes* is not represented in the NIV translation) most naturally includes Paul and all other believers, another aspect of the mutuality to which Paul has repeatedly brought attention in the letter (cf. 1:1–2, 3–11, 24; 2:2). Very much like Moses, who removed his veil when entering the presence of the Lord (Exod. 34:34), all believers, from whom the veil of hard-heartedness has been removed, are being progressively transformed into **his likeness,** that is, into the image of the Lord. Paul's defense is vulnerable at this point, for to admit that all believers have direct access to, and actual participation in, the glory of God, might seem to diminish the apostle's own unique role in mediating that glory. Potentially, the opposition in Corinth could then argue against Paul as Korah had done against Moses: "All the congregation are holy, everyone of them, and the Lord is among them. So why then do you exalt yourselves above the assembly of the Lord?" (Num. 16:3; see further on 2 Cor. 3:6). Nevertheless, Paul seems intent on showing that, through Christ, access to God's presence has now been granted to all believers, who, without fear of death, are free to gaze upon and to be transformed by the revelation of God's presence, that is, the glory of God (cf. Renwick). In any case, however, Paul is the one who originally mediated the Spirit to the Corinthians (and hence the presence of God among them) and who in some special sense remains the spokesman of God and Christ (cf. 2 Cor. 5:20).

A physical transformation derived from speaking with God is evidently the result of having beheld the divine glory (cf. Exod. 34:29). According to the Psalm 68:18 tradition, Moses saw God's throne on Mount Sinai. Seen in this light, Paul's own encounter with the *merkabah* throne that he mediated to the Corinthians (cf. 2 Cor. 2:14) becomes, through the Spirit, their portion as well. Believers thereby behold the **glory** of God itself, even as Moses did (cf. Exod. 33:18; 34:6, 29; Num. 12:8). Furthermore, the **likeness** to which Paul refers here is undoubtedly the anthropomorphic "likeness of the glory of the Lord" that Ezekiel saw in his vision of the *merkabah* (Ezek. 1:26, 28; cf. Dan. 7:9–10). This interpretation is reinforced by Paul's choice of the verb "behold as in a mirror" *(katoptrizesthai),* for the idea of the mirror and reflected divine glory are likewise drawn from Ezekiel 1 and *merkabah* tradition based on Ezekiel 1 (cf. D. J. Halperin and others cited in Additional Notes below). Ezekiel saw his vision as in a mirror, either in the water of the river Chebar (see Additional Notes below) or in the "gleaming amber" in the midst of the fire that accompanied the theophany (cf. Ezek. 1:4, 27).

According to the apostle, those who are in Christ are in a process of transformation into the image of God "from glory to glory" (which the NIV translates as **with ever-increasing glory**). What has already partially begun by the life-giving Spirit will be consummated through the Spirit at the Parousia (cf. Rom. 8:29–30). Hence, 2 Corinthians 3 describes the double process of transformation by means of the Spirit: a moral/ethical transformation in the heart (vv. 3ff.), which contrasts with Israel's hardened heart "to this day" (v. 14), and a physical transformation in the body (v. 18). Interestingly enough, *merkabah* mysticism included both aspects as goals of ascending to the divine throne-chariot.

4:1–6 / In 2:14–4:6, Paul defends the legitimacy of his apostleship by focusing on the glory of God that his ministry mediates. In the final section of this argument (4:1–6) Paul asserts the integrity of his ministry and claims that those who reject his apostleship and his gospel message are blinded by Satan. Paul goes back to his encounter with Christ on the Damascus road to establish the legitimacy of his apostleship. 2 Corinthians 4:1–6 concludes Paul's argument as it began in 2:14–17, with reference to Paul's vision of God's throne. There are also several other striking correspondences between the beginning and the end of 2:14–4:6.

4:1–2 / In 3:12–18, Paul argues that the reason he is so bold is that, in contrast to Moses' ministry, his own ministry transforms lives and mediates the glory of God to believers. In 4:1–2 Paul reiterates his point from 3:12–13. Here Paul returns to using the apostolic plural **(we)**, referring to himself. **Through God's mercy** (lit., "as we have received mercy"), Paul has the ministry of the new covenant (cf. 3:6ff.). The mercy to which Paul refers here is his call to apostleship on the way to Damascus, when the persecutor encountered the risen Lord (cf. 1 Cor. 15:9–10; also Rom. 1:5; Gal. 1:15–16). If he has something to commend him, it is the gracious working of God in and through him. His sufficiency is from God (2 Cor. 3:5).

Since he has graciously received the ministry of the new covenant, with its transforming work of the Spirit, Paul does not **lose heart;** for although Paul's proclamation of the gospel is not being met with open arms by his people Israel, neither Paul nor his gospel is really to blame. This obduracy fits into a historical pattern of hard-heartedness and rebellion. For his part, Paul focuses on presenting the gospel and conducting himself with candor and honesty (cf. 2:17), since he is mediating divine revelation (**the word of God** and **the truth**). To counter his opponents' personal attack against him (see further on 7:2), Paul hopes to **commend** himself to the Corinthians (v. 2). Although this may sound like a contradiction to Paul's opening salvo in 3:1 ("Are we beginning to commend ourselves again?"), his point is similar to what he has been arguing all along, because Paul's commendation stems from tangible evidence that the Corinthians can access because of their familiarity with him and the results of his gospel in their midst (cf. 1:12; 3:2; 5:11). Therefore, Paul commends himself **to every man's conscience,** and particularly to the Corinthians' conscience (cf. 5:11). This appears hyperbolic at first sight, but Paul has already stated that, through his evangelistic ministry, God reveals knowledge of himself "in every place" (2:14). From Paul's perspective, the divine origin of his message is apparent. But realizing that human conscience is not the ultimate authority (see on 1:12), Paul also states that he commends himself **in the sight of God.** As we have seen in 2:17 (cf. 12:19), the apostle states that in Christ he speaks sincerely "in the presence of God," that is, the actual physical presence of God seated on his heavenly throne.

4:3 / From the beginning of his defense, Paul claims that, through his apostolic preaching, God reveals the fragrance of the knowledge of himself to the whole world (2:14), even though Paul admits that there are two different perceptions of that fragrance. Besides being a "fragrance of life" to those who are being saved, it can also be a "smell of death" to those who are perishing (2:15–16a). In 4:3 the apostle reiterates the negative effect of his his preaching, for having characterized his preaching as a "revelation of the truth" (4:2), he acknowledges that some people remain hardened to it. Paul admits that his gospel is **veiled** to some people, since not everyone accepts his message, including most Jews (cf. Rom. 9–11). Here again the figure of a veil is used as a metonymy of effect for cause (hard-hearted rebellion). This represents another direct comparison between Paul and Moses, for Israel has the same reaction to Paul's message as it had to Moses' (cf. 2 Cor. 3:15).

As Paul goes on to explain, his message is veiled to **those who are perishing** *(apollymenoi)*. Paul uses the same participle in 2:15 in contrast to "those who are being saved." Hard-hearted rebellion under both the Sinaitic covenant and the new covenant produces the same result, that is, judgment and death (cf. Num. 17:13; 1 Cor. 10:9–10). This provides yet another direct comparison between the ministries of Paul and Moses. Furthermore, Paul may have in mind here specifically his opponents in Corinth, who have rejected both his message and his apostleship.

4:4 / Paul explains the (Satanic) source of the hard-hearted, veiled state of those who have rejected his apostolic message. The full expression **the god of this age** *(ho theos tou aiōnos toutou)* occurs nowhere else in the NT; hence, there has been some debate whether the articular noun *ho theos* refers to God (as usual in Paul) or to Satan (unattested in Paul). It seems to have gone unnoticed that Daniel 5:4 LXX decries those who have praised idols made with their own hands rather than "the God of the age/world *[ton theon tou aionos]* who has power over their [life-]spirit." Similarly, Tobit 14:6 (in Codex Sinaiticus) expects that "all the nations in the whole world" will one day praise "the God of the age/world *[ton theon tou aionos]*." Hence, our passage apparently refers to God himself as the one who has blinded the minds of unbelievers, an idea supported by other Pauline passages (cf. 2 Cor. 3:14; Rom. 11:8). Such a notion, however, is as repugnant to the modern mind as the Markan explanation of Jesus' use of parables (Mark 4:12, citing Isa. 6:9–10). Therefore, commentators usually prefer to interpret the expression as a reference to Satan, even though such a designation seems to have no parallels. In Paul's writings, "this age" refers to the present evil age that is perishing (cf. Gal. 1:4; 1 Cor. 2:6, 8; 3:18; Rom. 12:2), as opposed to the age to come that brings resurrection of the dead and consummation of the new creation (cf. Eph. 1:21; 2:7; Rom. 8:18–25; 1 Cor. 15:20–28). The present evil age is governed by "the rulers of this age" (1 Cor. 2:6, 8) and "the prince of the kingdom of the air, the spirit who is now at work in the sons of disobedience" (Eph. 2:2). Hence, the ruler of this age (apparently Satan) could also be called "the god of this age." In that case, it is Satan who causes people to harden their hearts to the truth. We may compare the many statements about Belial (cf. 2 Cor. 6:15) in Second Temple literature, according to which Belial is the ruler of this world and of this age (*Mart. Isa.* 2:4; 4:2–6; *T. Reu.* 4:11; 1QS 1.23–24; 2.19) and the one who leads people's hearts astray (*Jub.* 1:20; *T. Reu.* 4:7; *Sib. Or.* 3:63–74; CD 4.12–19). It is not easy to choose between these options, and each has its own plausibility. We may give a slight preference to interpreting the expression as referring to God, who frequently hardens people's hearts against him (e.g., Exod. 4:21; 7:3, 13; 9:12, 35; 14:4, 8; Deut. 2:30; Isa. 63:17).

The **unbelievers** whose minds are blinded include all those who reject the Pauline gospel, especially the opponents of the apostle in Corinth (cf. 6:14, 15), who are really servants of Satan (cf. 11:12–15). Such people cannot see **the light of the gospel.** According to Acts 13:47, Paul understood his commission in terms of Isaiah 49:6: "I have made you a light for the nations, that you may bring salvation to the ends of the earth." In our passage, the content of the light of the gospel is further described as **the glory of Christ.** When Paul met the resurrected Christ on the way to Damascus, God revealed his Son to Paul (Gal. 1:16). At that time, Paul saw Christ (cf. 1 Cor. 9:1), and this made Paul an eyewitness apostle (cf. 1 Cor. 15:1–11). In the previous context of our passage, much has been said about "glory" as the representation of God's presence. Thus, Moses' face so shone with the glory of God that the Israelites could not gaze at it (2 Cor. 3:7). The glory of Christ is likewise a manifestation of God's presence, for the text goes on to describe Christ as the **image of God.** Paul has already referred to the Lord's "likeness" in 3:18, presumably alluding to the anthropomorphic appearance of God in Ezekiel's throne-chariot vision (Ezek. 1:26–27). If God and Christ sit side by side in the divine throne-chariot, that would explain why Christ is viewed here as the glorious manifestation of the image of God that one sees in a *merkabah* vision.

4:5 / Having identified the content of his gospel as the glory of Christ, the very image of God, Paul goes on to reinforce this content, evidently in the face of criticism that he champions himself ("we do not **preach ourselves**"). Perhaps the very defense of his apostleship has opened him up to the charge of preaching himself. Perhaps his opponents in Corinth have charged the apostle with selfish ambition, extortion, and power mongering (cf. 1:24; 2:17). After all, Paul's preaching put him in a unique mediatorial position, which demanded respect and compliance. From Paul's perspective, the situation he faces in Corinth is not much different from the opposition Moses encountered during Korah's rebellion. After being charged with exalting himself above the assembly of the Lord and lording it over the people (Num. 16:3, 13), Moses felt compelled to affirm his divine sending and to deny both that he had taken tribute (v. 15) and that the works he was doing were of himself (v. 28). Paul's opponents considered him a fraud as an apostle (cf. 2 Cor. 5:16), preaching his own Damascus-road vision, which was nothing more than a delusion (cf. 5:13).

The apostle responds to these (implicit) accusations by emphasizing that he is not interested in promoting himself, even if he is forced to do so in the face of heavy opposition. Rather, the central content of Paul's gospel is Jesus Christ as **Lord,** just as the latter was revealed to him on the way to Damascus. Both Paul and the early church understood Jesus Christ in terms of Psalm 110:1: "The Lord says to my Lord: 'Sit at my right hand until I make your enemies a footstool for your feet' " (cf. Rom. 8:34; 1 Cor. 15:25). As we have seen, the application of this text to Jesus Christ strongly implies that Christ sits at the right hand of God on the *merkabah* throne-chariot (cf. Mark 14:62). Also, this psalm is part of the background for calling Christ "Lord." Hence, the one whom Paul preaches is none other than the co-occupant of the divine throne of glory, the Lord of all (cf. Rom. 10:12; Acts 10:36).

Far from lording it over the Corinthians and promoting his own selfish interests, Paul characterizes himself as their **servant,** or even their "slave," for Jesus' sake. This actually subordinates Paul to the Corinthians, following the model of Jesus himself (cf. Phil. 2:7; Mark 10:44–45; 1 Cor. 9:19).

4:6 / The apostle goes on to explain that he preaches Jesus Christ as Lord because he experienced a revelation of Jesus Christ on the way to Damascus. Here, as throughout 2:14–4:6, Paul continues to refer to himself with the first person plural. He is recounting the divine revelation that brought him personal knowledge of gospel on the way to Damascus. Ultimately, Paul cannot get behind the seminal revelation that made him an apostle in the first place, even with the additional signs of the apostle that attest to his ministry (cf. 12:12).

God is described as the author of the revelation in terms of an allusion to Genesis 1:3–4 LXX ("And God said, 'Let there be **light**,' and there was light. And . . . God divided between the light and the darkness") and/or to Isaiah 9:1 LXX ("O people who walk in darkness, behold a great light; you who dwell in the region and shadow of death, a light will shine upon you"). While both passages contain key terms linking to the present text, the Isaiah passage seems particularly appropriate as the source of Paul's allusion, given the obviously "postexilic" perspective of 2 Corinthians 2:14–4:6. Even if Genesis 1:3–4 is deemed to have a greater affinity with our text by virtue of the common vocabulary **(God, said, light,** and **darkness),** the Genesis passage has been read in light of the Isaiah passage. The restoration of Israel, of which Paul is already a part (cf. Rom. 11:1–2), is tantamount to a new creation (cf. 2 Cor. 5:17). In fact, elsewhere in Isaiah the restoration is described in grandiose terms as inaugurating the new creation of the heavens and the earth (cf. Isa. 65:17–19; 66:22). This interpretation of our text would fit well with Paul's idea of "the light of the gospel" (2 Cor. 4:4), understood against the background of Isaiah 49:6 (see above on 2 Cor. 4:4). Isaiah is well known to be a major influence on the apostle's thinking (cf. R. B. Hays).

Paul moves from general (the scriptural allusion about Israel) to specific (Paul himself): The God who restores Israel to covenantal relationship made his light shine in Paul's heart to give him the light of the knowledge of the glory of God in the face of Christ. Paul is speaking here from his own personal experience in his **heart** (cf. Gal. 1:16). Paul's call to apostleship, like the call of Moses and the prophets, took place in his encounter with the glory of God, this time "in the face of Christ." This seminal experience provided Paul with the **knowledge,** so that through him, God reveals the fragrance of the knowledge of Christ in every place (2:14). Paul thereby becomes a revelatory mediator like Moses.

The revelation that Paul received was the light of the knowledge of **the glory of God in the face of Christ.** This alludes to Paul's vision of the risen Christ (1 Cor. 9:1; cf. 15:8; Acts 9:3; 22:6, 11; 26:13). On the way to Damascus (and often subsequently [cf. 2:14; 12:1]), Paul saw Christ as the "image of God," indeed as the anthropomorphous image or likeness of God that Ezekiel saw in his *merkabah* vision (Ezek. 1:26–27; see above on 2 Cor. 3:18; 4:4). In other words, "the same image" and "glory" in 3:18 is specifically the "glory of God" being revealed "in the face of

Christ" (4:6), who is "the image of God" (4:4; cf. Phil. 2:6; Col. 1:15). Seated next to God in the divine throne-chariot, Christ is the very image and glory of God (cf. *Gen. Rab.* 8:10 on Gen. 1:27 [cited above]; Ps. 8:5–7; see further N. Deutsch). Here it is interesting to note that in *Hekhalot Zutrati,* the story of the "Four Who Entered *Pardes*" to encounter the *merkabah* concludes with God's statement that R. Aqiba "is worthy to behold my Glory" (Schäfer, §346; cf. §673; Sir. 49:8: "It was Ezekiel who saw the vision of glory, which God showed him upon the chariot of the cherubim [*epi harmatos cheroubin]*"). Certainly it would have been important to Paul's defense if he could likewise claim to have been worthy to behold the divine glory (cf. 2 Cor. 2:16b).

Additional Notes §4

2:14–4:6 / Cf. Dieter Georgi, *The Opponents of Paul in Second Corinthians* (Philadelphia: Fortress, 1986), p. 335.

According to recent composition theories of 2 Corinthians, 2:14–7:4 (without 6:14–7:1) is a fragment of a letter that Paul wrote before 2 Cor. 1–8. This "apology for Paul's apostolic office" is usually considered either (1) part of the tearful letter, together with 2 Cor. 10–13, or (2) part of a separate letter that Paul sent the Corinthians before the painful visit. According to the first position, Paul became better acquainted with the stance of his opponents during the painful visit, and he responded to their attack on the legitimacy of his apostleship in the tearful letter (2:14–7:4; 10–13). According to the second position, Paul learned of the arrival of the opponents in Corinth, whom he did not consider legitimate apostles. Hence, Paul thoroughly presented his understanding of the apostolic ministry in a letter and hoped in this way to correct the situation in Corinth. When the situation worsened, however, Paul considered it necessary to visit Corinth himself (the painful visit). After this unsuccessful visit, Paul wrote 2 Cor. 10–13, which constitutes part of the tearful letter and contains Paul's reaction to the painful visit.

Cf. Thrall, *Second Corinthians,* vol. 1, pp. 20–25.

Perhaps there is yet another possibility for understanding the placement of 2:14–7:4 in the midst of the travelogue. In 2:12–13 and 7:5–7 Paul describes the inner turmoil he suffered in connection with the rebellion in Corinth. Later in the letter he lists his "anxiety for all the churches" (11:28) as part of the many tribulations he experiences as a servant of Christ (11:23b–29). If, as 12:1–10 would suggest, there is a relationship between the apostle's revelatory experience and his suffering (see esp. v. 7), then the extended apology for Paul's apostleship in

2:14–7:4, which focuses on Paul's revelatory experience as the basis of his apostleship (see esp. 2:14–4:6), would stand out all the more clearly in a framework of apostolic suffering (2:12–13; 7:5–7).

2:14–17 / In a prayer contained in the Qumran *Thanksgiving Hymns*, the Teacher of Righteousness begins by blessing God for not abandoning him (1QH 13.20–22) and then goes on to expresses the emotional effect that disaffection in the community has had on him (13.22–15.5). See further on 2 Cor. 2:5.

2:14 / The connection between vv. 12–13 and vv. 14ff. is extremely controversial. While many scholars posit a major break in the train of thought, others search for a plausible link between the two passages. S. Hafemann, for example, suggests that v. 14, with its idea of Paul being led to death in triumphal procession, continues the theme of Paul's anxiety in vv. 12–13, which is "yet another example of the 'death' which Paul undergoes as an apostle of Christ" ("The Comfort and Power of the Gospel: The Argument of 2 Corinthians 1–3," *RevExp* 86 [1989], pp. 325–44 [here p. 334, with n. 23]). M. Thrall regards 2:14 as a second introductory period, analogous to 1:3–11 (*Second Corinthians*, vol. 1, pp. 188, 191).

C. K. Barrett describes 2 Cor. 2:14 as "the most cheerful verse in the epistle so far" ("Conclusion," in *Paulo. Ministro del Nuovo Testamento [2 Co 2,14–4,6]* [ed. M. Carrez, et al.; Rome: Benedictina Editrice, 1987], pp. 317–29 [here p. 321]). On philological grounds, it is impossible to accept his conclusion that v. 14 pictures Paul as taking part in the triumph as one of the victorious army (ibid., p. 323).

Cf. G. Dautzenberg, "Motive der Selbstdarstellung des Paulus in 2 Kor 2,14–7,4," in *Apôtre Paul. Personnalité, style et conception du ministère* (ed. A. Vanhoye; BETL 73; Leuven: Leuven University Press, 1986), pp. 150–66 (here p. 154).

Gordon D. Fee argues that the imagery of Paul's being a captive in Christ's triumphal procession (2 Cor. 2:14) "deliberately echoes 1 Cor. 4.9 and thereby pushes back to the crucified Messiah in 1.18–25" ("'Another Gospel Which You Did Not Embrace': 2 Corinthians 11.4 and the Theology of 1 and 2 Corinthians," in *Gospel in Paul: Studies on Corinthians, Galatians and Romans for Richard N. Longenecker* [ed. L. Ann Jervis and Peter Richardson; JSNTSup 108; Sheffield: Sheffield Academic Press, 1994], pp. 111–33 [here p. 129]). However, this suggestion is extremely unlikely for several reasons. First, the alleged deliberate echo is muted by the painful visit and the tearful letter that came between the writing of 1 and 2 Corinthians. Second, there are substantial differences between the two passages in question. For example, in 1 Cor. 4:9 the apostle disparages being exhibited by God before the world in contrast to the Corinthians' self-commendation, whereas in 2 Cor. 2:14 he actually exults in being led in triumphal procession and in its positive revelatory benefit for the world.

Cf. Peter Marshall, "A Metaphor of Social Shame: *Thriambeuein* in 2 Cor. 2:14," *NovT* 25 (1983), pp. 302–17 (here p. 304): ". . . the triumphal procession must have been a familiar institution to Greeks and Romans of all levels of society. Approximately 350 triumphs are recorded in their literature and they were most sought after and frequent in the republican period. Traditional processional themes or triumphal motifs were portrayed on arches, reliefs, statues, columns, coins, cups, cameos, medallions, and in paintings and the theatre."

On the interpretation of *thriambeuein* in the sense of lead **in triumphal procession,** see Hafemann, *Suffering,* p. 33; Thrall, *Second Corinthians,* vol. 1, pp. 191–95; Roy Yates, "Colossians 2.15: Christ Triumphant," *NTS* 37 (1991), pp. 573–91 (esp. pp. 574–80). For a completely different reason, Paul refers to his co-workers as "fellow-prisoners" (cf. Rom. 16:7; Col. 4:10; Phlm. 23).

On the interpretation of v. 14 developed here, see further my essay, "The Triumph of God in 2 Cor. 2:14: Another Example of Merkabah Mysticism in Paul," *NTS* 42 (1996), pp. 260–81. Recently, there has been a renewed interest in the Jewish mysticism of the Apostle Paul, and particularly his *merkabah* mysticism. For example, Alan F. Segal attempts to understand Paul as having undergone a mystical conversion similar to those found in the Jewish mystical tradition (*Paul the Convert: The Apostolate and Apostasy of Saul the Pharisee* [New Haven: Yale, 1990]; see also idem, "Paul and the Beginning of Jewish Mysticism," in *Death, Ecstasy, and Other Worldly Journeys* [ed. John J. Collins and Michael Fishbane; Albany, N.Y.: SUNY Press, 1995], pp. 93–122). Martin Hengel has also focused on the *merkabah* experience of Paul, arguing that the apostle bears witness to an early Christian tradition based on Ps. 110:1, that the crucified Messiah, Jesus of Nazareth, was raised and seated "at the right hand" of God, that is, enthroned as a co-occupant of God's own "throne of glory" (cf. Jer. 17:12), located in the highest heaven (" 'Sit at My Right Hand!' The Enthronement of Christ at the Right Hand of God and Psalm 110:1," in *Studies in Early Christology* [Edinburgh: T&T Clark, 1995], pp. 119–225). Cf. Eusebius, *Demonstration of the Gospel* 4.15.33, 42. All of the basic elements of *merkabah* mysticism are already found in the visions of God reported in the OT: Exod. 24:10–11; 1 Kgs. 22:19; Isa. 6:1–13; Ezek. 1:1–28; 3:12–13, 22–24; 8:1–18; 10:9–17; Dan. 7:9–14.

On Hab. 3:8 see M. Haran, "The Ark and the Cherubim," *IEJ* 9 (1959), pp. 30–38 (esp. p. 37), 89–94; cf. also 1 Chron. 28:18 ("his plan for the golden chariot of the cherubim"); the description for the "great four-faced chariot of cherubim" in the gnostic *Hypostasis of the Archons* [NHC II,4, 95:13–14]; *3 En.* 22:11; 24:1. The paintings in the synagogue at Dura-Europos include a picture of the throne-chariot with wheels, which seems to reflect the *merkabah* tradition (cf. Jonathan A. Goldstein, "The Judaism of the Synagogues [Focusing on the Synagogue of Dura-Europos]," in *Judaism in Late Antiquity, Part Two: Historical Syntheses* [ed. Jacob Neusner; Handbuch der Orientalistik 1.17.2; Leiden: Brill, 1995], pp. 109–57).

Cf. David J. Halperin, *The Faces of the Chariot: Early Jewish Responses to Ezekiel's Vision* (TSAJ 16; Tübingen: Mohr Siebeck, 1988).

See also *1 En.* 60:2; 71; 90:20; Ithamar Gruenwald, *Apocalyptic and Merkavah Mysticism* (AGJU 14; Leiden: Brill, 1980), pp. 29–72.

Cf. John J. Collins, *The Scepter and the Star: The Messiahs of the Dead Sea Scrolls and Other Ancient Literature* (ABRL; New York: Doubleday,

1995), p. 140; also idem, "A Throne in the Heavens: Apotheosis in pre-Christian Judaism," in *Death, Ecstasy, and Other Worldly Journeys* (ed. J. J. Collins and Michael Fishbane; Albany, N.Y.: SUNY Press, 1995), pp. 43–58.

The concept of a throne-chariot in which someone is seated at the right hand of the deity is very ancient; e.g., on a Roman coin, divine Augustus and divine Claudius are shown enthroned together in an elephant quadriga; Diodorus Siculus 16.92.5; 95.1 records how Phillip II displayed himself as "co-occupant of the throne *[synthronon]* with the twelve gods"; according to Pseudo-Callisthenes (*Historia Alexandri Magni* 1.36.2; cf. 1.38.2 [ed. W. Kroll]), the Persian king claimed to be "king of kings, relative of the gods, co-occupant of the throne with the god Mithras" (*synthronos theō Mithra*). See also *Gen. Rab.* 8:9: "When the Holy One, blessed be he, came to create the first [man], the ministering angels mistook him [for God, since he was in the image of God] and wanted to say before him, 'Holy' [i.e., the *Trisagion* in Isa. 6:3]. To what may the matter be compared? To the case of a king and a governor who sat in a chariot, and his subjects wanted to acclaim the king, '*Domine!* (Sovereign!),' but they did not know which one of them was which. What did the king do? He pushed the governor out and and put him away from the chariot, so that the people would know who was king." In patristic literature, Jesus Christ is often called the *synthronos* of God (cf., e.g., Eusebius, *Demonstration of the Gospel* 4:15:33; 5:3:9 [both citing Ps. 110:1]). This is not the place to enter into a discussion of the name Metatron and its possible relationship to *synthronos* (cf. Gruenwald, *Apocalyptic and Merkavah Mysticism*, pp. 235–41 [an appendix by Saul Lieberman]).

C. Breytenbach suggests that **fragrance** *(osmē)* here refers to the incense or cinnamon that often accompanied a Roman triumphal procession ("Paul's Proclamation and God's 'Thriambos': Notes on 2 Corinthians 2:14–16b," *Neotestamentica* 24 [1990], pp. 265–69).

2:15–16a / The use of **aroma** in this context reminds us perhaps of the outbreak of plague after the people grumbled against Moses over God's judgment of Korah and his followers (Num. 16:41). Moses instructed Aaron to lay incense in his censer and carry it out to the congregation in order to make atonement for them: "He stood between the dead and the living" (Num. 16:48; cf. 4 Macc. 7:11). According to Jewish tradition (e.g., *b. Šabb.* 89a), Moses had learned the secret of the incense as a cure for the plague during his *merkabah* encounter with God on Sinai, and this is indeed one of the "gifts" to which Ps. 68.19 refers. Cf. Halperin, *The Faces of the Chariot,* p. 302.

The contrast between **those who are being saved** and **those who are perishing** is already found in 1 Cor. 1:18. In a similar way, Moses is said to have set before the people "life" and "death" (Deut. 30:15, 19, 39).

2:16b / The allusion to Exod. 4:10 is now well recognized in the literature. Cf., e.g., Hafemann, *Suffering,* pp. 87, 89–101; idem, *Paul, Moses, and the History of Israel: The Letter/Spirit Contrast and the Argument from Scripture in 2 Corinthians 3,* (WUNT 81; Tübingen: Mohr Siebeck, 1995), p. 100; Carol K. Stockhausen, *Moses' Veil and the Glory of the New*

Covenant: The Exegetical Substructure of II Cor. 3.1–4.6 (AnBib 116; Rome: Pontifical Biblical Institute, 1989), pp. 82–86; Thrall, *Second Corinthians,* vol. 1, p. 210.

If Paul's sufficiency is from God, we can understand why the apostle would regard boasting in his own strength as absolutely ludicrous (cf. 2 Cor. 11:17). Paul's motto is this: "Let him who boasts boast in the Lord" (10:17, citing Jer. 9:24).

A similar question to that in 2 Cor. 2:16b is found in *Hekhalot Zutarti* (Schäfer, §§348–352), which seems to allude to Moses. In the Hekhalot literature there is much discussion about who is "worthy" to ascend/descend to the *merkabah* and to see the throne of glory (cf. Schäfer, §§199, 229, 232, 234, 236, 258–259, 303, 333, 335, 346, 407, 408, 409, 411, 583, 584, 673, 712, etc.). The one who is considered worthy is he who, among other things, has read Torah, the Writings, and the Prophets, and obeys all the commandments that Moses gave on Sinai (§234). See further N. A. van Uchelen, "Ethical Terminology in Heykhalot-Texts," in *Tradition and Re-Interpretation in Jewish and Early Christian Literature: Essays in Honour of Jürgen C. H. Lebram* (ed. J. W. van Henten, et al.; SPB 36; Leiden: Brill, 1986), pp. 250–58.

2:17 / The literal use of *katenanti* is by far the most common in the LXX and in the NT. Cf. David A. Renwick, *Paul, the Temple, and the Presence of God* (BJS 224; Atlanta: Scholars Press, 1991), pp. 61–94.

Paul alludes to Exod. 32 in Rom. 9:3, again comparing himself to Moses: Just as Moses offered to sacrifice himself for his people (Exod. 32:32), so also Paul offers to sacrifice himself for the sake of Israel. Hence, we should not doubt that Paul consciously thinks of himself in terms of Moses.

Cf. Karl O. Sandnes, *Paul—One of the Prophets? A Contribution to Paul's Self-Understanding* (WUNT 2/43; Tübingen: Mohr Siebeck, 1991); Craig A. Evans, "Prophet, Paul as," *DPL,* pp. 762–65.

On the use of *kapēleuein* in the sense of **peddle**, see Hafemann, *Suffering,* pp. 106–26. For other interpretative options, see Thrall, *Second Corinthians,* vol. 1, pp. 212–15.

In the OT, the **word of God** was often used in the sense of a divine oracle delivered through the God-sent prophet (cf. Jer. 1:2; 9:19). In 2 Cor. 2:17b, the "word of God" is the unexpressed object of the verb "speak." For other occurrences of the "word of God," see Rom. 9:6; 1 Cor. 14:36; 2 Cor. 4:2; Col. 1:25; 1 Tim. 4:5; 2 Tim. 2:14; Titus 2:5.

On the use of *eilikrineia,* see Spicq, *TLNT,* vol. 1, pp. 420–23. As S. Hafemann points out, Paul's use of the term in 2 Cor. 1:12 underscores the divine source of Paul's sincerity (*Suffering,* p. 165).

Paul's words **before God** recall how the Lord used to speak to Moses "face to face *(enōpios enōpiō),* as someone might speak to his own friend" (Exod. 33:11; cf. Num. 12:7–8; Deut. 34:10; Sir. 45:5). Thus, according to LXX Exod. 32:11 (Codex Alexandrinus), while Moses was on Sinai (the *merkabah* experience!) and the people back in the camp had made the golden calf, God wanted to destroy the people and begin anew with Moses, but "Moses pleaded for mercy in the presence of the Lord God *(katenanti kyriou tou theou).*" In light of the other allusions to

Moses in the foregoing context (2 Cor. 2:14–16; cf. 3:1), Paul obviously has this passage in mind when he writes v. 17.

3:1 / **Letters** (plural!) **of recommendation** *(systatikai epistolai)* to or from the Corinthians may seem strange here, since one letter would seem sufficient. In Greek usage, however, the plural *epistolai* commonly refers to a single letter (cf. M. L. Stirewalt Jr., *Studies in Ancient Greek Epistolography* [SBLRBS 27; Atlanta: Scholars Press, 1993], pp. 77, 85), and indeed Paul uses the singular *epistolē* in v. 2. In view of the allusions to Moses and Aaron in the previous context (see on 1:1, 4, 19, 24; 2:6–7, 15), it is possible that the first person plural **(we)** includes Timothy, the co-sender of the letter, whom Paul seems to portray as an Aaron figure. In that case, the plural number of letters of recommendation is explained.

On Greek letters of recommendation, see William Baird, "Letters of Recommendation: A Study of II Cor 3:1–3," *JBL* 80 (1961), pp. 166–72; C.-H. Kim, *Form and Structure of the Familiar Greek Letter of Recommendation* (SBLDS 4; Missoula, Mont.: Scholars Press, 1972); Spicq, "*systatikos*," *TLNT*, vol. 3, pp. 342–43.

3:2–3 / Paul's apostolic ministry affects the heart, the center of a person's being (4:6). It is there that one receives the down payment of the Spirit (1:22), which is so essential to Paul's ministry of the new covenant (cf. Ezek. 11:19; 36:26; Jer. 31:31–34). Paul is bound to the Corinthians in his heart and writes to them from the heart (2 Cor. 2:4). He wants to be evaluated as an apostle on the basis of his heart (5:12).

Since the whole apology is purposely framed by the term **hearts** *(kardiai)*, the textual variant **our/your** *(hēmōn/hymōn)* should be decided in favor of the former, which in any case has the superior attestation and is the more difficult reading (cf. Bruce M. Metzger, *A Textual Commentary on the Greek New Testament* [2d ed.; Stuttgart: United Bible Societies, 1994], p. 509). See further Thrall, *Second Corinthians*, vol. 1, pp. 223–24; Baird, "Letters of Recommendation," pp. 166–72; Hafemann, *Suffering*, pp. 186–89.

The NIV makes no attempt to render the passive voice of the participle *diakonētheisa*. In light of the other cognate terms of service in the context *(diakonos* and *diakonia)*, it should almost certainly be translated "served, ministered," rather than "delivered" or "prepared." The text wants to emphasize Paul's mediatorial role in the *process* of revealing the Spirit to the Corinthians.

The tradition behind **tablets of stone** is found in *Lev. Rab.* 35:5 (cf. also *Song Rab.* 6:26): "In the same way the Holy One, blessed be he, said: 'The Torah is called a stone *('eben)* and the evil inclination is called a stone *('eben).*' That the Torah is called a 'stone' is proved by the text, 'The tables of stone, and the law and the commandment' [Exod. 24:12]; that the evil inclination is called a 'stone' is proved by the text, 'I will take away the heart of stone out of your flesh' [Ezek. 36:26]. Thus, the Torah is a stone and the evil inclination is a stone. The stone shall watch the stone." Here, as often elsewhere in rabbinic literature (cf. *b. Sukka* 52a; *b. Ber.* 32a; *Num. Rab.* 15:16; 18:1; *Deut. Rab.* 6:14; *Cant. Rab.* 1:15; 6:26; *Eccl. Rab.* 9:24), Ezek. 36:26 is cited as a future expectation that God will do away the stone heart/evil inclination. This is precisely what Paul sees being accomplished through his ministry of the Spirit. Moreover, *Lev. Rab.* 35:5 well illustrates the contrast in 2 Cor. 3:3 between "tablets of stone" and "tablets of fleshly hearts," for there Paul likewise assumes a relationship between the law as "stone" and the people's hearts as "stone."

In later Hekhalot literature, the goal of the ascent to the *merkabah* was to enable the ordinary person to assimilate the whole Torah instantly, directly, and permanently (cf. P. Schäfer, "The Aim and Purpose of Early Jewish Mysticism," in *Hekhalot Studien* [TSAJ 19; Tübingen: Mohr Siebeck, 1988], pp. 289ff.). At least one passage alludes in this connection to Ezek. 11:19–20 (cf. Jer. 17:1 MT), the promise that God would "remove the heart of stone from their flesh and give them a heart of flesh, so that they may follow my statutes and keep my ordinances and obey them" (note the reference to the *merkabah* and glory of God in Ezek. 11:22). Hence, according to *Ma'aseh Merkabah* (Schäfer, §578; cf. Halperin, *The Faces of the Chariot*, p. 429), the *merkabah* mystic adjures "the great prince of Torah, you who were with Moses on Mount Sinai and preserved in his heart everything that he learned and heard, that you come to me and speedily remove the stone from my heart. Do not delay." The purpose of this complete communion with God and complete knowledge of Torah was to attain the redemption of Israel in the here and now (cf. Schäfer, "The Aim and Purpose of Early Jewish Mysticism," p. 295). The transformation of the heart in order to obey the law was a central idea in *merkabah* mysticism (cf. Schäfer, §§656, 678, 680). As Rabbi Aqiba found out before the divine throne, even a proselyte could receive this direct knowledge of the Torah (Schäfer, §686).

The expression **written . . . on tablets of human hearts** may also allude to Prov. 7:3 LXX ("Write them [sc. commandments of God] on the tablet of your heart"). Cf. Prov. 3:3; Jer. 17:1; *Eccl. Rab.* 2:1.

For both Paul and his congregations there is no question that the **Spirit** has been poured out in their midst and that its manifestations are empirically verifiable (cf., e.g., 1 Cor. 12 and 14; Gal. 3:1–5). Hence, Paul can begin with this fact in his apologies.

For Hekhalot texts on the Torah in the heart, see Schäfer, §§278–279, 292, 293, 329–330, 340.

If Paul's opponents in Corinth claim to be *merkabah* mystics in their own right (cf. 1 Cor. 12–14; the Corinthians' realized eschatology in 1 Cor. 4:8–10; 15:12; see also on 12:1), they may be promoting a direct knowledge of God and the Torah that would eliminate the need for a revelatory mediator like Paul (see further on 3:6, 18). And, insofar as these opponents advocate the Torah, their program is comparable to Paul's opponents in Galatia.

3:4–6 / This paragraph, as well as the interpretation of the rest of the chapter, is particularly indebted to Hafemann, *Paul, Moses, and the History of Israel*.

On the protracted exile in Paul's thinking, see my essay, "Restoration of Israel," *DPL*, pp. 796–805. The Hekhalot literature has much to say about the exile of Israel and its continuation, frequently citing national confessions of sin like Neh. 9 and Dan. 9 (cf. Schäfer, §§130–139, 143, 148, 149, 281–283, 293, 297, 324–325, 331).

Note, however, that both Philo (*On the Embassy to Gaius* 210; *Allegorical Interpretation* 4.149) and Josephus (*Ag. Ap.* 2.171–178) refer to the law being "engraved" on Jewish hearts by precept and practice.

Cf. Hafemann, *Suffering*, p. 216.

3:4 / On the literal interpretation of **before God** suggested here, see, however, Hafemann, *Paul, Moses, and the History of Israel*, p. 96.

3:6 / The NIV causes v. 6 to begin a new sentence with the pronoun **He**. Actually, however, v. 6 continues uninterrupted from v. 5 by means of the relative pronoun "who" (namely, God), which serves to ground Paul's statement that his competence is from God (v. 5b). The Greek text of v. 6a includes the adverb "also" (*kai*), which is not translated in the NIV. C. Stockhausen (*Moses' Veil*, p. 84) suggests that, since it has no explicit antecedent in context, the "also" refers to Moses' being made competent in Exod. 4:10ff. In that case, Paul would be saying that, like Moses, God has "also" made him competent to be a minister. This competence was not merely given once at Paul's call but continually throughout his ministry, just as the *merkabah* visions and revelations on which his competence is based were recurrent (note the "always" in 2:14 and the plural "visions and revelations of the Lord" in 12:1). Cf. also Hafemann, *Paul, Moses, and the History of Israel*, p. 102.

On Paul's exilic perspective, see my "Restoration of Israel," *DPL*, pp. 796–805. On Paul's exilic perspective in Gal. 3:10, see James M. Scott, " 'For as many as are of works of the Law are under a Curse' (Galatians 3.10)," in *Paul and the Scriptures of Israel* (ed. James A. Sanders and C. A. Evans; JSNTSup 83; Sheffield: JSOT Press, 1993), pp. 187–221; Hafemann, *Paul, Moses, and the History of Israel*, p. 182.

According to a liturgical poem from Qumran, the renewal of the covenant with Israel would be accompanied "with visions of the glory" (4Q*508* frag. 97–98 i:7–8). The *Damascus Document* refers explicitly to the "new covenant" (CD 6.19; 8.21; 19.34; 20.12). A new Qumran fragment can be interpreted as a reference to the new covenant of Jer. 31 "to perform and to cause the performance of all the law" (cf. Erik Larson, "4Q470 and the Angelic Rehabilitation of King Zedekiah," *DSD* 1 [1994], pp. 210–28).

When Paul describes himself as a minister **of a new covenant**, he is open to critique by his opponents, for if Korah could oppose Moses for setting himself above the nation when in fact the whole congregation was holy (Num. 16:3; cf. Exod. 19:6), how much more could Paul's opponents criticize him for elevating himself to the position of revelatory mediation when Jer. 31:34 explicitly states that there would be no mediator under the new covenant, but rather direct knowledge of the Lord (cf. 2 Cor. 3:18). As we have seen, later Hekhalot literature holds out the possibility of direct and permanent knowledge of the Torah for the *merkabah* mystic. Nevertheless, the Hekhalot literature also seems to expect a *merkabah* mystic like Paul who would herald the eschatological redemption, cf. Schäfer, §218.

3:7–18 / According to Exod. 34:29–35 LXX, when Moses descended from Mount Sinai with the two tablets in his hand, he did not know that his face was glorified. However, when Aaron and the elders of Israel saw Moses' face, they were afraid to come near him. After giving the people the commandments, Moses put on a veil and wore it whenever he spoke with the people, except when he entered the tent of meeting and spoke to God.

3:7–8 / The **glory** of Moses' ministry is, of course, commonly assumed in early Judaism (cf., e.g., Philo, *On the Life of Moses* 2.70; 4 *Ezra* 3:19, 31, 36–37; *Tg. Ps.-J.* Exod. 34:29). See further Hafemann, *Paul, Moses, and the History of Israel,* pp. 287–98. On Paul's concept of glory (*doxa*) and its background, see also Carey C. Newman, *Paul's Glory-Christology: Tradition and Rhetoric* (NovTSup 69; Leiden: Brill, 1992); Renwick, *Paul, the Temple, and the Presence of God,* pp. 99–121.

According to the *Ascension of Isaiah,* the progressively greater glory of each successive heaven has a counterpart in the physical transformation that Isaiah undergoes as he ascends. In the third heaven, the prophet notices that "the glory of my face was being transformed" (7:25). In the seventh heaven, he is transformed so that he becomes like an angel (9:30). Nevertheless, he and the angels are capable only of glancing at God, whereas Isaiah sees the righteous [dead] "gazing intently upon the Glory" (9:37–38).

On Paul's use of *katargein* in the sense of "abolish, annul," see Hafemann, *Paul, Moses, and the History of Israel,* pp. 301–13.

3:9–11 / Cf. Hafemann, *Paul, Moses, and the History of Israel,* p. 330.

In 1 Cor. 10:1–14, Paul alludes to the golden calf incident and the ensuing divine judgment. On the OT/Jewish background of Paul's understanding of this incident and its significance for the history of Israel, see Karl-Gustav Sandelin, "Does Paul Argue Against Sacramentalism and Over-Confidence in 1 Cor. 10.1–14?" in *The New Testament and Hellenistic Judaism* (ed. Peder Borgen and Søren Giversen; Peabody, Mass.: Hendrickson, 1997), pp. 165–82 (esp. pp. 177–79).

3:12–13 / On the term **bold** (*parrēsia*), see Spicq, *TLNT,* vol. 3, pp. 56–62; Hafemann, *Paul, Moses, and the History of Israel,* pp. 338–47. Josephus (*Ag. Ap.* 2.168–169) proudly contrasts the openness of Moses to the masses with the great Greek philosophers Phythagoras, Anaxagoras, Plato, and the Stoics, who did not venture to disclose their true beliefs to the masses.

On the interpretation of *to telos* here, see esp. Hafemann, *Paul, Moses, and the History of Israel,* pp. 347–62 (here p. 359). The exegetical options on this complex text are too numerous to list here; cf. Thrall, *Second Corinthians,* vol. 1, pp. 255–61.

3:14 / The connection of v. 14 to the foregoing is difficult, for it is not immediately obvious what the opening *alla* **(But)** relates to; in other words, what the hardening of the Israelites' minds is contrasted with (cf. Thrall, *Second Corinthians,* vol. 1, pp. 262–63). The simplest answer is to suppose that Paul is contrasting his own apostolic boldness

(v. 12) with the Jews, whose minds have been hardened from the time of Moses to Paul's day (v. 14). One might have expected a perfect tense verb to express this idea, but the aorist is regularly used in the LXX to refer to a past action with results that continue to the contemporary period (cf., e.g., Gen. 47:26; Deut. 3:14; 29:3; Josh. 6:25; 7:26; 22:17; 23:8; Judg. 1:21; 10:4; 18:12; 1 Kgs. 9:13; 12:19; 2 Kgs. 2:22; 8:22; 10:27).

Cf. Craig A. Evans, *To See and Not to Perceive: Isaiah 6:9–10 in Early Jewish and Christian Interpretation* (JSOTSup 64; Sheffield: JSOT Press, 1989).

On **their minds were made dull** see Philo, *On the Life of Moses* 2.271.

On the formula **to this day,** see further Brevard S. Childs, "A Study of the Formula, 'Until this Day,'" *JBL* 82 (1963), pp. 279–92. When passages such as Deut. 4:25–31 (cf. also 2 Kgs. 17:23; 1 Chron. 5:26) were read in the ancient synagogue, the words "to this day" would have been interpreted as a description of the contemporary condition of Israel in exile, as indeed Dan. 9:4–19, 2 Chron. 29:9, Ezra 9:7, 1 Esd. 8:74, and Josephus, *Ant.* 11.133 show. Cf. also Bar. 1:19–20; Rom. 11:8 (citing a combination of Deut. 29:4 and Isa. 29:10; cf. Isa. 6:9–10). According to *m. Sanh.* 10:3 (cf. *b. Sanh.* 110b), Rabbi Aqiba contends that "the Ten Tribes are not destined to return" from exile, citing Deut. 29:28 to support this point: "And he [sc. God] will cast them out to another land *as at this day.*" Cf. *Exod. Rab.* 42:9 (on Exod. 32:9): "R. Abin said: 'To this very day Israelites in the Diaspora are called the stiffnecked people." See also Saebø, "*yôm,*" *TDOT,* vol. 6, pp. 7–32 (here pp. 15–16). For the expression "from the days of Moses until now" in the context of sin and exile, see *Hekhalot Rabbati* (Schäfer, §293). See also 2 Kgs. 21:15; *b. Yoma* 53b–54a contains an interesting controversy about whether the scriptural expression "until this day" applies only to the time of writing or to anytime thereafter as well.

Cf. James M. Scott, "Paul's Use of Deuteronomic Tradition," *JBL* 112 (1993), pp. 645–65.

On *b. Ber.* 32b ("From the time the Temple was destroyed, an iron wall cut Israel off from its Father in heaven" or "the iron wall that was between Israel and its Father in heaven has come to an end"), see Baruch M. Bokser, "The Wall Separating God and Israel," *JQR* 73 (1983), pp. 349–74. Cf. Eph. 2:14.

3:15 / Cf. Hafemann, *Paul, Moses, and the History of Israel,* p. 384.

3:16 / Cf. N. T. Wright, *Climax of the Covenant: Christ and the Law in Pauline Theology* (Minneapolis: Fortress, 1992), p. 183: ". . . the basic point of the chapter: those who are in Christ, the new-covenant people, are *unveiled* precisely because their hearts are *unhardened* (3.1–3, 4–6)."

Cf. Hafemann, *Paul, Moses, and the History of Israel,* pp. 394–95.

There are a number of OT citations in Paul's letters that originally refer to Yahweh, but Paul applies them to Christ (cf. Rom. 10:13; 1 Cor. 1:31; 10:26; 2 Cor. 10:17). On Paul's use of **Lord** *(kyrios),* see L. W. Hurtado, "Lord," *DPL,* pp. 560–69.

3:17 / On the problems of interpretation in v. 17a (**Now the Lord is the Spirit**), see Thrall, *Second Corinthians*, vol. 1, pp. 278–82 (Excursus III).

The **Spirit of the Lord** *(pneuma kyriou)* occurs frequently in the LXX (cf. Judg. 3:10; 6:34; 11:29; 13:25; 14:6, 19; 15:14; 1 Sam. 10:6; 16:13, 14; 1 Kgs. 18:12; 22:24; 2 Kgs. 2:16; 2 Chron. 18:23; 20:14; Isa. 11:2; 61:1; Ezek. 11:5; Mic. 2:7; 3:8).

S. Hafemann sharply distinguishes here between **freedom** "from" and freedom "for," arguing that Paul has in mind the latter, that is, freedom for obedience to the law *(Paul, Moses, and the History of Israel,* pp. 405–7). The distinction becomes untenable, however, when we consider the Exodus typology in the passage: Just as God once delivered Israel from slavery in Egypt to a covenantal relationship with himself at Sinai, so also he now delivers his people from slavery to a new covenantal relationship which requires obedience.

3:18 / In omitting the word "all" in the translation, the NIV evidently accepts the reading of P[46]. The omission there, however, is most likely due to a scribal error.

Cf. Renwick, *Paul, the Temple, and the Presence of God,* pp. 97–98.

According to Exodus, Moses' face was charged with glory because of his exposure to the resplendent presence of the Lord (Exod. 34:29–30; cf. Philo, *On the Life of Moses* 2.70; *Pesiq. Rab.* 10:6; 2 Cor. 3:7, 13). His encounter with the living God resulted in physical transformation. One who ascends to the *merkabah* is also subsequently transformed in the process into the likeness of the divine glory. Cf. C. R. A. Morray-Jones, "Transformational Mysticism in the Apocalyptic-Merkabah Tradition," *JJS* 43 (1992), pp. 1–31; Segal, *Paul the Convert,* pp. 34–71; idem, "Paul and the Beginning of Jewish Mysticism," p. 111; M. Himmelfarb, "Revelation and Rapture: The Transformation of the Visionary in the Ascent Apocalypses," in *Mysteries and Revelations: Apocalyptic Studies since the Uppsala Colloquium* (ed. John J. Collins and James H. Charlesworth; JSPSup 9; Sheffield: JSOT Press, 1991), pp. 79–90; idem, *Ascent to Heaven in Jewish and Christian Apocalypses* (New York: Oxford University Press, 1993), p. 29. In 1QH 12.5 the psalmist gives thanks to God because the Lord has brightened his face with his covenant. A physical transformation is also evident in Rom. 8, which expects that believers, who already have the indwelling Spirit of adoption (vv. 11, 15), will be glorified at the Parousia (v. 30), when they are conformed to the "image" *(eikōn)* of God's Son (v. 29; cf. Phil. 3:21), who is the "image of God" (2 Cor. 4:4; cf. Ps. 8:5–7).

The **Lord's glory** *(hē doxa kyriou)* occurs frequently in the LXX with reference to the glory of Yahweh (cf. Exod. 16:7, 10; 24:16, 17; 40:34, 35; Lev. 9:6, 23; Num. 14:10, 21; 16:19, 42; 20:6; 1 Kgs. 8:11; 2 Chron. 7:1, 2, 3; Pss. 104:31; 138:5; Isa. 35:2; 40:5; 58:8; 60:1; Ezek. 1:28; 3:12, 23; 10:4, 18; 11:23; 43:4, 5; Hab. 2:14). In view of our interpretation of 2 Cor. 2:14, it seems significant that the Targum interprets Ps. 68:19 particularly with reference to proselytes: "You ascended to the expanse, O prophet Moses; you led captivity captive; you taught the words of the Law; you gave gifts to the sons of men. But as for the rebellious who are becoming proselytes (and) are turning in repentance, there rests upon them the Shekinah of the glory of the Lord God."

The difficult hapax legomenon *katoptrizesthai* probably denotes "to behold as in a mirror" (cf. Diogenes Laertius 2.33; 3.39) rather than merely "to see" or "to **reflect**" (so NIV). Cf. Hafemann, *Paul, Moses, and the History of Israel*, p. 409; Thrall, *Second Corinthians*, vol. 1, pp. 290–95 (Excursus IV). Cf. 1 Cor. 13:12, where Paul refers to seeing in mirror in order to describe believers' current perception of heavenly realities in contrast to the face-to-face vision at the Parousia.

On Ezek. 1 as the background of 2 Cor. 3:18, see, e.g., Segal, *Paul the Convert*, p. 60 with n. 94; Halperin, *The Faces of the Chariot*, p. 212 with n. 22; Seyoon Kim, *The Origin of Paul's Gospel* (2d ed.; WUNT 2/4; Tübingen: Mohr Siebeck, 1984), pp. 231–33. Cf. a passage from the *Visions of Ezekiel* referring to what Ezekiel saw *"at the river Chebar* [Ezek. 1:1]," in Halperin *The Faces of the Chariot*, p. 230; also p. 265. Cf. also *b. Yebam.* 49b; *Lev. Rab.* 1:14: "All prophets saw [the divine vision] through the medium of nine mirrors. So it is written: *Like the appearance of the vision that I saw, like the vision I saw when I came to destroy the city, and visions like the vision I saw at the river Chebar. And I fell on my face* [Ezek. 43:3]. Moses saw through the medium of a single mirror: *By vision, and not in riddles* [Num. 12:8]. The rabbis say: All the prophets saw [the divine vision] through the medium of a dirty mirror. So it is written: *I speak to the prophets, and I multiplied visions, and so forth* [*and I liken myself through the prophets* (Hos. 12:11)]. Moses saw through the medium of a sparkling mirror. So it is written: *He sees the Lord's appearance* [Num. 12:8]." See further Halperin, *The Faces of the Chariot*, pp. 231–38, 265. Note that Wis. 7:25–26 refers to Wisdom as a "spotless mirror of the working of God" and a "pure emanation of the glory of the Almighty."

Another interpretation sees the reference to the Lord's **likeness** against the background of Gen. 1:26–27 and of Christ as the "Second Adam." Cf. Hafemann, *Paul, Moses, and the History of Israel*, p. 424. We have seen evidence, however, that Gen. 1:27 was interpreted in light of the *merkabah* vision of Ezek. 1 (cf. *Gen. Rab.* 8:10 [cited above]). This dovetails with Ps. 8:5–7, where the psalmist exults in the fact that Yahweh has made "man/the son of man" a little lower than "God" (MT only; LXX: *than the angels*), has crowned him with "glory" *(doxa)*, and has put all things under his feet (cf. Ps. 110:1; 1 Cor. 15:27).

On the present and future aspects of the transformation by the Spirit in Rom. 8, see James M. Scott, *Adoption as Sons of God: An Exegetical Investigation into the Background of* ΥΙΟΘΕΣΙΑ *in the Pauline Corpus* (WUNT 2/48; Tübingen: Mohr Siebeck, 1992), pp. 221–66.

4:1–2 / On **God's mercy** as a reference to Paul's Damascus road christophany, see Kim, *Origin of Paul's Gospel*, pp. 11, 26, 288–96; Thrall, *Second Corinthians*, vol. 1, p. 298. See further on v. 6.

On the use of *enkakein* in the sense of **lose heart**, see Spicq, *TLNT*, vol. 1, pp. 398–99. M. Thrall argues that the verb here denotes "be remiss" (*Second Corinthians*, vol. 1, pp. 298–300).

4:4 / The expression **the god of this age** *(ho theos tou aiōnos toutou)* is unique in the NT, although 1 Tim. 1:17 refers to God as "the King of the ages *(ho basileus tōn aiōnōn)*." Nevertheless, Paul can use the articular term "god" *(ho theos)* in a sense other than God, as Phil. 3:19 shows: "their end is destruction *(apōleia)*; their god *(ho theos)* is their belly." See further Origen, *Commentary on Matthew* 11.14; Thrall, *Second Corinthians,* vol. 1, pp. 306–8; Susan R. Garrett, "The God of this World and the Affliction of Paul: 2 Cor. 4:1–12," in *Greeks, Romans, and Christians* (ed. D. L. Balch, et al.; Minneapolis: Fortress, 1990), pp. 99–117 (here pp. 104ff.).

The Christ-hymn in Col. 1:15–20 refers to Christ as the "image of the invisible God, the firstborn of all creation."

S. Kim makes an interesting case that several epiphanic visions, including that in Ezek. 1:26–27, should be read together as the background of Paul's christological conception (*Origin of Paul's Gospel*, pp. 137–268).

4:6 / Cf. Richard B. Hays, *Echoes of Scripture in the Letters of Paul* (New Haven: Yale University Press, 1989), p. 162.

Cf. Carol Stuhlmueller, *Creative Redemption in Deutero-Isaiah* (AnBib 43; Rome: Pontifical Biblical Institute, 1970).

On the interpretation of 4:6 as a reference to Paul's Damascus road christophany, see Kim, *Origin of Paul's Gospel*, pp. 229–32.

Cf. Nathaniel Deutsch, *The Gnostic Imagination: Gnosticism, Mandaeism and Merkabah Mysticism* (Brill's Series in Jewish Studies 13; Leiden: Brill, 1995), pp. 99–111.

§5 Body (2 Cor. 4:7–5:15)

In 2:14–4:6, the first step in his defense of the legitimacy of his apostolic claim, Paul repeatedly refers to heavenly realities he has known as an apostle: He has entered the heavenly throne room of God; he speaks in the presence of Christ; and he has seen the glory of God in the face of Christ (cf. 2:14, 17; 4:6). The emphasis in the previous section has thus been on the glory of Paul's apostolic ministry. The problem is that Paul's body does not manifest the glory of God in a tangible way. According to Jewish tradition, however, one who ascends to the *merkabah* is bodily transformed in the process into the likeness of the divine glory. Moses himself, to whom Paul has already alluded, had to veil his face because the Israelites could not bear the resplendent glory visible there (cf. 3:7, 13; Philo, *On the Life of Moses* 2.70; *Pesiq. Rab.* 10:6; *Zohar* 1.31b). Therefore, the question is this: If Paul has ascended to the throne-chariot of God in the highest heaven, and if greater glory attends Paul's ministry than even that of Moses, why does Paul not have to wear a veil as Moses did (cf. 2 Cor. 3:13; 5:12)? According to *Merkabah Rabbah,* the face of one who ascends to the divine throne-chariot should shine (cf. Schäfer, §§705, 706). Furthermore, according to *Hekhalot Rabbati,* the one who ascends to the divine throne-chariot becomes invincible and greater than all other humans (Schäfer, §§84–85; cf. G. A. Wewers). So why does Paul's suffering and dying body look so unimpressive (cf. 10:10)? Why does Paul have a "thorn in the flesh" (12:7)? Why, in short, is Paul's glory so different from the glory of Moses?

In answer to these questions, which probably stem from Paul's opponents and resonate in the Corinthian church, Paul emphasizes in 4:7–5:15 that a simultaneous process of destruction and reconstruction is currently taking place in his body, a process that will reach its completion only at the Parousia, when his mortal body will be transformed into immortality, and Christ will judge him on his *merkabah* throne for what he has done in the body. Paul thus contrasts his earthly suffering as an apostle to the heavenly prospects that he still earnestly awaits. Yet, while the verdict on Paul must await the final judgment, there is evidence even now of God's power working through Paul in his mortal body (4:7). Ultimately, however, Paul rejects the opponents' physical criterion for assessing the legitimacy of his apostleship and seeks instead to establish valid criteria (5:11–15). Hence, the present section forms a solid, second step in Paul's defense strategy.

4:7 / Having shown the transcendent power and glory of his apostleship in 2:14–4:6, Paul is careful not to claim personal credit for these things. Paul wants to avoid the appearance of self-commendation (3:1) and claims instead that his competence is from God (3:5). **This treasure** probably refers to the revelation of the glory of God in the face of Christ through which Paul received his apostolic commission (4:6). Paul has this revelatory treasure **in jars of clay**. It is difficult to know exactly why Paul has chosen this metaphor for his physical body (cf. *b. Taʿan.* 7a; Acts 9:15). In the ancient world, the most common vessels were earthenware. They were used for storing and transporting (of water, oil, grain, and olives), cooking, eating, drinking, and presenting offerings. They are found in every domestic excavation site and in graves, where they accompanied the deceased with provisions. Pottery vessels became the main type of containers in most Near Eastern cultures. Yet the vessels were fragile and their usual life spans were probably a few years at the most. Therefore, when Paul refers to his body as a clay jar, he may be regarding himself, on one level, as quite ordinary and transitory (cf. Lam. 4:2; *Song Rab.* 1:19: "Just as water does not keep well in a vessel of silver or gold but in the commonest of vessels, so the Torah resides only in one who makes himself like a vessel of earthenware").

Paul's metaphor, however, has a deeper significance: His body is a "jar of clay" because "the Lord God formed man (*ʾādām*) from the dust of the ground (*ʾadāmāh*)" (Gen. 2:7; cf. Ps. 103:14; Isa. 29:16; 45:9; Sir. 33:10, 13; 1QH 1.15; 3.21; 1QS 11.21–22). The Hebrew verb *yāṣar* here is most often used of a potter who "forms" a vessel out of clay (cf. Isa. 29:16; 41:25; Jer. 18:4, 6; 1 Chron. 4:23; Lam. 4:2). In the account of the curse, Genesis goes on to underscore the relationship of human beings to the soil: "You are dust, and to dust you shall return" (Gen. 3:19; cf. Ps. 104:29; Job 10:9; 17:16; 21:26; 34:15; Eccl. 3:20; cf. Schäfer, §973).

Therefore, when Paul refers to his body as a clay jar, he regards himself as having a mortal human body.

Verse 7b goes on to give the purpose for which the revelatory treasure is contained in the clay jar of Paul's mortal body. In the previous context, Paul has been careful not to claim any credit for the surpassing glory and power of his apostolic ministry (cf. 3:6, 10). In fact, the apostle strictly denies any sufficiency in and of himself (3:5). If his body fails to emanate this glory and power, that merely underscores the point, for while Paul considers himself to possess **all-surpassing power,** this power is not inherently Paul's own; it is **from God** (v. 7b; cf. 6:7; 12:9; 12:12).

4:8–18 / In this section, Paul elaborates on his "earthenware" apostolic experience by a series of antithetic statements designed to show that, despite the apostle's suffering and dying, God is the source of power in his ministry. By the power of the death and resurrection of Jesus, God enables Paul to persevere in the midst of persecution; he makes Paul's ministry of suffering to redound to the benefit of the Corinthians; and he gives Paul confidence in the future resurrection of the dead.

4:8–9 / The section begins with a series of antitheses that express God's providential preservation of Paul despite severe persecution. The Corinthians are well informed of Paul's sufferings: In 1 Corinthians 4:11–13 he lists his apostolic trials and tribulations, and in 2 Corinthians 1:8–11 he describes his nearly fatal experience in Asia, which made him despair even of life. Yet, as we have seen, God comforts Paul in "all our troubles" (1:4), in the sense that he rescues the apostle from all his trials. Since the power of God is at work in his life, Paul can withstand persecution without being destroyed. Acts even records an incident in which Paul was stoned and left for dead, but he walked away from the scene (Acts 14:19–20). In all of these trials, Paul is **not abandoned,** that is, not forsaken by God (cf. in LXX Pss. 26:9; 36:25, 28, 33; 37:22; 70:9, 18; 118:8; 139:9). God always preserves him from destruction and death.

4:10–11 / Paul explains the paradoxical result of his perseverance in persecution by the power of God. Paul considers all of the deprivations, efforts, and persecutions that he incurs in the course of his apostolic ministry as participation in the sufferings of Christ, including the cruciform **death of Jesus** itself (cf. 1:5). As the apostle states in Philippians 3:10–11, he shares in Christ's sufferings and the power of his resurrection, "becoming like him in his death, and so, somehow, to attain to the resurrection from the dead." According to Galatians 3:1, before the Galatians' very eyes Jesus Christ was clearly portrayed as crucified. In all likelihood, this means that, through seeing the apostle and his sufferings, the Galatians saw in human form a revelation of the death of Jesus. This seems to be confirmed in Galatians 6:17, where Paul states that he bears on his body "the marks of Jesus," referring to the wounds and scars that he received in the service of Christ. Paradoxically, however, Paul's suffering shows the resurrection **life** of Jesus in his body. Sharing in Christ's sufferings here and now is a prerequisite for sharing in his resurrection glory in the future (Rom. 8:17). In the present, however, Paul is constantly being delivered from demise, which is a revelation of the resurrection life of Jesus at work in Paul's mortal body (cf. 1:9–10; 4:14). Hence, a simultaneous process of death and resurrection is currently taking place in Paul's body.

4:12 / There is another paradoxical result of Paul's perseverance in persecution by the power of God: **So then, death is at work in us, but life is at work in you.** As Paul has already explained in the thanksgiving of 1:3–11, the persecution that he endures is for the benefit of the Corinthians. Hence Paul's suffering is a special suffering related particularly to his apostolic ministry, since it mediates benefits to the churches that he founds. Among these benefits is the life-giving Spirit (cf. 3:6).

4:13–15 / In this section, Paul elaborates on his hope of and confidence in the resurrection of the dead, again stressing the benefit to the Corinthians.

4:13 / The apostle begins in verse 13 with a citation from Psalm 116:10 (115:1 LXX) in order to allude to the context of the psalm. The psalmist, who identifies himself as the Lord's "servant," speaks of his great humiliation (v. 1) and refers to the death of the Lord's pious ones (v. 6). Evidently, the psalmist has been delivered from great persecution (v. 7), and he now, in accordance with vows given during the trial, seeks to render praise to God before the people in the house of the Lord (vv. 9–10). The psalmist **believed** that God could deliver him, and therefore he has **spoken.** Having been delivered from many perilous situations in the past and expecting to be delivered in a full and final way in the future, Paul likewise speaks in **that same**

spirit as this psalm. We have already noted Paul's use of psalmic form and content in the opening thanksgiving (cf. 2 Cor. 1:3–11).

4:14 / Paul gives the reason he can speak with the same spirit of faith as Psalm 116:10: despite his present plight, Paul has an indomitable confidence in the resurrection of the dead, or, more particularly, in "the God who raises the dead" (2 Cor. 1:9–11). He describes this confidence by means of the early Christ creed, "God raised Jesus" (cf. Rom. 10:9; 1 Thess. 1:10; Acts 3:15; the participial construction used here is also found in Rom. 4:24; 8:11; Gal. 1:1). At the Parousia, the apostle will stand together with the Corinthians before God. This ties together with themes that Paul developed in the previous section (2:14–4:6), that Paul has often stood in the presence of God (cf. 2:14, 17; 4:6), and that believers are being transformed into the likeness of the Lord (3:18). Paul's confidence and hope is that believers are just one step behind the risen Lord, who is "the firstfruits of those who have fallen asleep" (1 Cor. 15:20). In this sense, God will raise Paul up **with Jesus.** The christological context of the believer's experience is quite pronounced (cf. 2 Cor. 4:10–11).

4:15 / The reason (*gar*, untranslated NIV) that God will raise up Paul is ultimately doxological. On the one hand, Paul's deliverance is for the benefit of the Corinthians (2 Cor. 1:3–7). On the other hand, Paul's final deliverance is expected to result in overflowing **thanksgiving** to God (cf. 1:11). The culmination of the Pauline mission is that Jews and Gentiles would glorify God together for his mercy (cf. Rom. 15:5–13). In this way, the goal of the Pauline mission coincides with the general message of Isaiah.

4:16–18 / In this section Paul draws a conclusion (**Therefore**, *dio*) from what he has said previously about his sharing in both the death and life of Jesus (vv. 10–12, 13–15), using the same antithetical style as previously. In the process, Paul reiterates what he has said in verse 1 (**we do not lose heart**), thus bringing closure to chapter 4.

4:16 / The apostle begins in verse 16 with the conclusion itself and the substantiation for it. Paul contrasts the ongoing destructive and reconstructive processes that are simultaneously at work in his "outer man" and in his "inner man." On the one hand, Paul's suffering and sharing in the death of Jesus have him **wasting away** outwardly, that is, physically. In the context of degenerative processes, the term is used of rust's eating into iron, of moths' eating clothes, and of the bodies of starving persons. Paul has already referred in verse 7 to his body as a "jar of clay," alluding to the original composition of human beings from the dust of the ground (Gen. 2:7) and to their subjugation to death and decomposition to dust after the curse (Gen. 3:19). The creation, too, has been subjected to futility and decay (Rom. 8:20). The mortal material out of which humans are made is the problem. Hence, in Romans 7:24 we find the anguished cry (perhaps of Adam after the fall), "Who will rescue me from this body of death?"

On the other hand, Paul's sharing in the resurrection of Jesus causes him continually to be **renewed**. Paul has already described the transformation of believers (3:18; cf. Col. 3:9–10). In 2 Corinthians 5:17, he declares: "Therefore, if anyone is in Christ, he is a new creation; the old has gone, the new has come!" Hence the renewal that Paul envisions is not just a matter of outer versus inner, but also of past versus present and future. The consummation of the renewal process takes place at the Parousia, when the bodies of believers will be redeemed (Rom. 8:23), that is, resurrected and conformed to the likeness of the Son of God (v. 29), and the whole creation "will be liberated from its bondage to decay and brought into the glorious freedom of the sons of God" (v. 21).

Paul wants to stress against his opponents that the real test of his apostleship is not external glory, which is observably deficient at present, but rather the process of internal transformation (see further on 5:12). Given these values, the apostle does not **lose heart**, despite his hardships and their negative effect on his body.

4:17 / Paul gives a second reason he does not lose heart: the weight of his current tribulation is relatively small compared to the immeasurably greater weight of glory that still awaits him. Paul thereby makes a play on the corresponding Hebrew word for **glory** *(kābôd)*, which literally means "weight, heaviness." Although Paul's temporary and earthly suffering is actually quite *excruciating* in the sense of sharing in Christ's sufferings (cf. 1:8–11), this suffering is **light**. It pales in comparison with the future eternal glory that he expects as a result of the present process of transformation. For Paul, sharing in Christ's sufferings is the prerequisite to sharing in Christ's glory (Rom.

8:17). In fact, suffering is a normal part of the Christian experience (Phil. 1:29), and especially so for the apostle. Paul already enjoys a substantial measure of glory through his apostleship (2 Cor. 3:7–18). The process of transformation into the visible likeness of the Lord has already begun (3:18). However, there is even more glory in store for him in the future, when he is given a resurrection body in the likeness of the glorious resurrection body of Jesus Christ himself (cf. 1 Cor. 15:43; Phil. 3:21).

4:18 / Paul states here the result of his future expectation of glory on his present perspective. He does not lose heart (v. 16a) because he has his sights set on as yet intangible heavenly realities rather than on the tangible earthly vicissitudes and physical frailty that currently mark his **outwardly** being ("the external man" of v. 16). Paul has already had a foretaste of the coming glory through his experience of the *merkabah* (cf. 12:1–7). Looking beyond the transitory moment, Paul knows that the transformation taking place within him is eternal.

5:1–10 / This section continues the theme of Paul's earthly apostolic existence and his heavenly expectation. While this much-discussed passage is crucial for understanding Pauline eschatology, it admits of various interpretations, depending on which religious background is seen here (Jewish apocalyptic, Hellenistic dualism, or Gnosticism). The interpretation of the passage is also beset by the tensions within the text and by the question of its relation to 1 Thessalonians 4:13–18 and 1 Corinthians 15. In particular, there is some question as to when Paul thinks the transformation of the body takes place, whether during a person's present life, at the time of one's death, or at the Parousia. If, according to the present passage, the transformation of the body takes place at the time of death, then that would mean that Paul had changed his mind about the eschatological expectation expressed in 1 Corinthians 15, where the transformation is expected to take place at the Parousia. If, on the other hand, our passage is taken to refer exclusively to the transformation at the future resurrection at the time of the Parousia of Christ, then it is difficult fully to integrate the references in the text to death as the destruction of the earthly tent (2 Cor. 5:1) and being away from the body (v. 8). Furthermore, if the text is interpreted as an explication of the present process of death and renewal in 4:16–18, then that does not do justice to the fact that Paul must appeal to the future consummation to substantiate the expected goal of his present apostolic existence of suffering. In view of this knotty problem, it is not surprising that combined interpretations have been suggested. For example, the supposition that Paul speaks of dying in verse 1 and of the transformation at the Parousia in verses 2–4 leads to the idea of an "intermediate state," whereby the "nakedness" is evaluated as a reason for fear or for hope. Very often, verse 3 is understood as a polemic against the expectation of liberation from the material body, which Paul's gnostic opponents supposedly hold. In the midst of this confusion over Paul's intention, we must be very careful to pay strict attention to the apostle's own formulation, in order to avoid foisting an extrinsic system onto the text and asking questions that Paul did not ask in the time of an imminent expectation.

The passage can be divided into two sections: In verses 1–5 Paul describes his longing to dwell in heaven with a new, immortal body; in verses 6–10 this longing is further described in terms of intimate communion with Christ at the time of the consummation.

5:1 / Paul commences the first section (vv. 1–5) with a statement that substantiates the idea in 4:17–18, that the expected heavenly glory far outweighs the momentary troubles on earth. At first, the first person plural **(we)** seems to refer not just to Paul but to believers in general, thus introducing a generally accepted, traditional Christian conviction **(we know)**; however, the previous context always uses "we know" of the apostle's personal knowledge, albeit a knowledge that has implications for the Corinthians (cf. 1:7; 4:13b–14). Therefore, if 4:7ff. has already been using the first person plural to refer exclusively to Paul, it seems reasonable to assume continuance here, although the apostle's experience and hope are here, as often elsewhere, prototypical for all believers.

Yet how does Paul "know" that he has an eternal house in heaven? Is the source of his knowledge exclusively Jewish and/or Christian tradition? Or, has he received a special revelation? In answering these questions, it is well to remember that in 2 Corinthians Paul claims to have personal experience with the heavenly realm. As we have seen, the apostle refers to his Moses-like encounter with the throne-chariot of God (2:14) and his speech in the presence of God (2:17). He has seen the glory of God in the face of Christ (4:6), and he has been caught up to the third heaven or paradise (12:2–4). Yet, as we would expect, his own personal experience is often expressed in terms of traditional expectations.

The contrast here is between a transient **tent** and a permanent **house,** just as the tabernacle was to the temple (cf. 2 Sam. 7:2, 5–7). Paul knows that if his earthly tent (i.e., his mortal body) is destroyed, he has an eternal house in heaven. The present tense **we have** suggests that Paul already has the heavenly house in some sense, but that he occupies it sometime after death. This corresponds to the idea in verse 5 of the Spirit as a "deposit, guaranteeing what is to come." In other words, just as Paul already has possession of the guarantee that promises full payment at a specific time in the future, so also he already has the eternal house prepared for him in heaven (cf. John 14:2; 2 *Bar.* 48:6; 5Q15). This thinking is typical of Paul's notion of the "already" and the "not yet." It is likely, therefore, that the "eternal house" is not referring to a continued *bodily existence* in heaven but rather to a kind of *heavenly dwelling* that is different from the individual's resurrection body. According to 1 Corinthians 15:23, 52, the spiritual body is received at the Parousia—unless, of course, Paul's thinking has undergone significant development since the writing of that passage (so M. Thrall). Furthermore, 2 Corinthians 5:8 contrasts being away from the earthly body with being "at home with the Lord," rather than with receiving a new body.

The expression that Paul uses for his mortal body is not just **the earthly tent** (NIV) but rather "our earthly house of the tent." The language is drawn from 1 Chronicles 9:23 LXX, which refers to the tabernacle as "the house of the tent" (cf. also 1 Chron. 6:17 LXX). Just as the tabernacle was the temporary dwelling of God from the time of the wilderness wanderings and until the building of a permanent temple in Jerusalem, so also Paul's mortal body is merely temporary. In 1 Corinthians 6:19 Paul refers to the body as "the temple of the Holy Spirit within you." It may also be significant for Paul's metaphor that the glory of God filled the tabernacle (Exod. 40:34–35), for Paul is arguing in context for internal criteria for evaluating his apostleship.

The eternal house in heaven is **not built by human hands.** This term occurs elsewhere in connection with the temple (cf. Mark 14:58). The contrast here is between what humans make and what God makes (cf. Acts 7:48; 17:24). In Jewish tradition, the eschatological temple will be built either by God himself (*Jub.* 1:17; cf. 1:27; 11QTemple 29.8–10; *Sib. Or.* 5:420–425) or by his

Messiah (*Tg. Isa.* 53:5). The Qumran community evidently understood itself as a sort of interim, spiritual temple, a "sanctuary of men," until the eschatological temple could be built (cf. 4QFlor 1.2–7). Very likely, Mark 14:58 reflects a similar idea of a spiritual temple composed of Jesus and his followers. According to Matthew 12:6, Jesus says, possibly referring to himself, "Something greater than the temple is here" (cf. 12:41–42; Luke 11:31–32; John 2:19–21). Hence, when Paul refers to a house not made with hands, he evidently looks beyond believers as the present temple of the living God (2 Cor. 6:16) to the corresponding heavenly reality (cf. Gal. 4:26–27). The word *oikos*, **house**, is frequently used of the temple of God (cf. 1 Kgs. 7:31; Matt. 21:13; Mark 11:17; Luke 19:46; John 2:16; Acts 7:47, 49). Moreover, **eternal house** (*oikos aiōnios*; Heb. *bēth ʿôlāmîm*) is a common name for the (Solomonic!) temple in Jerusalem (e.g., Josephus, *Ant.* 8.107; *Gen. Rab.* 54:4; 99:1; *Num. Rab.* 9:26, 32, 42; 10:24; *b. Yoma* 44a, 53a, 67b; *b. Sukka* 5b; *b. Soṭa* 16a; *b. Mak.* 12a).

Paul evidently knows the heavenly temple through his prior *merkabah* experience (cf. *T. Levi* 3:4: the Great Glory dwells in the holy of holies in the third heaven). The fact that he holds open the possibility of an out-of-body experience during his ascent to the third heaven (cf. 2 Cor. 12:2–4) shows how he may have conceived of a bodiless existence in heaven before the resurrection at the Parousia.

5:2–3 / Paul explicates and substantiates what he claims to know in verse 1 by means of two parallel statements (vv. 2–3 and v. 4), both introduced by *kai gar*, both speaking of his present groaning and his longing for the heavenly dwelling, and both alluding to OT texts as part of the substantiation. The metaphor is hopelessly mixed, since people do not clothe themselves with buildings. Moreover, Paul seems to shift the emphasis from the heavenly temple that he will enter if he dies before the Parousia, to the spiritual body that he expects to receive at the Parousia, for as the parallel to Romans 8:23 clearly shows, believers groan in their present travail, longing for the redemption of their bodies *at the resurrection*. This means that the "eternal house (*oikia*) not made with hands in the heavens" (2 Cor. 5:1), which Paul now "has" proleptically in the event of his death before the Parousia, is different from **our heavenly dwelling** (lit., "our dwelling which is from heaven") with which Paul longs to be clothed at the Parousia. Even the words used to describe the two are different.

Perhaps the apostle signals by this subtle shift in focus his earnest desire to live until the Parousia and so to avoid death altogether.

How should we understand this process of transformation at the Parousia? M. Himmelfarb argues that in Jewish apocalyptic and Hekhalot literature the ascent to heaven, conceived as a royal court and temple, involved transformation by a heavenly version of priestly investiture. The idea that there are special garments for the righteous after death is widespread in Jewish and Christian literature (cf. Zech. 3:4, 5; *1 En.* 62:15–16; *Apoc. Zeph.* 8:3; *4 Ezra* 2:39, 45; *Apoc. Ab.* 13:14; Rev. 3:4–5; 6:11; 7:9, 13, 14). When Paul speaks of a spiritual body for believers after death (1 Cor. 15:42–50), he seems to have in mind something similar to these heavenly garments. Indeed, his description of the transformation process at the resurrection (1 Cor. 15:51–54) explicitly refers to *putting on* new clothes: "For the perishable must clothe itself with the imperishable, and the mortal with immortality" (v. 53). Hence, the conception in 2 Corinthians 5:2 coincides to a certain extent with that in 1 Corinthians 15.

In 2 Corinthians 5:2, however, Paul is not concerned with the resurrection of all believers; he yearns to be clothed himself. As we have suggested (p. 102), Paul is open to the charge of fraud, since his body does not show any visible signs of having been transformed as a consequence of his heavenly ascents. His opponents could at least expect that his face would be charged with glory as Moses' face was (cf. 3:7, 13). Instead, however, Paul's appearance is quite unimpressive (cf. 10:10). Paul explains this fact by reiterating twice that he does not know whether his heavenly journeys were "in the body or out of the body" (12:2, 3). Ezekiel, for example, speaks of the Spirit of the Lord transporting him from place to place in visions, which may imply an "out-of-body" experience, although at one point he is picked up by a lock of his hair (cf. Ezek. 3:12, 14; 8:3; 11:1, 24). Of course, if Paul's heavenly journeys were out-of-body experiences, that would account for the lack of perceptible transformation in the apostle's physical constitution. Paul's claim not to know, however, could also sound like the excuse of a charlatan. Therefore, Paul has a twofold motive for wishing to be transformed as soon as possible: (1) to end the process of his current suffering and dying, and (2) to stifle the critique of his opponents.

Meanwhile, Paul's present condition (**we groan**) is an expression of the "not yet" of the eschatological consummation as a result of his having received the Spirit. In a progressively climatic series, Romans 8:22–27 attributes groaning first to the creation in general, then to believers, and finally to the Spirit. The creation groans because it has been subjected to futility as a result of the fall. Believers groan, despite the fact that they are a "new creation," because in their present suffering the indwelling Spirit makes them conscious that their bodies have not yet been redeemed in the newness of resurrection. And the Spirit groans as a way of helping believers in their weakness and interceding for them before God. Like the groaning of the Israelites in Egypt (cf. Exod. 2:23b–24; 6:5–6), groaning is a precursor to redemption from bondage, albeit in this case a bondage to decay (cf. Rom. 8:21).

But what does Paul mean in his desire not to be found **naked?** While most commentators interpret "naked" either as "disembodied" or as "moral nakedness" or "shame," there is another possibility if the allusion is to Ecclesiastes 5:14–15 LXX: "As he [sc. the rich man] came forth naked from his mother's womb, he shall return back as he came, and he shall receive nothing for his labor, in order that it might go with him in his hand." Seen in light of this passage, Paul does want to be found "naked" in the sense of being physically buried without receiving a reward for his apostolic suffering and labor. As he stated in 4:17, "our light and momentary troubles are achieving for us an eternal glory that far outweighs them all." If Paul were to die without attaining to the resurrection and receiving what he expects at the final judgment (cf. 5:10), his whole apostolic ministry will have been in vain, a striving after the wind. Furthermore, the transformation of his body is essential to authenticating him as an apostle who has encountered the *merkabah*. If this interpretation is correct, then 2 Corinthians 5:3 is not as tautological as it may at first seem. Paul is saying that he wants to receive his resurrection body so that he will not be found **naked** in the grave, having lived and died in vain, without recompense.

5:4 / The second, parallel step in explicating and substantiating the apostle's knowledge in verse 1 is given in verse 4, but it does not go much beyond what has already been stated in verses 2–3. The redundancy underscores the fervency of Paul's eschatological expectation, not to mention its urgency in view of the situation in his mission field. The expression, **so that what is mortal may be swallowed up by life,** makes it clear that here, as in 1 Corinthians 15:53–54, Paul is thinking of the eschatological consummation at the Parousia. The allusion is to Isaiah 25:8, which is explicitly cited in 1 Corinthians 15:54. In the context of a vision of an eschatological banquet on Zion that includes "all peoples," Isaiah 25:7–8a MT reads: "And he will destroy on this mountain the shroud that is cast over all peoples, the sheet that is spread over all nations; he will swallow up death forever." The citation in 1 Corinthians 15:52, however, uses a proto-Theodotian version, which translates Isaiah 25:8a slightly differently: "Death is swallowed up in victory." Hence, Paul yearns for the day of resurrection, when "the one who raised the Lord Jesus from the dead will also raise us with Jesus and present us with you in his presence" (2 Cor. 4:14).

5:5 / The theological reason that Paul can expect this future transformation of his body is given in verse 5: since God, according to his own purpose, has given believers the Spirit, they can expect the resurrection of their bodies at the Parousia. Romans 8:29 traces the process of transformation in terms of a sorites that progresses from divine predestination to conformity to the likeness of his son at the resurrection. Moreover, just as in Romans 8:23, where the Spirit is the "firstfruits" of the coming redemption of the body (cf. Rom. 8:11), the Spirit is here the **deposit**, which, in a binding way, promises and guarantees the rest of the expected payment (i.e., the resurrection of the body) within a specified period of time (cf. 2 Cor. 1:20). Paul's confidence about his heavenly destination and his imminent expectation are based on an intimate knowledge of God's ultimate purposes for his life and the inner working of the Spirit.

5:6 / In verses 6–10, Paul's longing for bodily transformation is further described in terms of a desire for more intimate communion with Christ at the time of the consummation, for while he is on earth, Paul is still distant from Christ who is in heaven, and so he looks forward to being with the Lord. Paul begins this section in verse 6 by drawing a hopeful inference (**Therefore,** *oun*) from the previous discussion, especially in view of his possession of the Spirit as a guarantee of the future resurrection. This verse reiterates what Paul states in verse 1: If his body dies, then he has a home in the heavenly temple. For the time being, however, **we are away from the Lord** (lit., "we are in exile from the Lord"). This statement has caused much consternation among Paul's interpreters. How is it possible for a believer like Paul to be at home in the body and away from the Lord, as if life in the body is incompatible with life in Christ? Is not the apostle already "in Christ"? Has he not been reconciled with God (2 Cor. 5:19)? Is he not being progressively transformed into the image of Christ (3:18)? The problem is so acute that J. Murphy-O'Connor argues that Paul is not stating his own position but quoting his opponents' point of view, which supposedly denied any importance to the body. Nevertheless, the problem is easily solved if we consider that it is not until the Parousia that believers, including Paul, are fully conformed to the likeness of the Son and finally take up residence with him, so that he becomes the firstborn "among many brothers" (Rom. 8:29; cf. Phil. 3:20–21). As Paul states in 1 Thessalonians 4:17, referring to being caught up in the clouds to meet the Lord in the air, "And so shall we be with the Lord forever." In the interim, Paul, along with other believers, is "away from the Lord" in the sense that he does not yet dwell with Christ in heaven. This remains true for Paul even if he has gone on repeated heavenly journeys, for the apostle does not know whether they were in-body or out-of-body experiences (2 Cor. 12:2, 3), and in any case they certainly represent only temporary departures from his earthly existence. For the moment, therefore, Paul is truly "at home in the body" in the sense that that is his normal apostolic experience, and his body has not yet been fully redeemed from its bondage to decay (Rom. 8:23). Believers are never away from the Lord in the absolute sense, but, relatively speaking, there is more to experience in the future (cf. 1 Cor. 13:12).

5:7 / Paul proceeds to give a reason (*gar*, untranslated NIV) for his confidence in the future resurrection of his body. The prepositional phrase **by faith** is positioned forward in the sentence for emphasis. As in Hebrews 11:1, where faith is defined as "the assurance of things hoped for, the conviction of things not seen," with many examples of such faith being given in the subsequent context, Paul founds his confidence in his life of faith, which does not need already to see the outcome in order to believe that it will happen. He simply trusts in God. The meaning of **sight** here is similar to that in Numbers 12:8: "I [sc. God] will speak to him mouth to mouth, by sight, and not in riddles; and he has seen the glory of the Lord." In both cases it denotes a visible form of the phenomenon (cf. 2 Cor. 2:17; 3:18; 4:6). Elsewhere,

Paul equates speaking this "mouth to mouth" with seeing "face to face" in the eschatological consummation, a time when believers will no longer see in a mirror dimly (cf. 1 Cor. 13:12). Thus, 2 Corinthians 5:7 differentiates Paul's present life in faith from his future existence in the consummated kingdom of God, when the Lord's visible form will be manifest, and the apostle will no longer live in anguished exile from the Lord's presence. Paul has already stated that he fixes his eyes "not on what is seen, but on what is unseen" (4:18), that is, on the eternal glory which far outweighs his current plight.

5:8 / Paul again expresses here his earnest desire to be with the Lord. For the apostle, death (being **away from the body**) is preferable to life in the body, for it means being at home with the Lord. He realizes, however, that may be necessary for him to continue living in order to carry out God's purposes (cf. Phil. 1:21–24).

5:9 / Paul draws an inference (**So,** *dio*) from the fact that he has both the hope that he will dwell with the Lord and the knowledge that he must presently carry on in his mortal body. Paul does not put his own preferences first. Like the synoptic portrayal of Jesus in Gethsemane (Mark 14:36 par.; cf. John 12:27), Paul subordinates his own will to the will of God. To **please** God in all things is the apostle's highest goal (cf. Rom. 12:1, 2; 14:18; Phil. 4:18; Col. 3:20). To bring praise and honor to God is Paul's constant aim. The expression **whether we are at home . . . or away** corresponds to "whether we wake or sleep" (1 Thess. 5:10) and to "whether we live or die" (Rom. 14:8). These expressions describe the present life and the eschatological existence in the new body. Even Paul's afterlife will be a life of dedication, service, and praise to God. This marks an unbroken continuity of purpose from present to future.

5:10 / The reason that Paul endeavors to please God while in his mortal body is the coming eschatological judgment. The **we all** includes first and foremost Paul and all other believers, but it also points to a universal judgment, which he calls "the day of the Lord Jesus" (1:14). That believers are justified by faith in Christ does not mean that they are excused from the judgment according to their works (cf. Rom. 14:10, 12; 1 Cor. 3:12–15; 2 Cor. 11:15). The merciful God remains also a holy God; the reconciler is also the righteous judge.

Whereas Paul states here that "we must all appear before the **judgment seat** of *Christ (to bēma tou Christou),*" he states in Romans 14:10 that "we must all stand before the judgment seat of *God (to bēma tou theou)."* As Martin Hengel argues, the explanation for this is that, since Christ has been seated at the right hand of God (cf. 1 Cor. 15:25; Rom. 8:34), God and Christ share the same throne-chariot *(merkabah);* hence they carry out activities either together or interchangeably (cf. 2 Cor. 5:19), including the eschatological judgment (cf. Rom. 2:6, 16; 14:10; 1 Cor. 3:13–15; 4:4–5).

We must remember that Paul claims to have seen the divine throne-chariot (cf. 2:14, 17; 4:6; 12:2–4), and that fact is very much at issue in the present section of his defense. He is open to the charge of being a fraud, since there are no visible signs of his having encountered the *merkabah.* Paul's conclusion to the issue in this section is tantamount to a warning, similar to the one he gave in 1 Corinthians 4:3–5, that he should not be judged before the time. However, the one who claims to have the revelatory treasure of the *merkabah* vision in his mortal body is confident that the power of God is at work in him (cf. 2 Cor. 4:7).

The purpose of the appearance before the judgment seat is that believers may receive recompense for their conduct in the body, whether it be good or bad. Paul is motivated to please God both in order to receive a reward for his sufferings and labors (cf. 2 Cor. 5:3) and in order to avoid condemnation.

5:11–15 / In this section, Paul draws a conclusion (note the "therefore," **Since, then** *[oun],* in v. 11) to the previous discussion. He rejects the opponents' physical criterion for assessing the legitimacy of his apostolic office and seeks instead to establish valid, internal criteria.

5:11 / The conclusion begins in verse 11, the expression **fear the Lord** tying in with what Paul has said about the judgment seat of Christ in verse 10. Since he is well aware that all people must give an account of their actions in the final judgment, Paul carries out his apostolic ministry in reverence before the "Lord," which means here either God or Christ, since both are seated together on the *merkabah* and perform activities interchangeably (see on v. 10). His previous encounters with the divine *merkabah* (cf. 2 Cor. 2:14; 12:1–4) have probably contributed to this fear and reverence of the Lord. Already in the biblical account of Isaiah's commission, the prophet displayed great fear at the sight of the the Lord seated on a high and exalted throne and attended by seraphs (Isa. 6:1–5). In subsequent Jewish tradition, the standard reaction of the *merkabah* mystic when confronted with the throne-chariot is awe and terror of the divine (cf. Ezek. 1:28; *1 En.* 71:11; *4 Ezra* 10:29–30, 34; *Apoc. Ab.* 16:1–4; *Hekhalot Rabbati* [Schäfer, §92]).

Since Paul knows the fear of the Lord, he tries to **persuade** men. While it is unclear exactly what Paul tries to **persuade** men of, the verb seems to be used in Acts as a technical term for the apostolic proclamation (cf. Acts 18:4 ["Every Sabbath he reasoned in the synagogue, trying to persuade Jews and Greeks"]; 19:8; 28:23). Indeed, it is Paul's responsibility to "win" both Jews and Gentiles with the message of the gospel (1 Cor. 9:19–22). In that case, Paul would be saying that his knowledge of the fear of the Lord causes him to preach the gospel and to try to persuade people. The thought is, again, similar to that in 1 Corinthians 9: The Apostle Paul, who has "seen" the Lord Jesus as the very basis of his apostleship (v. 1; cf. 15:8–9), has a divine "obligation" upon him to preach the gospel, "and woe to me if I do not proclaim the gospel" (v. 16). Obviously, the fear of the Lord is upon the apostle as he proclaims the message in accordance with his "commission" (v. 17), and the subsequent reference to an ultimate "reward" for his preaching (vv. 17–18) fits well with the reference in our passage to the judgment seat of Christ, before which each one will receive what is due (2 Cor. 5:10). All this goes to say that Paul is driven by pure and honorable motives.

Paul substantiates his assertion that the fear of the Lord and the coming judgment motivate him to preach the gospel, by appealing to two witnesses—God and the Corinthians themselves. On the one hand, Paul appeals to God as his witness: **What we are is plain to God** (lit., "We are made known to God"). In 1 Corinthians 13:12, Paul claims to be fully known by God (cf. Gal. 4:9). His motives and actions are completely laid bare to the one who will be his judge at the final tribunal. As Paul states in 1 Corinthians 4:4–5, "It is the Lord who judges me. [. . .] He will bring to light what is hidden in darkness and will expose the motives of men's hearts." This is not the first time in the letter that Paul has appealed to God as his witness (cf. 2 Cor. 1:18, 23).

Paul's second witness is the Corinthians themselves. As thoroughly as God already knows the apostle, Paul hopes that **it is also plain to your conscience** (lit., "it is also made known to your conscience"). Just as Paul has already appealed to his own clear conscience in order to testify that he has conducted himself in his relations to the Corinthians with the holiness and sincerity that are from God (1:12), so also here Paul appeals to the Corinthians' conscience in order to testify to his integrity (cf. 4:2). Thus, if Paul claims that he is motivated to preach the gospel by the fear of the Lord and the coming judgment, he appeals to their conscience to verify that fact. The Corinthians themselves provide some of the strongest, tangible evidence for the legitimacy of Paul's apostleship (cf. 3:1–6). Paul realizes, however, that the Corinthians will not understand him fully until the day of the Lord (1:14).

5:12 / Having asserted the motivation for fulfilling his apostolic commission and offering supporting testimony as to its veracity, Paul clarifies a possible misunderstanding over his self-commendation. At first, this may seem like a semantic game. The word **again** refers back to Paul's statement in 4:2, that "by setting forth the truth plainly we commend ourselves to every man's conscience in the sight of God." Prior to that, Paul had denied that he was commending himself again (3:1). Paul seems to have a delicate tightrope to walk between defense and self-commendation. As the apostle bitterly contests in 12:11, "I ought to have been commended by you. . . ." The reason for this is simple: The Corinthians themselves are supposed to be Paul's letter of recommendation for all to read (2 Cor. 3:2). Therefore, if he needed first to commend himself to the Corinthians before they could commend him, Paul would be placed in an awkward, if not compromising, situation. Instead, Paul appeals to what they already know in their consciences about him as the basis for commending him.

In this way, Paul wants to give them **an opportunity to take pride** (lit., "boast") in him. In 1:14, Paul has already stated his hope that in the day of the Lord Jesus the Corinthians can boast of Paul just as he will boast of them. Paul seeks to avoid every appearance of boasting in himself and in his own accomplishments (cf. 1 Cor. 9:16; 2 Cor. 12:5), although he would gladly accept external authentication in the form of boasts from the Corinthians (but cf. 1 Cor. 3:21). When his apostolic authority is questioned, however, Paul does, paradoxically, engage in self-boasting, although he acknowledges it to be foolish (cf. 2 Cor. 10:8; 11:16–17, 21; 12:1, 11).

The purpose (**so that,** *hina*) for which Paul wants to give the Corinthians an opportunity for boasting about him is given in verse 12b. The expression used here *(echein pros tina)* has puzzled scholars because it is usually assumed that an object for the verb "have" must be inferred from context. The NIV evidently understands the object to be **answer** and thus shortens the whole expression ("**so that** you may have an *answer* to those who . . .") to **so that you can** *answer* **those who** . . . . Instead of **answer,** other suggestions for the missing object include "occasion," "boast," "some means of reply," or simply "something," each of which assumes that Paul wants to supply the Corinthians with arguments against the attacks of those who would oppose his apostolic office. More likely, however, Paul is using an abbreviated Greek idiom that means "to be hostile or ill-disposed toward someone." This is made clear by the adverbs that are normally included in the construction (e.g., *allotriōs, apechthōs, dysmenōs, echthrōs, kakoēthōs, kakōs, chalepōs*). Thus, when Ptolemy, filled with wrath (3 Macc. 5:1), had ordered the execution of the Jews, "he returned to his feasting, gathering together those of his friends and of the army who were most hostile to the Jews" (v. 3). The idiom occurs frequently in the writings of Josephus (cf. *Ant.* 1.166; 7.186; 8.117; 13.35, 85, 195, 288; 14.8, 164, 404; 15.81; 16.267; 17.290; 20.162; *Life* 375, 384, 392; *War* 7.56). By using this expression, Paul seems to be urging the Corinthians to side with him against his opponents: "in order that you may be hostile toward those who boast in the face and not in the heart."

Paul describes his opponents as **those who take pride in what is seen** (lit., "in the face" [NRSV: "outward appearance"]) **rather than in what is in the heart.** This is the first reference to Paul's opponents in Corinth since 2:17 and 3:1. The allusion is to 1 Samuel 16:7, where the Lord says to Samuel: "Look neither at his face nor at the outward appearance of his stature, for I have rejected him with contempt. For God sees not as a man looks: Man looks at the face, but God looks at the heart" (cf. *Ps.-Philo* 59:2; *b. Sanh.* 106b; Gal. 2:6). As we have discussed, Paul is open to the charge of being a fraud, because his glorious claims (cf. 4:6) cannot be verified by any physical change in his body like the one that Moses experienced in his face (cf. 3:7–18; p. 102). Indeed, the process of heavenly ascent itself could have been expected to transform Paul's face (cf. *Ascen. Isa.* 7:25: "the glory of my face was being transformed as I went up from heaven to heaven"). Paul's opponents evidently allege that Paul is a fraud because he does not need to wear a veil in public (cf. 3:13), his bodily presence face-to-face is so weak (10:1, 10), and he has a thorn in the flesh (12:7). In response to these allegations, Paul characterizes the opponents' position as "boasting in the face," and his allusion to 1 Samuel 16:7 makes it clear that the opponents' criterion for assessing the legitimacy of Paul's apostleship is not God's. As Paul has already stated to the Corinthians, he will stand before the judgment seat of Christ (2 Cor. 5:10), which will expose the inner motives of his heart (cf. 1 Cor. 4:4–5). Meanwhile, any appeal to bodily evidence of Paul's veracity is strictly illegitimate. By failing to realize the flow of thought in context—from the discussion of Moses' face in 3:7–4:6, through the discussion of the transformation of Paul's mortal body in 4:7–5:10, through to the present passage—many commentators misunderstand the reference to "face" in 5:12 as figurative, i.e., the opponents' boasting in their own outward achievements (cf. 11:22–23).

The opponents' criterion for boasting (i.e., the face) is juxtaposed to Paul's own, that is, the **heart.** In 2 Corinthians, the apostle repeatedly emphasizes the condition of his heart in relation to the Corinthians (cf. 2:4; 3:2; 6:11; 7:3). Paul puts great stock in this aspect, for the heart is the place of the working of the Holy Spirit of the new covenant, of which he has been appointed a mediator (cf. 3:6). Hence, the rejection of the external criterion of assessing apostolic legitimacy in favor of the internal is not a way of retreating to the inaccessible, but rather essential to everything Paul stands for. Paul rejects the opponents' claims based on their "deeds" (cf. 11:15) and supports his own legitimacy based on his own behavior (4:2; 5:9–10; 6:4–10; 10:12–18; 11:23–33; 12:5, 9–10). It is interesting to note that according to later Hekhalot literature, the *merkabah* mystic is able to perceive every word and deed of humans, even in the innermost sanctum (Schäfer, §§83, 86).

5:13 / Paul goes on to give the reason the Corinthians have an occasion for boasting about him. The use of the term translated here **to be out of one's mind** *(existanai)* is equivocal: It can refer either to the ecstatic experience of the enraptured mystic (cf. Philo, *Questions and Answers on Genesis* 1.24; *On Drunkenness* 146–147) or to insanity (cf. Mark 3:21). Hence, picking up a theme related to his previous discussion of being at home in the body or with the Lord, Paul touches here on another accusation with regard to his encounter with the *merkabah*: In what sense was it an "out-of-mind" experience? Paul's opponents apparently allege that he is crazy, whereas Paul claims to have had a genuine revelatory experience. The crucial question is how the apostle can authenticate his *ekstasis* as revelatory experience in the face of opponents who think he is a fraud.

The opponents' perspective on Paul's mental infirmity is rooted in Jewish tradition. The charge reflected here may be directly related to Paul's claim to have encountered the *merkabah* (the so-called Fool's Speech in 11:1–12:13 comes back to this charge and to his *merkabah* experience). Interestingly enough, in 1 Corinthians 14, one of the key passages that informs us that Paul is an ecstatic mystic who speaks in the "tongues of angels" (1 Cor. 14:18; cf. 13:1), Paul expresses the concern that speakers of these heavenly languages would appear to outsiders to be out of their minds (14:23). According to *Hekhalot Rabbati*, however, hearing the voices of the angels who sing before the throne of glory causes one immediately to go mad (Schäfer, §104).

In reconstructing the opponents' attitude toward Paul's mental state, we may also compare the use of the Hebrew *mešuggaʿ* ("mad, crazy") in the critique of OT prophets by their enemies (cf. 2 Kgs. 9:11; Jer. 29:26; Hos. 9:7), a term which has been understood by some as an indication of ecstasy in OT prophecy (see the reference to "babbling" in 2 Kgs. 9:11; see also Jer. 29:26; Josephus, *Ant.* 10.114). Although he never calls himself a prophet, Paul has many similarities to an OT prophet (cf. K. O. Sandnes). According to Philo, prophetic "ecstasy" *(ekstasis)* is not the same as that associated with "madness" *(mania)*; rather, it is a relaxation of the senses and a retreat of the reason that causes the senses to "depart" *(existanai)* from those who perceive (*Questions and Answers on Genesis* 1.24; cf. *1 En.* 71:11: At the sight of the "Ancient of Time" [cf. Dan. 7:13], Enoch fell on his face, his whole body became relaxed, and his spirit was transformed).

On the one hand, Paul is arguing here that if his opponents are right that he is out of his senses, then it is **for the sake of God** (*theō* is a dative of advantage here). Paul equivocates on the term *existanai* in order to imply that his alleged madness is actually the ecstatic revelatory experience of a man of God. Furthermore, as the apostle has already stated, he is motivated by the fear of the Lord (v. 11). On the other hand, Paul states that if he is in his right mind (as he himself would maintain), then it is **for you** (*hymin* is another dative of advantage). Paul has repeatedly insisted that his apostolic ministry redounds to the benefit of the Corinthians (cf. 1:6–7; 4:12).

5:14–15 / The reason that Paul's complete existence is a life for the sake of God and others is given in terms of a sorites in verses 14–15, which puts a capstone on everything Paul has been saying in this section on his apostolic existence in a mortal body. Paul has been urging the Corinthians to abandon the opponents' physical criteria for assessing the legitimacy of his apostleship and to focus instead on the process of renewal that is taking place within him and within his heart. In keeping with this argument, Paul reveals here once again what kind of convictions and compulsions motivate him at the core of his being: not only "the fear of the Lord" (v. 11), but also **Christ's love.** While, at first glance, we may wonder whether Paul means the love which he has for Christ or the love which Christ has shown to him, the next line makes it clear that Paul intends the latter. The love of Christ is expressed in the fact that Christ **died for all** (cf. Gal. 2:19–20: *"who loved me and gave himself for me"*). Paul is motivated by devotion to the crucified Christ who died "on behalf of all [people]." At this point at the latest, we see that some of the arguments that Paul uses in defense of his apostleship actually apply more generally to others as well.

But what does it mean that Christ died for all and **therefore all died?** At first, the inference that Paul makes here does not appear compelling, for it is not immediately obvious how the death of a single individual effects the death of others, let alone why that might be a desirable event and a motivation for Paul's apostolic ministry. According to Paul, all people are sinners who are estranged from God, sold into slavery under the power of sin, and condemned to death (Rom. 1–3; 7:14). In order to rectify this situation, the OT law of atonement prescribes that the sinner must identify himself/herself with a sacrificial victim (Lev. 1:4), so that when the victim is sacrificed, the sinner in effect dies with it. Sprinkling the blood of the victim on the altar (Lev. 1:5) signifies giving the life to God, for according to Leviticus 17:11, "the life of the flesh is in the blood." This is not so much a matter of placating an angry God as it is providing restoration both of the life of the condemned sinner and of his/her relationship with God. In other words, Jesus became sin, or rather a sin-offering for humanity, so that people could be justified before God through his blood (2 Cor. 5:21; Rom. 3:25; 5:9) and reconciled with God (2 Cor. 5:18).

The purpose (**that,** *hina*) of Christ's universal atonement is that those who live might have a new life dedicated to Christ and to obedience to him. In other words, Christ died "for all" in order **that** they might live **for him.** Those who have been baptized into Christ were baptized into his death, so that as Christ was raised from the dead, they might walk in newness of life (cf. Rom. 6:2–11). As Paul explains it, believers are not free to live as they wish, but are under the authority of a new master and are controlled by the power of the indwelling Spirit. This is Paul's motivation for apostolic ministry, and the criterion by which he would like to be evaluated.

Additional Notes §5

4:7–5:15 / On the bodily transfromation into the likeness of the divine glory cf. C. R. A. Morray-Jones, "Transformational Mysticism in the Apocalyptic-Merkabah Tradition," *JJS* 43 (1992), pp. 1–31; M. Himmelfarb, "Revelation and Rapture: The Transformation of the Visionary in the Ascent Apocalypses," in *Mysteries and Revelations: Apocalyptic Studies since the Uppsala Colloquium* (ed. John J. Collins and James H. Charlesworth; JSPSup 9; Sheffield: JSOT Press, 1991), pp. 79–90.

4:7 / On **treasure,** Col. 2:3 refers to Christ as the one "in whom are hidden all the treasures of wisdom and knowledge" (cf. *1 En.* 46:3; Schäfer, §77 ["all the treasuries of wisdom" were opened to Moses on Sinai, including various aspects of the seventy languages of the seventy nations]). "This treasure" has also been understood as an allusion back to the "gospel" (cf. Thrall, *Second Corinthians,* vol. 1, pp. 321–22) or to the divine glory lost by Adam and being restored through the righteous suffering of Christ, the last Adam (C. Marvin Pate, *Adam Christology as the Exegetical and Theological Substructure of 2 Corinthians 4:7–5:21* [Lanham, Md.: University Press of America, 1991], pp. 77–106). For Pate, therefore, 2 Cor. 4:16–5:4a is a "midrashic type of interpretation of Gen. 1–3" (ibid., p. 126). On this, see the review by Scott Hafemann, *JBL* 113 (1994), pp. 346–49.

On **jars of clay** see also 1QH 3.23–25; *Apoc. Mos.* 31:4.

According to Herodotus (3.96), Darius used to store *(thēsaurizei)* the tribute he had collected from the whole inhabited world by melting it down and pouring it into large earthen wine-jars *(pithous keraminous),* which served as molds; when the vessels were full, he would break them away and use the resulting ingots to mint new coins. Hence, the jars were merely of utilitarian value and had to be broken in order to complete their function.

If, as we have argued, 2 Cor. 2:14–4:6 is based on Israel's salvation history and reflects the nation's sin, exile, and restoration, then it may be significant to note that in Jewish tradition Israel's story is seen as a direct parallel to Adam's, so that "Israel's sin and exile are a reiteration of Adam's sin and exile" (Paul Morris, "Exiled from Eden: Jewish Interpretations of Genesis," in *A Walk in the Garden: Biblical, Iconographical and Literary Images of Eden* [ed. Paul Morris and Deborah Sawyer; JSOTSup 136; Sheffield: JSOT Press, 1992], pp. 117–66 [p. 123]). Cf. *Pesiq. Rab Kah.* 15:1:1 (cf. also *Gen. Rab.* 3:9; 19:9).

On the verb *yasar*, see B. Otzen, *"yasar," TDOT*, vol. 6, pp. 257–65.

4:8–9 / On the tribulation catalogues in Rom. 8:35; 1 Cor. 4:10–13; 2 Cor. 4:8–9; 6:4–10; 11:23–33; 12:10; and Phil. 4:12, see Niels Willert, "The Catalogues of Hardships in the Pauline Correspondence: Background and Function," in *The New Testament and Hellenistic Judaism* (ed. Peder Borgen and Søren Giversen; Peabody, Mass.: Hendrickson, 1997), pp. 217–43.

The phrase that the NIV translates **on every side** *(en panti)* is literally translated "in everything" or "in every way," and may apply to all four of the following antitheses. Compare the pleonastic use of *pas* ("all, every") in 1:3, 4; 6:4; 7:5, 11, 16.

How can we explain the apparent tension between our text (**perplexed, but not in despair**) and 1:8, where the apostle states that he "despaired even of life" during his tribulation in Asia? Perhaps our passage reflects Paul's normal response to various kinds of affliction, whereas the severity of the situation in Asia caused a momentary lapse.

4:10–11 / On the **death of Jesus**, see J. Lambrecht, "The Nekrōsis of Jesus: Ministry and Suffering in 2 Cor. 4:7–15," in *Apôtre Paul. Personnalité, style et conception du ministère* (ed. A. Vanhoye; BETL 73; Leuven: Leuven University Press, 1986), pp. 120–43.

Although for the most part v. 11 merely explains v. 10 in other words, it does add the idea that Paul is being **given over** to death. The same verb is used of Jesus' being "given over" (cf. Rom. 4:25; 8:32; 1 Cor. 11:23; Gal. 2:20).

4:12 / Steven J. Kraftchick argues that in 2 Corinthians the death and resurrection of Jesus is a "generative metaphor" ("Death in Us, Life in You: The Apostolic Medium," in Hay, ed., *Pauline Theology*, pp. 156–81). Specifically, Kraftchick concludes that in 2 Corinthians "the structure by which terms such as death, life, the glory of God, and power are related to one another by the resurrection of Jesus from the dead is transferred by Paul to the terms of his ministry and by extension to the life of the Christian in the present time before the eschaton" (ibid., p. 164). See the response to this proposal by Beverly Roberts Gaventa, "Apostle and Church in 2 Corinthians: A Response to David M. Hay and Steven J. Kraftchick," in Hay, ed., *Pauline Theology*, pp. 182–99 (here pp. 187–93).

This is the first explicit OT quote in 2 Corinthians (cf. also 6:2, 16, 17, 18; 8:15; 9:7, 9, 10; 10:17). Cf. D. Moody Smith, "The Pauline Literature," in *It Is Written: Scripture Citing Scripture: Essays in Honour of Barnabas*

Lindars (ed. D. A. Carson and H. G. M. Williamson; Cambridge: Cambridge University Press, 1988), pp. 265–91, here p. 275: "In 2 Corinthians Paul's use of the OT is if anything more incidental, and even casual, than in 1 Corinthians." As we shall see, however, Scripture is much more fundamental to Paul's argument than Smith suggests.

4:16 / On *diaphtheirein*, see BAGD, p. 190.

How may we understand the contrast between **inwardly** and **outwardly?** H.-P. Rüger ("Hieronymus, die Rabbinen und Paulus. Zur Vorgeschichte des Begriffspaars 'innerer und äußerer Mensch'," *ZNW* 68 [1977] 132–37) suggests that, for the benefit of his readers in Corinth, Paul employs "the inner man" and "the outer man" as Hellenistic substitutes for the Jewish expressions "the good inclination" and "the evil inclination," respectively. In that case, the renewal of the inner man Paul refers to in 2 Cor. 4:16 is none other than the work of the life-giving Spirit in the heart associated with the new covenant (cf. 3:6; Eph. 3:16). As we have seen on 2 Cor. 3:3, however, the evil inclination is usually understood in rabbinic sources to be at work in the heart. In fact, it is sometimes identified with the heart of stone that will be replaced by a heart of flesh in accordance with Ezek. 36:26 (*Lev. Rab.* 35:5; *Song Rab.* 6:26). The possibility that Paul has in view here a Jewish tradition seems to be underscored by his use of the expression **day by day** (lit., "day and day"), which is apparently a Hebraism meaning "each day" (cf. Esth. 2:11; 3:4 [translated *kath' hekastēn hēmeran* in the LXX]; 11QPs. 27.6; 11QTemple 15.1; 17.12). For example, corresponding to the notion that "the evil inclination of a man grows in strength from day to day and seeks to kill him" (*b. Sukka* 52b) is the idea that in the future the Spirit of God will spread throughout the whole body in accordance with Ezek. 36:27 and not merely through one of the limbs as presently (*Gen. Rab.* 26:6).

The earliest clear use of the phrase "evil impulse" is found in the "Plea for Deliverance," a hymnic text from Qumran (11QPsa 19.15–16) dated to the first century A.D. (for possibly earlier Qumran texts, see now Torleif Elgvin, "Admonition Texts from Qumran Cave 4," in *Methods of Investigation of the Dead Sea Scrolls and the Khirbet Qumran Site: Present Realities and Future Prospects* [ed. Michael O. Wise, et al.; Annals of the New York Academy of Sciences 722; New York: The New York Academy of Sciences, 1994], pp. 179–94 [here 186–87]). Cf. also 2 Esdr. 4:30; 7:48, 92; Sir. 15:14–17.

According to W. D. Davies, Paul seems to connect the evil impulse to the flesh, whereas the rabbis do not (*Jewish and Pauline Studies* [4th ed.; Philadelphia: Fortress, 1984], p. 196). In light of 2 Cor. 4:7, where Paul refers to his body as a "jar of clay," we may point out the frequent wordplay in rabbinic texts between God as potter (*yōser*) and the evil inclination (*yeser*) that he created in humans (cf. *b. Ber.* 61a; *ʿErub.* 18a; *Exod. Rab.* 46:4; *Ruth Rab.* 3:1).

C. M. Pate argues that the man of 2 Cor. 4:16 is an allusion to Gen. 1:26–28, associated with Ps. 8:5–6, so that the "outer man" refers to the believer's existence under the decaying mortality inherited from Adam, whereas the "inner man" is the believer's existence in the new age

Additional Notes: 2 Corinthians 4:16–5:1

already inaugurated by Christ as the Last Adam, "an age characterized by the renewal of the image and glory of God in the heart of the believer (cf. 4:16 with 3:18; 4:4, 6)" (*Adam Christology,* p. 110; cf. p. 112).

4:17 / On the use of *kabôd* in the sense of "weight," see C. Westermann, "*kbd,*" *TLOT,* vol. 2, pp. 590–602, here p. 593.

5:1–10 / This passage is fraught with exegetical difficulties. See, besides the commentaries, E. Earle Ellis, "The Structure of Pauline Eschatology (II Corinthians v. 1–10)," in *Paul and His Interpreters* (Grand Rapids: Eerdmans, 1961), pp. 35–48; Rudolf Bultmann, "Exegetische Probleme des zweiten Korintherbriefes," in *Exegetica. Aufsätze zur Erforschung des Neuen Testaments* (ed. Erich Dinkler; Tübingen: Mohr Siebeck, 1967), pp. 298–322 (here pp. 298–312); J. Osei-Bonsu, "Does 2 Cor. 5.1–10 Teach the Reception of the Resurrection of the Body at the Moment of Death?" *JSNT* 28 (1986), pp. 81–101; T. Francis Glasson, "2 Corinthians 5:1–10 versus Platonism," *SJT* 43 (1990), pp. 145–56; W. L. Craig, "Paul's Dilemma in 2 Corinthians 5.1–10," *NTS* 34 (1988), pp. 145–47; A. C. Perriman, "Paul and the Parousia: 1 Corinthians 15.50–7 and 2 Corinthians 5.1–5," *NTS* 35 (1989), pp. 512–21.

On the supposed development in Pauline eschatology between the writing of 1 Thess. 4:13–18, 1 Cor. 15:51–52, and 2 Cor. 5:1–10, see Rainer Riesner, *Die Frühzeit des Apostels Paulus. Studien zur Chronologie, Missionsstrategie und Theologie* (WUNT 71; Tübingen: Mohr Siebeck, 1994), pp. 343–49.

5:1 / The perishable **tent** *(skēnos)* here signifies Paul's mortal earthly body. Cf. Wis. 9:15–16. Paul holds out the possibility **(if)** that he may die before the Parousia.

Cf. Craig R. Koester, *The Dwelling of God: The Tabernacle in the Old Testament, Intertestamental Jewish Literature, and the New Testament* (CBQMS 22; Washington, D.C.: Catholic Biblical Association of America, 1989).

The meaning of **we have** has been the subject of considerable debate. It has gone unnoticed, however, that in conditional sentences having *ean* **(if)** + the aorist subjunctive in the protasis and the present indicative of *echō* (**have**) in the apodosis, the latter expresses a possession that an individual already has had (or not had) all along (cf. 1 John 2:1; Matt. 5:46; John 6:53), not just reception immediately consequent upon the action of the protasis.

On the concept of the dwellings in the heavenly Jerusalem (John 14:2; cf. Michael Chyutin, "The New Jerusalem: Ideal City," *DSD* 1 [1994], pp. 71–97).

On Mark 14:58, whose authenticity can scarcely be doubted, see E. P. Sanders, *Jesus and Judaism* (Philadelphia: Fortress, 1985), pp. 61, 364 nn. 2–3.

On the Qumran idea of the community as a spiritual temple, see Bertil Gärtner, *The Temple and the Community in Qumran and the New Testament: A Comparative Study in the Temple Symbolism of Qumran Texts and the New Testament* (SNTSMS 1; Cambridge: Cambridge University

Press, 1965), pp. 49–56. On Paul's appropriation of the tradition of the community as temple, see on 2 Cor. 6:16.

On the correspondence between the heavenly and the earthly, the liturgy performed in the heavenly temple corresponds to the offerings in the earthly temple, which is a copy of the heavenly temple (cf. Isa. 6:1).

On the future eschatological temple that God himself would make, see 11QTemple 29.7–10; *Jub.* 1:17. Cf. Yigael Yadin, *The Temple Scroll* (3 vols.; Jerusalem: The Israel Exploration Society/The Institute of Archaeology of the Hebrew University of Jerusalem/The Shrine of the Book, 1983), vol. 1, pp. 182–87, vol. 2, p. 129; Daniel R. Schwartz, "The Three Temples of 4QFlorilegium," *RevQ* 10 (1979), pp. 83–91.

Both Kings and Chronicles report that when Solomon dedicated the Jerusalem temple, he brought the tabernacle into the temple (cf. 1 Kgs. 8:4; 2 Chron. 5:5), where it remained (cf. 2 Chron. 29:5–7) until it was destroyed with the temple in 587 B.C. (cf. Ps. 74:7; Lam. 2:6–7). Perhaps our passage implies the apostle's hope that the resurrected tabernacle of his body will be brought into the eternal heavenly temple built by God himself.

5:2 / On **clothed with our heavenly dwelling**, cf., for example, 2 *En.* 22:7–10, where Enoch is transformed in the seventh heaven during a face-to-face encounter with the Lord. God initiates the process of transformation with the command, "Let Enoch join in and stand in front of my face forever" (v. 7). Then God commands Michael: "Take Enoch, and extract (him) from his earthly clothing. And anoint him with delightful oil, and put (him) into the clothes of my glory" (v. 8). This results in Enoch's being transformed into an angel: "And I looked at myself, and I had become like one of his glorious ones, and there was no observable difference" (v. 10). Likewise, the patriarch Levi is instructed on his ascent to put on "the vestments of the priesthood, . . . the robe of truth, . . . and the turban for the head" (*T. Levi* 8:2). According to *Exod. Rab.* 42:3, God spread his garment *(talito)* over Moses. Cf. Martha Himmelfarb, *Ascent to Heaven in Jewish and Christian Apocalypses* (New York and Oxford: Oxford University Press, 1993), pp. 29–46.

Note that in Josephus, *Ant.* 8.114, Solomon acknowledges in his prayer of dedication for the temple that "the whole vault of heaven and all its host is but a small **dwelling** *(oikētērion)*—how much less this poor Temple!" Earlier in the same context (*Ant.* 8.107) the temple was described as an "Eternal House" *(oikos aiōnios)*. Likewise in 2 Cor. 5:1–2, the "eternal house *(oikian aiōnion)* in the heavens" is not necessarily the same as "our dwelling *(oikētērion)* which is from heaven."

Pate (*Adam Christology,* pp. 121–23) suggests that the mixed metaphor "**clothed** with a building" can be explained as the overlap of three traditions here: the Jewish motif of the heavenly temple, the tradition of Christ's body as equated with the temple of God's presence (cf. Mark 14:58; John 1:14; 2:21), and the later Christian tradition in which all believers are seen to share in Christ's resurrection as the temple of God (cf., e.g., 1 Cor. 3:16–17; 6:19–20; 15:50–55; 2 Cor. 6:16).

According to Gal. 3:26–27, believers, who are sons of God through faith in Christ Jesus, have clothed themselves with Christ. In other words, they already participate by the indwelling Spirit in the sonship of the messianic Son of God (cf. Gal. 4:1–7). Believers already have within and around them the means by which they will be transformed in the future.

5:3 / Pate argues that **naked** refers to Adam's nakedness as a result of losing his glory, interpreted in *3 Bar.* 4:16; *2 En.* 22:8; 30:12; *Gen. Rab.* 20:12 in terms of a garment or "clothing" that was lost at the fall (*Adam Christology*, p. 115). This loss of glory is interpreted by Paul as being "bodiless" in 5:3 (ibid., p. 116). The believer is now naked of bodily glory, and it is this bodiless existence in the intermediate state that Paul fears (pp. 116, 125), longing instead in 5:2–3 for the manifestation of divine glory in his body that has already begun in his heart (p. 120). According to Paul's understanding of Gen. 3:21, Adam's nakedness (i.e., his glory-less state after the fall), was covered with human skin, so that all humanity must now live in a mortal, tent-like body (p. 120).

A few manuscripts have the variant reading "when we have undressed ourselves" or "when we have taken it off" (so NRSV), instead of the participle **when we are clothed.** This variant, however, is probably a later modification attempting to avoid the seemingly tautological statement that being clothed means not being naked. Following Rudolf Bultmann, supporters of the variant reading understand the text as Paul's polemic against his alleged gnostic opponents, who yearn to strip themselves of the body and yet not be naked (cf. *Mart. Isa.* 4:17; *Apoc. Mos.* 31:1; 32:4). In response to this suggestion, we must recognize that the text does not show any particular evidence of this polemic, and the reading "when we are clothed" goes well with the preceding line. Furthermore, as we have seen, Pauline eschatology expects a bodily resurrection. On the textual problem in v. 3, see Bruce M. Metzger, *A Textual Commentary on the Greek New Testament* (2d ed.; Stuttgart: United Bible Societies, 1994), p. 511.

5:5 / Paul maintains an imminent expectation of the consummation throughout his correspondence (cf. 1 Thess. 2:19; 3:13; 4:13–5:11; Phil. 2:12–18; 3:20–21; Gal. 5:5; 6:7–10; 1 Cor. 15:20–58; Rom. 13:11–14; 14:10).

5:6 / Cf. Jerome Murphy-O'Connor, " 'Being at Home in the Body We are in Exile from the Lord' (2 Cor. 5:6b)," *RB* 93 (1986), pp. 214–21.

By stating that he knows he is at home in the body, Paul may also be addressing the accusation that he is "out of his mind" (cf. v. 13).

Pate argues that the "exile" described by Paul in 5:6–10 is based on Adam's own exile in Gen. 3:24–25 (*Adam Christology*, p. 127).

Cf. C. Spicq, "*ekdēmeō*," *TLNT*, vol. 1, pp. 453–54 (here 454): "The Pauline use of moving as a metaphor for death, expressed as a play on words, is clear: it is a matter of moving from one country to another, that is, moving out of here in order to move in elsewhere, leaving the body behind to gain heaven and see Christ. Here below, Christians are in exile 'apart from the Lord.' They live as exiles *(ekdēmeō)* so long as they dwell in this body, which is likened to a tent *(skēnos*—2 Cor. 5:1, 4—a symbol of nomadic life) because their citizenship is in heaven (Phil. 3:20)." Paul's idea is very close to that of Philo at this point (e.g., *On the Confusion of Tongues* 78). The trials that Paul faces on earth are typical of one who is in exile in a foreign land (see further on 2 Cor. 11:23b–29).

5:10 / Cf. Martin Hengel, " 'Setze dich zu meiner Rechten!' Die Inthronisation Christi zur Rechten Gottes und Psalm 110,1," in *Le Trône de Dieu* (ed. Marc Philonenko; WUNT 69; Tübingen: Mohr Siebeck, 1993), pp. 108–94 (here esp. pp. 142, 164). In light of Hengel's argument, it is interesting to note that, according to Josephus (*Ant.* 13.84), Alexander Balas compelled his ally, the high priest Jonathan, when he came to Ptolemais, to take off his own garment and to put on a purple one, "making him sit with him on the judgment seat *(bēma).*"

The Greek word *bēma* **(judgment seat)** is rare in the LXX. Josephus describes the grand and glorious throne of Solomon as being "in the form of a tribunal *(bēma)*, with six steps leading up to it" (*Ant.* 8.140; cf. 17.201).

In rabbinic literature, *bēma* is a loanword. Cf. Daniel Sperber, *A Dictionary of Greek and Latin Legal Terms in Rabbinic Literature* (Bar-Ilan University Institute for Lexicography: Dictionaries of Talmud, Midrash and Targum 1; Ramat-Gan: Bar-Ilan University Press, 1984), pp. 70–72. The normal term for the judgment seat of God is *kissē' dîn* ("throne of judgment"). Cf. *Gen. Rab.* 93:11; *Lev. Rab.* 29:3, 4, 6, 9, 10.

Corinth itself had a *bēma*, or governor's tribunal, in the forum. As Corinth was the capital of the province of Achaia, the governor and his staff were often present in the city on legal business. Paul was brought before Cornelius Gallio at this site in A.D. 51 by the Jewish community of Corinth (Acts 18:12). For a description of the *bēma* in Corinth see James Wiseman, "Corinth and Rome I: 228 B.C.–A.D. 267," *ANRW,* 17.1, pp. 438–548 (here pp. 515–17).

One of the main difficulties with Rudolf Bultmann's attempt to make anthropology and the gift of God's declaration of acquittal the sole subject of Paul's theology is that it caused him to demythologize the future aspects of Paul's apocalyptic eschatology for the sake of the present. Hence, Bultmann's position was unable to incorporate Paul's statements concerning the final judgment according to one's works, which believers must also endure (cf. 1 Thess. 3:13; 5:23; 1 Cor. 1:8; 2:12–15; 4:4–5), into his purely forensic theological scheme.

5:11 / In the OT, the **fear of the Lord** is a central concept, and only a very brief sketch can be given here (see further H. F. Fuhs, *"yārē',"* *TDOT,* vol. 6, pp. 290–315). The presence of God is considered a terrifying sight (Exod. 6:3; 20:18) because its holiness is potentially deadly (Gen. 16:13; 32:30; Exod. 19:21; 24:10–11; 33:18–23; Judg. 6:22–23; 13:22; 1 Sam. 6:19; 1 Kgs. 19:13; Isa. 6:5). An individual may experience the terrifying aspect of God's presence in a dream or vision as well as in a theophany (cf. Gen. 28:17; Job 4:12–16; Dan. 10:8–9, 15–17). Israel fears the Lord because he delivered the people from Egypt (Exod. 14:31). In general, the mighty acts of God in history and in nature instill fear and reverence in people (cf. Isa. 25:3; Hab. 3:2; Zech. 9:5; 1 Kgs. 18:39; Job 37:1, 24; Pss. 33:8; 65:6–9; Jer. 5:22, 24; 10:7), and the Lord's universal judgment brings fear upon the whole earth (cf. Ps. 76; Isa. 41:5). In Deuteronomic tradition, fear most often means "worship" in the sense of fidelity to the covenant of God (cf., e.g., Deut. 5:29; 6:2; 10:12, 20; 2 Kgs. 17:7–41). In the Psalms, "Yahweh-fearers" always refers to the community or nation that worships Yahweh (cf., e.g, Pss. 15:4; 22:24, 26; 31:20; 60:6; 66:16; 85:10), or to the devout who are faithful to Yahweh (cf. Pss. 25:14; 33:18; 34:8, 10; 103:11, 13, 17; 111:5; 119:74, 79; 145:19; 147:11). The "fear of the Lord" can even be used in a metonymy for torah (Ps. 19:10). In Wisdom literature, the "fear of the Lord" is a key concept, which teaches wisdom (Prov. 15:33), including proper conduct toward God, the king, and those in authority (cf. Prov. 24:21). According to Prov. 1:7, "The fear of the Lord is the beginning of wisdom" (cf. also Job 28:28; Ps. 111:10; Prov. 1:29; 2:5; 9:10; 15:33). Since God's ordinances are immutable and God is beyond human knowledge, "to fear God" means that mortals have no choice but absolute submission and strict obedience, relying on whatever God may decree (Eccl. 3:14).

For Paul, too, fear or reverence of God or Christ is foundational for the believer's relationship to God (see Stanley E. Porter, "Fear, Reverence," in *DPL*, pp. 291–93). The completion of the Corinthians' sanctification, which includes cleansing themselves from every defilement of body and spirit, is to be grounded "in the fear of God" (2 Cor. 7:1). In Col. 3:22 Paul exhorts slaves to obey their earthly masters (*kyrioi*, pl.) in everything even as they fear the Lord (*kyrios*, sg.). Slaves should put themselves into the task, whatever it may be, as done for the Lord and not for their masters, since they know that from the Lord they will receive the inheritance as their reward (Col. 3:23–24). Paul exhorts the Philippians to follow Christ's example of obedience (Phil. 2:6–11) and to work out their salvation with "fear and trembling" directed toward God (Phil. 2:12).

M. Thrall (*Second Corinthians*, vol. 1, p. 403) suggests that there is a certain circularity in Paul's appeal to the Corinthians' conscience in judging his apostolic integrity, since the apostle must have in mind the standards that have emerged by implication in his own description of apostolic ministry in the preceding chapters. This overlooks, however, that the Corinthians themselves know Paul and have experienced the effects of his ministry in their midst, particularly through his mediation of the Spirit (cf. 2 Cor. 3:1–6). It is on this basis that the Corinthians are Paul's "letter" of recommendation.

5:12 / It is not impossible that the opponents boast in their own glorified faces (cf. 11:13). Here, however, their critique of Paul's lack of a gloried face like that of Moses is more to the point (cf. Thrall, *Second Corinthians*, vol. 1, p. 405).

5:13 / A similar contrast of terms is found in Acts 26:24–25: Festus believed that Paul's great learning had driven him mad, whereas Paul claims to be speaking "words of truth and mental soundness" (v. 25). The word "mental soundness" (*sōphrosyne*) here is a derivative of the verb used in 2 Cor. 5:13 (*sōphronein*, to be in one's **right mind**).

On ecstasy and 1 Cor. 14, see Markus N. A. Bockmuehl, *Revelation and Mystery in Ancient Judaism and Pauline Christianity* (WUNT 2/36; Tübingen: Mohr Siebeck, 1990), pp. 168–70. Cf. Sandnes, *Paul—One of the Prophets?*

5:15 / Of course, Paul's view of Jesus as an atoning sacrifice goes well beyond the OT law of atonement as given in Leviticus. According to Paul, the single sacrifice of Jesus provides universal atonement in a way that repeated cultic rites could not. As the Son of Man, Jesus came to give his life as a ransom for many (Mark 10:45). Likewise, Paul understands Jesus as the Suffering Servant of the Lord, who bears the iniquities of the many (cf. esp. Isa. 53:4–5, 11–12; 1 Cor. 15:1–5; Rom. 4:25).

§6 Ambassador (2 Cor. 5:16–6:2)

In 5:16–6:2 Paul proceeds to the third step in the defense of the legitimacy of his apostleship, which climaxes in a direct appeal to the Corinthians not to receive God's grace in vain (6:1). In essence, Paul urges the Corinthians to quit seeing him as a suffering and dying apostolic imposter and to acknowledge him instead as the divinely appointed representative of Jesus Christ on earth and the minister of reconciliation that he really is. Otherwise, they risk forfeiting the eschatological salvation of the Lord. For the Corinthians to defect from Paul and to reject his apostolic ministry is to abandon Christ and the Spirit, and thus the very love of God.

5:16 / The new section begins in verse 16 with a conclusion (**So,** *hōste*) that draws together what Paul has been saying in the previous section and makes a transition to a new subject. In the previous section (4:7–5:15) Paul has been arguing that the opponents' physical criterion for assessing the legitimacy of his apostleship is distorted. The apostle's suffering and dying body and his lack of a glorified face like that of Moses cannot be used to show that Paul is a fraud. Therefore, Paul now applies his own principle to himself in a kind of reverse psychology: **we regard no one from a worldly point of view.** A more literal translation shows what Paul is really trying to say: "we know no one according to the flesh." Implied in this is that Paul's opponents do "know" him "according to the flesh." In context, the opposite of knowing according to flesh would be to know "according to the heart," as Paul has been urging the Corinthians (cf. v. 12). Ultimately, of course, only the Lord really knows the hearts of people and rewards each person according to his or her works (cf. vv. 10, 11; Rom. 8:27; 1 Kgs. 8:39; Prov. 24:12).

In contrast to Paul's present practice of refusing to know anyone according to the flesh, he admits that in the past he did so with regard to Christ: **Though we once regarded** [lit., "knew"]

Christ in this way [lit., "according to the flesh"], **we do so no longer.** The argument here is as subtle as it is powerful. At one time, Paul erroneously used the same physical criterion to evaluate Christ as the apostle's opponents presently use on him! Paul is saying that he once knew Christ according to the flesh as a crucified messianic pretender. The word "Christ" *(christos)* here denotes Messiah (cf. M. Hengel); this is particularly clear from the reference to "him who knew no sin" in verse 21. By all appearances, Jesus of Nazareth was merely one of several such messianic pretenders who had come on the scene in recent years and who had received their just deserts at the hands of the Romans (cf. C. A. Evans). From a Jewish perspective based on Deuteronomy 21:22–23, Paul the Pharisee saw the crucified messianic pretender as accursed by God, for according to Deuteronomy 21:23, which Paul later cites in Galatians 3:13, "anyone hung on a tree is under God's curse" (cf. M. Hengel). As Paul's life ebbs from his mortal body in a process of daily dying, the opponents recognize Paul in a similar fleshly way as an apostolic pretender (cf. 2 Cor. 6:8, which makes it clear that Paul was considered a *planos*, i.e., a false prophet and religious seducer of the people, just as Jesus had been [cf. A. Strobel]). The previous section (2 Cor. 4:7–5:15) has been at pains to show that, despite appearances to the contrary in Paul's body, the evidence points in another direction precisely because of the resurrection of Christ.

What made the difference for Paul? Why does he no longer know Christ according to the flesh? The emphasis of the text at this point is on the *manner* of knowing rather than on the object per se. Paul's radical change of mind about Jesus came about as the result of his encounter with the resurrected Lord on the way to Damascus. At that time, the one whom Paul thought was crucified and "accursed" in the body confronted him in the splendor of divine glory (cf. 2 Cor. 4:6; 1 Cor. 9:1). Exalted to the right hand of God to share God's throne on the *merkabah*, Christ revealed himself to Paul as the Son of God, as Messiah of Israel, and as redeemer of all who believe. What had previously been a stumbling block—a crucified Messiah! (cf. 1 Cor. 1:23)—became the center of Paul's new existence (15:3–11). The new "knowledge of Jesus Christ my Lord" had radical consequences for Paul's entire life, requiring him to abandon old values and to reorient himself on new ones (Phil. 3:7–11; cf. Gal. 1:13–16). Now Paul wants "to know Christ and the power of his resurrection and the sharing of his sufferings by becoming like him in his death, if somehow I may attain the resurrection from the dead" (Phil. 3:10–11; cf. 1 Cor. 2:2). That fairly well summarizes what Paul says in 2 Corinthians 4:7–5:15 about his mortal body.

Through subsequent reflection on the Scriptures, Paul recognizes the error of his ways as a Pharisee: He saw Christ according to the flesh in the same way as the "we" of Isaiah 53:3–4 viewed the Suffering Servant of the Lord: "He was despised and rejected by others; a man of suffering and acquainted with infirmity; and as one from whom others hide their faces, he was despised, and *we* held him of no account." Now, however, as a result of encountering the resurrected Lord, Paul recognizes Christ as the Suffering Servant who bears the iniquities of the many (2 Cor. 5:15; cf. Isa. 53:4–5, 11–12). Similarly, the suffering apostle of Jesus Christ—the one who shares in the sufferings of Christ (1:5; 4:10)—is despised and rejected by opponents (cf. E. Baasland). Paul changed his mind and his method of assessment; his opponents, however, are still operating on the old method of observing the mortal body (so also M. Thrall). Their position is contrary to Scripture (see the aforementioned allusion to 1 Sam. 16:7 in 2 Cor. 5:12).

5:17 / Paul draws a general conclusion (**Therefore,** *hōste*) from the fact that, since his encounter with the resurrected Lord on the way to Damascus, he no longer knows Christ according to the flesh as a crucified messianic pretender. The contrast in verse 16 between Paul's old and new ways of perceiving Christ prompts a further contrast between old and new that makes Paul's experience prototypical of all believers. Being **in Christ** (e.g., 1 Thess. 2:14; 5:18; Gal. 1:22; 2:17; 3:26; 5:6; 1 Cor. 1:4; 15:22; 2 Cor. 3:14) or "in the Lord" (e.g., 1 Thess. 5:12; Gal. 5:10; 1 Cor. 7:22, 39; 11:11; 15:58; 2 Cor. 2:12) results from having been baptized into Christ by faith (Gal. 3:27), so that one now forms part of the church, which is the "body of Christ" (cf. 1 Cor. 12:12–31; Rom. 12:4–8; Col. 1:18, 24; 2:16–19; 3:15; Eph. 1:23; 4:4–16; 5:23). Believers are personally united with Christ, who is a corporate figure like Adam and indeed his typological counterpart (cf. 1 Cor. 15:22, 45).

Being in Christ ("the last Adam") causes one to be a **new creation.** In the "postexilic" time of distress, Nehemiah's prayer (Neh. 9:6–37) takes creation as the ground for hope (v. 6). If the God who elected Abraham and led Israel out of Egypt is really the creator God, then he can and will lead Israel out of the present situation of degradation and distress (cf. R. Rendtorff). In Isaiah, the expectation of Israel's restoration as a second exodus redemption included the idea that God would make "new heavens" and a "new earth" (Isa. 65:17–19; 66:22–23; cf. *1 En.* 45:4–5; 72:1), and that there would be a return to the ideal conditions in Eden (Isa. 51:3; cf. *Jub.* 4:26 [no sin]). Within this new creation, "all flesh" would come to Zion in order to worship God (Isa. 66:22–23). Obviously, we are dealing here with much more than individual transformation (cf. 2 Cor. 5:18 ["the world"]). Paul calls believers a "new creation" (cf. also Gal. 6:15) because they, with the rest of creation (cf. Rom. 8:19–22), undergo a physical and spiritual transformation (see on 4:7–5:15), which is an act of creation on a personal level (see the allusion to Gen. 1:3–4 in 2 Cor. 4:6).

Paul's radical distinction between the **old** *(ta archaia)* and the **new** *(kaina)* is also drawn from Isaiah. This in the context of Israel's future redemption from exile, which recalls the exodus from Egypt, Isaiah 43:18–19 reads: "Do not remember the former things, and do not consider the old things *(ta archaia)*. Look *(idou)*, I am doing new things *(kaina)* which will now spring up, and you will know them. And I will make a road in the desert and rivers in the dry land." This OT text plays a major role in the NT (cf. O. Betz). Paul identifies these "new things" with the redemptive work of Jesus Christ in the world. In the process, he recalls the "old *(palaia)* covenant" and the "new *(kainē)* covenant" mentioned in 2 Corinthians 3:6, 14, which is also understood in the traditional context of the second exodus redemption. The condemnation of the law that sent Israel into exile under the "old covenant" (and expelled Adam from Eden) is being reversed.

5:18–21 / In this section Paul goes on to elaborate on the new creation and the new things in terms of the divine **reconciliation** and his own official, apostolic function in relation to this reconciliation.

5:18 / The new world order in Christ is **from God** in the sense that God took the initiative in providing it in accordance with his divine plan. Apocalyptic literature of the OT and early Judaism consistently emphasizes that in the last days God himself will intervene in world affairs to establish his kingdom. Ultimately, joint effort plays no part in this process; God is at work from start to finish.

God is described by means of two, parallel participial clauses that emphasize his reconciliatory *deed,* on the one hand, and the consequent reconciliatory *word,* on the other. About the *deed,* the first clause makes clear that participation in the new creation presupposes that God **reconciled** Paul to himself through the substitutionary death of Christ. Here again the apostle portrays his experience as prototypical of that of all believers (cf. 5:1, 16–17), although it is not impossible that the first person plural actually includes all believers at this point. As we have seen, Paul's use of the first person plural can shift quite suddenly in any given context (cf. 1:3–11). But in verse 20, which draws an inference from the previous context, the first plural clearly refers to the apostle. Furthermore, the second participial clause almost certainly refers to Paul's own ministry of reconciliation.

The verb **reconciled** is used in the sense of making peace between enemies (cf. Rom. 5:10–11; 1 Cor. 7:11). In Hellenistic-Jewish texts, it is hoped and prayed that God will turn away his wrath and reconcile himself either with individual people or with Israel as a whole (cf. 2 Macc. 1:4; 7:33; 8:29; Philo, *On the Life of Moses* 2.166; Josephus, *Ant.* 3.315). Ephesians 1:14–18 gives us an encompassing picture of the reconciliation that Christ, in his body, has accomplished between former enemies—between Jews and Gentiles, on the one hand, and between God and humanity, on the other—creating "one new man" and making "peace." Likewise, according to Isaiah 53:5, the Suffering Servant of the Lord was expected to be "wounded for our transgressions, crushed for our iniquities; upon him was the punishment that brought us peace, and by his bruises we are healed" (O. Hofius). The "peace" of Isaiah 53:5 is the same as the "reconciliation" of which Paul speaks in 2 Corinthians 5:18–21. The atoning, substitutionary death of Christ for sinners effects "peace with God" and "reconciliation" (Rom. 5:1–10). Hence, Paul begins his letters with the formulaic greeting that refers to this peace: "Grace to you and *peace* from God our Father and the Lord Jesus Christ" (e.g., 2 Cor. 1:2).

The second participial clause, about the reconciliatory *word,* shows the apostle's involvement in proclaiming God's reconciliatory *deed:* Paul has already used the word **ministry** *(diakonia)* and "minister" *(diakonos)* in the previous context to refer to his own ministry of the new covenant in contradistinction to Moses' "ministry" of the old covenant (cf. 3:6, 7, 8, 9; 4:1). Here, too, he implies a typological comparison to Moses. Both Philo *(On the Life* *of Moses* 2.166; *Questions and Answers on Exodus* 2.49) and Josephus (*Ant.* 3.315) portray Moses as "reconciler" *(katallaktēs, diallaktēs)*, in the sense that he intervened before God on behalf of the people after the golden calf incident (Exod. 32:11–13; cf. *Exod. Rab.* 43:2; *Deut. Rab.* 3:15). Paul sees himself as being commissioned with a similar ministry of reconciliation and mediation, although, as we shall see, Paul's ministry is greater since it encompasses the whole world and comes solely from divine initiative. Paul's role is primarily one of preaching the gospel and of persuading people (cf. 2 Cor. 5:11). On the way to Damascus, God himself revealed his Son to Paul and gave Paul the commission to preach the gospel of the Son of God among the nations (Gal. 1:16). When Paul states that God gave him the ministry of reconciliation, this is another way of saying that he has an apostolic office directly from God.

5:19 / This verse elaborates on God's reconciliatory *deed* and Paul's commission to a ministry of reconciliation proclaiming the reconciliatory *word* in verse 18. Whereas verse 18 speaks very specifically about Paul as the object of God's reconciliatory *deed*, verse 19 expands the scope to include the world. The idea that **God was reconciling the world to himself in Christ** puts the matter on a grand scale.

It possible that in 2 Corinthians 5:19 Paul is using imperial imagery of the Pax Romana (cf. K. Wengst) in order to communicate his point about God's reconciling the world (sinful humanity or the nations) to himself in Christ. As we have seen in 2:14, Paul uses another imperial image—the triumphant emperor—in order to suggest that he has encountered the throne-chariot of God, who is always leading him in triumphal procession "in Christ" in every place. Furthermore, Paul may have the same motive for using Roman imperial imagery in the present context, for by using the reconciliation of the world under the Pax Romana as a metaphorical vehicle, Paul can bring up the image of Christ enthroned next to God on the *merkabah* in accordance with Psalm 110:1, the most important christological text in the NT (cf. M. Hengel). Interestingly enough, Origen's *Commentary on the Gospel of John* (6.57 §295) already interprets 2 Corinthians 5:19 in light of Psalm 110:1, because the Psalm text expresses reconciliation in terms of the subjugation of enemies: "The Lord says to my Lord, 'Sit at my right hand until I make your enemies your footstool.'" The image is one of world domination (cf. Ps. 2:8;

72:8; *Sib. Or.* 3:741–762, 785–795), which is quite consistent with Paul's previous reference to the "judgment seat of Christ" before which all people must appear (2 Cor. 5:10). We may note that, in Jewish tradition, the enthronement of Messiah is associated with the aforementioned "new creation" (cf. *1 En.* 45:3–5; *2 Bar.* 73:1–74:4). If our interpretation is correct, then verse 19 goes beyond verse 18 by stating that the reconciliation of sinners to God effected by Christ's atoning death also entails a reconciliation of the world to the lordship of God and Christ, who sit enthroned together on the *merkabah*.

Two parallel clauses follow, linked by **And** *(kai)* to the main clause. The first relates to the world and the second to Paul's commission. The first participial clause states that, in reconciling the world to himself, God is not **counting men's sins against them.** By this, Paul is merely reaffirming that under the new regime those who were formerly enemies through sinfulness (cf. Rom. 5:8, 10) are now brought into fellowship and allegiance. Their former sins are not counted against them; they are absolved. The expression is traditional, as Psalm 32(31):2; *Joseph and Asenath* 11:10; and *Testament of Zebulun* 9:7 show.

The second participial clause, about the "word" (**message,** *ton logon*), links Paul's apostolic commission with God's reconciliation of the world. Unfortunately, the NIV translation obscures the parallelism between the two circumstantial participles by making the second one an independent clause. The point, however, is that God's reconciling the world manifested itself both in not counting humanity's sins against them *and* in entrusting **the message** (lit., "word") **of reconciliation** to Paul. In other words, Paul's apostolic ministry of preaching the gospel (cf. 1 Cor. 1:18 ["the word of the cross"]) is integral to God's reconciliation of the world. As such, Paul is an official "coworker" with God (cf. 2 Cor. 6:1; 1 Cor. 3:9), an apostle to the nations (cf. Rom. 11:13). With this bold, self-confident assertion, Paul completely dismisses the opposition to his apostleship and appeals once again to the divine commission upon which his ministry is solidly based. The reason Paul's ministry is integral to God's reconciliatory program is that preaching is necessary for the people to hear the message of the gospel in order to believe (cf. Rom. 10:14–17, citing Isa. 52:7 and Isa. 53:1).

5:20 / Having presented himself as a minister of reconciliation with a message of reconciliation (vv. 18–19), Paul draws a conclusion (**therefore,** *oun*) from the preceding discussion about his stately apostolic commission and appeals directly to the Corinthians in light of it. This is crucial for Paul's defense of his apostolic office in 2:14–7:4, for he states in no uncertain terms that Christ and God speak though him. First, Paul is one of Christ's **ambassadors.** The term is frequently used of imperial legates, who represent the Roman emperor in foreign lands and govern there on his behalf with legionary troops (cf. H. Mason). As we have seen, Paul is thinking of his apostolic role in a world empire established by God and Christ analogous to the Pax Romana (cf. 2 Cor. 5:19). The expression **Christ's** in this context does not mean "for the cause of Christ," but rather "on whose behalf." Thus, in the word of the apostolic ambassador, Christ himself speaks. In this sense, the apostle represents Christ and is endowed with all the authority of the one he represents. Not appointed by human authorities (Gal. 1:1, 12), but by the risen Christ himself, Paul regards himself as the personal representative of Christ on earth (cf. 1 Thess. 1:6; 1 Cor. 11:1; Phil. 3:17). This explains, in part, why the apostle shares in the sufferings and death of Christ (cf. 4:10–11) and also otherwise takes on the functions of Christ (e.g., his suffering and dying benefits others [1:6; 4:12]). Furthermore, although Paul's opponents in Corinth fancy themselves to be "apostles of Christ" (11:13) and "servants of Christ" (11:23), Paul in effect disputes their claim by asserting that he is the personal representative of Christ on earth.

As an ambassador for Christ, Paul speaks **as though God were making his appeal through us.** Here again, we see the unity of Christ and God in undertaking activities together, including speaking: Paul is the ambassador of Christ, yet it is God who speaks through the apostle. The God who in Christ reconciled the world to himself uses the apostle as a mouthpiece to announce the good news and to summon people to accept the message. In the situation with the opponents, of course, Paul can appeal to no higher authority than God Almighty as the source of his apostolic ministry and message.

Having established his apostolic credentials as the spokesman of Christ and God, Paul gives a sample of his gospel preaching: **We implore you on Christ's behalf: Be reconciled to God.** The NIV supplies the object **you** in the first line. But it is very unlikely that the exhortation is directed toward the Corinthians, since they are already believers and hence have already accepted the message of reconciliation that the apostle originally delivered to them. Elsewhere Paul does, of course, entertain the idea that the Corinthians may not be "in the faith" (cf. 6:1; 13:5), and he does exhort them to reconciliation (cf. 13:11). More probably, the implied object of Paul's imploring here is the world (*kosmos*, cf. v. 19), and the **Be reconciled to God** is a direct citation of the message that, as an ambassador "for Christ" *(hyper Christou)*, Paul preaches to the world "on behalf of Christ" *(hyper Christou)*. In that case, Paul's gospel message is an exhortation (cf. 5:11) to desist from rebellion against God and to appropriate by faith the reconciliation that God has accomplished in Christ. The application of the present section to the Corinthians does not come until 6:1 (so also M. Thrall).

5:21 / Since there is no transition between verses 20 and 21, it is difficult to know exactly how verse 21 relates to the foregoing. Apparently, verse 21 continues the direct citation of Paul's message of reconciliation from verse 20, providing, in effect, substantiation for the exhortation to be reconciled with God. As in verse 19, the acting subject is God; however, unlike verse 19, Christ is the object of the action. This is the only passage in which Paul refers directly to the sinlessness of Christ **(who had** [lit., "knew"] **no sin)**, although other passages seem to presuppose it (cf. Rom. 5:19; 8:3; Phil. 2:8). Paul's description of Christ in our text conforms to a traditional expectation about the Messiah, as well as to the statement about the Suffering Servant of the Lord (cf. Isa. 53:9: "For he did no lawlessness *[anomia]*").

Can the same be said for what follows? God made Messiah **sin for us.** Interestingly enough, a text from Qumran (CD 14.18–19) expects that the Messiah of Aaron and Israel will appear and "atone for their iniquity." The expression "Messiah of Aaron and Israel" may be elliptical for "Messiah of Aaron *and Messiah of* Israel" (so A. S. van der Woude). Even so, this text does not necessarily include the substitutionary aspect which 2 Corinthians 5:21 has. The sinless Christ was made sin "for us" *(hyper hēmōn)* in the sense that he took on the sinners' curse in his atoning death on the cross. According to Galatians 3:13, Christ redeemed believers from the curse of the law by becoming a curse "for us" *(hyper hēmōn)*, for it is written in Deuteronomy 21:23, "Cursed is everyone who hangs on a tree." As we have seen above, Paul the Pharisee probably applied this OT text against the crucified Christ while he knew Christ "according to the flesh" (cf. 2 Cor. 5:16). After his encounter with the resurrected Lord on the way to Damascus, however, he saw Christ in a different light, but continued to apply Deuteronomy 21:23 to the death of Christ, this time in a positive way as a reference to the substitutionary death of Christ for sinners. Paul realized that Christ was not the accursed sinner before God, but rather the deliverer who had come to die for the remission of sins of others. As he states in 2 Corinthians 5:14, "one died for all" (cf. 1 Cor. 15:3; Gal. 1:4; Rom. 4:25; 5:6, 8; 6:10; 1 Thess. 5:10). Paul understood the death of Christ in light of the sinless Suffering Servant of the Lord: "The Lord has laid on him the iniquity of us all" (Isa. 53:6); "he poured out himself to death, and was numbered with the transgressors" (cf. Isa. 53:12). It is also possible that becoming "sin" *(hamartia)* refers to becoming a "sin offering," for in the LXX *hamartia* is sometimes used of the sin offering (cf. Lev. 4:21, 24; 5:12; 6:18). The Suffering Servant is said to be made an "offering for sin" (Isa. 53:10).

The purpose for which God made sinless Christ a substitute for sinners is that **in him we might become the righteousness of God.** As Paul stated in a previous letter to the Corinthians, "It is because of him [sc. God] that you are in Christ Jesus, who has become for us wisdom from God—that is, righteousness, holiness and redemption" (1 Cor. 1:30). It is clear that **the righteousness of God** comes from him and is conferred on believers who are in Christ. Godless sinners, who previously possessed no righteousness of their own, receive righteousness in sinless Christ who, by a process of substitution, became a sin offering for them. In other words, believers identify with Christ in such a way that they die with Christ to the penalty for their sin (i.e., the curse of the law) and also share with Christ in his resurrection life and vindicated status.

6:1–2 / Here Paul concludes 5:16–6:2 and urgently applies what he has been saying directly to the Corinthians. As in 6:14–7:1, the causal circumstantial participle in 6:1 introduces the conclusion in a way that draws together what has been said. Thus, in 6:1, **as God's fellow workers** (lit., "Since we are fellow workers") recalls 5:20 (cf. 1 Cor. 3:9: "For we are God's fellow workers"). Furthermore, the verb to **urge** is the same as the verb "to make an appeal" in 5:20, although the subject is different in each case (God and Paul, respectively). In his mediatory role as minister of reconciliation, Paul now urges the Corinthians **not to**

receive God's grace in vain. The apostle assumes thereby that the Corinthians have indeed received the message of reconciliation that he originally delivered to them, and therefore that they have received the grace of God. But there is a thinly veiled threat here: If the Corinthians continue on their course of denying the legitimacy of Paul's apostolic office, then they will have undermined their own salvation, for it is through Paul that they received the message of reconciliation and thus the grace of God itself (cf. 13:5). As we have seen, Paul's ministry of reconciliation is inseparable from God's reconciliation of the world. The tacit argument here is much the same as the one that we have already seen several times in the letter. Ultimately, the Corinthians cannot deny Paul's original message to them and his mediatory role without at the same time rejecting the gospel and denying their own Christian existence (cf. 1:19; 3:1–6).

6:2 / The reason (**For,** *gar*) that Paul urges the Corinthians not to receive the grace of God in vain is underscored in verse 2 by a verbatim citation of Isaiah 49:9 LXX, which stresses the eschatological timing of this grace. The introductory formula to the citation *(legei gar)* can be translated either "**For he** [sc. God] **says**" (so NIV) or "For it [sc. the Scripture] says" (so D.-A. Koch; cf. Rom. 9:17; 10:11; 1 Tim. 5:18). In the original context of Isaiah, however, Paul's citation is introduced by "Thus says the Lord," and so Paul most likely understands God as the unexpressed subject of 2 Corinthians 6:2a. The Lord himself, whom Paul represents and whose grace he has just mentioned, makes a pronouncement in the OT that has application in the present. Evidently, Paul understands the authoritative interpretation of Scripture as one way in which God makes his appeal though the apostle (cf. 5:20).

In its original context, Paul's citation is part of the second Servant Song (49:1ff.), in which the Servant of the Lord is called to proclaim the restoration of Israel and the salvation of the world: "It is too light a thing that you should be my servant to raise up the tribes of Jacob and to restore the survivors of Israel; I will give you as a light to the nations, that my salvation may reach to the end of the earth" (Isa. 49:6). This is the passage that is so determinative to Paul's understanding of his own apostolic commission to the nations (cf. Gal. 1:15–16). As a text on the restoration of Israel, Isaiah 49:1ff. coheres with Paul's emphasis in 2 Corinthians 5:16ff. on the new creation (Isa. 65:17–19;

66:22–23), which has been inaugurated through Christ, the Suffering Servant of the Lord (Isa. 53).

Paul goes on to draw the significance of the citation of Isaiah 49:8 for the Corinthians: "**I tell you** [lit., "Look!"], **now is the time of God's favor, now is the day of salvation.**" The word "Look!" links 6:2 with the "Look!" in verse 17 (not rendered in the NIV): The present time is the time of both the "new creation" and the "new things" that God promised in Isaiah. For Paul, the day of salvation and reconciliation that Isaiah prophesied has dawned. The fulness of time has come (Gal. 4:4). Therefore, the Corinthians must not forfeit the opportunity to take advantage of God's mercy. The twofold "Look, now" in 6:2 reveals a sense of urgency in Paul's authoritative, ambassadorial exhortation to the Corinthians.

Additional Notes §6

5:16 / The relation of v. 16 to the previous context is crucial for Paul's whole apology. If, however, most interpreters fail to recognize the point of 4:7–5:15, they also fail to see the function of 5:16, i.e., to draw a conclusion to Paul's previous argument.

Cf. Martin Hengel, " 'Christos' in Paul," in *Between Jesus and Paul* (Philadelphia: Fortress, 1983), pp. 65–77, 179–88 (esp. p. 71); idem, "Christological Titles in Early Christianity," in *The Messiah: Developments in Earliest Judaism and Christianity* (ed. James H. Charlesworth; Minneapolis: Fortress, 1992), pp. 425–48 (esp. pp. 444–46).

Cf. Craig A. Evans, "Messianic Claimants of the First and Second Centuries," in *Noncanonical Writings and New Testament Interpretation* (Peabody, Mass.: Hendrickson, 1992), pp. 239–52.

Cf. Martin Hengel, *The Pre-Christian Paul* (Philadelphia: Trinity Press International, 1991), pp. 64, 83–84.

Cf. August Strobel, *Die Stunde der Wahrheit. Untersuchungen zum Strafverfahren gegen Jesus* (WUNT 21; Tübingen: Mohr Siebeck, 1980).

Cf. Ernst Baasland, "Persecution: A Neglected Feature in the Letter to the Galatians," *ST* 38 (1984), pp. 135–50.

5:17 / Other interpreters understand the two *hōste*-sentences in vv. 16 and 17 as parallel to one another, both drawing out the consequences of vv. 14–15.

On the **new creation** and the restoration of Israel in Paul, see my article, "Restoration of Israel," *DPL*, pp. 796–805. Paul's concept of "comfort" in the thanksgiving of the letter (1:3–11) is drawn, in part, from the

"Book of Comfort" (Isa. 40–55), which announces the restoration of Israel.

Cf. Rolf Rendtorff, "Some Reflections on Creation as a Topic of Old Testament Theology," in *Priests, Prophets and Scribes: Essays on the Formation and Heritage of Second Temple Judaism in Honour of Joseph Blenkinsopp* (ed. Eugene Ulrich, et al.; JSOTSup 149; Sheffield: JSOT Press, 1992), pp. 204–12.

On Isa. 43:18–19, see Carroll Stuhlmueller, *Creative Redemption in Deutero-Isaiah* (AnBib 43; Rome: Pontifical Biblical Institute, 1970).

According to *Ma'ase Merkabah* (Schäfer, §680), the *merkabah* mystic experiences the transformation within his heart as if he had come into a "new world."

Unfortunately, the NIV fails to translate the demonstrative particle "Look!" *(idou)* in the last line of our verse ("[Look,] the new has come!"). Although the particle seems superfluous, it actually provides important evidence of the verbal parallel to Isa. 43:18–19.

Rabbinic literature draws the comparison between the expulsion of Adam from the garden and the exile of Israel from the land (cf. *Pesiq. Rab Kah.* 15.1.1).

5:18–21 / This section, whether in whole or in part, is sometimes thought to contain pre-Pauline tradition. On these various hypotheses see Thrall, *Second Corinthians*, vol. 1, pp. 445–49.

5:18 / Cilliers Breytenbach's comprehensive study examines the whole vocabulary of reconciliation in Greco-Roman, Hellenistic-Jewish, and NT sources (*Versöhnung. Eine Studie zur paulinischen Soteriologie* [WMANT 60; Neukirchen-Vluyn: Neukirchener Verlag, 1989], pp. 45ff.); see also now Stanley E. Porter, Καταλλάσω *in Ancient Greek Literature, with Reference to the Pauline Writings* (Estudios de Filologia Neotestamentaria 5; Cordoba: Ediciones El Almendro, 1994); idem, "Peace, Reconciliation," *DPL*, pp. 695–99.

In Qumran, the messianic "Son of God" or "Son of the Most High" was expected to effect worldwide peace: "He will judge the earth in truth and all will make peace. The sword will cease from the earth and all provinces will worship him" (4Q246 2.5–6). Cf. John J. Collins, "The *Son of God Text* from Qumran," in *From John to Jesus: Essays on Jesus and New Testament Christology in Honour of Marinus de Jonge* (ed. M. C. de Boer; JSNTSup 84; Sheffield: JSOT Press, 1993), pp. 65–82.

5:19 / Cf. Klaus Wengst, *Pax Romana and the Peace of Jesus Christ* (trans. John Bowden; Philadelphia: Fortress, 1987).

Cf. Martin Hengel, " 'Setze dich zu meiner Rechten!' Die Inthronisation Christi zur Rechten Gottes und Psalm 110,1," in *Le Trône de Dieu* (ed. Marc Philonenko; WUNT 69; Tübingen: Mohr Siebeck, 1993), pp. 108–94 (here esp. p. 142).

If the second participial clause in v. 19 (". . . and placed in us the word of reconciliation") alludes to Ps. 104:27 LXX ("[God] placed in them [sc. Moses and Aaron] the words of his signs"), then Paul is making another comparison between himself and Moses in context (cf. 2 Cor. 5:18).

5:20 / Cf. Hugh J. Mason, *Greek Terms for Roman Institutions: A Lexicon and Analysis* (American Studies in Papyrology 13; Toronto: Hakkert, 1974).

Ambassadors were typically "worthy and excellent men" (cf. Josephus, *Ant.* 13.260; 14.251). An ambassador was not to be treated in a lawless manner, whether by persecuting him or killing him, for that would violate the "law of envoys" and would thereby constitute an act of war (cf. Josephus, *Ant.* 7.120; Philo, *On the Life of Moses* 1.258). Instead, an ambassador is to be shown "hospitality" *(xenia)*, which includes lavish entertainment and gifts (cf. Josephus, *Ant.* 12.165, 171; 14.198).

5:21 / Cf. A. S. van der Woude, *Die messianische Vorstellung der Gemeinde von Qumran* (Studia Semitica Neerlandica 3; Assen: van Gorcum, 1957), pp. 32–33, 60–61, 74.

According to N. T. Wright, v. 21 means to say that, as ambassador for Christ through whom God makes his appeal, Paul himself becomes a revelation in person of the covenant faithfulness of God ("On Becoming the Righteousness of God: 2 Corinthians 5:21," in Hay, ed., *Pauline Theology*, pp. 200–208).

6:1 / On **receive grace in vain**, see Judith M. Gundry Volf, *Paul and Perseverance: Staying In and Falling Away* (WUNT 2/37; Tübingen: Mohr Siebeck, 1990), pp. 277–80.

Cf. Hafemann, *Paul, Moses, and the History of Israel*, p. 345: "Whether those in Corinth accept or reject Paul's final defense of his ministry in this letter [sc. 2 Corinthians] will determine whether or not they too have been brought into this new covenant relationship with God, and thus, whether they too will be able to stand before the judgment of God (cf. 2 Cor. 5:10–12). Given the unity between Paul's person and his proclamation of the Gospel, to reject the former is to be excluded from the latter." Paul calls for the Corinthians to test the genuine nature of their faith by their stance toward him, whether or not they accept his legitimacy as an apostle and his admonitions (cf. 2 Cor. 13:5).

6:2 / Cf. Dietrich-Alex Koch, *Die Schrift als Zeuge des Evangeliums. Untersuchungen zur Verwendung und zum Verständnis der Schrift bei Paulus* (BHT 69; Tübingen: Mohr Siebeck, 1986), pp. 25 n. 5, 261–63. On the comparison of Paul's citation technique here with the Qumran biblical commentaries *(pesharim)*, see Hays, *Echoes of Scripture*, pp. 171–72.

Cf. Jan Lambrecht, "The Favorable Time: A Study of 2 Cor. 6,2a in Its Context," in *Vom Urchristentum zu Jesus. Für Joachim Gnilka* (ed. Hubert Frankemölle and Karl Kertelege; Freiburg: Herder, 1989), pp. 377–91.

§7 Self-Commendation (2 Cor. 6:3–10)

Having exhorted the Corinthians to recognize his God-given ministry of reconciliation (5:16–6:2), Paul continues the discussion of his ministry in 6:3–13 by declaring that he is completely innocent of any aspersions that have been cast on his ministry. Paul claims that, in word and deed, he commends himself as a genuine apostle who is motivated by sincere love.

6:3 / The new section opens quite defensively. Paul knows that his ministry has come under fire because of his alleged inconsistency and double-mindedness, and he has handled such accusations in 1:12–2:13. In the face of these accusations, Paul forcefully asserts with an unmistakable apologetic tone that he did not put a **stumbling block** in anyone's way. Paul uses similar terms in admonitions to "strong" believers not to cause "weaker" believers to stumble, particularly with reference to food (Rom. 14:13, 20–21; 1 Cor. 8:9). The weak were being tempted to compromise their integrity by going against their conscience and participating in what they considered to be idolatry (1 Cor. 8:7, 10) or impurity (Rom. 14:14, 15). In 2 Corinthians 6:3 Paul completely exonerates himself from any wrongdoing in this regard, although he is aware that his gospel of a crucified Messiah is a stumbling block to Jews (cf. 1 Cor. 1:23; Gal. 5:11; Rom. 9:32–33).

The apostle puts no personal stumbling block in anyone's way so that his **ministry will not be discredited.** The "ministry" to which Paul refers is, of course, the "ministry of reconciliation" mentioned in 5:18. His concern is that no one will be able to find fault with what he is doing and saying (cf. Philo, *Allegorical Interpretation* 3.180). The apostle wants it to be as blameless in this regard as the believers who, having been reconciled through his ministry of the gospel, will be presented "holy and blameless and beyond reproach" before God if they continue in the faith (cf. Col. 1:22–23).

6:4–10 / Far from discrediting his ministry through his allegedly scandalous behavior in word and deed, Paul presents his behavior in verses 4–10 as genuine and exemplary in every way. He is one of the **servants of God** *(theou diakonos)*, a term that he applies elsewhere to the Roman emperor (Rom. 13:4; cf. Wis. 6:4). More to the point, Paul describes himself in 2 Corinthians 11:23 as a "servant of Christ" *(diakonos Christou)*, and gives a list of his greater tribulations and sufferings to prove that he excels his opponents in this role (vv. 23–29).

As a servant of God, Paul commends himself. We have already seen that Paul walks a fine line in 2 Corinthians between self-commendation and defense. Fundamentally, he abhors any appearance of self-commendation (3:1; 5:12; 10:12, 18). By siding with the opponents and failing to commend Paul themselves (3:2; 5:12; 12:11), however, the Corinthians have forced the apostle into a kind of self-commendation that emphasizes both what the Corinthians already know about Paul in their conscience (4:2) and the evident power of God at work in him despite suffering (4:7–12; cf. 12:9). Hence, when Paul states in 6:4 that he commends himself **in every way**, the subsequent list of these ways (vv. 4–10) includes many references to suffering and tribulation, and the "power of God" is explicitly mentioned, together with Paul's offensive and defensive weaponry (v. 7). By presenting this list, Paul wants to give the Corinthians an opportunity to boast in him, so that they can shun those who evaluate Paul's apostleship on external factors (cf. 5:12).

The three-part list in verses 4b–10 is meant to exemplify all the ways and situations in which Paul commends himself by his behavior, often despite the circumstances. The first part (vv. 4b–7a; cf. *2 En.* 66:6) gives a straight catalogue of various things organized, in part, into groups and introduced by the preposition **in**—*persecutions* **(beatings, imprisonments and riots)**, *deprivations* **(hard work, sleepless nights and hunger)**, *fruits of the Spirit* **(purity, understanding, patience and kindness; Holy Spirit, sincere love, truthful speech, power of God)**. The second part of the list (vv. 7b–8a) gives a shorter catalogue of paired items introduced by the preposition **with** to describe the attendant circumstances **(with weapons of righteousness in the right hand and in the left; glory and dishonor; bad report and good report)**. Finally, the third part of the list gives a series of contrasting pairs that begin with **as** and show Paul's positive character in the face of negative circumstances **(genuine, yet** regarded as imposters; known, yet regarded as unknown; dying, and yet we live on; beaten, and yet not killed; sorrowful, yet always rejoicing; poor, yet making many rich; having nothing, and yet possessing everything)**. In all these ways, Paul commends himself and his ministry as motivated by **sincere love** and as proven **genuine**. The underlying problem in the letter is that the Corinthians have come to doubt the legitimacy of Paul's apostleship and particularly his motives for claiming authority. Under the influence of the opponents, they now regard their founding apostle as one of the **imposters** or as a "deceiver" *(planos)*. Just as Jesus was executed as a messianic pretender, a "deceiver" *(planos)* of the people, so also Paul—the apostle of Jesus Christ who shares in Christ's death and life (cf. 1:5, 9–10; 4:10–11, 14)—is also regarded as a *planos* (see on 5:16). Hence, as Paul goes on to say later in the letter, he has received forty lashes by the Jews and has even been stoned (cf. 11:24, 25). Yet, it is the apostle's contention that his behavior is evidence of the working of the **Holy Spirit** in his heart. Indeed, the ministry that he defends is the "ministry of the Spirit" (3:8).

Additional Notes §7

6:3 / For **stumbling block**, compare Paul's strong language in 1 Cor. 8:11 and Rom. 14:15, 20, 22–23, reflecting the gravity of the danger the strong were setting before the weak. In his concern for the weak, Paul could not help but be deeply agitated when the weak were "scandalized" (2 Cor. 11:29). In Rom. 16:17 Paul warns his readers to take note of those who create dissensions and *skandala* in opposition to the teaching they had learned. Paul's strong language is strikingly similar to Jesus' stern warning against "scandalizing" one of the little ones (Mark 9:42 par.), and to other dominical sayings about *skandala* (Matt. 18:7 par. Luke 17:1; Matt. 13:41–42; 16:23).

Cf. Scott Hafemann, " 'Self-Commendation' and Apostolic Legitimacy in 2 Corinthians: A Pauline Dialectic?" *NTS* 36 (1990), pp. 66–88.

6:4–10 / The practice of compiling lists of virtues (and vices) was widespread in the ancient Mediterranean world. Cf. John T. Fitzgerald, "Virtue/Vice Lists," *ABD*, vol. 6, pp. 857–59.

During Korah's rebellion, Moses was accused of deceiving the people (cf. Num. 16:14).

§8 Hearts (2 Cor. 6:11–7:4)

In 2:14ff. Paul has given a sustained defense for the legitimacy of his apostleship. He has already pointedly urged the Corinthians not to receive the grace of God in vain by rejecting his God-given apostleship (6:1). In 6:11–7:4 Paul turns once again to exhortation and, in the process, draws the whole apology to a fitting conclusion that recalls its beginning (this rhetorical device is called an *inclusio*). The appeal pivots on the word **hearts**, which Paul has used extensively in the course of his apology, not only in the context of his ministry of the new covenant (3:1ff.) but also as the only valid criterion for assessing Paul's apostleship (5:12). Hence Paul exhorts the Corinthians to open their **hearts** to him, even as his heart is open to them and they are in his heart, explicitly referring back to what he has said in 3:2. The main point of the whole apology is contained in 6:14–7:1, which has often been mistakenly interpreted as either misplaced and/or non-Pauline, for there Paul exhorts the Corinthians to live in light of the new covenant and to dissociate from the opponents (cf. 5:12).

6:11 / Paul begins the final section of his apology with a summarizing statement that looks back on everything he has said since 2:14. He attempts to personalize his language by directly addressing the church as **Corinthians** for the first time in the letter. In using this rare form of direct address (elsewhere only in Gal. 3:1; Phil. 4:15), he also draws special attention to the concluding section. The apostle has **spoken freely** with the Corinthians, meaning simply "to open the mouth" in the sense of "to speak" (cf., e.g., Job 33:2; Sir. 51:25; Ezek. 33:22; Dan. 10:16; Luke 1:64; Acts 18:14). Paul has opened his heart to the Corinthians in that he affectionately has them in his heart (2 Cor. 3:2). Thus, by an *inclusio* the word **hearts** ties in this last section of the apology with the first (2:14–4:6). As we shall see, there is even more that links these two sections together.

6:12 / Paul blames the Corinthians for the discord between them. Literally, the text states that "you are not restricted in us [i.e., in the open heart of the apostle; cf. verse 11], but rather in your own hearts." The Corinthians seem to question whether Paul really loves them (cf. 11:11). The apostle reassures them that he does. From his perspective, any restraint upon the relationship has been caused by the Corinthians.

6:13 / In view of this situation of disproportionate love, Paul exhorts the Corinthians to respond reciprocally to his affection as his own **children.** He has spiritually fathered them (cf. 1 Cor. 4:15) and thus has fatherly affection for them (cf. 1 Cor. 4:14). As the founding apostle, Paul has authority over the church and a special responsibility in raising the Corinthian believers to maturity in Christ. Paul admonishes the Corinthians as his children to **open wide your hearts also.** Just as Paul already has his heart open to the Corinthians, Paul calls upon them to do likewise. The word **hearts** is not actually represented in the Greek text but is understood from the same construction in verse 11.

6:14–7:1 / This section, which has caused so much controversy in the secondary literature, is sandwiched between two exhortations for the Corinthians to open their hearts to the apostle (6:13; 7:2). Paul demands from the Corinthians not merely affection but also complete separation from his opponents. As we have seen in 5:12, Paul wants the Corinthians to "be hostile or ill-disposed" against the opponents, who boast in the face rather than in the "heart." The main criterion for the authenticity of Paul's apostleship is the changed "heart," both in himself and in others. Hence, the apostle calls upon the addressees, who have the Spirit of the new covenant in their heart (3:3), to live in light of the new covenant situation and to separate themselves from fellowship with those who are not in the realm of Christ. As we shall see, the whole section forms a fitting conclusion to Paul's defense of his apostleship in 2:14–7:4.

Taken as a whole, 2 Corinthians 6:14–7:1 is a paraenetic section with a ring structure, in which the initial command not to be allied with unbelievers (6:14a) is reiterated in other words by the closing exhortation (7:1). Between these exhortations come two separate lines of substantiation: the rhetorical questions in verses 14b–16b and the Scripture citations in verses 16c–18. There can be no doubt that the function of these citations is to substantiate verse 14a, for the exhortation in verse 17, which reiterates verse 14a, comes at the center of two sets of corresponding scriptural promises (vv. 16def and 17b–18b), which provide the theological basis of verse 17 and thus of verse 14a. Quite logically, therefore, these promises also provide the basis for the concluding exhortation in 7:1, thereby closing the ring. Hence, it is clear that the promises carry the main argument of the passage.

6:14a / The passage is controlled by the opening exhortation. The exact meaning of the verb **yoked together** *(heterozygein)* remains unclear, for it is used only here in the entire NT, and there are no metaphorical uses of the verb in Greek literature outside the NT. The only metaphorical use of the word-group *heterozyg-* occurs in Plutarch, *Cimon* 16.10, where, apparently, the word *heterozyga* means something like "ally." In that case, Paul would be exhorting the Corinthians not to be "allied" with unbelievers, that is, not to make common cause with them. This sense is borne out by the subsequent context, for the whole section is controlled by three exhortations (6:14, 17; 7:1), which make it clear that the Corinthians should not be allied with, and should actually separate from, the sphere of those opposed to Christ (note especially the contrast between "Christ and Belial" in v. 15). The whole concept of yoking in this sense should be compared to Psalm 2:2–3, according to which the kings of the world conspire to throw off from themselves the yoke *(zygos)* of the Lord and his "anointed one" *(christos)*, the king of Israel (cf. *Pss. Sol.* 17:30). Clearly in this case as well, the yoke is a metaphor for (political) alliance and vassalage (cf. 2 Cor. 5:19a). The end of Psalm 2 pronounces a blessing on "all who trust in him [sc. the Lord]." This may help explain part of the motivation for using the term **unbelievers** *(apistoi)* in 2 Corinthians 6:14a (cf. 4:4). Those who are allied with God and his Christ trust in the Lord; those who are set against God and his Christ are **unbelievers.**

But who are these **unbelievers** with whom Paul prohibits any alliance? Although the term is anarthrous (i.e., without the definite article "the") and the word is used elsewhere as a general technical term (cf. 1 Cor. 6:6; 7:12–15; 10:27; 14:22–24), it is doubtful that the apostle is referring here generally to relationships with unbelievers through marriage, business partnership, table fellowship, and the like. The apologetic context of this paraenetic section demands a more specific reference. Even if the term **unbelievers** is general (as indeed all the references to Paul's opponents have been to this point [cf. 2:17; 3:1; 5:12]), it seems clear that the apostle is talking about specific people who are allied against God and his Christ. If we follow the flow of thought in Paul's defense of his apostleship in 2:14–7:4, we recognize that he has repeatedly polemicized against his opponents in Corinth, including their slanderous charges and false values (cf. 2:17; 4:2; 5:12). Paul actually wants the Corinthians to become hostile to his opponents and to shun them completely (5:12), for by siding with the opponents against Paul the Corinthians risk forfeiting their own salvation (cf. 6:1–2; 13:5). For Paul, the issue is black and white (6:14b: "light" and "darkness"), depending on how one responds to his message (cf. 2:15–16a: "those who are being saved" and "those who are perishing"). There is no middle ground. Those who are closed to the apostle's message are "unbelievers" who are "perishing" (4:3–4). If the Corinthians continue on their course of siding with the opponents and of denying the legitimacy of his apostolic office, then they will have effectively denied their own salvation, for it is through Paul that they received the message of reconciliation and thus the grace of God itself. Ultimately, the Corinthians cannot deny Paul's original message to them and his mediatory role without at the same time rejecting the gospel and denying their own Christian existence (cf. 1:19; 3:1–6). Hence, to make common cause with Paul's opponents is tantamount to being an unbeliever, for the apostle's message is inseparable from his person and commission (cf. 5:18–20). Paul's description of the opponents as "false apostles," who disguise themselves as apostles just as Satan disguises himself as an angel of light (2 Cor. 12:13–15), certainly fits with our interpretation that they are the **unbelievers** to whom Paul specifically refers in 2 Corinthians 6:14, for as we shall see, the context makes clear that these **unbelievers** are allies of Belial (i.e., either Satan himself or a Satanic figure).

6:14b–16b / The first line of substantiation (**For**, *gar*) for verse 14a contains a series of five antithetical questions that begin with the interrogative **what** *(tis)* and expect a negative answer. In the form of proverbial truth familiar from Hellenistic Wisdom tradition (cf. Sir. 13:2, 17–18), these questions set up a contrast between two mutually exclusive spheres. Thus, believers are not to be allied with unbelievers because they belong to the sphere of **Christ** rather than Belial. As servants of Satan, Paul's opponents can be classified as "unbelievers" who are making common cause with **Belial,** that is, with either Satan himself or a Satanic figure (cf. S. D. Sperling).

Why does Paul use the rare name **Belial** instead of the more common "Satan"? The answer may lie in a subtle wordplay. The Talmud explains *benê belîyyaʿal* ("sons of Belial") punningly as *benê belîʿōl* ("sons without the yoke"), that is, "sons who have thrown off the yoke of Heaven from their necks" (*b. Sanh.* 111b; cf. *Vitae Prophetarum* 4:6: "those who belong to Beliar become like an ox under yoke *[hypo zygon]*"). In that case, there might be a play on words between Paul's exhortation not to be "yoked together" with unbelievers (2 Cor. 6:14a) and the reference to "Belial" (v. 15a; see also 2 Cor. 2:11, where Paul may be playing on the meaning of "Satan" as "Slanderer"). Although this rather obscure pun would presumably be lost on all but the most alert Jewish scholars, who were conversant both in Greek and Hebrew and knew the traditional pun on the name Belial, it is not impossible that Paul himself could have thought of it while writing our text. Otherwise, it is difficult to account for the use of **Belial** here, the only occurrence of the word in the entire NT. Of course, it is always possible that Paul is relying on a source at this point. We may note, for example, the many affinities of our passage with *Jubilees* 1 (e.g., Beliar [=Belial, v. 20], covenant formula [v. 17], adoption formula [v. 24], restoration theology [vv. 22–25], sanctification [v. 23]).

6:16c–18 / The second line of substantiation (**As,** *kathōs*) for verse 14a picks up where the first leaves off. Having mentioned in verse 16b that believers are the temple of the living God, the text continues in verse 16d with the related idea that God dwells among his people. It is not the purpose of verses 16c–18 to substantiate from Scripture that believers are the temple of the living God (cf. M. Thrall). It is obvious that none of the citations actually asserts this, not even verse 16d. Furthermore, as mentioned above, the citations center at verse 17 and thereby give a reason for the exhortation in verse 14a.

The six citations in verses 16d–18b are treated as a single quotation introduced by an introductory formula and concluded by a closing formula, rather than by six separate formulas. The passage has corresponding beginning and ending premises with practical implications in the middle. Hence, the citations form three parts consisting of three lines each. In fact, the citation combination in our passage is so symmetrical that "says the Lord" *(legei kyrios)* in verse 17 bisects the citations into equal halves and thus lies precisely equidistant from the opening and closing formulas. Thus, God's promises of a reciprocal relationship between himself and his people expressed in the first person singular **(I)** bracket a center section that gives the practical implications of this relationship to God. The bilateral symmetry of the citation combination corresponds to the bilateral relationship between God and his people (vv. 16ef, 18ab). As a result, form and content blend beautifully in these modified citations to communicate Paul's message.

The citation combination in 2 Corinthians 6:16c–18 comes toward the end of Paul's long apology for his apostolic office (2:14–7:4), concluding this major section.

6:16d / The first OT quote is a conflation of Leviticus 26:11–12 and Ezekiel 37:27. Paul has combined two similar passages into a single citation, for both texts refer to God's dwelling among Israel, and both contain a version of the covenant formula. In the OT, the full, twofold covenant formula (**"I will be their**/your **God, and they**/you **will be my people"**) is used basically in two contexts: historical (the birth of Israel) and eschatological (the consummation of the promises to Israel).

Paul began his defense for his apostleship (2:14–7:4) by drawing a typological comparison between his ministry and that of Moses. In that context, Paul calls himself a "minister of the new covenant" (3:6), and his argument turns on allusions to Ezekiel 36:26–27 and Jeremiah 31:33. As we shall see, it is no coincidence that Paul now returns to the subject of the new covenant at the end of the apology, as he makes a final appeal to the Corinthians.

6:17abc / After the citation of the covenant formula in verse 16, the text goes on in verse 17 to introduce a modified citation of Isaiah 52:11. In its original context, Isaiah 52:11 is an exhortation to the exiles to go out from Babylon (cf. Rev. 18:4), the land of their captivity, and to return in purity to the Holy Land with the temple vessels. Here, however, the passage is crafted to fit the new context in accordance with Paul's purpose. By rearranging the lines of the citation and changing the pronouns, the apostle makes the text begin with an exhortation to **come out from them**, that is, the "unbelievers" of verse 14a. This shows once again that the citation combination centering at verse 17 is designed to substantiate the opening paraenesis of verse 14a.

The quotation of Isaiah 52:11 is presented here as a consequence (**Therefore,** *dio*) of the reciprocal new covenant relationship between God and his people in 2 Corinthians 6:16d. The exhortation to separate is based on a relationship, on God's living among his people. The text does not imply that obedience is a stipulation either for the entrance into or for the maintenance of the covenant relationship. Unlike the conditional Sinaitic covenant, the new covenant was to be unconditional and inviolable, because God would supply his people with a new heart and his Spirit, whereby the righteous requirement of the law might be fulfilled (cf. Rom. 8:4). Paul cites Isaiah 52:11 at this point because it fits the exodus typology of the new covenant. In Isaiah 52, God addresses the exiles and promises to "redeem" them in a second exodus that would outstrip the first (vv. 3, 9, 12). It is in the context of this second-exodus redemption that the returning exiles are to separate themselves (v. 11). Hence, the exhortation is naturally read in light of the related expectation of the second exodus, that is, the reestablishment of the covenantal relationship between God and his people. Just as in 1 Corinthians 10:1–13, exodus typology is used here in instruction directed to the church in Corinth.

The point of the exhortation in 2 Corinthians 6:17 (and hence all the exhortations in the passage) is that the Corinthians should practice the implications of the new covenant situation for their sanctification. Opening their Spirit-filled hearts toward the apostle (6:13) demands separation from Paul's opponents (v. 14a), because God said in the OT that the new covenant relationship that he would establish through a second-exodus redemption requires separation (v. 17).

6:17d–18b / The quotation of Isaiah 52:11 is immediately followed by a mixed citation of Ezekiel 20:34, 2 Samuel 7:14, and Isaiah 43:6. In its original context, Ezekiel 20:34–35 clearly refers to the second exodus. In 2 Corinthians 6:17d, therefore, the idea of God's gathering Israel from the lands in the second exodus (Ezek. 20:34) is merely the other side of the idea expressed by the citation of Isaiah 52:11, that in the second exodus Israel should "come out from among them."

In verse 18 **and** *(kai)* is added editorially to join the citation of Ezekiel 20:34 to that of 2 Samuel 7:14. The original text of 2 Samuel 7:14 has undergone some modifications. For one thing, the adoption formula is applied to the addressees of the citation combination (**you**), that is, the ones referred to by the second person plural of Isaiah 52:11 and Ezekiel 20:34 in the preceding citations. Thus, the modified citation of 2 Samuel 7:14 in our passage closely parallels that in *Testament of Judah* 24:3, a passage that speaks of God the **Father** adopting the Messiah and his people of God and pouring out his Spirit on them at the time of the eschatological restoration of Israel. Furthermore, the adoption formula in 2 Corinthians 6:18 is expanded under the influence of Isaiah 43:6 to include not just **sons** but **daughters** as well (cf. *b. Menaḥ.* 110a). Although the influence of Isaiah 43:6 has sometimes been denied, the exodus typology of Isaiah 43:1–7 fits well with the exodus typology in the rest of the citations in 2 Corinthians 6:16–18. Thus, the Davidic promise is interpreted as a promise of restoration associated with the second exodus.

7:1 / Paul concludes 2 Corinthians 6:14–7:1 with a final exhortation to the Corinthians that reiterates the paraenesis in 6:14, 17 and thus closes the ring. In the Greek text, this verse begins with the word "therefore" (**Since,** *oun*), which underscores that Paul is drawing an inference from his preceding scriptural argument. Based on the **promises** quoted in the citation combination of 6:16 and 18, Paul concludes that the Corinthians should, once again, separate themselves from pernicious influences. This is what the apostle means by **perfecting holiness,** for **holiness** or "sanctification" denotes "separation."

The Israelites were originally charged to maintain a holiness through obedience to the law. This obligation is the result of Yahweh's separating them from other nations, redeeming them from Egypt, and entering into a covenantal relationship with them. As their God, he enjoins them to be holy as he is holy (cf. Lev. 11:44–45; 19:2; 20:7–8, 24–26; 22:32–33; Num. 15:40–41; cf. Exod. 31:13; Ezek. 20:12). Paul merely carries over this conception and applies it to the community that has experienced a second-exodus redemption through Christ.

Hence, when 2 Corinthians 7:1 exhorts the Corinthians to cleanse themselves from **everything that contaminates body and spirit,** we must not think that this is foreign to Paul's thinking. Although it is true that Paul does not elsewhere use the term "defilement" (*molysmos*), 1 Corinthians 7:34 does speak of being "holy both in body and in spirit," and 1 Corinthians 8:7 uses the cognate verb (*molynein*) metaphorically of defiling the conscience. Furthermore, the purity language of our passage could have been suggested by the image of the church as the "temple of God" (2 Cor. 6:16), which is definitely a Pauline concept (cf. 1 Cor. 3:16).

7:2–4 / Here, Paul resumes his train of thought from 6:13, that the Corinthians should open wide their hearts to him just as he has done to them. This incidently shows that 6:14–7:1 must be integral to the present context, for otherwise 7:2 would sound redundant coming directly after 6:13. The intervening exhortation in 6:14–7:1 explains how they are to open their heart. As was shown above, 6:14–7:1 exhorts the Corinthians to put into practice the implications of the new covenant for their sanctification, particularly as it pertains to the situation with the opponents. By separating from the opponents (and other pernicious influences), the Corinthians, who are in Paul's heart (7:3; cf. 3:2!), open their Spirit-filled hearts to the apostle and remain a "letter of Christ" written by the Spirit of the living God (3:3; cf. 6:16b!), and their new covenant lifestyle remains a reason for boasting (7:4) for the apostle, an apology for the legitimacy of Paul's apostolate. Seen in this light, 6:14–7:1 does not interrupt the context, but rather contributes to the argument of the passage and provides closure for the whole apology.

7:2 / After Paul exhorts the Corinthians to live in light of the new covenant situation by separating from his opponents (6:14–7:1), he renews his plea from 6:13, that the Corinthians should open their hearts to him, and he reiterates his claim of innocence from 6:3. As in 6:13, the word **hearts** is not represented in the Greek text but is clearly assumed from the context (cf. 6:11–12). As we have seen, the word "heart" dominates the whole final section of the apostle's defense.

Paul desperately wants to normalize his relations with the Corinthians; therefore, he tries defensively to remove the stones of stumbling that have gotten in the way of complete reconciliation. Lingering doubts about his character and conduct are at issue. Paul claims to have **wronged no one,** using the same verb as in 7:12, where he refers to the wrong he suffered from a Corinthian (probably by a severe attack on his apostleship). Interestingly enough, Moses defends himself against the charges of Korah and his followers by stating that he has harmed no one (Num. 16:15). Likewise, Paul may be responding to his critics in Corinth in terms of the type, rather than thinking of a particular wrong. Paul also claims to have **corrupted no one.**

It is unclear exactly what Paul may be referring to here. Elsewhere, he uses the verb in a variety of senses: "to destroy" (1 Cor. 3:17), "to corrupt morally" (1 Cor. 15:33; Eph. 4:22), "to lead astray" (2 Cor. 11:3). This last usage might be meant here, since the apostle has been accused of leading others astray (cf. 5:16; 6:8). Finally, Paul claims to have **exploited no one.** He deals more with this accusation in 12:14–18, using the same verb. Evidently, it constitutes a major cause or at least a contributing factor in the breakdown of relations between Corinthians and the apostle. In all likelihood, Paul is alluding generally to the charge of fraud and self-aggrandizement that was prevalent in Corinth, and particularly to mismanagement of the church contributions to the collection for Jerusalem (cf. 2 Cor. 4:2; 7:2; 8:20–21; 11:7–8; 12:13–18). Paul has already turned this argument back on his opponents in 2:17, where he accuses them of peddling the word of God (cf. 11:20).

7:3 / Paul explains that it is not his purpose to condemn the Corinthians by defending himself against these accusations. As we saw above on 6:11, the final section of Paul's apology for his apostleship refers back to the previous context of his defense, particularly to the very beginning of it. Here again in 7:3, Paul refers back to the previous discussion. When the apostle states that **I have said before,** he makes reference to passages where he has expressed that the Corinthians are **in our hearts.** In the immediate context, of course, he stated this fact in 6:11–12. However, in the broader context of the defense as a whole, Paul stated that the Corinthians were in his heart already in 3:2 ("You yourselves are our letter, written in our hearts"). Therefore, the concept of **hearts** not only ties together the final section of Paul's defense (6:11–7:4) but also provides closure for the whole apology (2:14–7:4).

7:4 / Paul concludes his great apology for the legitimacy of his apostolic office with a statement of confidence in the Corinthians. In light of the Corinthian accusations and disaffection reflected in 1:12–2:13 and 2:14–7:4, it is unlikely that Paul has complete **confidence** (cf. 7:16) in this troubled church. Some of the paraenesis in the apology is inexplicable if Paul is so assured of the Corinthians' cooperation. After all, Paul has gone so far as to warn the church members that the outcome of their current course could spell spiritual disaster for them (cf. 2 Cor. 6:1). However, Paul wants to end his defense on a positive note, with plenty of hope for the future. As he states in 1:7, his hope for the Corinthians is "firm" or "sure." Also in 1:15 and 2:3 (cf. 13:14!), Paul expresses confidence in the church (even in "all" the members!). He furthermore states that the Corinthians reveal that they are a letter authored by Christ written by the Spirit (3:3) and as such a source of his "confidence" as an apostle (v. 4). Moreover, the subsequent section (esp. 7:7–13) reports that Titus had brought Paul good news from Corinth of some positive developments in Paul's relationship with the church, providing at least some basis for Paul's optimism (cf. 1:13–14).

Nevertheless, we cannot help thinking that Paul's claim of "great confidence" in the Corinthians may have been designed more to engender loyalty than to compliment them for already having it. As V. Furnish observes, Paul's expressions of confidence in his addressees are often implicitly hortatory. Ultimately, Paul hopes to be able to boast in the Corinthians in the day of the Lord (cf. 1:14; 1 Thess. 2:19). For the present, the apostle needs the church at Corinth as a letter of recommendation that will be "known and read by all men" (2 Cor. 3:2).

Additional Notes §8

6:11 / Paul directly addresses the church at Corinth with an appellative like **Corinthians** three other times in the letter, in each of those cases with the word "brothers" (cf. 2 Cor. 1:8; 8:1; 13:11).

6:14–7:1 / This difficult and controversial section is sometimes regarded as a "Qumran fragment" (cf. Joseph A. Fitzmyer, "Qumran and the Interpolated Paragraph in 2 Corinthians 6:14–7:1," in *Essays on the Semitic Background of the New Testament* [London: Chapman, 1971], pp. 205–17) or even an "anti-Pauline fragment" (cf. Hans Dieter Betz, "2 Corinthians 6:14–7:1: An Anti-Pauline Fragment?" *JBL* 92 [1973], pp. 88–108; idem, "Corinthians, Second Epistle to the," *ABD*, vol. 1, pp. 1148–54 [here p. 1150]). One must agree with M. Thrall (*Second Corinthians*, vol. 1, pp. 471–80) that there is no necessary connection with Qumran in this section. On the literary-critical problem posed by this section, see M. Thrall, *Second Corinthians*, vol. 1, pp. 25–36. For the interpretation suggested here, see James M. Scott, "The Use of Scripture in 2 Corinthians 6.16c–18 and Paul's Restoration Theology," *JSNT* 56 (1994), pp. 73–99; idem, *Adoption as Sons of God: An Exegetical Investigation into the Background of ΥΙΟΘΕΣΙΑ in the Pauline Corpus* (WUNT 2/48; Tübingen: Mohr Siebeck, 1992), pp. 187–220. See further G. K. Beale,

"The Old Testament Background of Reconciliation in 2 Corinthians 5–7 and its Bearing on the Literary Problem of 2 Corinthians 6:14–7:1," *NTS* 35 (1989), pp. 550–81; Heinz-Wolfgang Kuhn, "The Impact of the Qumran Scrolls on the Understanding of Paul," in *The Dead Sea Scrolls: Forty Years of Research* (STDJ 10; Leiden: Brill, 1992), pp. 327–39 (here p. 335); William J. Webb, *Returning Home: New Covenant and Second Exodus as the Context for 2 Corinthians 6:14–7:1* (JSNTSup 85; Sheffield: JSOT Press, 1993); Michael D. Goulder, "2 Cor. 6:14–7:1 as an Integral Part of 2 Corinthians," *NovT* 36 (1994), pp. 47–57.

6:14a / The adjective **yoked together** *(heterozygos)* occurs in Lev. 19:19 in a prohibition against mating different species of cattle (cf. Deut. 22:10). Cf. also Plutarch, *Cimon* 16.10 where, after a severe earthquake, Sparta, about to be attacked by the Helots, requested help from Athens. This precipitated a hefty debate in Athens, since the two cities were not on the best terms, but Cimon exhorted the Athenians "not to allow Hellas to be crippled, nor their city to be robbed of its yoke-fellow [i.e., Sparta]."

Even if a metaphorical usage of the verb *heterozygeō* is uncommon, the idea of being yoked in a metaphorical sense is well known (cf., e.g., Philo, *On Dreams* 2.83; Phil. 4:3). After the apostasy in Moab, Moses instructed the judges of Israel, "Each of you shall kill any of your people who have yoked themselves to the Baal of Peor" (Num. 25:5 [MT only]; cf. *Num. Rab.* 20:23). According to *2 En.* 34, antediluvian humanity cast off the "yoke" of God in favor of another "yoke," i.e., the worship of other gods. The Talmud speaks of "the yoke of the commandments" (*b. Ber.* 12b, 13a, 14b; *b. Yebam.* 47b), "the yoke of the kingdom of heaven" (*b. Ber.* 13a, 13b, 14b, 61b; *Num. Rab.* 14:6), "the yoke of the Torah" (*b. Sanh.* 94b; *Gen. Rab.* 98:12; *Num. Rab.* 13:16; 18:21; 19:26), and "one who throws off the yoke" (*b. Šebu.* 13a; *b. Ker.* 7a; *Gen. Rab.* 67:7). If 2 Cor. 6:14a alludes specifically to Ps. 2:2–3, then it is important to recognize that this same psalm refers to divine adoptive sonship (Ps. 2:7; cf. 2 Cor. 6:18). Cf. 4Q418 fr. 103 ii 7–8: ". . . lest it become a case of forbidden mixtures (Lev. 19:19), like the mule, and you will become like a garment [of linsey-woolsey] or of wool and flax mingled; or your work might be like one who plows with an ox yoked to a donkey. . . ." See further Charles L. Tyer, "Yoke," *ABD*, vol. 6, pp. 1026–27.

6:14b–16b / Cf. S. D. Sperling, "Belial," *Dictionary of Deities and Demons in the Bible* (ed. Karel van der Toorn, et al.; Leiden: Brill, 1995), pp. 322–27. *Vitae Prophetarum* 4:6 reads in full: "Concerning this mystery it was revealed to the holy man [sc. Daniel] that (Nebuchadnezzar) had become a beast of the field because he was fond of pleasure and stiffnecked, and because those who belong to Beliar become like an ox under yoke." For other references to **Belial** see *Jub.* 1:20; 15:33; *Ascen. Isa.* 1:8–9; 2:4; 3:11, 13; 4:2, 4, 14, 16, 18; 5:1; *Sib. Or.* 3:63, 73; *T. Levi* 3:3; 18:12; *T. Dan.* 5:1, 10–11.

The dualistic contrast between the mutually exclusive spheres of **Christ** and **Belial** is well illustrated by Levi's exhortation to his children: "Choose for yourselves light or darkness, the Law of the Lord or the works of Beliar" (*T. Levi* 19:1; cf. *T. Jos.* 20:2). Likewise, the Qumran scrolls (cf. 1QS 1.17, 23–24; CD 4.13, 15; 5.8) describe an ongoing struggle between good and evil, in which the Teacher of Righteousness represents the forces of light and good, whereas his opponent, the wicked priest, represents the forces of darkness and evil. The present age is the time of Belial's rule. He is the leader of "people who are opposed to the people of the lot of God" (1QS 1.16–2.8). It is possible to become entrapped in "the scheme of Belial" (4QMMT C 29). The parallel to our text and its concern about opponents is obvious. Paul himself is fully capable of such dualistic thinking (cf. 1 Thess. 5:5; Rom. 6:19).

On the community as the **temple of God**, see, e.g., D. R. de Lacey, "οἱ τινές ἐστε ὑμεῖς: The Function of a Metaphor in St. Paul," in *Templum Amicitiae: Essays on the Second Temple Presented to Ernst Bammel* (ed. William Horbury; JSNTSup 48; Sheffield: JSOT Press, 1991), pp. 391–409; P. W. Comfort, "Temple," *DPL*, pp. 923–25. See further on 2 Cor. 5:1.

6:16d–18b / Cf. Rom. 3:10–18, which, interestingly enough, has a threefold structure similar to that in 2 Cor. 6:16–18, beginning and ending with axiomatic statements whose practical implications appear in a middle section. The citation combination in Rom. 3:10–18 also marks a clear end to a major section of Paul's argument (Rom. 1:18–3:20).

6:16cd / The introductory formula to the citations (**as God has said**) is unique in Paul's letters and indeed in the rest of the NT as well.

6:16d / When Paul cites from the OT that God will **live with** (or *among*) **them and walk among them**, this could be used as an argument against his unique role as a revelatory mediator, just as a similar argument was used by Korah against Moses (cf. Num. 16:3: "All the congregation are holy, every one of them, and the Lord is among them. So why then do you exalt yourself above the assembly of the Lord?"). Nevertheless, Paul is willing to risk his mediatorial role as apostle by arguing that believers themselves experience the revelation of the presence of God in their midst (cf. 2 Cor. 3:18).

On the **people** of God, see, e.g., Brevard S. Childs, *Biblical Theology of the Old and New Testaments: Theological Reflection on the Christian Bible* (Minneapolis: Fortress, 1992), pp. 138–40.

The covenant formula is used, as in Lev. 26:12, of *Israel's birth as a nation*, when God led the people out of Egyptian bondage at the exodus, established the nation and the covenant relationship between Israel and himself, and began to dwell among them as their God (cf. Exod. 6:7; Deut. 29:12; 2 Sam. 7:24 = 1 Chron. 17:22; Jer. 7:23; 11:4). When the OT prophets declared that Israel had broken the covenant with God and had thereby forfeited both the reciprocal relationship with God and his presence in their midst (cf. Hos. 1:9), they also prophesied that one day Israel would be restored to covenantal relationship with God. As in Ezek. 37:27, therefore, the covenant formula is used, secondly, of *Israel's eschatological hope*. At the time of the restoration, God would lead Israel out of the bondage of exile in a second exodus; he would reconstitute the nation under the Davidic Messiah and reestablish a covenantal relationship between Israel and himself by means of a new covenant;

and he would again dwell among them in the land as their God (cf. Jer. 24:7; 30:18–22; 31:1, 33; 32:38; Ezek. 11:20; 14:11; 30:22; 36:28; 37:23, 27; Zech. 8:8; 13:9). The second, eschatological use of the covenant formula is the circumlocution of the promise of the new covenant and all that that entails (cf. Jer. 31:33).

How do the covenant formula and the promise of a new exodus come to be applied to the Gentiles in the Pauline churches? Part of the answer is that already in the OT covenant formula contexts mention how the nations are affected (cf. Ezek. 36:36; 37:28; Zech. 8:13). Furthermore, the OT treats exodus from Egypt as a paradigm of liberation, which is seen alongside of creation and thus transcends the historical specificity of Israel. Cf. John J. Collins, "The Exodus and Biblical Theology," *BTB* 25 (1995), pp. 152–60 (here p. 157).

6:17 / Cf. Paul's citation of Isa. 52:11 approvingly as paraenesis for the new covenant situation in Rom. 10:15, where the apostle applies Isa. 52:7 to the apostles of Jesus Christ who preach the gospel.

On the idea of not touching the unclean thing, cf. Col. 2:21. It is interesting to note that the same negative imperative *mē haptesthe* **(do not touch)** is found in the context of Korah's rebellion (Num. 16:26), as a divine command given through Moses that the people should separate themselves from the tents of Korah and should not touch anything belonging to the rebels who were about to be judged. If Paul has Num. 16:26 in mind as he cites Isa. 52:11, then that would support the idea that separation from Paul's opponents is the main thrust of 2 Cor. 2:14, 17; 7:1.

6:17d–18b / The adoption formula ("I will be to him a Father, and he will be to me a son") originally applied to the future "seed" of David (cf. 2 Sam. 7:14). Cf. James M. Scott, "Adoption, Sonship," *DPL*, pp. 15–18; idem, "Restoration of Israel," *DPL*, pp. 796–805.

By setting a period after v. 17 and beginning v. 18 without the original "and" *(kai)*, the NIV fails to recognize the fundamental link between vv. 17d and 18. The forward position of *egō* combines with *kai* to form *kagō*, representing a stylistic improvement to the combined LXX text (cf. the citation of 1 Kgs. 19:10 in Rom. 11:3). Therefore, the *kagō* in 2 Cor. 6:17d is not only proof that the two quotations have been welded into one, it is also evidence that Paul himself was responsible for the conflation.

7:1 / Assuming the integrity of 2 Cor. 6:14–7:1 within the letter, the use of **promises** in 7:1 in reference to the Scriptures (including 2 Sam. 7:14) recalls 2 Cor. 1:20, the only other use of the terms **promises** and "Son(s) of God" in 2 Corinthians.

If, as Paul seems to suggest in 2 Corinthians, his opponents have mounted an attack against him that is similar to Korah's rebellion against Moses, then it is worth noting that Paul's idea of progressive **holiness** differs from Korah's notion of static holiness. Korah argued against Moses' position of authority that "All the congregation are holy, every one of them" (Num. 16:3; cf. Exod. 19:6).

Cf. Hengel, *Pre-Christian Paul*, pp. 40–53.
Cf. Anthony J. Saldarini, "Pharisees," *ABD*, vol. 5, pp. 289–303.

7:2 / In light of the theme of the new covenant in 6:14–7:1, it becomes apparent that Paul's notion of opening the heart in 6:13 and 7:2 can be compared to the idea in 2 Macc. 1:4–5: "May he (namely, God) open your heart to his law and his commandments, and may he bring peace. May he hear your prayers and be reconciled to you, and may he not forsake you in the time of evil." According to *Hekhalot Rabbati*, a closed heart is a continuing effect of Israel's exiles (Schäfer, §293).

7:4 / M. Thrall (*Second Corinthians*, vol. 1, pp. 484–85) suggests that *parrēsia* should be translated "frankness of speech, candor" (cf. 3:12) rather than **confidence.** Yet Paul's reference to "comfort" in "tribulation" recalls his words in 1:7, where he likewise expresses confident hope in the Corinthians in the context of his "comfort" in "tribulation" (cf. 1:3–11).

Cf. Victor Paul Furnish, *II Corinthians* (AB 32A; New York: Doubleday, 1985), p. 121.

§9 Repentance (2 Cor. 7:5–16)

After giving an extensive apology for the legitimacy of his apostleship in 2:14–7:4, Paul now resumes his travelogue from 2:12–13. Paul had mentioned there that he had abandoned an open door in Troas because of his concern for the Corinthians' reaction to his tearful letter, and so he had gone to Macedonia in order to find Titus and hear his report. Paul began the defense without actually stating whether he managed to meet with Titus in Macedonia. Hence, the present section resumes the earlier narrative by recording Paul's elation when Titus finally arrived and reported on the Corinthians' repentant attitude following the tearful letter. The terms that Paul introduced in verse 4 (comfort, joy, tribulation, and confidence) are taken up and further developed in this section.

7:5–13a / Paul describes the joy he received from hearing about the Corinthians' repentant attitude toward himself and recalls the comforting news that Titus brought to him in Macedonia.

7:5 / In order to set the stage, Paul recollects the tremendous difficulty he had been facing until he received the news from Titus. Paul refers to **this body of ours** (lit., "our flesh"), recalling the discussion about his suffering and dying body in 4:7–5:15. From every side, Paul encountered difficulty in Macedonia. He was persecuted on the outside by Jews and Gentiles. He was oppressed on the inside by **fears**, particularly regarding the church at Corinth (cf. 2:12–13; 11:28). Paul had no **rest** *(anesin)* (cf. 2:13: "I still had no peace *[anesin]* of mind, because I did not find my brother Titus there").

7:6 / In sharp contrast to this tribulation in Macedonia, Paul expresses the comfort he received at the coming of Titus. The very fact that Titus found Paul in Macedonia is a cause of comfort for Paul. Evidently, he had been deeply concerned when Titus did not arrive as planned. Perhaps he was worried that Titus had met with disaster. The apostle does not credit human intervention for the positive turn of events that encouraged him so much; rather, he ascribes all the credit to God. God comforted Paul through the instrumentality of Titus's coming. Paul characterizes **God** here as one **who comforts the downcast** *(ho parakalōn tous tapeinous)*. This alludes to Isaiah 49:13 LXX: "Rejoice, O heavens, and let the earth be glad; let the mountains break forth with joy; for the Lord has had mercy on his people, and has comforted the downcast of his people *(tous tapeinous tou laou autou parekalesen)*." Paul has already alluded to Isaiah 49:9 in the previous context (cf. 2 Cor. 6:2), and this passage is also crucial to Paul's apostolic self-concept (cf. Gal. 1:15–16; Isa. 49:1). Just as in 6:2 Paul views the Corinthians as in danger of forfeiting the eschatological salvation prophesied in Isaiah 49, so also in 7:6 he perceives his own relief over the coming of Titus as an evidence of God's comfort of his people in the endtime.

7:7 / Paul was comforted not only by the actual coming of Titus to him in Macedonia but by the report that Titus was able to give him about the Corinthians. Evidently, Titus's mission to Corinth had succeeded in bringing the Corinthians to repentance in their attitude toward the apostle. Paul is comforted by the fact that Titus had received **comfort** from the Corinthians. But how exactly was Titus comforted? Does this imply that, like Paul, Titus was anxious about the situation in Corinth? Did Titus receive mental relief that the Corinthians were making a significant turnabout in their stance toward Paul? If so, Titus's relief about the situation resulted in Paul's relief, too. The principle of vicarious comfort was expressed in the opening thanksgiving: Paul's comfort results in the Corinthians' comfort (1:6). Titus was able to report that the church had a **longing** for Paul and earnestly desired his visit. Evidently, the Corinthians had already begun to open their hearts to the apostle, just as he now exhorts them to do more fully and finally by completely cutting themselves off from the remaining opponents in the congregation (cf. 6:11–7:4). The church expresses its **deep sorrow** for temporarily defecting from its founding apostle (or at least not adequately supporting him), and is now ready to obey Paul with a renewed sense of commitment and **ardent concern.** This latter term, which can be translated simply "zeal," may imply their punishment of the offender (cf. 2:5–6; 7:11). All of this good news causes Paul to rejoice all the more, thus putting an end to his fears about the church (cf. 7:5).

Yet we may wonder whether Paul's rather optimistic recollection of Titus's report about the Corinthians tells the whole story. If we accept the letter as a unity in its present form, the text bristles with tensions. The Corinthians are not so completely restored to fellowship with their founding apostle as this passage would suggest (cf. 1:12–2:13; 2:14–7:4; 10–13).

7:8–9a / Having stated the joy with which he received the good news from Titus about the Corinthians' repentance (vv. 5–7), Paul now proceeds to recall why he originally sent the tearful letter and Titus to Corinth (vv. 8–13a). Paul begins in verses 8–9a by explaining *(hoti)* his joy over their deep sorrow in verse 7. Instead of returning to Corinth as he promised during the painful visit, Paul wrote a **letter** (the so-called tearful letter), which caused him considerable anguish and tears (cf. 2:4) because he knew that it would cause the Corinthians deep **sorrow.** He could only hope that such a heavy-handed letter would not embitter the addressees against him, further aggravating the situation or even causing a complete and final break between the Corinthian church and its founding apostle. As he waited for a response, Paul was intermittently plagued by **regret** (note the imperfect tense) about the harsh tone and the possible negative reaction it might elicit from the Corinthians. Hence, Titus's report was able to dispel Paul's fears, for the apostle learned not only that, as expected, the letter did in fact hurt the Corinthians, but also that it caused them to repent. Therefore, Paul does not regret the ultimate effect that the letter had, but rather rejoices in it (7:9a). Yet, as Paul has already pointed out, he never wanted to grieve the ones who really should make him glad (cf. 2:2).

Paul uses the noun **repentance** *(metanoia)* only in 2 Corinthians 7:9, 10 and in Romans 2:4 (cf. 2 Tim. 2:25), and the verb *(metanoein)* in 2 Corinthians 12:21. In each case, the term is used in the context of divine judgment, which results from an impenitent heart. The Corinthians were in danger of accepting the grace of God in vain because of their stance toward the apostle (cf. 6:1). Paul and his gospel of reconciliation are so inextricably intertwined that it was impossible for the Corinthians to accept one without the other, for Paul was the divinely-chosen ambassador of Christ, as though God were making his appeal through him (5:20). Therefore, the Corinthians needed to change their minds about Paul and their behavior toward him in order to avert divine judgment. This point is developed in the subsequent context of the present chapter.

7:9b / Paul then explains the reason (**For,** *gar*) for his joy over the Corinthians' repentance. The Corinthians became **sorrowful** to repentance **as God intended.** It is God's will that sinners repent and thus avert judgment (cf. Ezek. 18:32). Paul rejoices over the Corinthians' repentance because they also averted disaster. The verb translated **be harmed** here denotes "suffer loss." What kind of loss was averted by the Corinthians' sorrowful repentance? In 1 Corinthians 3:15 the same verb is used in the context of divine judgment: "If it [sc. what a man builds] is burned up, he will suffer loss *(zēmioun);* he himself will be saved, but only as one escaping through the flames." Evidently, if the Corinthians had not repented, then he would have come to them in judgment. Indeed, 2 Corinthians 12:21 warns the Corinthians that when he comes for the third time those who are still impenitent face a judgment that will cause Paul to mourn. Furthermore, as he states in 10:6, "we will be ready to punish every act of disobedience" (cf. also 1 Cor. 4:21; 2 Cor. 1:23; 13:1–3). Paul regards himself as possessing apostolic authority and power to execute divine judgment in their midst. Already he has ordered and obtained the punishment of the troublemaker who had offended him during his painful second visit to Corinth (cf. 1:5–11).

7:10 / Paul explains what he has just stated in verse 9b about being sorrowful as God intended. Paul's distinction here between **godly sorrow** (lit., "sorrow according to God") and **worldly sorrow** (lit., "sorrow of the world") remains somewhat unclear. Evidently, the apostle wants to distinguish between two different motivations for sorrow and their outcomes. On the one hand, there is a kind of godly sorrow that effects a change of mind and behavior. This kind of sorrow leads to salvation in accordance with the will of God. On the other hand, there is a kind of worldly sorrow that brings death, probably because it is not characterized by a genuine change of mind and heart and a corresponding change of behavior. Hence, the sinner incurs the full wrath of God in judgment.

7:11 / Paul elaborates on the kind of repentance that the Corinthians have shown. Seven terms connected by the adversative particle *alla* ("[not only this,] but rather") are listed here that describe with rhetorical intensification the Corinthians' repentance. The apostle thereby takes up the terms **longing** and "zeal" (here translated **concern**) from verse 7. The issue had been Paul's apostleship, and now the Corinthian church has repented of its previous attitude and actions toward Paul. Moreover, its members have manifested fruit in keeping with repentance, including, as Paul had instructed in the tearful letter, the "punishment" (*ekdikēsis*, here translated **readiness to see justice done**) of the troublemaker who had offended the apostle during his painful visit (cf. 1:5–11). They show thereby that the conflict with Paul during the second visit was not their fault, and that they were in fact **innocent** (lit., "holy, pure") in this matter, since they did not actually cause it. Apparently, the Corinthians had not adequately supported Paul when the troublemaker called his authority into question. The majority of the congregation (cf. 2:6) has now provided an effective "defense" (*apologia*, here translated **eagerness to clear yourselves**) of their position.

There is a palpable tension in the text. If the Corinthians had been completely innocent during the debacle, as they seem to claim and as Paul now seems to accept, then they would have no need for sorrow and repentance. If, however, the Corinthians were culpable so as to require repentance, then it becomes difficult to explain why Paul had only one person punished rather than the whole congregation. The answer seems to lie in degrees of guilt. The troublemaker openly denounced Paul, while the Corinthians either passively stood by and watched or secretly agreed with the malefactor.

7:12 / Paul reveals that the real purpose of the tearful letter was to test the Corinthians (cf. 2:9) and to help restore them to a proper relationship with himself as their apostle. His intent was not first and foremost to punish the evildoer or to seek vengeance for himself any more than it was Moses' purpose to punish Korah and his followers. Paul speaks of himself here in the third person as the **injured party** (lit., "the one who was wronged") in an attempt to be less direct (cf. 12:2–4, where he likewise speaks of himself in the third person). Since his relationship with the Corinthians is one of revelatory mediator, they come to their insight *(phanerōthēnai)* about their devotion to the apostle ultimately **before God** (*enōpion tou theou*; cf. 4:2), before whom Paul speaks (cf. 2:17).

7:13a / Now that the "painful letter" has accomplished its purpose of restoring the Corinthians to a proper relationship with their founding apostle, Paul concludes that encouragement has been the general outcome (lit., "Therefore, we have been comforted").

7:13b–16 / Here Paul goes beyond describing the joy that he received from hearing about the Corinthians' repentant attitude toward himself (vv. 7–13a) by describing the joy that he derived from hearing about Titus's reception in Corinth.

7:13b / Just as the comfort with which Titus was comforted was a reason for Paul's **encouragement** (or comfort, cf. v. 7), so also the **happy** state of Titus is here a reason for Paul's joy (lit., "we rejoiced still more at the joy of Titus"). When Titus originally delivered the tearful letter to the Corinthians, he was undoubtedly apprehensive about how the church would receive him. Had Titus already had a difficult encounter with the Corinthians, perhaps in connection with the collection? That would help to explain his uneasiness. After the Corinthians welcomed him, however, Titus's worry turned to joy, and his mind was set at ease. The verb translated **refreshed** can also be used in the sense of giving someone rest (cf. Matt. 11:28), although Paul himself admittedly uses it most often in the sense of "refresh" (cf. 1 Cor. 16:18; Phlm. 7 [in the context of "joy and comfort"], 20). The term **spirit** is used here of the inner life of a person, the source and seat of feeling and volition (cf. 1 Cor. 16:18; Rom. 1:9; 8:16). According to 2 Corinthians 2:13, Paul "had no rest for my spirit" when he was waiting for the news from Titus.

In view of the apologetic nature of 2 Corinthians as a whole, it is interesting to note that Titus's spirit was refreshed **by all of you** (cf. v. 15). This would appear to be an exaggeration, if there was still an anti-Pauline faction in Corinth (cf. 2:6). Paul is probably addressing the majority of the congregation who have chosen to side with him. At the very end of the letter, however, Paul writes in a similar vein, "the fellowship of the Holy Spirit [is] with you *all*" (13:14).

7:14 / The reason that Paul rejoiced over the fact that Titus found joy in his reception in Corinth was that the apostle had **boasted** to Titus about the Corinthians. Paul had evidently done so in order to encourage Titus in his difficult mission to Corinth. If the church had refused both to punish the one who had offended Paul and to repent, then Paul's praise of the Corinthians would have been exposed as unfounded optimism; Paul would have been **embarrassed;** and his credibility would have been further eroded even among his coworkers.

Paul is very concerned here about the correspondence of what he says with reality, for his veracity has been severely questioned in Corinth. Changing his announced travel plans, for example, has left Paul with a credibility gap (cf. 1:13, 17). Paul tries to counter these charges by affirming his sincerity as one who speaks the truth in the presence of God without deception (cf. 2:17; 4:2; 6:7; 12:6; 13:8). Indeed, the "truth of Christ" is in him (11:10). And just as he has always spoken the truth to the Corinthians, so now there is positive evidence that what he had told Titus about the Corinthians was also **true.** This serves to reinforce Paul's credibility in Corinth, where the situation has significantly improved but has not yet been totally resolved.

7:15 / Paul goes on to describe the afterglow of Titus's positive reception in Corinth. When he was in Corinth, Titus evidently developed a close personal relationship with the Corinthians and a warm **affection** for them. Now that he has returned to Paul, Titus looks back with fondness at the time he spent with the church, particularly at the way in which they received him.

The obedience that Titus recalls is the Corinthians' submission to Paul's directives in the tearful letter that Titus delivered. Yet why were the Corinthians **obedient?** The OT formula **fear and trembling,** which Paul uses also in Philippians 2:12 and 1 Corinthians 2:3 (cf. Eph. 6:5), most often describes the fearful attitude of people before God (cf. Exod. 15:16; Deut. 2:25; 11:25; Jdt. 15:2; Isa. 19:16; Ps. 2:11; but see Ps. 55:5; Jdt. 2:28). In that case, the Corinthians received Paul's messenger with the same fear and trembling that is due God himself. This indirectly underscores Paul's apostolic role as an ambassador of Christ through whom God makes his appeal (cf. 5:20). Moreover, Paul has already stated that the Corinthians came to their insight about their devotion to the apostle *before God* (7:13a).

7:16 / Paul concludes this section on the Corinthians' repentance by reaffirming the joy and confidence stated already at the end of the previous section (7:4). In the present section, Paul rejoices over the Corinthians and the outcome of the embassy of Titus (cf. 7:7, 9, 13). His renewed confidence in the Corinthians is especially important in view of his imminent third visit to Corinth.

Clearly, however, Paul is not as confident about the Corinthians as he seems to indicate. His repeated statements of confidence and joy do not completely obscure the fact that Paul is still very much contending for the hearts and minds of the Corinthians in the face of disaffection and lingering doubts about his apostleship, at least among a minority of the congregation (cf. 2:6). Nevertheless, Paul wants to conclude the first part of the letter on a positive note that both recognizes the progress made to date and holds out hope for the future. By ending on this positive note *(captatio benevolentiae)*, Paul is in a better situation to request the completion of the collection (2 Cor. 8–9), which will demand a financial sacrifice from the Corinthians.

Additional Notes §9

7:6 / Paul's use of relative and participial clauses to describe God is sometimes based on OT and Jewish tradition (cf., e.g., Rom. 4:17; Gal. 1:1; Col. 2:12; 1 Thess. 2:12) and sometimes not (cf., e.g., 1 Thess. 4:8; 2 Cor. 5:18; Gal. 2:20).

7:10 / Cf. *T. Gad* 5:7: "for according to God's truth, repentance *(metanoia)* destroys disobedience, puts darkness to flight, illumines the vision, furnishes knowledge for the soul, and guides the deliberative powers to salvation."

7:14 / How could Paul boast to Titus about the Corinthians before the delivery of the tearful letter, at a time when the apostle himself was in anguish over the situation in Corinth? The problem cannot be solved by assuming that there was no rebellion in Corinth at the time of Titus's dispatch (on such hypotheses, see Thrall, *Second Corinthians*, vol. 1, pp. 498–99). Before resorting to such options, we should ask what the content of Paul's boast to Titus may have been. Very probably it was general and future-thrusting. For it seems that no matter how desperate the situation in Corinth becomes, Paul still refers to the Corinthians as "the church of God," "saints," "beloved children," and the like. As he states in 1:7, his hope for the Corinthians is "firm" or "sure." Also in 1:15 and 2:3 (cf. 13:14!), Paul expresses confidence in the church (even in "all" the members!). He even states that the Corinthians reveal they are a letter authored by Christ written by the Spirit (3:3) and as such a source of his "confidence" as an apostle (v. 4).

7:15 / On the theme of obedience in Paul, see Don B. Garlington, *The Obedience of Faith* (WUNT 2/28; Tübingen: Mohr Siebeck, 1991).

7:16 / For another example of *captatio benevolentiae*, see 2 Cor. 9:2.

§10 Gift (2 Cor. 8:1–9:15)

The first part of this letter to the Corinthians (1:12–7:16) is concerned primarily with a defense of Paul's apostolic authority. The second part (chs. 8–9), which deals with the collection for the church in Jerusalem, has a related issue. When Paul went with Titus to the so-called apostolic council in Jerusalem in order to present his gospel, the other apostles not only unequivocally acknowledged his gospel, his apostolic authority, and his mission to the nations, but they also added nothing to him, except that he should "remember the poor" in Jerusalem (Gal. 2:1–10; cf. Rom. 15:26). As a result, the collection for Jerusalem became one of Paul's major objectives as an apostle over the course of the next two decades. He wanted to conclude his evangelistic work in the eastern Mediterranean area (Asia Minor, Macedonia, and Achaia) by taking a collection among the churches that he had established there and by bringing that gift to the Jerusalem "saints," as he called them. From there, Paul planned to advance the gospel in the western Mediterranean area, by way of Rome, as far as Spain (Rom. 15:19, 22–24, 28). In other words, the collection was to come at approximately the halfway point in Paul's mission to the Japhethites in Asia Minor and Europe (see Introduction). Therefore, the collection was important to Paul both because it was to be a significant milestone in his mission and because it was associated with his official recognition as an apostle at the apostolic council.

The words that Paul uses to refer to the collection—"grace, gift" (8:6, 7, 19), "service" (8:4; 9:1, 12, 13), "liberal gift" (8:20), "generous gift" (9:5)—show that it is not merely a philanthropic endeavor, but rather a profound theological program. Hence, when Paul accepts the obligation to "remember the poor" (Gal. 2:10), it fits very well with his commission as apostle to the nations, for he would be fulfilling the eschatological expectation of restoring Jerusalem's fortunes through the nations. The nations that have come to share in the Jerusalemites' restoration ("their spiritual blessings") ought also to be of service to them in material blessings (cf. Rom. 15:26–27). For Paul, the collection was part of the OT motif of the eschatological pilgrimage of Israel and the other nations to Jerusalem (cf. 2 Cor. 9:9–10, citing Isa. 55:10 and Hos. 10:12).

According to Isaiah 66:18–21, Yahweh will gather "all nations," who will come and see his glory in Zion and bring an "offering to the Lord" to the "house of the Lord" in Jerusalem. This strongly religious language prompts Paul to characterize the collection for Jerusalem in similar terms. In 2 Corinthians 8–9 he draws an implicit comparison between giving to Jerusalem and the Israelites' freewill offering for the building of the tabernacle in Exodus 25:1–9; 35:4–29; 36:3–7. Interestingly enough, the only explicit reference in Acts to the collection seems to suggest that Paul and his companions delivered the gift to the Jerusalem temple (Acts 24:17–18). Moreover, Paul was mobbed for allegedly bringing Gentiles—the very Gentiles who had helped him with the collection—into the temple (Acts 21:27–30).

Paul wanted to encourage the wealthy Corinthians to complete the collection that he had previously instructed them to begin (1 Cor. 16:1–4). During the heat of the conflict between Paul and the Corinthians the preparations for the collection had come to a standstill. One wonders whether the severe famine that afflicted all Achaia in A.D. 51 (cf. Tacitus, *Annals* 12.43.1; J. Wiseman) may have supplied a ready excuse for the Corinthians' change of heart about the collection. In any case, now that the majority of the church members had repented of their attitude toward Paul (7:9–10), and the apostle could again put "complete confidence" in them (v. 16), it seemed natural that he would refocus their attention on the collection. Hence, although many scholars conclude that 2 Corinthians 8 presupposes a different situation from that in the immediately preceding section (7:5–16), there is evidence of continuity that should not be overlooked. Especially important in this regard is the continuation of the imagery of building the tabernacle and temple from Paul's defense in 2:14–7:4 (cf. 5:1; 6:16). Paul wants the collection to be completed before his imminent third visit to Corinth, so he makes the necessary preparations to ensure that it happens.

8:1–6 / In 2 Corinthians 8:1–24 Paul calls upon the Corinthians to complete the collection. He begins his appeal by holding up the poverty-stricken Macedonians as an outstanding example of sacrificial giving to the cause (vv. 1–6). Paul hopes thereby not only to explain why he sent Titus back to Corinth in order to oversee the collection, but also to encourage the wealthy Corinthians to contribute as generously as possible.

8:1 / The direct address of the Corinthians as **brothers** marks the transition to the new subject of the collection for Jerusalem. The word *charis* runs like a leitmotif throughout 2 Corinthians 8–9, displaying a variety of senses (cf. 8:1, 4, 6, 7, 9, 16, 19; 9:8, 14, 15). Here it is used in the sense of the **grace** that God gives people so that they can abound in good works (cf. 1 Cor. 15:10; 2 Cor. 9:8). The collection was to be a work of God in the hearts of the people, just as the freewill offering for the building of the tabernacle was (see below on v. 3a). Paul refers in the text to a plurality of **Macedonian** churches. According to Acts, Paul's first foothold in Europe was Macedonia (cf. D. W. J. Gill; R. Riesner). Macedonia was the province through which the Via Egnatia ran, linking the eastern provinces of the Roman Empire with Rome itself. Two of the main cities that Paul visited, Philippi and Thessalonica, were on this strategic road, and three of Paul's letters are addressed to the churches that Paul founded in these cities. Very likely, therefore, these are the Macedonian churches to which Paul refers here.

8:2 / Paul goes on to describe the grace that God gave the Macedonians. As Paul acknowledges in 1 Thessalonians, the Macedonian church at Thessalonica had suffered severely for the cause of the gospel (cf. 1 Thess. 1:6; 2:14–15). The term that Paul uses for **trial** in 2 Corinthians 8:2 is the same one he uses elsewhere in 2 Corinthians to refer to his own physical and mental tribulations (cf. 1:8; 2:4; 4:17; 6:4; 7:4; 8:13). In the case of the Macedonians, the trials may have included financial reversal, for Paul says that they gave out of their **extreme poverty.** Indeed, elsewhere Paul stresses the persecution suffered by particular groups of Macedonians (cf. 1 Thess. 1:6; 2:14; 3:3–4; Phil. 1:29–30). Perhaps, however, the text refers to the lot of the Macedonians as a whole, for first-century Jews were still very much aware that the Macedonians—former masters of the inhabited world—had been subjugated to the Romans, with all that that entailed (cf. Philo, *On the Life of Joseph* 134–136; *That God is Unchangeable* 173; Josephus, *War* 2.360, 365, 387; *Ant.* 15.385–387; *Sib. Or.* 3:161, 172, 188–190, 610; 1 Macc. 8:10). Hence, Paul may be thinking in terms of world empire when he refers to the Macedonians in general. Ultimately, however, we do not know the cause of the Macedonian poverty to which Paul refers.

Despite their abject poverty, the Macedonians gave to the collection **in rich generosity.** The churches of Macedonia were well known for their generosity, as the church at Philippi illustrates (cf. Phil. 4:10–19). Romans 15:26 also notes that "Macedonia" was pleased to make a contribution to the poor in Jerusalem.

8:3a / Paul elaborates on the Macedonians' sacrificial giving. Since the Macedonian churches were in all likelihood much poorer than the church at Corinth, their sacrificial giving would have been a powerful example to the Corinthians. The Macedonians gave **beyond their ability.** According to Exodus 25:1–9, the Lord told Moses to instruct the Israelites to take for him for a freewill offering for making the tabernacle and its equipment. According to Exodus 35:4–29, these instructions for a collection were met with an overwhelming response by the people. The people were bringing much more than enough to do the work (Exod. 36:5), so much so that Moses had to issue a restraining order (vv. 6–7). In fact, Josephus (*Ant.* 3.104) records that each person was ambitious to contribute "even beyond [his] ability," vying to outdo everyone else (cf. also *Ant.* 3.107). This is the kind of friendly rivalry that Paul hopes to stimulate among the Corinthians and that the Macedonians had already taken up as a challenge.

8:3b–4 / The description of the Macedonians' sacrificial giving continues. Just as Exodus 25:2 and 35:5 emphasize that the collection for the tabernacle was to be given freely and from the heart, Paul emphasizes that the Macedonians' contribution was **entirely on their own** (lit., "of their own free will") and from the heart. This is important for Paul to point out, because he has evidently been accused of lording over the congregation in Corinth (cf. 2 Cor. 1:24). The Macedonians' participation was so voluntary that they actually **pleaded** with Paul for the opportunity to contribute, as if Paul did not initiate the idea (but cf. v. 17) and was somehow unwilling to allow them to participate. The text makes it clear that the Macedonians begged Paul **urgently** (lit., "with much entreaty"), as if it took sustained pressure for them to convince Paul that they should participate. Perhaps this implies again that the Macedonians were extremely impoverished and could not really give without depriving themselves. Verse 5 makes it clear, however, that Paul did expect some contribution from the Macedonians, however small. Paul's reluctance can perhaps be compared to that of Moses, who had to hold the Israelites back from giving too much (cf. Exod. 36:5–7).

The collection is described as **service** *(diakonia)* to the saints of Jerusalem (cf. also 9:1, 12, 13). Paul has already used the term "ministry" *(diakonia)* several times of himself: He has the ministry of the Spirit (3:8) and the ministry of reconciliation (5:18). Now he reveals that he has the ministry of the collection for Jerusalem. The Macedonians pleaded with Paul for the **privilege of sharing** with him in this ministry. In Romans 12:13 Paul exhorts his Roman addressees to "share in the needs of the saints," probably referring again to the contribution for Jerusalem (cf. Rom. 15:26). The apostle exhorts the Romans to pray that "my service to Jerusalem may be acceptable to the saints" (Rom. 15:31).

It is interesting to note that the Jerusalemites are not mentioned by name in 2 Corinthians 8. Paul expects that his addressees would know that the collection is for the Jerusalemites, even though the term **saints** elsewhere refers to believers as a whole (e.g., 1 Cor. 6:1–2; Rom. 8:27; 12:13; 15:25). In 1 Corinthians 6:2 the term includes the Corinthians and clearly alludes to the "saints of the Most High" in Daniel 7:18, 21, 22, 25, 27. When Paul first announced to the Corinthians the collection for Jerusalem, he called it "the collection for the saints," which he would take to Jerusalem (1 Cor. 16:1–4).

8:5 / Paul's description of the Macedonians' sacrificial giving continues. The Macedonians far exceeded the response that Paul had hoped from them. They not only donated money (and things), but **they gave themselves.** In this self-sacrificial giving, the Macedonians' motivation and priorities were clear: **first to the Lord** and then to the Lord's apostle (**and then to us**). Thus the Macedonians acknowledged not only that the collection was of the Lord, but also that Paul had an ambassadorial role (cf. 2 Cor. 5:20) in administrating it. Throughout 2 Corinthians to this point Paul is seen to have a mediatorial role. The Macedonians were submitting to Paul in response to their obedience to the Lord. As if to underscore this point, the apostle states that the Macedonians gave **in keeping with God's will** (lit., "by the will of God"). Like the freewill offering for the tabernacle, the collection was seen as a project commanded by God. It is no coincidence that in both canonical letters to the Corinthians Paul emphasizes that he is an "apostle by the will of God" (1 Cor. 1:1; 2 Cor. 1:1). Indeed, as we have seen, there is a connection between the official recognition of Paul's God-given apostleship and the collection (cf. Gal. 2:9–10).

8:6 / The apostle uses the Macedonians' exemplary attitude and behavior toward the collection in order to spur on the Corinthians' participation in the campaign. **Titus** is the one who had recently carried the tearful letter to Corinth and had brought back news to Paul of the Corinthians' repentance. Now the same Titus was to be sent back from Macedonia to Corinth, in order to deliver the second canonical letter and to oversee the **completion** of the collection before Paul arrives.

8:7–15 / After giving this brief historical background, explaining why he sent Titus back to Corinth to oversee the collection after seeing the example of the Macedonians (8:1–6), Paul directly exhorts the Corinthians to complete the collection they had begun under Titus during the previous year (8:7–15).

8:7 / Paul exhorts the Corinthians to exceed in the matter of giving just as they have in other areas. The implication is that the Corinthians **excel** the Macedonians in many ways. In 1 Corinthians Paul had emphasized the richness of the Corinthians "in all things" in Christ, including all speech and knowledge (1:5). Here he adds several more items to that list, including **earnestness** and reconfirmed **love** for Paul (cf. 7:7, 11, 12). Of course, the rich possession of spiritual gifts had also led the Corinthians to a realized eschatology that evidently elevated such riches, including material wealth, in a presumptuous and self-contented way (cf. 1 Cor. 4:8–13). Perhaps it was difficult, therefore, for the Corinthians to donate to a cause with such future goals as the collection for Jerusalem. In any case, Paul exhorts the Corinthians to **also excel** in the **grace** of giving to the collection for Jerusalem. Everything that the Corinthians have is a gracious gift from God; therefore, they should give commensurately, particularly now in the matter of the collection.

8:8 / Paul clarifies the nature of his exhortation to the Corinthians by stating that he wants them to respond to the collection for Jerusalem in the same way that the Macedonians did—voluntarily and from the heart. Only in this way would their gift be an expression of grace. Hence, Paul is not simply **commanding** them (although he has the authority to do that); he appeals to them by means of the example of others like the Macedonians, hoping to create a friendly rivalry between brothers (see above on vv. 1 and 3a). The Corinthians are thereby given an opportunity to prove the genuineness of their **love** for the apostle (cf. v. 7). Love, in this case, is not primarily an emotion, but rather solidarity that comes to expression in tangible deeds.

8:9 / Paul supplies the christological reason (**For,** *gar*) the Corinthians should excel in the grace of giving to the collection for Jerusalem. The illustration turns on the word **grace** *(charis),* in the sense of self-sacrificial giving. The Corinthians are to abound in the **grace** of self-sacrificial giving to the Jerusalem saints, because **Christ** gave himself. As often elsewhere, Paul's admonition is based on the example of Christ (e.g., Phil. 2:5–11; 1 Cor. 11:1; 1 Thess. 1:6). Like the Macedonians who gave themselves (2 Cor. 8:5), Christ gave himself for the sake of others. Thus the Corinthians have both the Macedonians and Christ as examples of self-sacrificial giving.

Yet what does it mean that Christ **became poor?** Does it mean simply that he became a human being? That might be the meaning if we compare Philippians 2:5–11. More to the point is Galatians 3:13–14: "Christ redeemed us from the curse of the law by becoming a curse for us, . . . so that we might receive the promise of the Spirit through faith." On the analogy of this text, that Christ "became poor" means that he came under the curse of the law on behalf of others so that, through his sacrifice, others might know the riches of the Spirit.

8:10–11 / Paul goes from making an appeal to giving an opinion. As in 1 Corinthians 7:12, the apostle provides his **advice** to help the Corinthians in their practice of godly living. The Corinthians had already begun the collection a year earlier. In the meantime, the weekly collection for Jerusalem as directed in 1 Corinthians 16:2 had apparently come to a halt. Now that at least partial reconciliation had taken place between the Corinthians and their founding apostle, they should, in Paul's opinion, **finish the work,** that is, complete the collection. This advice is in the Corinthians' best interest, for the collection is the will of God (cf. 2 Cor. 8:5).

The apostle considers the **willingness** to give to be more important than the actual accomplishment of giving itself. Against the background of the freewill offering for the building of the tabernacle (see above on v. 3a), the reason for this seems clear: The attitude of the heart and the willingness of the spirit are the crucial factors in proper giving (cf. Exod. 35:21). The Corinthians have the same fervent willingness as the ancient Israelites had (cf. Josephus, *Ant.* 3.106). Hence, the Corinthians had already begun to take the collection with the proper motivation of the heart; now they are encouraged to carry through their original intention.

Paul stipulates that the Corinthians should complete the task **according to your means** (lit., "out of what you have"). Seen in light of the freewill offering for building the tabernacle, Paul's phrase suggests not so much that the Corinthians should follow the example of the Macedonians by giving beyond their means (cf. 2 Cor. 8:3a; Sir. 14:11), but rather that they should give according to what they happen to have on hand in their possessions, as did the Israelites in Exodus 35:23–24. In other words, the Corinthians are encouraged to offer gifts in kind, which could include a variety of commodities and not necessarily just money (see above on 2 Cor. 8:2; cf. Ezra 7:22). On the analogy of Ezra's mission, however, we might expect that the offering consisted mainly of silver and gold (cf. Ezra 7:15–16; 8:25–30, 33–34; *Sib. Or.* 3:290–294).

8:12 / The explanation (**For**, *gar*) of Paul's advice is that what counts is not the kind of offering but the heart of the offerer (**the willingness**). Giving sacrificially of one's substance, no matter what it may be, makes the offering acceptable to God (cf. Mark 12:41–44).

8:13 / Paul clarifies (*gar*, NIV untranslated) his position on the Corinthians' giving to the Jerusalemites. The point is not that the Jerusalemites (**others**) will be relieved of their poverty while the Corinthians are afflicted. Rather, from Paul's perspective, Jerusalem, which has suffered impoverishment at the hands of the nations (Isa. 42:22; 55:1), requires the promised influx of tribute from the nations in order to complete the restoration of Israel (cf. Isa. 45:22; 53:12; 60:3–16; 61:6–7; 66:12). Only then will there be what Paul here calls **equality**, that is, between Israel and the nations. Just as Israel shares in the wealth of the nations, so also the nations share in the restoration of Israel (cf. Isa. 2:2–5; 11:10; 25:6–10).

8:14 / Paul elaborates on this notion of equality. He is not so much concerned here that the Corinthians' physical needs will be covered in the future if they give toward the needs of the Jerusalemites now. Rather, the issue seems to be more related to the fact that the Corinthians, as part of the nations to which Paul directs his mission, participate in the restoration of Israel both in the **present** and in the future. According to Romans 15:27, "if the nations have come to share in their [sc. the Jerusalem saints'] spiritual blessings, they ought also to be of service to them in material things." This is the present aspect of equality. Ultimately, the salvation of "all Israel," when the full number of the nations comes in, will usher in the consummation **(their plenty)**, including the coming of the Deliverer from Zion (Rom. 11:25–26) and the resurrection of the dead (Rom. 11:15). This is the future aspect. The Corinthians' need for the resurrection is made clear in 1 Corinthians 15:12–19.

8:15 / An illustration of Paul's point about equality is drawn from a citation of Exodus 16:18, in the story of the feeding of the wilderness generation by means of manna. Paul's concentration on the wilderness generation continues here (see above on 8:3a). It is interesting to see that his argument to the Corinthians consists largely of an allusion to two stories from Exodus about the collecting activity of the wilderness generation: the collection for building the tabernacle (Exod. 25:1–9; 35:9–29; 36:2–7) and the daily collection of manna (Exod. 16:1–30). Each person received from God the manna he or she needed for daily subsistence—not more and not less.

8:16–24 / Having exhorted the Corinthians to complete the collection that they had begun (8:7–15), Paul recommends the emissaries he will send to take it to Jerusalem (8:16–24; cf. 1 Cor. 16:3–4, where Paul's original plan was different). In doing so, Paul takes up where he left off in verse 6, with the sending of Titus. Paul wants to send Titus back to Corinth with two companions in order to bring the collection to a fitting conclusion. Paul did not need letters of recommendation to or from the Corinthians (cf. 2 Cor. 3:1), but his coworkers did. Paul is concerned to protect against any appearance of evil in the delivery of the collection. Hence, the present section prepares the way for Paul's emissaries to be well received in Corinth. Paul did not write the present passage after he had already sent the three emissaries; rather, he probably sent the letter along with the delegation to Corinth. The past tense verbs in verses 17, 18, and 22 are to be understood from the perspective of the recipients (so-called epistolary aorists).

8:16–17 / Paul begins this section by highlighting **Titus,** whom Paul has asked to supervise the collection in Corinth. Titus is said to have the **heart** for the Corinthians as Paul does. The **heart** is the same criterion for Paul's apostolic authenticity as was emphasized in 5:12. The transformed heart is a hallmark of Paul's ministry of the Spirit. There is a concept here of mutual devotion: Just as the Corinthians have zeal for Paul (cf. 7:11–12; 8:7), so also Paul and his coworker Titus have zeal (translated here **concern**) for the Corinthians.

Paul made an **appeal** to Titus to return to Corinth for the collection, just as he evidently appealed to the Macedonians to contribute to the collection. By the same token, just as the Macedonians gave to the collection from their own free will (8:3), so also Titus is returning to Corinth **on his own initiative** (lit., "from his own free will").

8:18–22 / Having reinforced his selection of Titus as the leading person in the delegation to Corinth (vv. 16–17), Paul now turns to the second (vv. 18–21) and third (v. 22) members of the delegation to Corinth, both of whom remain anonymous. Perhaps their names were to be introduced by Titus when he arrived in Corinth. In any case, their official function is similar to that of the twelve priests whom Ezra entrusted with the safe and honorable transport of the freewill offering from Babylonia to the Jerusalem temple (cf. Ezra 8:24–30).

8:18 / Paul describes the second emissary. The first verb (**we are sending**) is an epistolary aorist, that is, a verb whose action will be past by the time the addressees receive the letter. The companion of Titus is a missionary **(brother)** who enjoyed a good reputation in all the churches for his service in the gospel.

8:19 / The second member of the team is one who was **chosen by the churches** to aid Paul in carrying out the collection. Paul sees the collection in a theological context. He personally commits himself to **honor** the Lord (lit., "for the glory of the

Lord"). According to Isaiah 66:18–21, a pivotal passage for understanding Paul's mission to the nations, those who organize the ingathering of the nations to Zion and the offering of the nations for the Lord, declare the "glory" of the Lord among the nations (v. 19).

8:20–21 / Paul handles a possible misinterpretation of the collection. Paul has already been accused of embezzlement (cf. 12:16ff.), a charge that he addresses in a preliminary way in 2:17. In order to prevent any **criticism** about his handling of this gift, Paul avoids making the delivery himself. Instead, he has commissioned representatives of the participating churches to deliver the collection. The analogy to Ezra's procedure is obvious (Ezra 8:24–30).

The collection is referred to as a **liberal gift**, literally "abundance." This is certainly an apt description of the collection if Paul has in mind the freewill offering for building the tabernacle in Exodus.

8:22 / Paul follows with a description of the third member of the delegation. Like Paul and Titus, this man **(our brother)** is also **zealous** (cf. 8:16, 17). Paul recommends the third man as someone whom he knows well and who has proved himself to the apostle through repeated experience.

8:23 / Paul summarizes his recommendation of the three emissaries to Corinth. Titus has been a companion of Paul at least since the apostolic council (Gal. 2:1). He had helped Paul in the conflict with the Corinthians. The two brothers are **representatives of the churches** (lit., "apostles of the churches" [cf. Phil. 2:25, where Epaphroditus is described as "your apostle and a minister to my need"]). This use of the term *apostolos* can be compared to the Jewish use of the term of one who is commissioned for a particular mission. Both of these representatives are described as a "glory" (here translated **honor**) to Christ. The impression given by verse 23 is that the two brothers had been appointed by the churches to assist Paul in the collection. At Paul's insistence, they were there to ensure that Paul would not falsely be accused of embezzlement (vv. 20–21).

8:24 / Paul draws his recommendation of the three emissaries to a conclusion (**Therefore**, *oun*), emphasizing the Corinthians' responsibility in view of all the churches. Paul boasted to the Macedonian churches about the Corinthians (7:14; 9:3) and presumably to others as well (cf. 7:4). For this reason, the Corinthians should receive Paul's emissaries in **love** and support them. In this way, the Corinthians preserve the brotherly fellowship in the love of Christ and, at the same time, they substantiate Paul's boast about them to the other **churches.** If the Corinthians fail to cooperate, then Paul will lose face.

9:1–15 / Having exhorted the Corinthians to complete the collection (8:1–24), Paul now generalizes his remarks about the collection to apply to Achaia as a whole but still including the Corinthians. This makes sense insofar as 2 Corinthians was obviously designed as a circular letter, addressed "to the church of God in Corinth, together with all the saints throughout Achaia" (1:1). While most of the letter has focused on Paul's relationship with the Corinthians in particular, Paul broadens his scope to include also the recipients of the letter in the rest of the Roman province. The presence of chapter 9 in 2 Corinthians may well explain why Paul addressed the letter more generally in the first place. The collection to be taken when he comes for the third time to Corinth would include not just the capital of Achaia but the province as a whole.

9:1–5 / The apostle now turns to Achaia as a whole and recommends the brothers mentioned in 8:18, 22–23.

9:1 / Paul wants to give a warrant and explanation for his exhortation to accept the three delegates who are coming to Corinth and to be ready to make the contribution to the saints. The NIV unfortunately leaves untranslated the word "for" *(gar),* which links 9:1 to 8:24. As in 1 Thessalonians 4:9 and 5:1, Paul tells his addressees that they do not really need his exhortations on a particular topic and then he goes on to remind, reinforce, and clarify what they already know. The apostle has already mentioned the **service to the saints** (8:4).

9:2 / The reason that Paul does not need to write to the Corinthians about the collection is given in verse 2. Paul does not need to exhort the Corinthians about the collection because he already knows their **eagerness** to participate from a year earlier (cf. 8:10–11). This time, however, he includes **Achaia** among those who were eager to contribute. Corinth was the chief city (and capital) of Achaia. Taken together, therefore, verses 1 and 2 express Paul's confidence in the willingness of the Corinthians to contribute.

Paul states that his **boasting** about the Achaian's eagerness to contribute to the collection has encouraged the Macedonians to contribute all the more. In this way, Paul hopes to provide another reason that the Achaians (including the Corinthians) should finish their own collection. The logic, however, is somewhat circular: the Corinthians should give because the poor Macedonians are giving so enthusiastically (8:1–5); yet the Macedonians are giving because the Achaians (Corinthians) are giving so enthusiastically (9:2). Therefore, the Corinthians should give both because of the example of the Macedonians to them and because of their example to the Macedonians. In reality, Achaia has not been **ready** since the previous year, as the Corinthian church dramatically illustrates. Therefore, Paul's boast to the Macedonians about the Achaians seems to stretch the truth. The weak link in Paul's logic and boasting is, of course, the Corinthian church, since eagerness of that church had flagged during the recent conflict, and the collection had certainly not been completed. The whole point of 2 Corinthians 8 is that the Corinthians should now complete the collection and accept the envoys who will deliver it to its destination.

The zeal of the Achaians (Corinthians) is said to have **stirred** most of the Macedonians to action. The verb suggests that the Macedonians were encouraged to emulate the example of the Achaians (cf. above on 8:3a).

9:3 / Very likely realizing that his boasting to the Macedonians about the Achaians stretched the truth, Paul wants to ensure that the Achaians (including the Corinthians) are ready as he has boasted they would be. The simplest hypothesis is that **the brothers** to whom Paul refers here are none other than the ones he has already mentioned in 8:18, 22–23. In both cases, **the brothers** are being sent by Paul to Corinth and Achaia in order to oversee the collection before he arrives. Paul's word is on the line, and he wants to present himself as a man of sincerity and integrity (cf. 2:17). The apostle has already acknowledged that the Corinthians are ready to give (cf. 8:11); now they need to be **ready** with the actual offering.

9:4 / Paul's goal in sending the advance party to Achaia is that neither he nor the Corinthians will suffer embarrassment. When Paul comes to Achaia on his way to Corinth for the third time, he evidently plans to be accompanied by **Macedonians**, i.e., further representatives from the Macedonian churches (cf.

Acts 17:14–15; 20:4). Paul would be put to shame if these Macedonians were to discover that the apostle's boasts about the Achaians and Corinthians were unfounded. In that case, Paul's apostleship would be further discredited, not only in the eyes of the Corinthians and the Macedonians, but eventually even before the Jerusalemites. The whole collection enterprise threatens to unravel if the Corinthians do not cooperate.

Just as Paul boasted to Titus about the Corinthians before sending him to Corinth with the tearful letter, and Paul was not embarrassed by the Corinthians at the outcome (7:14), so also now Paul is hoping that the boasting that he had made to the Macedonians about the Achaians will turn out well.

9:5 / The section (vv. 1–5) concludes with an explanation of why Paul is sending the brothers to Achaia before his own coming. Paul wants the Achaians' gift to come from the heart in advance of his third visit to Corinth, not to be wrung out of them after he arrives. The Achaians' contribution to the collection is to be a **generous gift** and not "stinginess." Again, the freewill offering for the building of the tabernacle in Exodus provides a good model of such giving. The Achaians were capable of a substantial gift, so Paul does not hesitate to take steps to ensure that it is collected.

9:6–15 / In this section, Paul speaks of the blessing that results from cheerful giving as another reason for the Corinthians to participate in the collection.

9:6 / The argument begins in verse 6 with the concept of metaphorically reaping what is sown, which is part of the common stock of OT and Jewish wisdom tradition (cf. Prov. 22:8; Job 4:8; Sir. 7:3; Philo, *On the Confusion of Tongues* 21, 152; *On the Change of Names* 268–269; *On Dreams* 2.76; *On the Embassy to Gaius* 293). The prophetic tradition challenges the direct relationship between reaping and sowing by announcing that there can be an inverse relationship: those who sow wheat can reap thorns (Jer. 12:13), and those who sow in tears can reap with shouts of joy (Ps. 125:5). Paul partakes of the wisdom tradition when he states in Galatians 6:7–8: "A man reaps what he sows. The one who sows to please his sinful nature, from that nature will reap destruction; the one who sows to please the spirit, from the Spirit will reap eternal life." Likewise in the present context, Paul applies the wisdom principle to the matter of giving generously to the collection for Jerusalem (cf. Prov. 11:24).

9:7 / With this principle in mind, Paul exhorts the Achaians to give. Paul does not want to imply that the wisdom tradition that he uses in verse 6 reflects a merely mechanical process of sowing and reaping. He wants to emphasize that the wisdom tradition itself regards giving as a matter of the **heart**, and only cheerful giving is acceptable (cf. Sir. 35:8–9). As we have seen, the freewill offering for building the tabernacle is a prime example of giving that one decides in the **heart** (cf. Exod. 25:2; 35:5, 21, 22, 26, 29). Likewise, 1 Chronicles 29:16–22 speaks of a freewill offering for the temple that is given freely and joyously. Someone who gives grudgingly cannot expect a blessing from God in accordance with the wisdom principle. To establish this point, Paul gives a modified citation of Proverbs 22:8 LXX: "God blesses a **cheerful** and generous man." In the previous line, this same proverb states that "he who sows wickedness shall reap evils."

9:8 / Paul relieves the Achaians' anxiety about giving liberally by pointing to God and his resources. God so meets needs according to his abundant riches (cf. Phil. 4:19)—note the repeated use of the world "all"—that the recipients have enough left over to help others. Paul is further developing a theme that he started in 8:15 (citing Exod. 16:18), i.e., that everyone should have no more and no less than is required. The term that Paul uses here is **all that you need** (lit., "sufficiency"). This is by no means a purely Stoic concept. According to *Pss. Sol.* 5:16–17 (cf. Prov. 30:8; 16:8), "Happy is (the person) whom God remembers with a moderation of sufficiency, for if one is excessively rich, he sins. Moderate (wealth) is adequate—with righteousness; for with this comes the Lord's blessing: to be (more than) satisfied with righteousness" *(OTP)*. According to this principle of moderation, the wealthy Corinthians might be in danger of overstepping the bounds of what is rightfully theirs to keep if they did not give generously to the collection.

9:9–10 / Paul substantiates his statement in verse 8 by means of two OT citations, while maintaining the imagery of sowing and reaping (v. 6). In verse 9, he substantiates his point by means of a citation from Psalm 111:9 LXX: "As it is written: 'He has scattered abroad his gifts to the poor; his righteousness endures forever.'" A wisdom psalm that contrasts the fate of the righteous and the wicked, Psalm 112 emphasizes particularly the rewards of the righteous (vv. 1–9). The Psalm links the divine provision of riches (v. 3) with the righteous person's responsibility to give to the poor (v. 4). Paul has already shown that there are really only two different kinds of people—the righteous and the wicked (cf. 6:14–16). Therefore, from a scriptural perspective, the works corresponding to righteousness clearly include giving to the poor.

In verse 10, Paul substantiates the other point that he makes in verse 8—that God is able to make all grace abound to the Achaians, so that they can in turn give. Here, again, the apostle uses an OT citation. Although there is no introductory formula to mark the citation as such, it is possible to tell from the distinctive style of the statement that Paul is citing Isaiah 55:10 (cf. D.-A. Koch). Isaiah 55:1–13 is a hymn of joy and triumph that celebrates the approaching consummation of Israel's restoration. God's promise about Israel's restoration will be fulfilled as surely as the rain from heaven that falls upon the earth causes germination and ultimately provides seed to the sower and bread to the eater (vv. 10–11). More than any other statement in 2 Corinthians 8–9, this citation of Isaiah 55:10 shows that Paul's concept of the collection is determined by the OT expectation of Israel's restoration and the eschatological pilgrimage of the nations. Isaiah 55 offers the impoverished Israelites the hope of restored fortunes (vv. 1–2) and expects that the nations will come to the glorified Israel (vv. 4–5). Therefore, when Paul substantiates his claim that God is able to make all grace abound to the Achaians on the basis of Isaiah 55:10, he in effect sees them as involved in fulfilling the promise to restore Israel's fortunes (see above on 2 Cor. 8:14).

The text also alludes to Hosea 10:12 LXX: "Sow for yourselves in righteousness, . . . seek the Lord until the fruits of righteousness come to you." Here, again, the restoration of Israel is in view. Paul evidently interprets the "fruits of righteousness" as the Achaians' wholehearted participation in the collection for Jerusalem, which contributes toward Israel's restoration.

9:11 / Paul goes on to restate his assertion in verse 8 (cf. the similar redundant use of the word "all") that God's grace to the Corinthians should issue in a generous gift to Jerusalem. However, Paul goes beyond what he has previously said by emphasizing that the Achaians' gift will effect **thanksgiving** to

God (the goal of Paul's entire missionary endeavor, cf. 4:15). Indeed, the doxological purpose of history is realized in the eschatological praise of God by all nations in Zion (cf. Rom. 15:9–11).

This thanksgiving to God is the result of a partnership and mutuality between Paul and the Corinthians, which the apostle had stressed repeatedly in the earlier chapters of the letter (cf. 1:1–2, 3–11, 14, 24; 2:2; 3:18; 6:11–13; 7:2; 8:16–17). Moreover, we observe here that Paul's mediatorial role **(through us)** extends even to the doxological outcome of the collection.

9:12–15 / Paul elaborates on the theme of "thanksgiving" in verse 11 and appropriately concludes with a thanksgiving of his own. In verse 12, Paul goes back to the principle established in 8:14–15, that the Corinthians should supply the **needs** of the Jerusalemites (cf. 8:4).

In verse 13, Paul anticipates the **praise** to God that will issue from the Jerusalemites who receive the collection. According to Acts, when Paul arrived in Jerusalem (with the collection), he declared to the leaders of the Jerusalem church what God had done among the nations through his "ministry" or **service**, a word that Paul himself uses of the collection (Acts 21:19; cf. 2 Cor. 8:4; 9:1, 12, 13; Rom. 15:31). Then, Luke states, "Those who heard it praised God" (Acts 21:20).

As verse 14 goes on to state, the Jerusalem saints are bound together with the Achaians. The **grace** of God recalls the beginning of Paul's discussion of the collection, where he refers to "the grace of God given to the Macedonian churches" (8:1), thus providing closure for these two chapters. Ultimately, God is the one responsible for the tremendous outpouring of love and wealth for Jerusalem, and so the praise belongs to him. The Jerusalemites, for their part, reciprocate the love that is shown to them. Thus the gift of God produces a gift for Jerusalem, which, in turn, binds together in love the church that is formed of both Jews and Gentiles.

Finally, in verse 15, Paul concludes his discussion of the collection and its doxological purpose with a doxology: "Thanks be to God for his indescribable gift!" The **gift** of God is the gift that sets all the others in motion. Here Paul is probably alluding to Christ (cf. 8:9), the supreme example of self-sacrificial giving, to motivate the Corinthians to give generously.

Additional Notes §10

8:1–9:15 / If the collection had simply been a matter of relief for an acute situation (cf. Acts 11:27–30), Paul would not have taken so many years to complete the collection. Numerous texts show that the expectation of Isa. 66:20, that the nations would bring gifts to Jerusalem in connection with the restoration of Israel, was kept alive in the Second Temple period (cf. 4QDibHam frag. 1–2 iv 4–12; *Pss. Sol.* 17:31; Tob. 13:1–17; *Sib. Or.* 3:772–775; *Hekhalot Rabbati* [Schäfer, §144]; *Song Rab.* 4:19 [citing Isa. 66:20]).

According to Isa. 61:1–2, another text on the restoration mission to Zion, which Jesus incidently applies to himself (cf. Luke 7:22//Matt. 11:5) and which a Qumran text apparently interprets messianically (11QMelch), the Spirit-endowed anointed one is sent to bring the good news to the oppressed "poor" that the Lord is bringing liberation to the exiles (cf. also 4Q521). The Qumran community is called "the congregation of the poor (*ʾebyônîm*)" (4QpPs37 3.10; cf. also 1QpHab 12.3; 1QH 5.22; 4Q434, 436), and an early Christian sect of observant Jews called the Ebionites (from the Hebrew *ʾebyônîm*, "the poor") continued to use the appellation of themselves well into the third century.

Paul's collection for Jerusalem also echoes Ezra's freewill offering for the second temple (Ezra 7:1–8:34), an offering to be donated not only by the Jews themselves but also King Artaxerxes, his counselors, and the whole province of Babylonia (Ezra 7:15–23). Ezra entrusted the enormous offering to twelve of the leading priests for safe transport back to the Temple (Ezra 8:24–30), and apparently had nothing to do with the offering en route, perhaps in order to avoid even the appearance of evil.

On Paul's collection for Jerusalem, see Jouette M. Bassler, "Perspectives from Paul, 1: Money and Mission, 2: The Great Collection," in *God and Mammon: Asking for Money in the New Testament* (Nashville: Abingdon, 1991), pp. 63–115; Dieter Georgi, *Remembering the Poor: The History of Paul's Collection for Jerusalem* (Nashville: Abingdon, 1992); S. McKnight, "Collection for the Saints," *DPL*, pp. 143–47.

Corinth had the reputation of being very wealthy because of its location at the great crossroads of the ancient world (cf. Strabo, *Geography* 8.6.20) and its importance as a commercial and financial center. The most common adjective applied to Corinth was "wealthy" (cf., e.g., Strabo, *Geography* 8.6.20–23; Dio Chrysostom, *Orations* 37.36); even the former Greek city was commonly referred to as "wealthy Corinth" (cf., e.g., Homer, *Iliad* 2.570; Pindar, *Eulogies* 122; Aelius Aristides, *Orations* 46.22; J. B. Salmon, *Wealthy Corinth: A History of the City to 338 B.C.* [Oxford: Oxford University Press, 1984]; Jerome Murphy-O'Connor, *St. Paul's Corinth: Texts and Archaeology* [Good News Studies 6; Wilmington, Del.: Glazier, 1983]).

Cf. Stanley K. Stowers, "*Peri men gar* and the Integrity of 2 Corinthians 8 and 9," *NovT* 32 (1990), pp. 340–48.

On Isa. 66:18–21 as foundational to Paul's missionary strategy, see James M. Scott, *Paul and the Nations: The Old Testament and Jewish Background of Paul's Mission to the Nations with Special Reference to the Destination of Galatians* (WUNT 84; Tübingen: Mohr Siebeck, 1995). On the eschatological pilgrimage of the nations to Zion, see further Isa. 2:2–4; 55:5; 56:6–8; 60:5–7; Mic. 4:2; *Pss. Sol.* 17:30–35; *T. Zeb.* 9:8; *T. Ben.* 9:2; *2 Bar.* 68:5; and particularly, 4QDibHam 4.4–12.

It seems possible that 2 Cor. 8–9 also has in mind Ps. 72, a prayer for God's blessing on the Davidic king. The psalm makes reference to the "poor" of his people, whom the king will deliver during his universal reign (vv. 2, 4, 12). Cf. *Sib. Or.* 5:414–419; *Apoc. Ab.* 31:6–10; *2 Bar.* 72:2–6.

Cf. S. Talmon, "The Concepts of *Mashîah* and Messianism in Early Judaism," in *The Messiah: Developments in Earliest Judaism and Christianity* (ed. James H. Charlesworth; Minneapolis: Fortress, 1992), pp. 79–115 (esp. pp. 107–8).

Cf. James Wiseman, "Corinth and Rome I: 228 B.C.–A.D. 267," *ANRW* 17.1, p. 505. Wiseman notes there is some evidence that other famines may also have affected Corinth during the reign of Claudius (cf. Seutonius, *Claudius* 18.2).

8:1 / For a similar use of the direct address of the Corinthians as **brothers** in order to mark the transition to a new subject see 2 Cor. 1:8; 13:11.

On Macedonia, see David W. J. Gill, "Macedonia," in *The Book of Acts in Its First Century Setting, Vol. 2: The Book of Acts in Its Graeco-Roman Setting* (ed. David W. J. Gill and Conrad Gempf; Grand Rapids: Eerdmans, 1994), pp. 397–417; Rainer Riesner, *Die Frühzeit des Apostels Paulus. Studien zur Chronologie, Missionsstrategie und Theologie* (WUNT 71; Tübingen: Mohr Siebeck, 1994).

8:2 / In A.D. 51, a severe famine was felt throughout Greece. Perhaps it affected Macedonia as well.

8:3a / The expression **beyond ability** *(para dynamin)* is used elsewhere of levying tribute that was beyond the people's ability to pay (Josephus, *War* 1.219) and of contributing to the repair of a war-torn city (*Ant.* 14.378).

8:9 / According to texts like Deut. 28:15–68 and 29:20–29, **poverty** would be one of the curses that would come upon the people if they forsook the covenant. Hence, Isaiah 40–66 uses the notion of the "oppressed poor" as a technical term to refer to the sufferings of the exiles in Babylon. The entire nation has endured divine judgment, and, through its captivity in Babylon, Israel as a whole has become "poor."

8:13 / Paul's use of the term **equality** might lead us to think of a community of goods. Josephus, for example, knows that the Essenes had community of goods, so that there was equality among them (*War* 2.122). According to the book of Acts, the earliest church in Jerusalem practiced a similar community of goods (cf. Acts 2:44–45; 4:32–5:11).

8:15 / On the citation of Exod. 16:18 here, see Dietrich-Alex Koch, *Die Schrift als Zeuge des Evangeliums Untersuchungen zur Verwendung und zum Verständnis der Schrift bei Paulus* (BHT 69; Tübingen: Mohr Siebeck, 1986), pp. 258–60; Hays, *Echoes of Scripture*, pp. 88–91.

On the Jewish expectation of a second, eschatological miracle of manna, see *2 Bar.* 29:8; *Qoh. Rabbah* 1:9; *Sib. Or.* fr. 3:46–49; Rev. 2:17. Paul's point here could be that the Corinthians are participants in these eschatological events.

8:16 / C. F. D. Moule describes the "epistolary aorist" as an "idiom . . . whereby the writer courteously projects himself in imagination into the position of the reader, for whom actions contemporaneous with the time of writing will be past" (*An Idiom-Book of New Testament Greek* [Cambridge: Cambridge University Press, 1968], p. 12). Whether or not Paul uses the epistolary aorist in 2 Cor. 8, 9 and 12 depends on whether one views the letter as an original unity or as a composite of several letter fragments. Cf. K. L. McKay, "Observations on the Epistolary Aorist in 2 Corinthians," *NovT* 37 (1995), pp. 154–58.

8:20–21 / We may note that the temple tax was often delivered to Jerusalem in the company of multiple representatives of the sending Diaspora communities, although more for the purpose of protection and security than for preventing embezzlement.

8:23 / On the use of **representatives** (*apostolos, šālîaḥ*) for emissaries of the Jewish leadership, see C. Spicq, *TLNT*, vol. 1, pp. 186–94; P. W. Barnett, "Apostle," *DPL*, pp. 45–51.

9:1 / Literary-critical questions abound in 2 Cor. 8–9. In particular, ch. 9 is often taken as a document independent from ch. 8 (and from the rest of 2 Cor. for that matter). Cf. Hans Dieter Betz, *2 Corinthians 8 and 9: A Commentary on Two Administrative Letters of the Apostle Paul* (Hermeneia; Philadelphia: Fortress, 1985). For an answer to Betz's hypothesis, cf. Stowers, "Integrity of 2 Cor. 8 and 9," pp. 340–48.

9:6 / For another use of wisdom tradition in 2 Corinthians, see the antithetical questions in 6:14–16.

Gal. 6:6–10 is sometimes seen as an allusion to the collection (cf. L. W. Hurtado, "The Jerusalem Collection and the Book of Galatians," *JSNT* 5 [1979], pp. 46–62).

9:8 / Philo makes the same contrast between "sufficient" and "excess" (cf. *On Dreams* 2.47; *On the Life of Joseph* 111).

See *Lev. Rab.* 34:16, where Ps. 112:9 is used with Isa. 58:12 to suggest the means by which God will restore Israel.

9:10 / Cf. Koch, *Die Schrift als Zeuge*, pp. 14, 23.

§11 Accusations (2 Cor. 10:1–18)

Each of the three main sections of 2 Corinthians mentions Paul's imminent third visit to Corinth and in some way prepares the way for that visit (see Introduction). In the preceding section of the letter (chs. 8–9) Paul builds on the confidence that he has in the Corinthians by reactivating the plan for the collection. In the third section (chs. 10–13) he handles the problem of the opponents in a more frontal way. In the process, Paul reinforces the defense of his apostleship from 2:14–7:4, particularly in view of the opponents' attack against the legitimacy of his apostleship. He also warns that any unrepentant Corinthians will encounter the full power of his apostolic authority when he comes.

Second Corinthians 10–13 has a three-part structure. In the first part Paul deals with the opponents' accusations against him (10:1–18). In the second part the apostle boasts of himself against his will, at the provocation of the opponents (11:1–12:13). And in the third part Paul prepares for his third visit to Corinth (12:14–13:10). As in the first main section of the letter (chs. 1–7), Paul's person and his message are inextricably bound together. Paul's message of reconciliation in Christ is at stake in the question of his apostleship, and thus also the salvation of the Corinthian church. This helps to explain the pungency of Paul's statements.

10:1–18 / Paul confronts two accusations of the opponents against him that are shared by some members of the Corinthian church: (1) that he is weak (vv. 1–11), and (2) that he has overreached his apostolic jurisdiction (vv. 12–18). The accusations previously dealt with in 1:12–2:13 are charges that the Corinthians brought against Paul, although they too may have been inspired by the opponents.

10:1 / Putting great emphasis on himself, the apostle introduces the new section of the letter in a direct **appeal** to the Corinthians. Here again, the "apostle of Jesus Christ" portrays himself in light of Christ: He entreats the Corinthians **by the**

meekness and gentleness of Christ. Previously, Paul has presented himself as one who shares in the sufferings of Christ (1:5) and is himself the aroma of Christ (2:15), as one who speaks in Christ (2:17) and is compelled by the love of Christ (5:14). By identifying himself with Christ in this way, Paul can repel the accusation that his own meekness and gentleness are signs of weakness or lack of power and authority, for otherwise the power and authority of Christ himself would be impugned. At the same time, Paul wants to stress that his direct confrontation of the situation in Corinth is not a symptom of lording it over the Corinthians (cf. 1:24).

Paul ironically quotes the accusations of the opponents in Corinth, and the NIV correctly supplies quotation marks for the words **timid** and **bold.** The apostle is accused of being timid or bold depending on whether he is away or present **(face to face).** This recalls the illegitimate criterion by which the opponents evaluate him, i.e., according to the **face** and not the heart (5:12). By pointing to Paul's suffering and dying body, the opponents use the lack of glory and power in his physical appearance to discredit Paul's apostleship (see on 4:7–5:15). The opponents claim that Paul tries to compensate for this lack of real glory and power by being bold while away, that is, in the letters he writes. Perhaps the reference is to the tearful letter in particular (cf. 2:4; 7:8), which is regarded as a cowardly attempt to regain power at a safe distance.

10:2 / Paul appeals to the Corinthians not to make it necessary for him to show his boldness to them when he comes to Corinth. If we assume that 2 Corinthians is a unity, then we must take seriously that Paul is cautiously optimistic about the majority of the Corinthian congregation (chs. 1–9). If in the final section of the letter (chs. 10–13) he now changes his tone toward the Corinthians, it is probably in order to persuade and warn those members of the congregation who either remain hostile to him or may be inclined in that direction. Hence, although the reference to the Corinthians remains general (**you**), and positive comments about the majority are not wanting (e.g., 10:15), the appeal is obviously more specific at points. **Some people** refers either to the unrepentant members of the church in Corinth who follow Paul's opponents (cf. 2:6; 11:4; 12:21) or to the opponents themselves (cf. 3:1). It does not really matter whom Paul specifically has in mind here, for the position of both the unrepentant minority and the interlopers is the same, and their fate will also be the same when Paul comes to Corinth.

The apostle fully expects to deal severely with these people who regard him as behaving according to the **standards of this world** (lit., "according to the flesh"). In 1:17 Paul mentions that he has been accused of making his travel plans "according to the flesh." When he mentions the same kind of criticism in the present context, it may relate to his plans to come to Corinth in order to deliver the collection to Jerusalem. If Paul's plan to come to Corinth is construed by the opponents as a self-serving trip (cf. 12:14–18), then Paul's apostolic authority is being undermined. Here, as in 12:19–21, therefore, Paul warns of judgment when he comes.

10:3–6 / Paul elaborates on what he means when in verse 2 he writes that he will be bold toward the opponents and toward others in the Corinthian church who may be similarly minded.

10:3 / The elaboration begins with an admission that reverses the opponents' accusation. Paul admits that he walks "in the flesh," that is, that he still lives in an earthly body (see on 4:7–5:15; cf. Gal. 2:20). Yet Paul asserts that he does not **wage war** "according to the flesh." What he means by this becomes clear in the following verse.

10:4 / Paul amplifies on the idea that he does not wage war "according to the flesh": he fights not with **weapons of the world** [lit., *fleshly*], but with the "weapons of righteousness" (6:7) in spiritual armor (1 Thess. 5:8; cf. Eph. 6:14–17). **Demolish** (tear down) **strongholds** is commonly used to describe what invading forces do to the bulwark of a conquered city (cf. Lam. 2:2; 1 Macc. 5:65; 8:10). In Proverbs 21:22, the expression is used figuratively of the wise man who goes up against strong cities and tears down the "stronghold" in which the ungodly trusted. In Jewish tradition, this verse is applied to Moses' ascent to the *merkabah* ("you have led captivity captive,"*Midr. Ps.* 68:19).

10:5 / Paul continues the conquest theme, applying it now to the situation in Corinth. The argument is *a fortiori*: If Paul can successfully wage war and win by the power of God, then he can certainly handle the situation in Corinth. Practically speaking, Paul is determined to bring the Corinthians who still oppose him back into submission to Christ.

10:6 / Paul even more bluntly applies what he has been saying to the situation in Corinth. As soon as the renegade minority of the Corinthians again recognize Paul's apostolic authority (cf. 7:15) and participate in the collection, Paul will punish the opponents and anyone else in the church who remains in **disobedience**. This shows that Paul continues to hope for a positive outcome of the current situation. Exactly how he plans to **punish** the disobedient is left unstated, just as the punishment applied to the offender was left unsaid (cf. 2:5–11). It is perhaps worth noting, however, that according to the later Hekhalot tradition, anyone who says or does anything against the *merkabah* mystic will have all kinds of bad things happen to his body by the hand of God (cf. Schäfer, §§84, 85, 91).

10:7–11 / Paul further elaborates on the apostolic authority and power that will be demonstrated when he comes to Corinth for the third time.

10:7 / The apostle exhorts the Corinthians: "Look at the things according to the face!" (NIV: **you are looking only on the surface**), referring back to verse 1. Hence, Paul's exhortation seems to be an invitation for the Corinthians, especially those who remain hostile to him, to take a closer, more realistic look at him as an apostle, even if they are evaluating according to "the face" rather than the heart (cf. 5:12).

Paul maintains that he is also a genuine apostle of Jesus Christ. In particular, **anyone** *(tis)* who is confident in himself that he **belongs to Christ**, that is, anyone who regards himself as an apostle commissioned by the Lord, should consider that Paul also **belongs to Christ**. Paul obliquely refers here to the opponents who claim to be apostles of Christ (cf. 11:13–15). For the sake of argument, Paul is willing to entertain that they are genuine apostles, with whom he is on equal footing, even though he later unmasks their true identity.

10:8 / Paul states the reason (**For,** *gar*) for his claim to be an apostle of Christ. Paul has **authority** from the Lord. He is not self-appointed. He is not confident "in himself" (cf. v. 7). Paul has been personally commissioned to undertake his apostolic responsibilities (cf. 13:10). The purpose for which Paul was commissioned is **building up** and not **pulling down**. He has already stated that he has divine powers to demolish strongholds (cf. 10:4–5), but his real purpose is the edification of the church. He does not specify the means by which he could tear the Corinthians down, possibly because he is optimistic about a positive outcome to the situation in Corinth. Paul anticipates that the authority with which he has been invested will not be a cause of shame in the future.

10:9 / After mentioning possible punishment in verse 8, Paul wants to clarify his intentions, especially in view of the critique of the opponents cited in verse 1, who see the apostle as "timid" when present, but "bold" when away. Paul does not wish to **frighten** the Corinthians. He realizes that his boldness by letter plays into the hands of the opposition, but he has no alternative if he wants to warn the Corinthians before his imminent third visit.

10:10 / An explanation (**For,** *gar*) follows of how Paul is allegedly trying to frighten the Corinthians with his letters. This is another quote from the critique of Paul by his opponents (cf. v. 1). Again, it is possible that the reference is particularly to the tearful letter, which the opposition regards as a cowardly attempt to scare people into submission without confronting them in person. From Paul's perspective, the reason for painful letters was to avoid the need for painful visits (cf. 2:3).

The opponents attack Paul on two grounds: his physical appearance and his lack of rhetorical skill. On the one hand, his physical appearance is characterized as **unimpressive,** that is, "weak," suggesting that the apostle looked sickly and frail. Later in the letter Paul will explain the astounding cause of his "thorn in the flesh" (cf. 12:7). Clearly, the opponents expected that someone who had ascended to the *merkabah* would be a more powerful and imposing figure (see on 4:7–5:15). On the other hand, they allege that Paul's speaking ability **amounts to nothing,** that is, it is "despised." His efforts to make an oral presentation were met with utter contempt. Following Paul's denunciation of rhetoric in preaching for theological reasons (1 Cor. 1:17–2:5), his opponents made a stinging critique of his oratorical abilities, claiming that he lacked "presence," that is, "a beautiful body and a pleasant-sounding voice with appropriate gestures to match" (B. W. Winter).

There are striking parallels between this critique of Paul and the critique of Moses. Moses was chosen and made sufficient for his ministry in spite of his "insufficiency," which Exodus 4:10 links to a speech defect (cf. S. Hafemann). In the same way, Paul can assert his sufficiency in spite of his own personal weaknesses, which, according to 2 Corinthians 10:10; 11:6, consist in part in his unimpressive speech. Interestingly enough, *Num. Rab.* 18:9 attests to Moses' wisdom and rhetorical ability. Josephus records that Korah too was a capable speaker and very effective in addressing a crowd (*Ant.* 4.14).

10:11 / Paul denies the charge of his opponents that he is always weak in person and admonishes these people to **realize** [lit., "let such a person consider"] that soon his **actions** will match his words. The apostle promises a day of reckoning in Corinth, when his bold, threatening words in letters will be transformed into decisive action in person (cf. v. 1).

10:12–18 / Paul defends his apostolic right to territorial jurisdiction over Corinth against the encroachment of his opponents. The issue of territoriality is extremely important to Paul, especially after the apostolic council (see Introduction). Obviously, this is a matter that the apostle must handle before he comes to Corinth for the third time.

10:12 / With mock humility, Paul states that he cannot **compare** himself with his opponents in Corinth, whose very activity of comparing shows their false values. Paul has already referred to the way they **measure themselves by themselves** in self-appraisal (v. 7 "If anyone is confident in himself"). Nevertheless, he finds himself comparing favorably to the opponents as an apostle of Christ. Later in this same letter (cf. 11:21ff.) Paul will be forced to compare himself still further with his opponents, although he detests this kind of self-recommendation (cf. 5:12). The theological reason for this stance becomes clear in verses 17–18.

10:13 / In contrast to the self-recommendation of the opponents and their boasting in their own self-appointed apostolic status, Paul stakes his claim based on divine assignment. Although in the Greek text this sentence is somewhat convoluted, the basic sense seems relatively clear: Paul has a mission **field** or "jurisdiction," which has been apportioned to him by God. This jurisdiction **reaches even to you.** In other words, the Corinthian church falls within the swath of (Japhethite) territory from Cilicia to Spain that has been divinely allotted to Paul. Geographically, Corinth is located approximately in the middle of this territory, and so it forms the midpoint of Paul's westerly expanding mission (cf. Rom. 15:19). Unlike his opponents, who are trying to exert their influence over Corinth and thus to usurp Paul's territory, thereby overstepping the limits of their commission, Paul has not gone beyond the jurisdiction that God apportioned to him. Moreover, the territorial jurisdiction to which Paul appeals here was agreed to at the apostolic council, the same occasion on which his apostleship was recognized (cf. Gal. 2:6–7). As apostle to the nations, Paul was laying claim to his territorial jurisdiction over the Corinthian church, in which the opponents are "properly to be seen as interlopers and usurpers of apostolic prerogative" (R. P. Martin).

10:14–15a / Paul denies that his mission in Corinth constitutes an overextension of his apostolic prerogative. It is an undeniable fact that Paul founded the church in Corinth. The point of verse 14 is to underscore this fact. Paul was the one who originally came to Corinth with **the gospel of Christ** (cf. Rom. 15:19). Corinth was his apostolic work. That being the case, the apostle cannot be accused of **boasting** in work done by others (2 Cor. 10:15a). Who these **others** may have been has been the subject of considerable speculation. Perhaps Paul's opponents in Corinth allege that the Jerusalem apostles (especially Peter?) were the true founders of the Corinthian church (cf. 1 Cor. 1:10–12). A sustained anti-Pauline mission conducted by Peter himself (cf. M. Goulder) seems less likely. The identity of the intruders becomes more apparent in the subsequent context (see on 11:4–5).

10:15b–16 / Paul goes on to express his hope that Corinth will be instrumental in his projected missionary activities to the west. Paul acknowledges that the Corinthians' **faith** is growing. If 2 Corinthians is seen as a unity, this growing **faith** refers back to 8:7, where Paul exhorts the Corinthians to abound in the grace of giving, just as they already abound in **faith,** among other things. Hence, the difference in tone that is often detected between chapters 1–9 and 10–13 seems less pronounced than at first sight.

Paul hopes to preach the same gospel, which he brought to Corinth and which they believed (cf. 10:14), **in the regions beyond you.** Given the fact that in verses 13 and 14 Paul has come "as far as" the Corinthians, who are identified with Achaia (cf. 1:1; 9:2; 11:9–10), the idea of **beyond** in verse 16a is most naturally taken geographically as indicating lands to the west of Achaia, perhaps including Spain (cf. Rom. 15:24, 28). In the westward course he is pursuing, Paul seems confident that there are lands beyond the Corinthians where he can preach without encroaching on another's jurisdiction and that, at the same time, are legitimately part of the jurisdiction divinely allotted to him.

10:17–18 / Paul sums up his point in this subsection (vv. 12–18) by citing an OT prooftext and explaining its significance. The citation is drawn from Jeremiah 9:23–24 LXX: "Thus says the Lord, 'Let not the wise man boast in his wisdom, and let not the strong man boast in his strength, and let not the rich man boast in his wealth. But rather let him who boasts boast *in this,* that he understands and knows that I am the Lord who carries out mercy and judgment and righteousness upon the earth; for in these things is my will,' says the Lord." Here, as in 1 Corinthians 1:31, Paul modifies the citation by substituting **in the Lord** for the original "in this." His point in adducing this citation is made clear by the subsequent interpretation in verse 18. The opponents' self-recommendation shows a fundamental lack of understanding (cf. v. 12), for only a person whom the Lord specifically **commends** is **approved.** Paul implies by this that he alone is commissioned by God to undertake a mission in the territorial jurisdiction under discussion (cf. v. 13). Paul never lets the reader forget that he is an apostle "by the will of God" (cf. 1:1).

Additional Notes §11

10:1–18 / According to many interpreters, chs. 10–13 are written in a tone and about a subject so different from that of chs. 1–9 that they are considered a fragment of a letter written to Corinth at some other time, either before or after the writing of chs. 1–9. For the purposes of the present commentary, however, 2 Cor. 10–13 is treated as an integral part of a letter to the Corinthians that originally comprised all thirteen chapters (see Introduction for a complete discussion on the integrity of the epistle).

There is a kind of chronological progression to the presentation in 2 Corinthians: In the first part of the letter (chs. 1–7) Paul reflects on past events. In the middle part (chs. 8–9) he prepares the church to complete the collection under the supervision of his coworkers. In the final part (chs. 10–13) Paul warns about his own imminent third visit to Corinth.

For a detailed overview of the arguments for and against separating 2 Cor. 10–13 from the earlier part of the canonical letter, see M. Thrall, *Second Corinthians,* vol. 1, pp. 5–20.

See the Introduction for a discussion of the identity and character of the opponents who have infiltrated Corinth.

10:1 / Philo uses the same contrasting words—**timid** (humble) and **bold**—in his exposition of Gen. 15:2–18, where he argues that Abraham's boldness is not contradictory to his humility, for the patriarch has boldness to come before God precisely when he is humbled by perceiving his material nothingness (*Who is the Heir?* 24–29, esp. 29). Similarly, Paul argues that his bodily humility in no way contradicts the boldness of his apostolic letters. In fact, as he goes on to state, he may have to show his boldness on his next visit to Corinth.

10:3 / According to the the "law of envoys," mistreating an ambassador constituted an act of war (cf. Josephus, *Ant.* 7.120; Philo, *On the Life of Moses* 1.258). Since Paul considers himself an "ambassador for Christ" (cf. 2 Cor. 5:20), the warfare theme in our passage may also reflect that connection.

10:4 / Cf. William G. Braude, *The Midrash on Psalms* (Yale Judaica Series 13; New Haven: Yale University Press, 1959), vol. 1, p. 545.

Lev. Rab. 31:5 and its parallels explain the *gibborîm* ("the mighty") of Prov. 21:22 as angels whose "city" Moses raids when he brings down the Torah to humanity, again citing Ps. 68:18. This may explain why our text emphasizes that Paul's warfare is not "fleshly." The apostle has divine power successfully to wage war with angelic forces (cf. 2 Cor. 12:7–9). David J. Halperin develops the thesis that Moses storms heaven and forcibly takes the Torah from the angels (*The Faces of the Chariot: Early Jewish Responses to Ezekiel's Vision* [TSAJ 16; Tübingen: Mohr Siebeck, 1988]).

10:7 / We may note that the issue of equality was at the root of Korah's rebellion (16:3). The rebels wanted to usurp Moses' authority. Paul can compare himself positively with the intruders not because they are the Jerusalem apostles (although the interlopers may understand themselves as having been sent by the Jerusalem apostles) but because of the Korah typology. In the subsequent context Paul compares himself positively with the opponents at several points (e.g., 11:22).

10:10 / Cf. B. W. Winter, "Rhetoric," *DPL*, pp. 820–22 (here p. 821). Hafemann, *Paul, Moses, and the History of Israel*, pp. 42–47.

10:11 / Cf. H. Wayne Merritt, *In Word and Deed: Moral Integrity in Paul* (Emory Studies in Early Christianity 1; New York: Lang, 1993).

10:12–18 / On Pauline territoriality see Scott, *Paul and the Nations*, pp. 149–62.

10:13 / For a history of the word *kanōn*, see Bruce M. Metzger, *The Canon of the New Testament: Its Origin, Development, and Significance* (Oxford: Clarendon, 1987), pp. 289–93. On the interpretation of *kanōn* in the sense of "jurisdiction," see Scott, *Paul and the Nations*, pp. 159–62.

Cf. Ralph P. Martin, *2 Corinthians* (WBC 40; Waco, Tex.: Word, 1986), p. 322.

Cf. Gerd Theissen, "Legitimation und Lebensunterhalt. Ein Beitrag zur Soziologie urchristlicher Missionare," in *Studien zur Soziologie des Urchristentums* (2d ed.; WUNT 19; Tübingen: Mohr Siebeck, 1983), pp. 201–30 (here p. 212): "Wherever Paul had founded a church, other itinerant preachers appeared a short time later with amazing regularity."

10:14–15a / Cf. Michael D. Goulder, *St. Paul versus St. Peter: A Tale of Two Missions* (Louisville: Westminster John Knox, 1994); Gerd Luedemann, *Opposition to Paul in Jewish Christianity* (trans. M. Eugene Boring; Minneapolis: Fortress, 1989).

For a discussion of the character and identity of the intruders, see the Introduction.

10:17–18 / The exposition of Jer. 9:23–24 MT in *Num. Rab.* 22:7 illuminates how Paul is using the OT text in our passage. The entire passage is fascinating, but note especially, "Jeremiah, in the same vein, says: 'Thus says the Lord: "Let not the wise man boast in his wisdom, neither let the mighty man boast in his might, let not the rich boast in his riches; but let him who boasts boasts in this, that he understands and knows me"' (Jer. 9:23–24). These gifts, when they do not come from the Holy One, blessed be He, will ultimately fail a man." The passage also mentions Korah: "So also two rich men arose in the world, one in Israel and one among the nations of the world—*Korah* in Israel and Haman among the nations of the world—and both of them were destroyed from the world. Why? *Because their gifts were not from the Holy One, blessed be he, but they snatched them for themselves.*" Like Korah, Paul's opponents are attempting to snatch for themselves a gift (i.e., apostolic prerogative in Corinth) that God had not given to them. Their destruction is therefore certain.

§12 Boasting (2 Cor. 11:1–12:13)

In the last section of the letter (2 Cor. 10–13) Paul makes a frontal attack on his opponents to prepare the Corinthians for his third visit to Corinth. In chapter 10 he has already dealt with two of the opponents' accusations against him. Now, in 11:1–12:13, the apostle condescends to boasting about himself at the provocation of the opponents and in the face of a lack of concrete support from the Corinthians. These opponents, who evidently bill themselves as "apostles," had made a strong impression on the church at Corinth with their subversive teachings and robust appeal. Their boasting provoked Paul to engage in similar boasting, even though he recognized it to be utterly foolish. He had already resorted to self-commendation earlier in the letter (cf. 1:12–14; 6:3–10). Now, however, in this extended and, in part bitterly ironic "Fool's Speech" (11:21b–12:13), Paul boasts in an attempt both to counter the accusations of his opponents and to expose the false apostles as frauds who pervert the gospel and lead the Corinthians astray. To a certain degree, the apostle thereby stoops to the methods of the opponents, for they too boast and try to discredit Paul as a fraud; however, Paul uses these methods *self-consciously* and *openly*, aware of their foolishness.

The section can be divided into two parts. In the first part (11:1–21a) Paul prepares the Corinthians for his foolish boasting about himself, requesting that they endure it. For the apostle, such boasting must have been insufferable. In the second part (11:21b–12:13) Paul delves into the boasting itself, concentrating on two main points: (1) his apostolic activities and sufferings (11:21b–33) and (2) his apostolic revelations (12:1–10).

11:1–4 / In the first part of this section on Paul's self-praise, he prepares the Corinthians for his foolish boasting about himself (11:1–21a). He begins the preparation in verses 1–4 with the request that the Corinthians put up with his foolishness.

11:1 / Paul entreats the Corinthians to permit him the foolishness of boasting. **Foolishness** is another of the wisdom categories that Paul uses in 2 Corinthians. Based on what he has already said in 6:14–16, Paul would probably classify **foolishness** within the sphere of all things that stand opposed to Christ, who is the Wisdom of God (cf. 1 Cor. 1:24, 30). By calling his own boasting **foolishness,** Paul indirectly characterizes the opponents' self-praise as **foolishness** as well. The apostle asks the Corinthians' forbearance as he affects a foolish position for the heuristic purpose of exposing the ludicrous behavior of the opponents.

11:2 / The reason (*gar,* untranslated NIV) that Paul asks the Corinthians' forbearance is that he is jealous for them. The term **jealousy,** or rather "zeal," is drawn from the character of Yahweh as the sole husband of Israel (cf. Hos. 1–3; Ezek. 16; Isa. 50:1–2; 54:1–8; 62:5), which is spoken of, correspondingly, as his bride (cf. Isa. 49:18).

Mark 2:19 refers to the Messiah as a bridegroom, and Ephesians 5:22–33 applies this image to the relationship between Christ and the church. Just as Phinehas, the OT prototypical zealot (Num. 25:1–13; cf. Ps. 106:28–31; Sir. 45:23–24; 1 Macc. 2:26, 54), was eager to keep Israel pure from foreign influences, especially intermarriage, which would subvert its devotion to the one true God, so also Paul was zealous to keep the church a pure virgin until the Parousia, when Christ will receive the church for himself.

11:3 / The apostle fears that the Corinthians might be led astray by the false apostles. The bridal image that Paul introduces in verse 2 brings to mind the first human bride, **Eve,** and the intruder who beguiled her into disobedience (Gen. 3:1–7, 13). In Jewish tradition, the serpent is interpreted as Satan (cf. *1 En.* 69:6; *2 En.* 31:6; *Apoc. Ab.* 23; *L.A.E.* 9; *Apoc. Mos.* 17; *b. Yebam.* 103b; *Pirqe R. El.* 13:1; Wis. 2:23–24). Paul has already referred to "Satan" (2:11) and "Belial" (6:15), and in the subsequent context he refers again to "Satan" (11:14; 12:7) as an "angel of light" (11:14).

11:4 / The reason (**For,** *gar*) for Paul's fear is given in verse 4. Here, the apostle refers to an individual (**someone;** lit., "he who comes"), as if there were only one intruder. Perhaps Paul is thinking of the ringleader, for elsewhere he clearly refers to a plural number of opponents. These interlopers did not come on the scene, as some interpreters suppose, after Paul sent 2 Corinthians 1–9 to Corinth, for their presence is known in the earlier chapters of the letter as well (cf., e.g., 2:17; 3:1; 5:12; 6:14–7:1). The fact that Paul's opponents come into his divinely allotted apostolic territory (cf. 10:13–17) is also a major factor in the conflict in Antioch (cf. Gal. 2:11–12). Interestingly enough, Sirach 45:18 refers to those who were involved in Korah's rebellion as "outsiders" (*allotrioi;* cf. Num. 16:40). Of course, the problem is not just that the interlopers illicitly cross a territorial boundary line, but that they actually interfere with Paul's mission by preaching a **different gospel** (cf. Gal. 1:6–9) and thus causing the church to defect from its founding apostle. In a similar way, Jewish tradition portrays Korah as denying the Torah that was revealed through Moses (cf. *Ps.-Philo* 16; *Num. Rab.* 18:12; *b. Sanh.* 110a). The way that Paul defends himself in 2:14–4:6 shows that the opponents were promoting a gospel very much like the **different gospel** that had brought the Galatian churches into confusion, that is, one that emphasized obedience to the Mosaic law. Paul scolds the Corinthians for so easily accepting the opponents and their message. Earlier in the letter he has exhorted them to dissociate completely from the intruders (cf. 5:12; 6:14–7:1). Paul is the primary and legitimate mediator of the Spirit to the Corinthians (3:3, 6). The others proffer only what Paul rhetorically calls a **different spirit** (cf. Rom. 8:15) and even "a different Jesus" (cf. 2 Cor. 5:16, which refers to Paul's view of Jesus before his call/conversion). In Paul's view, the true gospel and the true Spirit are so inextricably bound together that to preach a false gospel is to preach a different spirit. Hence, by accepting a **different gospel** the Corinthians invalidate their own life in Christ and the Spirit.

11:5–11 / In this subsection Paul compares himself favorably with the rival preachers who have come to Corinth to usurp his authority. The transition from verse 4 to verse 5 is important for the identification of the opponents. According to some interpreters, the preachers in verse 4 are to be distinguished from the **"super-apostles"** in verse 5: the latter are the Jerusalem apostles and the former are their emissaries. However, there is nothing in the text to suggest a major shift in subject between these verses. In fact, the connector between verses 4 and 5 (*gar,* untranslated NIV) suggests that the term **super-apostles** in verse 5 elaborates on the preachers mentioned in verse 4. The NIV signals this relationship by translating *the* **super-apostles** as *those* **super-apostles.**

After stating his thesis (v. 5), Paul handles two accusations that the outsiders have lodged against him concerning his alleged inadequacies: (1) his lack of eloquence in public speaking (v. 6), and (2) his failure to accept support from the Corinthians (vv. 7–11).

11:5 / Paul affirms his parity with the **super-apostles.** The sarcastic term **super-apostles** *(tōn hyperlian apostolōn)* shows that, from Paul's perspective, the outsiders have come to Corinth in order both to subvert his own God-given apostolic authority and to usurp his God-given apostolic territory (cf. 10:13–18) by putting themselves above Paul. As we have seen throughout 2 Corinthians (1:24; 2:6–7, 15, 17; 3:1), Paul compares the opposition to Korah's rebellion, in which Korah and his followers rebelled against Moses and Aaron in order to set themselves up as the authorities in the congregation (Num. 16–17). Despite his lack of rhetorical ability, which recalls Moses (see on 10:10; 11:6), Paul will not allow that he is **inferior** to his opponents who seek to arrogate to themselves apostolic power and prestige. The implicit reason for this is that Paul, like Moses, received his apostolic authority from God (cf. 3:5–6; 10:18; Num. 16:11, 28, 30). Ironically, Paul goes on to state later in the same passage that he is "not the least inferior to the 'super-apostles,' even though I am nothing" (2 Cor. 12:11; cf. 10:7; 11:21–22). From Paul's perspective, therefore, the outsiders are less than nothing, despite their pretentious claims.

Very likely Paul refers to the opponents as **super-apostles** because they call themselves **apostles** *(apostoloi).* Perhaps they see themselves as envoys of the "pillar" apostles in Jerusalem (cf. Gal. 2:9), replete with letters of recommendation to attest their sending (cf. 2 Cor. 3:1). As we discussed on 8:23, which speaks of certain brothers who are "apostles of the churches," there is evidence in Jewish sources of "apostles" who are sent out on specific missions by Jewish authorities. Churches, including the mother church in Jerusalem, probably appropriated this practice. It appears that the opponents, who consider themselves "apostles" in a derivative sense (i.e, by the authority of the sending church), dispute Paul's apostleship, which allegedly relies on direct revelation of the resurrected Christ for its commission and authority (although 11:12 does refer to the "signs" of apostleship).

From Paul's perspective, this challenge to his authority compares with the situation Moses had to face with the wilderness generation, when he had to demonstrate that the Lord had sent him (cf. Num. 16:28).

11:6 / Paul explains the first way in which he is not inferior to the "super-apostles." He uses very compressed language here that cannot be translated unless it is unpacked. The singular subject of the first half of the verse (**I**) does not fit with the implied subject (perhaps **we**) of the plural participle in the second half. Literally, the first half reads as though the apodosis is missing: "Now if I am also an amateur in the speech, but not in the knowledge. . . ." Thereupon, the second half begins abruptly with the adversative conjunction *alla:* "but in every way [we] have revealed [the knowledge] in all things to you." The general sense is relatively clear if these two halves are pieced together and the appropriate words are supplied. Paul acknowledges his deficiency in public speaking very much as Moses did (see on 10:10). But, also like Moses, Paul exults in revealed **knowledge** mediated to others, albeit in this case it is the knowledge of Christ that God reveals through him to others, including the Corinthians (see on 2:14).

11:7–11 / Paul discusses a second way in which he is allegedly inferior to the outsiders, that is, in terms of accepting gifts from the Corinthians.

11:7 / The apostle begins with a rhetorical question expecting a negative answer. Was it wrong for him *not* to accept financial support from the Corinthians, when his opponents evidently did (cf. 2:17; 11:20)? According to Acts 18:3, Paul supported himself while in Corinth by means of manual labor (cf. also 1 Thess. 2:9), although he later accepted contributions from the Macedonians (2 Cor. 11:9; cf. Phil. 2:25; 4:10–20). Already in 1 Corinthians 9:14, Paul defended his right as an apostle to receive support from the churches, even as he also explained why he voluntarily relinquished that right (1 Cor. 9:15–17). Earlier in 2 Corinthians, Paul has touched on the subject of peddling the word of God (cf. 2 Cor. 2:17), and he returns to this contentious issue in the subsequent context (cf. 12:13–18). Since Paul has divine authority for his apostleship, he is not concerned with demonstrating his authority by taking advantage of his privileged position. But he is distressed by accusations of graft and avarice. Hence, he preaches the gospel **free of charge.** When Moses was charged with lording it over the congregation (Num. 16:3; see on 2 Cor. 1:24) he countered that he had not taken tribute from anyone (Num. 16:15). Evidently Paul follows the same general principle in exercising his apostolic ministry. Seen in this light, Paul could not be accused of exalting himself. Quite the opposite, he was elevating the Corinthians, whom he refused to bilk.

By selflessly refusing support from the Corinthians Paul exemplified among the Corinthians the Lord Jesus Christ, who, though he was rich, yet for their sakes became poor, so that they might become rich through his poverty (cf. 2 Cor. 8:9). Nevertheless, the following verses tend to detract from Paul's magnanimity.

11:8–9 / Paul explains the means by which he was able to preach the gospel free of charge to the Corinthians. This is a remarkable statement in several ways. First, Paul acknowledges that he received support from **other churches** (see on v. 7). If Paul's refusal to accept support from the Corinthians was a source of controversy in Corinth, then the fact that he accepted funds from other churches may have contributed to the problem in the first place, since it could have been construed as showing favoritism and a lack of love for the Corinthians (cf. v. 11; 12:13). To mention the receipt of support from other sources may also have exacerbated the situation, demonstrating once again how double-minded and inconsistent Paul really was (cf. 1:17). Second, Paul claims to have **robbed** (or "plundered") these other churches, a highly provocative formulation for someone who defends himself against the charge of exploitation in the previous context (cf. 7:2). His manner of speaking is, of course, hyperbolic and ironic, but it would seem to play into the hands of the opponents. Perhaps this is just what Paul wants in this prelude to the "Fool's Speech." Third, the apostle states that it was the brothers from **Macedonia** who supplied his need—members of the very church that is described as destitute in 8:2. With heightening intensity, Paul declares that even when he was very needy in Corinth he was so intent on not being a burden to the Corinthians that he chose to "rob" a church that was in abject poverty rather than risk offending the Corinthians. All of this was ultimately for the Corinthians' own benefit **(so as to serve you).**

11:10–11 / Paul expresses his determination to continue his policy of declining support from the Corinthians. Here again,

Paul uses an oath formula (**as surely as the truth of Christ is in me**) both to show his determination and to assert his claim (cf. 2 Cor. 1:18, 23; 11:31; Gal. 1:20; Rom. 9:1). The **truth of Christ** is in Paul in that Christ speaks through him (cf. 13:3). On the one hand, the apostle fears that, in the face of opposition in Corinth, to accept contributions from the Corinthians would deprive him of his **boasting.** As he states in 1 Corinthians 9:15, he would rather die than have anyone deprive him of the boast of voluntarily declining to exercise his apostolic rights. Like Moses, he wants to be able to declare, with all good conscience, that he has not accepted gifts from the congregation (cf. Num. 16:15). Paul's boast will not be stopped **in the regions of Achaia;** he will continue his policy of not accepting support in the territory allotted to him by God (cf. 2 Cor. 10:12–18). It is a question of apostolic prerogative.

On the other hand, Paul fears that his refusal to accept gifts will be interpreted as a lack of love for the Corinthians. Hence, he resorts again to the witness of God (cf. 1:18, 23; also 11:31; 12:2) in order to affirm his **love** for them (cf. 6:11–12; 12:15). The plethora of oath formulas in this letter shows the defensive position in which Paul finds himself.

11:12–15 / After denying that he is inferior to his opponents (vv. 5–11), Paul proceeds to expose them as frauds, indeed as servants of Satan (vv. 12–15). In this section Paul effectively turns the tables on the opponents, showing that they do not compare with him.

11:12 / Paul solemnly declares that in the future he will continue to refuse contributions from the Corinthians. He has previously stated (cf. 2:17) that the opponents dishonestly peddle the word of God for money, whereas he himself is free of this blameworthy practice. Hence, by refusing to accept support from the Corinthians, Paul deprives his opponents the opportunity to be considered **equal** with him (lit., "just as also we [are]"). We may recall that Korah and his followers were jealous of Moses and therefore claimed to be equal with Moses and Aaron in terms of holiness, probably because they wanted the privileges of a special priesthood for themselves (Num. 16:3, 8–11). In the same context, Moses denied that he had accepted any gifts from the congregation (Num. 15:16). In our text, there is a possibility that the clause **in order to cut the ground from under** may recall that Korah's followers were swallowed up by the ground as divine judgment on their impertinence (Num. 16:31–35; see on 2 Cor. 2:7), although here the expression is clearly metaphorical, for the word translated "ground" *(aphormē)* actually denotes "opportunity, pretext, occasion" (cf., e.g., Gal. 5:13; 2 Cor. 5:12).

11:13 / Paul further explains (**For,** *gar*) why the opponents in Corinth are not equal to him. First, he describes the opponents as **false apostles** *(pseudapostoloi)*. He thereby coins a term that recalls another neologism of his, i.e., "false brothers" *(pseudadelphoi)*. The latter refers to a Jew who pretends to be a believer, but whose claim is belied by his attempt to thwart the true gospel (cf. Gal. 2:4; 2 Cor. 11:26). Likewise, a false apostle is one who pretends to be an apostle but whose claim is belied by his attempt to work against Paul and his gospel; they have "another gospel" (v. 4). Perhaps Paul coined the term **false apostles** by analogy to the term "false prophets" *(pseudoprophētai)* in the OT (cf. Jer. 33:8 LXX). It may be that this derogatory term implies that the opponents called themselves "apostles" (also "servants of Christ," according to 2 Cor. 11:23). If so, this would not necessarily be a reference to the Jerusalem apostles, for the term "apostle" was used for others besides the Twelve (cf. 8:23; Phil. 2:25). Perhaps the opponents understood themselves as emissaries of the Jerusalem apostles (cf. C. K. Barrett). In any case, Paul's characterization of his opponents as **false apostles** fits very well with the Korah typology that he develops in this letter, for Korah and his followers aspired to honor and authority equal with Moses, and, according to Jewish tradition, Korah and his followers were "false," whereas Moses and Aaron were "true" (cf. *b. Sanh.* 110b; *b. B. Bat.* 74a; *Num. Rab.* 18:20).

Second, Paul goes on to describe the opponents as **deceitful workmen.** He uses a similar expression in Philippians 3:2 ("evil workers") to refer to his Jewish-Christian opponents, whom he characterizes as "those who mutilate the flesh" (i.e., practice circumcision). While this does not necessarily imply that the same Judaizing opponents are in view, the similarity is suggestive, especially as they preach "a different gospel" (2 Cor. 11:4; cf. Gal. 1:6–9).

Third, Paul describes the opponents as **masquerading as apostles of Christ.** Usually, the term is taken metaphorically to mean that the interlopers behaved like apostles in some way, and that is probably correct (note that in v. 15, the same opponents are said to masquerade as "servants of righteousness"). Elsewhere, however, Paul uses the term of literal, physical transformation. In Philippians 3:21, the hope is expressed that believers' lowly, earthly bodies will be transformed into the glorious, heavenly body of the Savior, the Lord Jesus Christ (cf. 4 Macc. 9:22). The term *metaschēmatizein* means "to transform, to change the outward appearance of a person or thing, to disguise" (cf. *T. Reu.* 5:6; Philo, *On the Eternity of the World* 79; *On the Embassy to Gaius* 80, 346; Josephus, *Ant.* 7.257; 8.267). In that case, the physical appearance of the opponents may be particularly in view here, just as Paul's frail physique has already come under discussion in the previous context (cf. 4:7–5:15; 10:10). Yet it is difficult to imagine how the opponents may have been disguised in a literal sense. Perhaps we may think of a glorified outward appearance either through ornamentation, (priestly?) vestment (cf. M. Himmelfarb), or even masking. As we have seen, the *merkabah* mystic was considered to have had an experience that altered his physical appearance. Hence, the verb in our passage may carry with it the literal sense of physical transformation, even if the primary sense is metaphorical.

11:14–15 / The opponents' masquerading is compared to that of **Satan.** The association of the opponents with Satan is based on the premise that there are only two opposing spheres—one of Christ and the other of Satan (see on 6:14b–16a). Those who align themselves against the apostle make common cause with the sphere of Satan. The prince of the darkness (cf. 6:14c) disguises himself as an **angel of light,** an idea based on Isaiah 14:12–15. Furthermore, according to *L.A.E.* 9:1, when Satan wanted to deceive Eve for a second time, he "transformed himself into the brightness of angels" (cf. *Apoc. Mos.* 17:2; on the deception of Eve, see further on 2 Cor. 11:3).

Paul strongly implies that his opponents are servants of Satan, although they disguise themselves as **servants of righteousness** *(diakonoi dikaiosynēs).* Rightfully, the term **servant of righteousness** applies to Paul, for he calls himself a "servant" *(diakonos)* several times in the letter (cf. 3:6; 6:4; 11:23), and his apostolic ministry *(diakonia)* is a "ministry of righteousness" (3:9), in contrast to the "ministry of condemnation" that leads to "death" (3:6–7). Hence, we see again that the main purpose of the opponents is to usurp Paul's authority in Corinth, just as the **angel of light** tried to make himself like God and even to usurp his throne of glory (cf. Isa. 14:13–14). In the end, however, this **angel of light** is brought down to Sheol, to the depths of the pit (Isa. 14:12, 15;

cf. *L.A.E.* 12–16; *2 En.* 29:4–5). Those who try to usurp Paul's apostolic authority and ministry will meet a similar fate, a fate that Korah and his followers met when they sought equality with Moses, the Lord's servant, and tried to usurp his authority (Num. 16:31–33). Paul warns ominously that his opponents' **end** will be what their actions deserve. In light of the allusions of the text, there can be little doubt that he means the opponents' demise.

11:16–21a / Paul prepares the Corinthians for the boasting in which he is about to engage by asking for their indulgence (cf. v. 1). Having mentioned that the opponents seek to boast in their equality with him (11:12), Paul does some boasting of his own. He knows it is foolish to vaunt his achievements, and perhaps even wrong (cf. 10:18; 12:1, 7), but he accepts the challenge (11:18) of some at Corinth who have forced him to assert his claims (12:11).

11:16 / The apostle reiterates his appeal for indulgence from verse 1. Paul is no **fool**, and in reality he should not be taken as one. He knows that any boasting, except boasting in the Lord, is illegitimate (cf. 10:17–18). Nevertheless, he is willing to engage in boasting because he knows that the Corinthians regard him as a fool. They have forced him into boasting (12:11). Furthermore, Paul uses this technique as a heuristic tool to expose his opponents as frauds and to win the Corinthians back to his cause.

11:17 / Paul stresses that the boasting in which he is about to engage is really illicit. He is affecting a role that is totally out of character for a true apostle of Jesus Christ, for he is not talking **as the Lord would** (lit., "according to the Lord"). In other words, Paul is not boasting in the Lord as he should (cf. 10:17).

11:18 / In affecting the role of boastful man, Paul is responding to the challenge of his opponents. The **many** to which he refers includes the opponents (cf. v. 20). They are boasting **in the way the world does** (lit., "according to the flesh"); hence, Paul does so, too. He means by this vaunting one's own achievements. There is a strong contrast in verses 17–18 between the prepositional phrases "according to the Lord" and "according to the flesh." Paul has already been accused of making his travel plans "according to the flesh" (see on 1:17). Now he turns the accusation of behaving "according to the flesh" back onto the opponents. He performs a similar maneuver in verse 20.

11:19 / Paul intensifies his critique by ironically calling the Corinthians wise in putting up with the opponents' foolish boasting. He uses the same rhetorical strategy in 1 Corinthians 4:10: "We are fools for Christ, but you are so wise in Christ!" Yet, as Paul had already argued in his first canonical letter, the Corinthians had a defective understanding of "wisdom," which led them to boast improperly in spiritual gifts and leaders according to Hellenistic standards of wisdom (1 Cor. 1:10–4:21). Here again, the Corinthians' particular brand of "wisdom" distorts their vision, causing them to put up with people who are really **fools**, from the divine perspective that Paul claims to have.

11:20 / Paul goes on to explain in five strong verbs how the opponents originally burst onto the scene in Corinth. From this description it seems obvious that the opponents moved into Corinth with the intent of taking over. Their actions were aggressive, and they began to assert their authority over the congregation, even to the point of enslaving the church (cf. Gal. 2:4) and extorting funds. Paul has already defended himself against the charges of lording it over the church (1:24) and exploiting the congregation (7:2; see also on 12:16–18). Now he turns the tables by reapplying similar charges to the opponents (cf. 2:17). With rhetorical acumen, Paul employs the very accusations that his rivals applied to him.

11:21a / In summary of his point in verses 16–21a, Paul admits with mock shame that he did not come to the Corinthians like a conquering ruler as his opponents did. The opponents allege that Paul's personal appearance is **weak** (10:10; cf. 1 Cor. 2:3). Picking up on that thought, Paul mockingly admits his weakness as a reason he did not come to Corinth to enslave and exploit the Corinthians. In actuality, of course, Paul considers his intentions with the Corinthians to have been forthright and honorable.

11:21b–12:13 / In this section, which constitutes what is called the "Fool's Speech," Paul boasts in two areas: the labors and sufferings he has endured in the course of apostolic service (11:22–33) and his extraordinary revelations of the Lord that he has received as an apostle (12:1–10). The latter category spills over into a boast that even the opponents would acknowledge as enviable.

11:21b–33 / The first area in which Paul boasts is that of the labors and sufferings that he has endured while engaged in apostolic service. These boasts prove doubly foolish, since boasting itself is foolish, and, by the opponents' standards, suffering and weakness do not count as meritorious qualities. The intricate structure of this subsection is best observed with a diagram (cf. R. P. Martin).

11:21b / Paul begins by taking up the challenge of his opponents to **boast**. He does not let us forget that he is affecting the role of a **fool** in order to make a rhetorical point about his opponents. Paul has been accused of being bold (cf. 10:1–2), so now he turns this accusation back on his opponents and then accepts it as applying to himself.

11:22 / Paul compares himself with his opponents point for point in terms of their Jewish heritage. Do these assertions mean that Paul's Judaism was called into question by the "super-apostles"? Or should we infer that Paul himself brings these points up in order to reinforce his connection with his Jewish heritage before proceeding further? First of all, Paul describes himself here, as in Philippians 3:5, as a Hebrew *(Hebraios)*. Perhaps he puts this self-description first in the list in order to recall his connection with the historic people of Israel. This point is reinforced by the next self-description.

Second, Paul describes himself as a Israelite *(Israelitēs)*. This tends to underscore and reinforce the archaicizing tendency of the first self-description. The apostle uses the same description of himself in Romans 11:1: "I myself am an Israelite, a descendant of Abraham, a member of the tribe of Benjamin." He states this in order to deny that God has rejected his "people." Because Paul stands in continuity with the historic people of Israel (cf. Rom. 9:4) he can serve as an example of the faithful remnant which preserves the continuity.

Third, Paul describes himself as Abraham's descendant (lit., "seed of Abraham"). With this term, the apostle stresses the fact of his genealogical descent (cf. Rom. 11:1) as well as his participation in the salvation-historical privileges of the elect people of God. To Abraham and his seed belong the promises of God (cf. Gen. 12:1–3, 7; 13:15–17; 15:18; 17:7–10, 19). Paul traces his gospel back to the Abrahamic promise (Gal. 3:8), and he regards Christ as the seed of Abraham in the strict sense (Gal. 3:16). In Christ, believers participate in the seed of Abraham and and thus become heirs to the Abrahamic promise (Gal. 3:29).

11:23a / After comparing himself favorably to the opponents in terms of membership in the historic Hebrew nation, Paul makes yet another comparison, this time directly in relation to the claim of apostleship. Whereas in the first three comparisons between himself and the opponents (v. 22) Paul was willing to acknowledge his adversaries' place in the historic people of God, here, in the fourth comparison, he balks at the idea that the opponents are **servants of Christ.** The apostle has already described the intruders as "servants" of Satan who disguise themselves as "servants of righteousness" (v. 15) and as "apostles of Christ" (v. 13). Therefore, it is obvious that he cannot seriously entertain the notion of their being true servants of Christ. He does so only to introduce several ways in which he is superior to the opponents as a servant of Christ (**I am more**). It is possible that the opponents described themselves as "servants of Christ," and that Paul uses their own honorific title in a similar way to his use of their own accusations in verse 20. By stating that it more properly applies to himself, Paul is asserting that he outstrips even the "super-apostles" (cf. 11:5).

11:23b–29 / Paul substantiates his claim in verse 23a that he is a servant of Christ more than his opponents are by adducing a list of his apostolic labors and sufferings. The opponents would not be impressed by this litany of troubles; they criticized Paul's suffering and weakness, and probably did not boast in such things themselves (cf. 5:12). The fact that Paul does so is part of the double "foolishness" of the section. With respect to literary form, this section constitutes a tribulation catalogue (see on 4:8–9). In 6:4–10 Paul uses a similar tribulation catalogue to show that "as servants of God we commend ourselves in every way." Indeed, several of the items in the list are repeated from the earlier catalogue. Furthermore, many of the sufferings mentioned in the present tribulation catalogue can be illustrated by specific episodes in the book of Acts. Some of the persecutions listed here may even have been practiced by Saul/Paul the Pharisee against believers in Jesus. Now the persecutor becomes the persecuted. Also in Romans 5:3, Paul boasts in tribulations.

11:23b / Paul lists the areas in which he is excels as a servant of Christ. The hyperbolic language in this list is unmistakable in the Greek text. Each noun in the series is modified by an adverb denoting superabundance: the first two nouns have *perissoterōs* ("far more, far greater"); the next one has *hyperballontōs* ("exceedingly, immeasurably"); and the last one has *pollakis* ("frequently"). Such hyperbolic language is characteristic of 2 Corinthians as a whole (cf. 1:5, 8, 12; 2:4, 7; 3:9, 10; 4:7, 15, 17; 7:4, 13, 15; 8:2, 7, 14; 9:8, 12, 14; 10:8, 15; 12:7, 15).

The catalogue begins with the boast that Paul has **worked harder** (lit., "with far greater labors"). Although this could refer to manual labor that he undertook in Corinth (and elsewhere) to support himself, here it probably refers specifically to apostolic labors as in 10:15, where boasting is also mentioned in connection with such labors. In 1 Corinthians 15:10 (cf. Gal. 1:14), Paul boasts that he has "worked harder" than any other apostle, although he quickly corrects his statement to acknowledge that it is actually the grace of God working through him (cf. 2 Cor. 10:17). If in our text, the apostle likewise boasts that he has worked harder than the "false apostles" (cf. 11:13), does that imply a connection between the Jerusalem apostles and the false apostles in Corinth? As we have seen, it is possible that the outsiders who infiltrated the Corinthian church regard themselves as having been sent by the Jerusalem church (cf. 3:1; see also on "false brothers" in v. 26b). However, there is an important difference between the two passages: Whereas in 1 Corinthians 15:10 Paul means the comparison between himself and the Jerusalem apostles positively, because he and they agree together on the essence of the gospel (cf. 1 Cor. 15:1–11), in 2 Corinthians 11:23b Paul can mean the comparison with the false apostles in Corinth only ironically, since the latter oppose Paul and proclaim a different gospel (cf. 11:4). For Paul, the "apostolic" labors of the false apostles cannot be seriously compared to his own genuinely apostolic labors. Here we have a good illustration of the doubly ridiculous nature of Paul's boasts in the "Fool's Speech."

Paul's second boast is that he has **been in prison more frequently** (lit., "with far more imprisonments"; cf. also 6:4–5). The book of Acts records only one imprisonment of Paul, in Philippi, before his arrest in Jerusalem (cf. Acts 16:23–30). It is possible, however, that he was incarcerated also in Ephesus. According to 1 *Clement* 5:6 Paul was in prison a total of seven times; however, this number may not preserve a reliable tradition, since along with "imprisonment," two other persecutions (banishment and stoning) are listed as having occurred seven times. Paul often had company while in prison; hence, he sometimes refers to his coworkers as "fellow-prisoners" (cf. Rom. 16:7; Col. 4:10; Phlm. 23). In the present context, however, the apostle mentions only his own imprisonments because of the apologetic situation.

Finally, Paul boasts that he has been **flogged more severely** (lit., "with more abundant floggings") and **exposed to death again and again** (lit., "with frequent deaths"). These tribulations are taken up in the following verses by the references to the "forty lashes minus one" (v. 24), to being beaten with rods (v. 25), and to stoning (v. 25). Previously (1:8–10), Paul has recounted a near-death experience he had in Asia.

11:24–26a / Having listed the various ways in which he is *more* a servant of Christ than his opponents, Paul begins simply to enumerate his tribulations without directly comparing himself to the opponents. The first two tribulations in this list are corporal punishments, which elaborate on the flogging mentioned in verse 23b. The **forty lashes minus one** refers to a form of corporal punishment administered in the synagogue (cf. Deut. 25:1–3; S. Gallas) and possibly practiced by Paul himself on believers (Acts 22:19) before his conversion. Whenever he entered a new city, Paul used the synagogue as a basis for evangelism (cf. Acts 9:20; 13:5, 14; 14:1; 17:1–2, 10, 17; 18:4, 19, 26; 19:8), since his gospel was "to the Jew first" (Rom. 1:16; cf. 1 Cor. 9:20). The fact that the apostle received a synagogal punishment not only tends to corroborate the testimony of Acts at this point, but also shows that he was taken seriously as a Jew who operated within the parameters of Judaism, as an erring member rather than as an outsider or an apostate. Hence, in a backhanded way, the "forty lashes minus one" further underscores Paul's claim to being an Israelite in verse 22. But what was it about Paul and his apostolic ministry to the nations that caused Jews in various localities to punish him by flogging? Perhaps Paul's own connection of persecution with the requirement of circumcision provides at least a partial answer (cf. E. P. Sanders).

With the words **beaten with rods** (v. 25) Paul indicates that he also received corporal punishment at the hands of the Romans. According to Acts 16:22–23 the Roman magistrates in Philippi ordered Paul and Silas to be beaten with rods before throwing them into prison. Since this form of punishment was usually reserved for slaves and provincials, it has often been argued that

Paul was not a Roman citizen as Acts reports (22:25). Even in Acts, however, Paul was beaten and scourged by the Romans unless he made his Roman citizenship known to the authorities in time (cf. Acts 16:37; 22:25–29). Furthermore, Roman officials sometimes ignored strict legality in their treatment of citizens. For example, before the outbreak of the Jewish War in A.D. 66 the procurator Gessius Florus had two Jews who were Roman citizens publicly flogged and crucified (cf. Josephus, *War* 2.308).

Paul mentions that he was **stoned** (or, more unequivocally, with the NRSV, "received a stoning") once. Stoning is the most common form of execution in the Bible, being used in the case of apostasy (Lev. 20:2; Deut. 13:10–11; 17:2–7), blasphemy (Lev. 24:14, 16, 23; 1 Kgs. 21:10), sorcery (Lev. 20:27), Sabbath violation (Num. 15:35–36), misappropriation of devoted things (Josh. 7:25), a disobedient son (Deut. 21:21), and adultery of a bride (Deut. 22:21, 24). Interestingly enough, Korah's rebellion incited the crowd to stone Moses (Josephus, *Ant.* 4.22), as they had almost done on other occasions (cf. Exod. 17:4; Num. 14:10). According to Acts 14:19, Jews from Antioch and Iconium came to Lystra and persuaded the people to stone Paul. Although Paul was left for dead outside the city, he miraculously walked away from the ordeal.

Three times Paul had been **shipwrecked.** This cannot refer to the shipwreck he experienced on the way to Rome (Acts 27:13–44), which came at a later time, but rather to earlier experiences not mentioned in the book of Acts.

11:26b / Next Paul lists the various situations in which he has been **in danger** (lit., "in dangers"). From this description it seems that, at one time or another, Paul has been **in danger** from almost every group (bandits, countrymen, Gentiles, false brothers) and in almost every place (rivers, city, country, sea). The apostle has frequently suffered persecution at the hands of his own **countrymen** (*genos;* lit., "race, nation"), i.e., his own people Israel. Yet in verse 22 Paul boasts that he is a Hebrew and an Israelite (v. 22). It is ironic, therefore, that the very nation of which Paul boasts is also the source of grave danger for him. The book of Acts contains many examples of Paul's persecution at the hands of his own people. In 1 Thessalonians 2:14–16, Paul puts the Jewish persecution of himself in salvation-historical perspective: Drawing a line from the OT prophets, through Jesus, to himself, Paul shows, in effect, that his countrymen have always resisted those whom God has sent.

It is also ironic that Paul cites danger from **false brothers** as part of the evidence that he is more a servant of Christ than the "false apostles," especially if, as is likely, both sets of opponents probably stem from the Jerusalem church and represent similar perspectives. In Galatians 2:4 Paul refers to "false brothers" who spied out the freedom that he and Titus had in Christ, so that they might enslave them. In 2 Corinthians 11:26b, the term **false brothers** may even include the aforementioned "false apostles" who tried to "enslave" the Corinthians (v. 20). In that case, Paul would be implying that he is more of a servant of Christ than his opponents in Corinth because he has been in danger by those very opponents. The seemingly ridiculous nature of such a proposition would not be out of character with the irony of the "Fool's Speech."

11:27 / More tribulations follow, this time without the word "dangers." These tribulations both reinforce the ones Paul has already listed (e.g., apostolic "labors" in v. 23b) and underscore the general impression of great suffering over an extended period of time. In particular, Paul may be detailing the kind of deprivations he experienced even in Corinth because he refused support from the Corinthians (see on 11:7–9).

11:28–29 / In addition to the tribulations that come upon the apostle from the outside (vv. 23b–27) Paul mentions here personal suffering that arises from his care and empathetic concern for the churches. The Corinthian correspondence itself is an eloquent testimony to Paul's pastoral care and concern for the churches. We may recall, for example, how much Paul fretted about the Corinthians and their reaction to his tearful letter before he heard back from Titus (cf. 2 Cor. 2:12–13; 7:5–7). In Paul's own words, "We were harassed at every turn—conflicts on the outside, fears within" (7:5). Paul is evidently still quite concerned about the situation in Corinth, particularly as some members have been led into sin by the intruders.

11:30–33 / Paul concludes the tribulation catalogue with a statement emphasizing his stance on boasting (v. 30), an oath formula (v. 31), and a concrete illustration of the persecution he endures (vv. 31–33).

11:30 / The apostle emphasizes his stance on boasting, carefully phrasing the sentence as conditional. He would rather not boast, since any kind of boasting, other than boasting in the Lord (cf. 10:17), is foolishness (cf. 11:1, 16–17). But if the apologetic situation in Corinth requires it (lit., "If it is *necessary* to boast"), then he will boast in such as way as to reveal his **weakness**. The long catalogue of Paul's adversities in 11:23b–29 is meant to illustrate this weakness. As we shall see, Paul is setting his readers up for a surprising insight into the relationship between suffering, weakness, and Paul's apostleship (see on 12:1–10).

11:31 / Paul invokes **God** as a witness to the veracity of his claim that he boasts only in his weakness. This is not the first time in the present letter that he invokes God as witness (cf. 1:18, 23; 11:10). The polemical situation in Corinth requires Paul to assert his claim in an elaborate oath formula (cf. 1:17).

11:32–33 / The generalized tribulation catalogue in 11:23b–29 illustrates the "weakness" of which Paul prefers to boast in verse 31. Likewise, in verses 32–33 Paul provides a concrete illustration of those tribulations ("dangers from nations," "dangers in the city," v. 26) in his dramatic escape from the clutches of "King Aretas." The emphatic position of **in Damascus** at the very beginning of the sentence suggests that the location of the incident is of some importance to Paul. We can deduce from Galatians 1:17 that Paul was in Damascus twice—once at or near his call to apostleship (cf. Acts 9; 22; 26:12–23), and once on his return from Arabia. It is reasonable to assume that the episode recounted here took place on one of these visits, since there is no indication that Paul was operating in this area in later years. Although this incident might seem to provide a fixed point in Pauline chronology, especially since it is linked with the reign of **Aretas** IV, king of Nabatea from ca. 9 B.C. to A.D. 40, there are still many uncertainties in the historical reconstruction (cf. R. Riesner), including the thorny question of whether, and if so when, the Nabateans controlled Damascus during the late 30s A.D. (cf. G. W. Bowersock).

Here Paul recounts the escape from Damascus in order to illustrate the weakness and apostolic tribulations to which he has referred in the previous context. Perhaps the Corinthians would recall the apostle's ignoble retreat from Corinth during his second, painful visit to the congregation. The staunch opposition to his gospel, no less than by his own people and by fellow believers in Christ, may have seemed to undermine his apostolic credibility.

Paul's escape from Damascus was effected by lowering him in a basket from a window in the wall—the antithesis of the assault on a city described in 10:4. Similar language is used in the story of the Israelite spies whom Rahab lowered down the wall of Jericho (Josh. 2:15). In fact, the same verb *([kata]chalan)* is used for **lower** in Joshua 2:15 LXX; Acts 9:25; and 2 Corinthians 11:33. Like the spies, Paul slipped through the enemies' hands. Here we see again that Paul relates his own experiences to OT events.

12:1–10 / Up to this point in the "Fool's Speech" Paul boasts that, as a servant of Christ, he is superior to his opponents (the so-called super-apostles) mostly in terms of his far greater sufferings (11:21b–33). In 12:1–10 the apostle goes on to boast of his surpassing revelatory experience. In contrast to the disgraceful descent from the wall in Damascus (11:33), Paul here recounts a glorious ascent into heaven (cf. *T. Jos.* 1:4 for a similar contrast between descent as humiliation and ascent as exaltation). Although Paul realizes that such boasting is futile, he nevertheless engages in it, succumbing temporarily to the pressure from his opponents (v. 1). Yet, having very briefly and discretely mentioned an example of this revelatory experience (vv. 2–4), Paul immediately returns to boasting about his weaknesses (v. 5), explaining that a thorn in the flesh was given to him *(passivum divinum)* to keep him from being too elated or conceited because of the abundance (or surpassing character) of the revelations (v. 7). In other words, the formal cause of Paul's weakness is none other than his extraordinary revelatory experience! With this tour de force, Paul is able to boast about his visions, at the same time explaining why he is so weak. All the while, he is boasting in the Lord (cf. 10:17), the fount of both his revelatory experience (12:1) and his strength in weakness (vv. 9–10).

We may surmise that the opponents deny Paul's revelatory experience (Paul is a fraud [see on 5:16]) and/or depreciate it in view of their own experience (they have independent access to revelation). As we suggested above in §5, the opponents' attack may well have concentrated on Paul's miserable body, arguing that a *merkabah* mystic would have been transformed in the process of the encounter with the divine. In the present text, Paul turns this argument around by making his miserable body actually become a proof of his superior revelatory experience!

12:1 / Paul makes the transition to his new topic of boasting with a disclaimer. Even though he fundamentally doubts the efficacy of such activity, Paul is being compelled to boast in order to counter the boasting of his opponents (cf. 11:22). In view of this "counter-boasting," we may assume that the opponents also claim to have **visions and revelations.** It is uncertain whether Paul intends a distinction between "visions" and "revelations." Perhaps he merely amplifies in order to impress his readers with the quantity of his revelatory experiences (compare the hyperbolic language in v. 7). If, as we argued, 2:14 refers to Paul's encounter with the divine throne-chariot and the revelation that derives from that experience, it is interesting to note that God "always" leads the apostle in triumph in Christ, perhaps indicating the frequent occurrence of these audiences with God. In any case, what Paul sees in visions is integrally connected with the revelations he mediates. More importantly, we may ask whether these visions are **from the Lord** (so the NIV) or "of the Lord" (objective genitive), for the genitive *kyriou* can legitimately be translated either way. The latter is more probable, since elsewhere Paul bases his apostolic commission on his having actually seen the risen Lord (1 Cor. 9:1; 15:8). That being the case, the opponents' claim to similar visions and revelations threatened to undermine Paul's apostolic authority unless he could point out a decisive difference between his own experience and that of his opponents.

12:2–4 / After announcing his topic as that of "visions and revelations of the Lord" (v. 1), Paul goes on in verses 2–4 briefly to mention a concrete example of his heavenly experience. He recounts the experience twice, in slightly different terms. The purpose for recounting this event is not to describe the revelation itself (indeed, little of its actual content is mentioned) but to intimate the extraordinary quality of Paul's revelatory experience.

12:2 / Paul portrays his heavenly experience as a datable, historical event. If Paul's point is to provide an example of his own "visions and revelations of the Lord" in order to counter his opponents' similar claims, then it seems strange that he would recount his experience in the third person, as if he were reporting about an acquaintance (**I know a man**). But by verses 5–7a at the latest the reader realizes that verses 2–4 refer to Paul's own experience, for the apostle boasts in the experience. The reason for this use of the third person remains unclear, although many explanations have been offered. It is perhaps worth pointing out that Jesus, whom Paul otherwise seeks to imitate (cf. 1 Cor. 11:1; 2 Cor. 1:5; 4:10; see below on 12:8), referred to himself in the third person as the "Son of Man" (cf. Mark 2:10, 28; 8:31, 38, etc.). In any case, Paul's evasiveness in 12:2–4 is not to be explained as shyness or humility; the apostle is being modestly decorous with his addressees when he says that he knows a man in Christ (cf. the similarly sensitive situation in 7:12), for, after the extensive discussion in 2:14–3:18, there can be little doubt that Paul regards his role as revelatory mediator (on par with, and even superior to, Moses) as being foundational to his whole apostolic ministry. Elsewhere in the Corinthian correspondence Paul adamantly claims that his apostleship is based on his vision(s) of Christ: "Am I not an apostle? Have I not seen Jesus our Lord?" (1 Cor. 9:1; cf. 15:1–8; Gal. 1:12, 16). Although his original christophany on the way to Damascus remains the pivotal encounter with the resurrected Christ, other revelations and visions should not be discounted (cf. Acts 16:9; 18:9; 22:17–18; 23:11; 27:23). The vision that Paul describes in 2 Corinthians 12:2–4 (and others like it) is crucial to Paul's claim to apostolic authority, which he is defending in chapters 10–13.

Paul describes himself as a man **in Christ** *(en Christō)*. Assuming the unity of the letter as it stands, **in Christ** recalls 2 Corinthians 2:14, 17, the only other place in the letter in which the apostle uses the phrase **in Christ** in reference to his own personal experience. In 2:14, where Paul describes his ongoing apostolic experience as one of God leading him in triumphal procession **in Christ**, he alludes, as we have seen, to the divine throne-chariot on which Christ is seated at the right hand of God. In 2:17 Paul has in mind the same *merkabah* experience when he refers to speaking before God **in Christ** (the same expression occurs in 12:19, which underscores that there is a relationship between 12:1ff. and 2:14–17). As we shall see, our passage is also otherwise linked with 2:14–4:6, where Paul argues that he is a revelatory mediator on par with Moses.

Even without the allusion to 2 Corinthians 2:14, 17, our passage has long been suspected of referring to Paul's encounter with the divine throne-chariot (cf. G. Scholem), for the text recounts that Paul was **caught up** to the third heaven. The verb *harpazein* is used here as elsewhere in the sense of being taken up and carried away at another's initiative. In regard to whether the experience was **in the body or out of the body,** the very fact that Paul's affliction in this connection was physical (v. 7) may indicate the former. In several apocalypses the verb *harpazein* refers to heavenly ascent (cf. *Gk. Apoc. Ezra* 1:7; 5:7; *Apoc. Mos.* 37:3–5; 1 Thess. 4:17). The description of Paul's being "caught up" to the third heaven (2 Cor. 12:2–4) and his being "led in triumphal procession" (2:14) may be mutually interpretive.

Paul reports that he was caught up **to the third heaven.** Although Jewish and Christian apocalypses often presuppose a cosmology of seven heavens (cf. A. Y. Collins), some texts do speak of three heavens, the third of which is the highest, the dwelling place of God himself (cf. *1 En.* 14:8–25; *T. Levi* 3:4). Since Paul goes on to characterize his revelatory experience as exceptional (v. 7), he probably has in mind an ascent to the highest of three heavens, for otherwise his opponents could claim to have penetrated a higher heaven. The preposition used here (**to,** *heōs*) may also indicate that the apostle had reached the uppermost limit. The equation of the **third heaven** with "paradise" (v. 4) confirms this view.

12:3–4 / Paul repeats the same account here in slightly different terms. Instead of stating, as in verse 2, that the man was caught up to the "third heaven," Paul substitutes **paradise.** According to *2 Enoch* 8:1–3 (cf. *Apoc. Mos.* 37:5; 40:1), Enoch was taken "up to the third heaven, and . . . looked downward, and . . . saw Paradise. . . . And in the midst . . . the tree of life, at that place where the Lord takes a rest when he goes into paradise" *(OTP).* The reference to paradise in our text has led many scholars to compare the account of the "Four Who Entered *Pardes*" (a Persian word meaning a walled garden, but also connected with the garden of Eden as the eschatological paradise in Jewish literature), which is found both in the Talmud and in the Hekhalot literature (cf. C. R. A. Morray-Jones). Of these four, only R. Aqiba was deemed worthy of beholding God's glory behind the curtain (Schäfer, §346).

In our passage, we are struck by the fact that Paul's description of his heavenly experience is so cryptic. He describes nothing of the vision itself and barely mentions the audition, if indeed a sharp distinction between prophetic visions and auditions can be maintained (cf. Amos 1:1 LXX: "The *words [logoi]* of Amos . . . which he *saw [eiden]* about Jerusalem"; also Mic. 1:1; Hab. 1:1). Part of the explanation for this vagueness can be found in verse 4, where the apostle states that he has heard ineffable things (**inexpressible things, things that man is not permitted to tell**). Paul does not usually disclose the content of his visions and revelations. This corresponds to the general reluctance in Jewish mystical and apocalyptic literature to describe certain aspects of the heavenly journey. According to *Hekhalot Zutarti,* the *merkabah* mystic is to keep quiet about the mysteries he contemplates (Schäfer, §335). In rabbinic Judaism, all study and discussion of the divine throne-chariot in public was prohibited, unless the person was a scholar who understood of his own knowledge (*m. Ḥag.* 2:1). Those who ignored these injunctions did so at their own peril. The story is told, for example, of a certain Galilean who announced that he would publicly lecture on the *merkabah,* but who was stung by a wasp and died (*b. Šabb.* 80b). Of course, Paul's revelatory experience is not completely ineffable; otherwise, he could not present himself as a revelatory mediator on par with Moses. Even in the present context, the apostle divulges the content of a personal revelation to him by the risen Lord (cf. v. 9), a revelation perhaps directly connected with Paul's heavenly ascent (vv. 2–4).

12:5–6 / In the following verses Paul at first continues the third person and only gradually reveals that the heavenly journey recounted in verses 2–4 is his own. Paul's point here is simply this: Although he would be fully justified in boasting about his extraordinary revelatory experience, he refrains from doing so in favor of boasting in his physical **weaknesses.** If Paul's weakness was one of the primary criteria the opponents were using to undermine his apostolic authority in Corinth, particularly with respect to Paul's alleged revelatory experience, then it would seem foolhardy for him to give his opponents additional ammunition against him. Yet this is precisely Paul's tactic in the so-called Fool's Speech. (Paul's strategy was never any different in Corinth [cf. 1 Cor. 2:3–4].) It is clear from 2 Corinthians 12:1–10 that Paul does not disparage the revelations as such; they are a reason for boasting (cf. vv. 5a, 6a) and elation (v. 7b, e). Nevertheless, he deftly chooses instead to stress the formal cause of his **weaknesses** as a means of indirectly reveling in his visions and heavenly journeys.

He refrains from boasting about ineffable revelatory experiences that the Corinthians could not see or hear for themselves. He relies instead on the outward manifestation of those experiences in **what I do or say.** In his first canonical letter to the Corinthians Paul reminded the church of how his manner among them "in weakness and in fear and in much trembling" served to emphasize that the persuasiveness of his message was not based on the latest wisdom of this world or rhetorical flair, but "in a demonstration of the Spirit and power" (1 Cor. 2:3–4). Paul had been sent to proclaim "Christ crucified" (1:23) and to live a correspondingly "cruciform apostolic" existence (2:1–4; 4:8–13), in order that their faith might not be in the wisdom of men but in the power of God (2:5), for to those being saved, the suffering of Christ and the suffering of his apostle were not a stumbling block or foolishness, but the vehicle through which the very power and wisdom of God were being displayed and revealed in the world (cf. 1:23–24 compared to 2:4–5). Clearly, therefore, Paul had not changed his approach; the Corinthians had changed theirs.

12:7–10 / In this section Paul makes a startling admission, one that would have been potentially damaging to him in the hands of his opponents. The apostle admits that God himself is ultimately responsible for his physical weakness! Just as God was responsible for his heavenly ascent (note the divine passives in vv. 2 and 4), so also God was responsible for his receiving a "thorn in the flesh" (note the divine passive in v. 7); however, the real crux of Paul's admission consists in the reason for which he was given this physical malady, that is, to keep him from becoming conceited. If a glorious outer appearance is missing in Paul, it can be explained by his superlative inner experiences, which might normally make him proud. By this argument, Paul can justify his obvious physical weakness and yet underscore his apostolic authority.

12:7 / In order to make his dramatic point, Paul refers back to his thesis in verse 1, that he has had a plurality of revelations. The phrase at the beginning of this verse (lit., "and/ also because of the extraordinary character of the revelations") does not go well with the end of verse 6, and it does not fit the grammar of verse 7, unless one deletes the inferential conjunction *dio* ("therefore"), as some manuscripts do. Yet there is no apparent reason why a scribe would have added the conjunction, whereas there is a good grammatical reason why a scribe would have omitted it. The NIV has seen fit to connect the clause in question to verse 7, to ignore the inferential conjunction, and to translate the sentence as if it began with the immediately following subordinate conjunction *hina* ("in order that"). This maneuver yields a tolerably coherent translation that may approximate what was originally meant. Unfortunately, the NIV fails to represent the fact that the Greek text twice repeats the purpose clause ("in order that I might not become conceited"), once at the beginning of the sentence and once at the end. The repetition obviously serves to emphasize the purpose of the thorn in the flesh.

The apostle has had many revelations, of which the encounter described in verses 2–4 is merely one example. Paul uses hyperbole (**surpassingly great**) to express the extraordinary quantity *and* quality of the revelations he has experienced. This is the same kind of exaggeration as he used in the tribulation catalogue in 11:23b (and throughout 2 Corinthians, for that matter). The inherent danger in such an amazing revelatory experience is that one could become boastful and proud. Paul admits to becoming **conceited** because of the revelations he had received. He seems to warn the Colossians against this kind of pride in Colossians 2:18. Humility was to be one of the characteristics of the *merkabah* mystic (cf. Schäfer, §§621, 683; but see §225, where the *merkabah* mystic is addressed as "son of the proud"). Warnings against self-exaltation with regard to visionary experience are common in the Hekhalot literature (cf. Morray-Jones). Perhaps Paul's tendency to be conceited because of his *merkabah* experience can be compared to that of the Teacher of Righteousness in the Qumran community, who boasted of his ascent to heaven (cf. 4Q427 f7.1.8–17; 4Q471 f6.4; 4Q491 f11.1.14, 18).

To keep Paul from becoming conceited because of his revelatory experience, a **thorn in my flesh** was given to him (i.e., by God). In other words, the formal cause of Paul's weakness, which the opponents so vehemently decry, is none other than his extraordinary apostolic revelations! By this subtle and ingenious maneuver, Paul deconstructs his opponents' most effective argument against his apostleship. In effect, Paul makes suffering and weakness—even the extreme sort that he constantly endures (cf. 11:23bff.)—a sign of genuine, and even exceptional, apostleship since the more often that an apostle ascends to the divine throne of glory, the more his pride will need to be held in check by earthly suffering.

It is difficult to ascertain whether the **thorn** *(skolops)* refers to a persecutor (cf. Num. 33:55; Ezek. 28:24) or to a physical ailment (cf. Ps. 32:4[LXX 31:4]). If the following clause ("a messenger of Satan to torment me") is meant to be an appositional modifier of "thorn," then the former interpretation is possible. On the other hand, the latter interpretation cannot be dismissed, especially if Paul is alluding to Psalm 32:4: "For day and night your [sc. the Lord's] hand was heavy upon me; I was tormented with bodily suffering while a thorn *(akanthan)* was stuck in me." Psalm 32, a thanksgiving for healing and forgiveness after confession of sin, concludes with an exhortation to boast: "And boast, all you who are upright in heart" (v. 11). The "thorn in the flesh" (not represented in the MT) is a metaphor for the psalmist's unspecified physical ailment. The parallel to 2 Corinthians 12:7 is obvious (cf. Gal. 4:12–20), for our passage also makes a connection between the thorn in the flesh and boasting in weakness (cf. 2 Cor. 12:9). The fact that Paul knew this psalm is shown by the citation of Psalm 32:1–2 in Romans 4:7–8 ("Blessed are those whose iniquities are forgiven, and whose sins are covered; blessed is the man *[anēr]* against whom the Lord will not reckon sin"). If our passage alludes to this psalm, then it may imply that Paul received divine forgiveness for his conceit.

The text goes on to state that, in connection with this thorn in the flesh, a **messenger of Satan** *(angelos Satana)* was sent to torment Paul. Seeing that the thorn is connected to Paul's revelatory experience (and particularly his encounter with the *merkabah*), we should think of an "angel of **Satan**" rather than of a human **messenger**. We may recall the role of Satan in the physical affliction of Job, which was sanctioned by God himself in the heavenly court (cf. Job 1:6–12; 2:1–8; also Zech. 3:1).

It is also possible that the satanic messenger tormented Paul during his heavenly ascent to the *merkabah*. Some texts speak of angelic opposition during the journey to reach the throne of God (J. Maier), especially to those travelers considered unworthy or impure (Schäfer, §§1, 213–215, 224–228, 258–259, 407–410; also §§346, 673). If such a situation can be inferred from the text, then the satanic opposition is susceptible of two interpretations. On the one hand, the satanic opposition to the apostle could be construed by the interlopers in Corinth as evidence that Paul was not worthy of ascending to the highest heaven. On the other hand, it could also be used to demonstrate that Paul is not on the side of Satan (cf. Mark 3:20–27, where Jesus uses a similar argument against the accusation of demon possession).

12:8–9a / Not only did God allow Paul to be given the physical affliction through the angel of Satan, but when Paul petitioned the Lord for relief, he was refused. In the Hekhalot literature, prayer is frequently used in order to overcome or avert danger to the *merkabah* mystic, especially to make certain that the ministering angels do not destroy the traveler (cf. Schäfer, §§1, 558, 586). The number **three times** helps to relate Paul's prayers in the midst of chronic suffering to the previous tribulation catalogue, which likewise indicates the number of times some ordeals occurred (cf. 11:24–25). According to Psalm 55:17, the psalmist utters his complaint and moans **three times** a day—evening, morning, and noon—and the Lord hears his voice. Paul **pleaded** with the Lord "about this" (the phrase is omitted by the NIV), that is, about the aforementioned thorn in the flesh. If **Lord** refers here to Jesus Christ (cf. v. 9b), then we have evidence that the apostle practiced prayer to the resurrected Lord (cf. 1 Thess. 3:12–13; 1 Cor. 1:2; 16:22; Acts 7:59). Furthermore, it is interesting to note that Jesus is reported to have pled with God three times that his "cup" be taken from him (cf. Mark 14:32–41 par.). In Romans 8:15, 17, Paul seems to allude to the Gethsemane experience when he cites Jesus' Aramaic address to God as "Abba" in the context of suffering with Christ (cf. Mark 14:36).

In verse 9a Paul gives the answer of the resurrected Lord to his threefold request. Although the apostle's repeated request is not directly denied, a negative answer is strongly implied by the words, "my grace is sufficient for you." The verb **be sufficient** *(arkein)* recalls what Paul has already said in 2 Corinthians 2:16 and especially 3:4–6, namely, that his "sufficiency is from God." In other words, just as Paul's sufficiency for being the revelatory mediator is God (who has made him sufficient [3:6]), so also Paul's sufficiency for coping with the thorn in the flesh (which God gave him) is also God (12:9). Hence, whether in strength or weakness, Paul's sufficiency and boast are the Lord. As Paul states in Philippians 4:13, he can do all things (even live in adverse circumstances!) through the Lord who gives him strength. God's/Christ's **grace** *(charis)* made Paul an apostle in the first place, causes his ministry to flourish, and sustains him in the process (cf. Gal. 1:15; 2:9; 1 Cor. 3:10; 15:10; Rom. 1:5; 12:3; 15:15).

The risen Lord goes on to state the reason his grace is sufficient for Paul in his physical distress: Christ's **power** is made perfect in Paul's **weakness.** The contrast of terms is striking. Ultimately, the quality and character of the revelatory mediator is inconsequential, a lesson that is abundantly reinforced by the example of the OT prophets (cf., e.g., 1 Kgs. 18:4–18). Moses is the prime example of divine power being made perfect in weakness of the human revelatory mediator (cf., e.g., Exod. 3:1–15:21).

Citing a personal revelation from the risen Lord suits Paul's apologetic purpose in context, for just as he mentions his thorn in the flesh in order to explain his weakness while reveling in his extraordinary revelatory experience (2 Cor. 12:7), so also here Paul cites this word from the risen Lord in order to do the same thing. Hence, in contrast to the opponents' position, there is practically no stigma attached to Paul's weakness. To the contrary, Christ's power is **made perfect** in the apostle's weakness (cf. 4:7).

12:9b–10 / If Christ's power is made perfect in Paul's weakness (and thus indirectly attests to Paul's revelatory experience and his apostolic authority), then the apostle's positive response to the revelation of the Lord seems quite logical: he will boast in his weaknesses. This idea of strength in weakness must seem counterintuitive, especially to the opponents, who "take pride in what is seen" (2 Cor. 5:12). However, Paul now realizes that everything that he once regarded as a cause for boasting is nothing in comparison with knowing Christ and sharing in his sufferings, so that he may participate in Christ's resurrection (cf. Phil. 3:5–11).

Paul boasts in his weakness **so that** *(hina)* Christ's power might **rest** on him. The verb actually denotes "take up one's abode, dwell" and may well recall that the presence of God dwelled in the tabernacle and the temple (cf. Exod. 25:8; Ezek. 37:27; 2 Cor. 6:16). If so, the verb ties our passage back to 2 Corinthians 5:1, where Paul refers to his mortal body as "our earthly house of the tent," alluding to the tabernacle in 1 Chronicles 9:23 LXX. Even during his earthly pilgrimage in the body, the apostle is conscious of the presence of God in his life through the Spirit. He was also conscious that the same power of the resurrected Christ would one day transform his mortal body.

Because Paul is the dwelling-place of the power of Christ, he takes **delight** in his weaknesses (v. 10a). Rather than continue his prayer for relief from the thorn in the flesh (cf. v. 8), Paul has now come to accept his infirmity and even to delight in it **for Christ's sake**. This sounds almost masochistic, as if Paul likes to be abused. Certainly it opens the door to later Christian ideas of asceticism and martyrdom. Yet the apostle has come to his understanding of suffering after realizing that the power of Christ manifests itself most fully and obviously when he is at his weakest. Paradoxically, **when I am weak, then am I strong**. His light and momentary troubles are achieving for him an eternal glory that far outweighs them all (4:17).

Paul's **weaknesses** are explicated in verse 10b by a short tribulation catalogue that resembles similar catalogues in 4:8–12; 6:4–10; and especially 11:23–29. This shows that, in discussing his revelatory experience in 12:1–10, Paul has not really left his theme in 11:23, namely, that he is more a servant of Christ than his opponents *because of* his greater sufferings. Yet it has become apparent that boasting in weakness and suffering is not so foolish as it might seem at first, for the extremity of his weaknesses only reflects the magnitude of his extraordinary revelatory experience, which is the very foundation of his apostolic authority. Furthermore, his boasting in his weakness is ultimately consonant with his principle of boasting only in the Lord, who gave him both his apostolic prerogative and his weakness (cf. 10:17).

12:11–13 / Paul concludes his Fool's Speech as he began it, with an admission that in commending himself he has made a fool of himself (cf. 11:1; 12:1). He chides the Corinthians for their part in forcing him to stoop to this level. This conclusion simultaneously serves as a transition to the next section of the letter.

12:11 / Paul starts with the admission and an accusation against the Corinthians. Having written the foregoing section on boasting, Paul realizes that he has been a **fool**. All the way along, the apostle has indicated his reluctance to engage in this kind of foolish boasting (cf. 11:21–23, 30). "It is necessary to boast," he states in 12:1, for in the face of the opponents' own boasting, to which the Corinthians were quite susceptible, the apostle had little choice but to respond in kind. As we have seen, however, his boasting was doubly foolish: Not only was it not boasting in the Lord, the only legitimate kind of boasting (cf. 10:17), but it was boasting about things that, except for the revelation in 12:2–4, his opponents would not recognize as praiseworthy.

The fact that he had to write the foregoing Fool's Speech at all can be blamed squarely on the Corinthians: They **drove** him to it. Paul should have been **commended** by the church in the face of the intruders, for the Corinthians are his letter of recommendation (cf. 3:2), that is, those who witness to his apostolic legitimacy in both word and deed (cf. 12:6). Instead of ousting the opponents, as Paul would have preferred (cf. 5:12), however, the Corinthians seem to have taken at best a neutral position (cf. 2:5–11) and, in some cases, a hostile stance by actually siding with the opponents.

The reason that the Corinthians should have commended Paul is that he is in no way **inferior** to the intruding opponents, whom he ironically calls **super-apostles**. He makes a very similar statement in 11:5. As we have seen, these opponents invaded the Corinthian church in order to subvert Paul's God-given apostolic authority and to usurp his God-given apostolic territory (cf. 10:12–18), even preaching a different gospel (11:4). To counter this, Paul has argued not only that he is in no way inferior to these **super-apostles** (11:5) but that he is actually superior *(hyper)* to his opponents as a servant of Christ (11:23). Actually, he considers himself to be **nothing** (cf. 3:5). By implication, then, the **super-apostles** are less than **nothing**. Paul's admission contains a rhetorical barb.

12:12 / Paul continues to describe how he is in no way inferior to the interlopers with examples of indisputable apostolic behavior. Implicitly, Paul argues here that the Corinthians should have commended him because, in contrast to the opponents, he performed **the things that mark an apostle** (lit., "the signs of the apostle") in their midst. These "signs" are accompanied by three manifestations that need not be sharply distinguished from one another: **signs, wonders,** and **miracles.** The combination "signs and wonders" occurs frequently in the OT in reference to divine displays that attest to the sending of a human messenger, especially Moses (cf. Exod. 7:3; Deut. 4:34; 6:22; 7:19; 13:1, 2; 26:8; 28:46; 29:3; 34:11; Isa. 8:18; 20:3; Jer. 32:20, 21; Ps. 78:43; 105:27; 135:9; Neh. 9:10). The same collocation of terms is used in the NT of Jesus (cf. Acts 2:22) and the apostles (cf. Acts 2:19, 43; 5:12), including Paul himself (cf. Rom. 15:19; Acts 15:12). Just as Jesus of Nazareth was accredited by God through **signs, wonders and miracles,** which God did among the people through Jesus (cf. Acts 2:22), so also Paul was accredited as an apostle (cf. Acts 14:3).

Of course, these **miracles** did not cure Paul of his own physical infirmity, which perhaps left him open to the opponents' cynical retort, "Physician, heal yourself!" (cf. Luke 4:23, a common proverb in antiquity). Despite his own human weakness and frailty, Paul could manifest the power of Christ in quite tangible ways. In the case of the Corinthians, the apostle appeals specifically to manifestations of the Spirit in their midst as incontestable evidence that his apostleship is genuine (cf. 2 Cor. 3:1–6). The fact that Paul performed these signs **with great perseverance** suggests perhaps that the Corinthians were slow to perceive their significance or actually rejected them at first (cf. 1 Cor. 1:22). Moses, we may add, had a similar problem with the wilderness generation.

12:13 / Paul states another reason *(gar)* that he should have been commended by the Corinthians, since he is not inferior to his opponents. Although left untranslated by the NIV, the *gar* ("for") connects verse 13 to verse 11 as a second line of substantiation. The Corinthians feel slighted by Paul both because he has changed his travel plans in order to avoid them for the time being (cf. 1:12ff.) and because he has declined to accept financial support from them (cf. 11:7–12). With his rhetorical question, however, Paul disputes that he has treated the church at Corinth as **inferior** to other churches. Paul may have temporarily distanced himself from the Corinthians in order to spare them from immediate judgment during his second visit (cf. 1:23), but that does not mean that he regards them as a second-class church.

The apostle has not been a burden to the congregation (cf. 11:9), although he implies that the opponents have been (cf. 11:20). While he has the apostolic right of support from the churches, he voluntarily declines to use it for the sake of the gospel (1 Cor. 9:1–18). For Paul, selflessness is more of a sign of true apostleship than taking advantage of the congregations (cf. 2 Cor. 2:17; 4:2; 11:7–12). Hence, the reason Paul refrains from accepting support is not that he is inferior to the other so-called apostles, but rather that he is concerned for the success of his mission. With the same irony as in 11:7, Paul asks the Corinthians to **forgive** him for not being a burden to them **(this wrong)**. Actually, the apostle maintains that he has wronged no one (cf. 7:2). This mention of financial support provides a transition to the next section.

Additional Notes §12

11:1 / Cf. E. J. Schnabel, "Wisdom," *DPL*, pp. 967–73.

11:2 / On jealousy in Paul, see David Rhoads, "Zealots," *ABD*, vol. 6, pp. 1043–54.

11:3 / Cf. D. G. Reid, "Satan, Devil," *DPL*, pp. 862–67.

11:4 / Cf. Fee, " 'Another Gospel Which You Did Not Embrace,' " pp. 111–33, arguing that the opponents' **different gospel** is a triumphalistic message rather than the true Pauline gospel of Christ crucified.

11:5–11 / On the identity of the **super-apostles** in 11:5 and 12:11, see Victor Paul Furnish, *II Corinthians* (AB 32A; New York: Doubleday, 1985), pp. 502–5.

11:8–9 / Note that in 6:9 Paul describes himself as "poor" and as "having nothing" (cf. v. 27; 1 Cor. 4:11–12).

11:10 / Most churches today would be more than happy to accept free service from a minister. Why, then, would the Corinthians be so annoyed by Paul's refusal to accept their offers of financial assistance (2 Cor. 11:10; 1 Cor. 9:15)? The answer(s) to this question may be found in the Corinthians' cultural context. Most considered manual labor degrading and unseemly for a philosopher (cf. R. F. Hock, *The Social Context of Paul's Ministry: Tentmaking and Apostleship* [Philadelphia: Fortress, 1980]). To make matters worse, Paul hints that his earnings hardly sufficed and that he was in need (2 Cor. 11:9; cf. Phil. 4:12; 1 Cor. 4:10–12). His poverty would hardly persuade others of the power of his gospel. A second irritant stems from Paul's acceptance of aid from the much poorer Macedonians (2 Cor. 11:9; cf. 8:2). This must have struck the Corinthians as a sign of Paul's inconsistency and as demeaning to them (2 Cor. 11:8–9a). The congregation's status was involved. In Roman societal structure, refusal of a benefaction was tantamount to a refusal of friendship and would have been construed as an act of social enmity (cf. Peter Marshall, *Enmity at Corinth: Social Conventions in Paul's Relations with the Corinthians* [WUNT 2/23; Tübingen: Mohr Siebeck, 1987]).

11:13 / Cf. C. K. Barrett, "*PSEUDAPOSTOLOI* (2 Cor. 11:13)," in *Essays on Paul* (London: SPCK, 1982), pp. 87–107.

Martha Himmelfarb argues that the transformation that takes place during heavenly ascent corresponds to priestly investiture (*Ascent to Heaven in Jewish and Christian Apocalypses* [New York/Oxford: Oxford University Press, 1993]).

11:14–15 / On **Satan,** see further on 2:11. In *b. B. Bat.* 16a Satan is called "the angel of death." On Satan's many disguises, see *T. Job* 6:4; 17:2; 23:1; *b. Qidd.* 81ab; *b. Sanh.* 95a, 107a.

Paul's use of the term "minister" of himself (cf. 2 Cor. 3:6; 6:4; 11:23) may have been prompted by the opponents' own self-understanding, for Paul elsewhere prefers the prophetic title "slave of Christ" (Rom. 1:1; Gal. 1:10).

If we would doubt that Paul could refer to "apostles" with letters of recommendation from the Jerusalem authorities as "**servants [of Satan]**," we need recall only Paul's severe condemnation of Peter in Antioch (cf. Gal. 2:11–14, with the anathema of Gal. 1:8–9).

11:21b–33 / For a structural diagram of this passage, see Martin, *2 Corinthians*, p. 370.

11:22 / In Hellenistic-Jewish literature, the term "Hebrew" occurs much less commonly than its synonyms *Israēl* and *Ioudaios*. It is used primarily in two senses: (1) as a term for the language and script (cf. Acts 6:1) and (2) as an archaic name and lofty expression for the Hebrew nation (cf. 2 Macc. 7:31), particularly with respect to ancestral lineage (cf. Ezekiel the Tragedian, *Exagoge* 7, 12, 35, 43, 107). In the OT, the people were known as **Hebrews** long before the exodus from Egypt. According to Acts 21:40–22:3 Paul spoke the language(s) of Palestine, even though he was a Diaspora Jew from Tarsus. In the present context, however, the term seems to have less to do with language than with Paul's nationality, although these two aspects are, of course, closely related (cf. Gen. 10:5, 20, 31). Cf. Niels Peter Lemche, "Hebrew," *ABD*, vol. 3, p. 95; K. G. Kuhn, "Israel," *TDNT*, vol. 3, pp. 365–69, 372–75. A late inscription (possibly fourth–fifth century A.D.) attests to the existence of a "synagogue of the *Hebrews*" in Corinth.

11:23b–29 / Cf. Scott B. Andrews, "Too Weak Not to Lead: The Form and Function of 2 Cor. 11.23b–33," *NTS* 41 (1995), pp. 263–76.

Ben Witherington III argues that Paul's boasts in his weakness are intended as a parody on the *Res Gestae*, the list of Augustus's achievements as Roman emperor (*Conflict and Community in Corinth: A Social-Rhetorical Commentary on 1 and 2 Corinthians* [Grand Rapids: Eerdmans, 1995], pp. 450–52). More to the point, however, Paul seems to describe himself here as someone who is in exile from his own country (and from his heavenly home [cf. 2 Cor. 5:6]) and who expresses his sufferings and endurance in that situation (cf., e.g., Ovid, *Tristia* 3–5; *Epistulae ex Ponto*). We may compare the teaching of Diogenes (ca. 400–325 B.C.), founder of the Cynic sect, who came to Corinth during the Isthmian games (cf. Dio Chrysostom, *Discourses* 8–9, esp. 8.13, 16; 9.12–13). In a list of other persecutions that Paul had to endure (i.e., imprisonment and stoning), 1 Clem. 5:6 explicitly refers to the apostle as one who has been "exiled" (*phygadeutheis*) from his own country.

It is worth noting that, according to Josephus, Moses boasted that he devoted himself to tribulations on behalf of the people (*Ant.* 4.42).

When Paul refers to having been **flogged**, we may also consider that the Romans used flogging as a form of interrogation (cf. Acts 22:24).

11:24 / Cf. A. E. Harvey, "Forty Strokes Save One: Social Aspects of Judaizing and Apostasy," in *Alternative Approaches to New Testament Study* (ed. A. E. Harvey; London: SPCK, 1985), pp. 79–96.

On Jewish disciplinary methods and attitudes in the Greco-Roman period, see Torrey Seland, *Establishment Violence in Philo and Luke: A Study of Non-Conformity to the Torah and Jewish Vigilante Reactions* (Leiden: Brill, 1995). On rabbinic loanwords for whipping, see Daniel Sperber, *A Dictionary of Greek and Latin Legal Terms in Rabbinic Literature* (Bar-Ilan University Institute for Lexicography: Dictionaries of Talmud, Midrash and Targum 1; Ramat-Gan: Bar-Ilan University Press, 1984), pp. 23–24, 181–82.

Cf. E. P. Sanders, "Paul on the Law, His Opponents, and the Jewish People in Philippians 3 and 2 Corinthians 11," in *Anti-Judaism in Early Christianity, Vol. 1: Paul and the Gospels* (ed. Peter Richardson; Studies in Christianity and Judaism 2; Waterloo, Ontario: Wilfrid Laurier University Press, 1986), pp. 75–90 (here pp. 85–87).

11:25 / On the Roman citizenship of Paul, see Hengel, *Pre-Christian Paul*, pp. 6–15. Hengel argues that Paul deliberately allowed such beatings in order to participate in the sufferings of Christ.

Stoning was not an exclusively Jewish form of execution (cf. Acts 14:5). As a spontaneous expression of rage by a mob, stoning was a very widespread form of lynch justice. The pre-Roman Corinthians are said to have practiced stoning (cf. Pausanias 2.3.6; see also Plutarch, *Philopoemen* 21.5).

11:26b / On Paul's persecution at the hands of Jews, see Ernst Baasland, "Persecution: A Neglected Feature in the Letter to the Galatians," *ST* 38 (1984), pp. 135–50; Colin G. Kruse, "Afflictions, Trials, Hardships," *DPL*, pp. 18–20. On 1 Thess. 2:14–16, see James M. Scott, "Paul's Use of Deuteronomic Tradition," pp. 645–65 (esp. pp. 651–57).

In the context of the mention of Israel as a "nation" (*genos*), the term *ethnē* (translated **Gentiles** in the NIV) should be rendered "nations." This prepares the way for the account of the incident under King Aretas in 11:30–33 (see further below). Paul thinks primarily in terms of nations (cf. Scott, *Paul and the Nations*.)

11:29 / The NIV translates the verb *pyroumai* as **I inwardly burn.** On the other hand, the verb can be understood figuratively as signifying "be inflamed with grief." Cf. William Horbury and David Noy, *Jewish Inscriptions of Graeco-Roman Egypt* (Cambridge: Cambridge University Press, 1992), pp. 64–69 (esp. p. 67). Note the other references to grief and sorrow in the letter (cf. 2 Cor. 2:1–5, 7; 6:10; 7:8–11).

11:32–33 / Cf. Rainer Riesner, *Die Frühzeit des Paulus. Studien zur Chronologie, Missionsstrategie und Theologie* (WUNT 71; Tübingen: Mohr Siebeck, 1994), pp. 29, 66–79; Justin Taylor, "The Ethnarch of King Aretas at Damascus: A Note on 2 Cor. 11, 32–33," *RB* 99 (1992), pp. 719–28.

The story of Paul's escape from **Damascus** is told in somewhat different terms in Acts 9:23–25. Cf. Mark Harding, "On the Historicity of Acts: Comparing Acts 9.23–5 with 2 Corinthians 11.32–3," *NTS* 39 (1993), pp. 518–38.

Cf. Jerome Murphy-O'Connor, "Paul in Arabia," *CBQ* 55 (1993), pp. 732–37.

Escaping through a city wall is a symbol of exile (cf. Ezek. 12:4–5, 7, 12). As we have seen, Paul portrays himself as an exile in this context (see on 11:23b–29).

If the reference to being **lowered in a basket from a window in the wall** is meant to contrast with the assault on a city described in 10:4 (citing Prov. 21:22), then the purpose for this contrast may be twofold: (1) to emphasize Paul's weakness in contrast to the wise, and (2) to prepare the description of the ascent to the third heaven in 12:2–4. According to our interpretation, both 10:4 and 12:2–4 relate to Paul's *merkabah* experience.

12:1–10 / When Paul implies that his opponents' **boasting** forces him to boast about his own superior revelatory experience, he may have in view Korah's rebellion, which attempted to eliminate the mediators of divine revelation by usurping the authority of Moses and Aaron (Num. 16:3; cf. Exod. 19:6; 29:45; Deut. 7:6; 14:2; 26:19; 28:9). After all, as a "holy nation," the people had received a direct divine revelation at Sinai, without mediators (Exod. 19:1–20:21). If Korah and his followers can claim that Moses and Aaron are superfluous as mediators, how much more can Paul's opponents claim in the new covenant situation that there is no need for mediators (cf. Jer. 31:34)?

12:1 / When Paul speaks here of **visions and revelations** in the plural, we are reminded that in *merkabah* mysticism the ascent to heaven was made during the lifetime of the mystic (i.e., not just after death!) and could be repeated numerous times. Moses' revelatory experience provides the prototype of repeated entrance into the presence of God. According to the book of Acts, Paul received a number of visions (cf. Acts 9:12; 16:9–10; 18:9–10; 22:17–21; 23:11; 27:23–24).

The genitive "of Christ" (**from the Lord** in the NIV) may be objective. In that case, just as *merkabah* mystics saw God enthroned at the climax of their heavenly ascents, so also Paul may have seen Christ enthroned.

12:2–4 / For the interpretation of 2 Cor. 12:2–4 that is developed here see further my essay, "The Triumph of God in 2 Cor. 2:14: Another Example of *merkabah* Mysticism in Paul," NTS 42 (1996), pp. 260–81. We may compare Paul's heavenly ascent to that of Philo (cf. Peder Borgen, "Heavenly Ascent in Philo: An Examination of Selected Passages," in *The Pseudepigrapha and Early Biblical Interpretation* [ed. James H. Charlesworth and Craig A. Evans; JSPSup 14; Sheffield: JSOT Press, 1993], pp. 246–68).

12:2 / Of course, Jesus' self-designation as the "Son of Man" is a huge problem in itself.

The Coptic *Apocalypse of Paul* from Nag Hammadi (NHC V,2), whose Greek original may stem from the second century A.D., provides a gnostic interpretation of 2 Cor. 12:2–4 in which Paul is made to allude to Ps. 68:18. Cf. Douglas M. Parrott, "The Apocalypse of Paul (V,2)," in *The Nag Hammadi Library in English* (3d ed.; San Francisco: Harper & Row, 1988), pp. 256–59 (here p. 259). This clear allusion to Ps. 68:18 provides evidence that Paul's ascent to heaven in 2 Cor. 12:2–4 was interpreted in light of Ps. 68:18 from an early period, even though the Pauline tradition may have undergone significant modification in the gnostic text. Hence, we see that 2 Cor. 2:14 and 12:2–4 are linked by their common basis not only in *merkabah* mysticism generally but also in the Ps. 68:18 tradition particularly.

Unfortunately, many interpreters have misunderstood Paul's rhetoric here to mean that he places no importance on his revelatory experience. Cf., e.g., Furnish, *II Corinthians*, p. 544.

The dating of Paul's vision to a time **fourteen years ago** is difficult to ascertain, for much depends on when 2 Corinthians itself (or at least this section of the extant letter) is dated. Furthermore, to which experience does the apostle refer? There is no necessary connection between our text and the "fourteen years" reported in Gal. 2:1. In view of these uncertainties, Riesner uses 2 Cor. 12:2–4 for the relative chronology only after the date of 2 Corinthians (A.D. 55/56) has been established on other grounds (*Die Frühzeit des Apostels Paulus*, pp. 242, 285). The suggestion that 2 Cor. 12:1–4 refers to Paul's conversion experience seems improbable, for *if* Paul's conversion took place about A.D. 33, and the heavenly experience recounted here took place fourteen years before the writing 2 Corinthians (assuming the unity of the letter), then the experience occurred about A.D. 42. With so many assumptions and uncertainties, however, this reconstruction must remain conjectural. Indeed, any reconstruction is bound to beg the question at some point.

Prophetic oracles are frequently dated. For example, Isaiah's encounter with the throne of God in the temple is dated to "the year that King Uzziah died" (Isa. 6:1). Perhaps the number **fourteen** has some traditional significance. We may note, for example, that Ezekiel's vision of the restored temple and land (Ezek. 40–48) took place "in the fourteenth year after the city [sc. Jerusalem] was struck down" (40:1). The text goes on to state that "on that very day, the hand of the Lord was upon me, and he brought me there." Jewish tradition has it that the Israelites spend seven years in conquering the land and seven years in dividing it among the twelve tribes (*Seder ʿolam Rabbah* 11; *b. Qidd.* 37a,b; *b. Zebaḥ.* 118b; *Gen. Rab.* 35:3; 98:15; cf. Josephus, *Ant.* 5.68). Furthermore, Jacob spent fourteen years secluded in the land and studying under Eber (*b. Meg.* 16b, 17a; *Gen. Rab.* 68:5, 11; *Exod. Rab.* 2:6).

Cf. Gershom Scholem, "The Four Who Entered Paradise and Paul's Ascension to Paradise," in *Jewish Gnosticism, Merkabah Mysticism, and Talmudic Tradition* (2d ed.; New York: Jewish Theological Seminary, 1965), pp. 14–19. On the connection of 2 Cor. 12:2–4 to Jewish mysticism see also Alan F. Segal, "Paul and the Beginning of Jewish Mysticism," in *Death, Ecstasy, and Other Worldly Journeys* (ed. John J. Collins and Michael Fishbane; Albany, N.Y.: SUNY Press, 1995), pp. 95–122 (esp. pp. 108–9).

On the verb **caught up** *(harpazein),* see Martha Himmelfarb, "The Practice of Ascent in the Ancient Mediterranean World," in *Death, Ecstasy, and Other Worldly Journeys*, pp. 123–37 (esp. pp. 128–33), who argues that "the dominant understanding of ascent in ancient Jewish and Christian literature is of a process initiated not by the visionary but by God" (p. 133). As John J. Collins observes, prophetic visions of the divine throne typically serve two functions: they establish the credentials of the visionary, thereby legitimating him as an intermediary between heaven and earth, and they provide revealed information (*The Scepter and the Star: The Messiahs of the Dead Sea Scrolls and Other Ancient Literature* [ABRL; New York: Doubleday, 1995], p. 140).

The connection between 2 Cor. 12:1–10 and 2:14–3:18 is further substantiated, if, as several scholars have suggested, the Lord's answer to Paul's request in 2 Cor. 12:9 reflects a midrash on Deut. 3:26, where God responds to Moses' request to enter the land (cf., e.g., Markus N. A. Bockmuehl, *Revelation and Mystery in Ancient Judaism and Pauline Christianity* [WUNT 2/36; Tübingen: Mohr Siebeck, 1990], p. 143; Furnish, *II Corinthians*, p. 530; but see Ulrich Heckel, *Kraft in Schwachheit* [WUNT 2/56; Tübingen: Mohr Siebeck, 1993], p. 89), for 2 Cor. 2:14–3:18 compares Paul and Moses in several ways. Moreover, Paul argues in 2 Cor. 2:16b that the reason for his sufficiency is really the same as that of Moses (cf. 12:9).

On the concept of the **third heaven**, see Adela Yarbro Collins, "The Seven Heavens in Jewish and Christian Apocalypses," in *Death, Ecstasy, and Other Worldly Journeys*, pp. 59–93 (esp. pp. 66–68).

In the body or out of the body could reflect the ambivalence that some *merkabah* mystics felt as to whether their experience was physical or mental, for example, *Merkabah Rabbah* (Schäfer, §680) states: "Rabbi said: When my heart heard this great secret, the world above me was transformed to clearness, and my heart was as if I had come into a new world. Day after day, it seemed to my soul as if I stood before the Throne of Glory." See also *1 En.* 14:8: "And behold I saw the clouds: And they were calling me in a vision; . . . and in the vision, the winds were causing me to fly and rushing me high up into heaven" (*OTP*). Most of the descriptions, however, seem to portray the heavenly journey in concrete, physical terms. In our text, the fact that Paul received a thorn in the flesh (2 Cor. 12:7) may indicate that his heavenly journey was in the body, if he received this affliction during the journey. Perhaps the apostle uses the uncertainty about his revelatory experience as a way of partially explaining why his body was not transformed by the ascents, for an out-of-body experience may not have been expected to produce physical change in the visionary. In that case, we may ask what difference, if any, Paul may have thought there was between believers' revelatory experience (cf. 3:18) and his own experience.

12:3–4 / On **paradise**, see Sandra R. Shimoff, "Gardens: From Eden to Jerusalem," *JSJ* 26 (1995), pp. 145–55; J. H. Charlesworth, "Paradise," *ABD*, vol. 5, pp. 154–55.

Cf. C. R. A. Morray-Jones, "Paradise Revisited (2 Cor. 12:1–12): The Jewish Mystical Background of Paul's Apostolate, Part 1: The Jewish Sources," *HTR* 86 (1993), pp. 177–217; idem, "Paradise Revisited (2 Cor. 12:1–12): The Jewish Mystical Background of Paul's Apostolate, Part 2: Paul's Heavenly Ascent and its Significance," *HTR* 86 (1993), pp. 265–92. For a rebuttal of this position, see now Alon Goshen-Gottstein, "Four Entered Paradise Revisited," *HTR* 88 (1995), pp. 69–133. For an answer to the objections of Goshen-Gottstein see James Davila, "The Hodayot Hymnist and the Four who Entered Paradise," *RevQ* 17 (1996) 457–77.

On the reluctance of Jewish mystics to recount certain aspects of their heavenly journeys, see Morray-Jones, "The Jewish Mystical Background of Paul's Apostolate, Part 2," pp. 271–72, 281, 283; Alan F. Segal, *Paul the Convert: The Apostolate and Apostasy of Saul the Pharisee* (New Haven: Yale, 1990), p. 58; Bockmuehl, *Revelation and Mystery*, p. 175. Cf. Dan. 12:4; *Apoc. Zeph.* 5:6; *4 Ezra* 14:4–6, 44–46. Perhaps one of the **things that man is not permitted to tell** is the name of YHWH himself, as often in Hekhalot literature (cf., e.g., Schäfer, §§670, 961; also Philo, *On the Embassy to Gaius* 353). Obviously, the *merkabah* mystic was not prohibited from telling everything that was revealed to him; otherwise, he could never be a mediator of revelation. See also Jean-Pierre Ruiz, "Hearing and Seeing but Not Saying: A Look at Revelation 10:4 and 2 Corinthians 12:4," *Society of Biblical Literature 1994 Seminar Papers* (ed. Eugene H. Lovering Jr.; Atlanta: Scholars Press, 1994), pp. 182–202.

12:7 / I am indebted to my colleague, Martin G. Abegg, for the parallel to the boasts of the Teacher of Righteousness. On the Hekhalot warnings against self-exaltation, see Morray-Jones, "The Jewish Mystical Background of Paul's Apostolate, Part 2," pp. 271–72. In *Hekhalot Rabbati* (Schäfer, §272), God is extolled as one who humbles the proud and exalts the humble.

Galen, the second-century medical writer, uses the expression **thorn in the flesh** several times in combination with participles (*De simplicium medicamentorum temperamentis ac facultatibus libri xi* 696; *In Hippocratis aphorismos commentarii vii* 17b.630; also Photius *Bibl.* 175b). These examples show that Paul uses the dative *sarki* in a locative sense, and that his elliptical expression *skolops tē sarki* means "a thorn (stuck) in the flesh." It is no use trying to specify what the precise nature of Paul's physical ailment might have been, whether epilepsy, depression, headaches, malaria, leprosy, a speech impediment, or some other. Our text is as unspecific about the ailment as the psalm that evidently lies behind it (Ps. 32:4). We have already noted Paul's use of psalmic form and context in 2 Cor. 1:3–11 and 4:13. Moreover, 2 Cor. 6:9 ("as disciplined and yet not put to death") is widely acknowledged as an allusion to Ps. 117:18 LXX ("with discipline the Lord disciplined me and yet did not give me over to death"). This shows that Paul did indeed seem himself as under divine discipline at points.

Sometimes Paul's "thorn in the flesh" is interpreted in light of Gal. 4:15 as an eye disease. Cf. T. J. Leary, " 'A Thorn in the Flesh'— 2 Corinthians 12:7," *JTS* 43 (1992), pp. 520–22. As with our passage, however, Paul's statements in Gal. 4:12–20 can be interpreted as referring either to an illness or to persecution. Cf. A. J. Goddard and S. A. Cummins, "Ill or Ill-Treated? Conflict and Persecution as the Context of Paul's Original Ministry in Galatia," *JSNT* 52 (1993), pp. 93–126.

12:8 / Cf. Michael D. Swartz, *Mystical Prayer in Ancient Judaism: An Analysis of Ma'aseh Merkavah* (TSAJ 28; Tübingen: Mohr Siebeck, 1992), who shows that in *Ma'aseh Merkabah*, a central text of Jewish *merkabah* mysticism, prayers are seen as the instruments by which the visionary ascends, experiences the vision of the *merkabah* and the heavenly realm, and protects himself from the terrifying dangers of that vision (pp. 5, 69, 128, 137, 141).

When Paul refers to the **Lord** here, he probably means the Lord Jesus Christ, for v. 9 interprets "the power" (NIV: ***my* power**) to mean "Christ's power."

It is interesting to note that Moses also made an entreaty to the **Lord** that was firmly denied (Deut. 3:23–26).

12:9 / On the connection between **power** and **weakness**, see Timothy B. Savage, *Power Through Weakness: Paul's Understanding of the Christian Ministry in 2 Corinthians* (SNTSMS 86; Cambridge: Cambridge University Press, 1995).

The stative verb *arkein* **(be sufficient)** falls within the same semantic field as *hikanos* ("sufficient"), *hikanotēs* ("sufficiency"), and *hikanoun* ("make sufficient") in 2 Cor. 2:16; 3:5, 6, and the two are often used synonymously (cf. Exod. 12:4, LXX; Plutarch, *Phocion* 30.1; Strabo, *Geography* 2.4.8). Hence, instead of *hikanon estin* in Luke 22:38, Codex Bezae has *arkei*.

If the "Lord" in v. 8 and the **he** in v. 9 refer to the Lord Jesus Christ, then this verse constitutes the earliest record of the words of Jesus in the NT, since Paul's letters constitute the oldest literature in the NT.

12:12 / For the expression "the signs of the apostle" *(ta sēmeia tou apostolou)*, we may also compare Isa. 66:19, where God promises to leave "signs" *(sēmeia)* and to "send out" *(exapostelō)* certain survivors to the nations. As we have seen, Isa. 66:19–20 is crucial to Paul's conception of his mission.

Signs and **wonders** can also be used by false prophets (cf. Deut. 13:1–2; Mark 13:22 par.). On Moses as a model of the sign prophets, even down to the first century, see Rebecca Gray, *Prophetic Figures in Late Second Temple Jewish Palestine: The Evidence from Josephus* (New York and Oxford: Oxford University Press, 1993), pp. 112–44 (esp. pp. 115, 125–28, 137, 141–42). Note also that in Num. 16:38 (17:3 LXX) the censers used in connection with Korah's rebellion were hammered into plates as a "sign" *(semeion)* to the sons of Israel. In fact, the Fragment Targum to Num. 17:3 MT uses the Greek loanword *sēmeion*. When Paul states that he performed **signs** and **wonders** in the midst of the Corinthians, one wonders whether he may include the punishment of the offender to which 2 Cor. 2:7 refers.

According to the book of Acts, Paul performed many healing miracles (cf. Acts 14:10; 15:12; 16:18; 19:11–12; 28:3–6, 8).

§13 Visit (2 Cor. 12:14–13:10)

The third and last section of 2 Corinthians 10–13 prepares the way for Paul's third visit to Corinth. His first visit was to found the church (Acts 18); his second visit was to check the church (2 Cor. 2:1); and now his third visit will be to judge the church. If Paul's ministry of the Spirit is convincing evidence for the legitimacy of his apostolic authority and ministry, a ministry that he attributes directly to God (cf. 2:14, 17; 3:5–6; 10:17), then the Corinthians' decision to reject that ministry becomes, from Paul's perspective, a rejection of God and his salvation as well. It is for this reason that Paul ends his second canonical letter to the Corinthians with the severe warning to test themselves in order to make sure they are still "in the faith" (cf. 6:1). Upon his arrival Paul will be forced to use his power to tear down all those who have failed this test by rejecting his apostleship (cf. 13:5, 10). Paul has been faced with a Korah-like rebellion in Corinth. He wants to give any rebels a chance to repent before he comes in judgment.

As we have seen, Korah's rebellion provides a useful model for understanding the complex situation in Corinth from Paul's perspective. Now, as we consider the possible relationship of 2 Corinthians 1–9 to 10–13, this model becomes helpful once again, for, as in Numbers 16, there are also evidently three parties to consider in Corinth: the congregation as a whole and two rebellious factions within the congregation. These factions do not necessarily correspond to those mentioned in 1 Corinthians 1:12, although that passage certainly illustrates the Corinthians' schismatic tendency, which the interlopers would have manipulated to their own advantage. Moreover, if the Corinthians were divided into separate house churches (cf. R. Banks), which only occasionally met together as a whole in one of the larger homes (cf. Rom. 16:23), then the very sociological structure of the church in Corinth lent itself to factions (see on 2 Cor. 13:12). These smaller assemblies would have been easy prey for intruders.

By the writing of 2 Corinthians Paul has already dealt with the faction led by the malefactor (cf. 2:5–6; also 1:13–14). When he comes to Corinth for the third time the apostle plans to deal with the remaining faction that continues to side with the false apostles (12:20–21). Like Moses, however, Paul must be concerned that the whole congregation might sympathize with the rebels, thus precipitating a full-scale purge when he arrives (cf. 10:8; 13:10; Num. 16:41–50). The apostle wants to avoid such a debacle at all costs; hence, he calls the factions to concord (12:20; 13:11).

12:14–18 / Some scholars take these verses as part of the theme of financial support in verse 13, thus making the next section of the letter begin with 12:19. More likely, however, verse 14 announces the theme of the next section—Paul's third visit to Corinth—since this announcement is repeated in 13:1 (cf. also 12:20, 21). Furthermore, the interjection "Look!" (**Now** in the NIV) dramatically signals the change of subject.

12:14 / Paul begins this subsection with an announcement of his coming. The adverb **third time** indicates that Paul has made two other visits: the founding visit and the second, painful visit. Simultaneously, the apostle announces that he will not be a **burden** to the Corinthians when he comes, just as he was not during the previous visits (cf. 11:9; 12:13). He wants to dispel any notion that he will exploit the Corinthians (7:2). Since one of his objectives in coming to Corinth is to complete the collection for Jerusalem (chs. 8–9), Paul feels he must reassure the church of his honest intentions, especially in light of their suspicions about him with regard to money. He wants the Corinthians themselves, not their possessions (cf. Phil. 4:17). This is in contrast to Paul's opponents in Corinth (cf. 11:20).

For Paul, relationships are more important than resources, and he wants to restore his relationship with the Corinthians. To this end, he reminds his readers that he and they are bound to each other by a parent-child relationship. He is their father, since he originally evangelized them (see on 6:13; 1 Cor. 4:15). The point that Paul draws from this parent-child relationship for his upcoming visit to Corinth seems plausible if he is referring metaphorically to minors: "For the children ought not to store up treasure for their parents, but rather parents for their children." Younger children can, of course, expect support from their parents, and Paul evidently considers the Corinthians to be "infants in Christ" (cf. 1 Cor. 3:1). However, if **the children** are adults (the term is frequently used simply of progeny, irrespective of age), then they may well be expected to support their elderly parents (cf. Exod. 20:12; 21:17; Mark 7:8–13). Elsewhere the apostle affirms that he does have an apostolic right to support (cf. 1 Cor. 9:1–18).

12:15 / Having stated that he will not be a burden to his spiritual children when he comes to visit in Corinth, Paul goes on to use this fact as an evidence of his love for them. This intensifies what Paul has said in verse 14: Not only is he willing to support himself during his visit in Corinth, he will very gladly **spend** *(dapanan)*. The words **for you everything I have** are not represented in the Greek text, although they are implied. Paul is saying that he is willing to "spend freely," referring particularly to his own support while in Corinth. Moreover, not only is the apostle willing to spend, he is willing to **expend** *(ekdapanan)* himself for the Corinthians's lives (the NIV does not include "for your lives"). The effect of the wordplay **(spend/expend)** is to underscore Paul's determination to exert himself fully on behalf of the Corinthians, using not only his material resources but also his time, his energy, his health, in short, anything and everything he has. Whatever suffering Paul endures, including apostolic labors (cf. 11:23, 27–28), is for the benefit of the Corinthians (cf. 1:6–7; Phil. 2:17).

Paul argues that his willingness to spend and to be spent is a sign of his love for the Corinthians **(If I love you more)**. Apparently the Corinthians do not perceive Paul's sacrifice as a token of his love (cf. 11:7, 11), for the more he refuses their support, the less the Corinthians love him. Bewildered by their irrational behavior, Paul asks incredulously, **[W]ill you love me less?** All along in the letter, the apostle has been trying to regain the Corinthians' love. He has already exhorted them as his "children" to open their hearts to him, just as he has opened his own heart to them (6:11, 13; 7:2). He has assured them that he is not withholding his affection from them, but rather that they are withholding their affection from him (6:12). Even in the matter of refusing support, Paul affirms his strong love for them (cf. 11:11). He desperately wants his love to be be requited, so much so that he brags about their love for him in the hope of actually receiving it (cf. 8:7).

12:16–18 / Here Paul handles a concrete accusation brought against him by the Corinthians. Whereas in verses 14–15 Paul has tried to reassure the Corinthians of his love despite the fact that he refuses to accept support from them, in verses 16–18, he must now defend himself against the charge of exploiting the Corinthians by means of his coworkers. In effect, Paul is being accused of a confidence game, in which he himself poses as the selfless apostle (**I have not been a burden to you**), while his accomplices carry out the actual exploitation. The collection for Jerusalem puts Paul in a difficult and sensitive position (cf. 2 Cor. 8–9). In the previous context he has steadfastly denied that he has **exploited** anyone (7:2), in contrast to the opponents (cf. 2:17; 11:20). Paul wants to avoid any criticism of the way he is administrating the collection (8:20), and, like Ezra before him (cf. Ezra 8:24–34), he has taken careful security measures to ensure that the collection will not become a scandal (cf. 8:21–22; 9:3–5). If we are correct that 2 Corinthians is a unity, and that therefore Titus has probably not yet arrived in Corinth to resume the oversight of the collection (cf. 8:16–24, which refers to Titus and *two* unnamed "brothers"), then Paul is referring in 12:18 to the earlier work of **Titus** and another anonymous **brother** in Corinth (cf. 8:6, although without mentioning the brother). Paul's question expects a negative answer: The Corinthians know full well that, when Titus began making the collection in Corinth over a year before, he did not try to exploit the Corinthians. Since Titus's integrity is above reproach, he becomes a key figure in Paul's defense against the allegation that the planned collection for Jerusalem will involve monetary gain for himself.

12:19–21 / In the previous part of the letter Paul has done everything possible to win the Corinthians back to his side. In this section Paul expresses his fears about what will happen if he finds an unrepentant faction in the church when he arrives. Not unlike an OT prophet, the apostle predicts impending judgment in order to effect repentance. The tearful letter has already promoted repentance among a majority of the congregation; the present letter is designed to promote repentance among the rest. The apostle wants to avoid yet another painful visit.

12:19 / Paul explains that he has not been defending himself in this letter, but rather trying to encourage the Corinthians. As we have seen, 2:14–7:4 is usually called Paul's "apology" for the legitimacy of his apostleship. He certainly does appear to defend himself both there and often throughout the letter. Where he does admit to defending himself (1 Cor. 9:3, "my defense to those who would examine me"), he makes it clear that he is speaking of a defense of his apostleship. Yet even in 1 Corinthians the apostle argues that ultimately only the Lord can judge him, not the Corinthians or any human court (cf. 1 Cor. 4:3–5; see further on 2 Cor. 1:12; 5:10).

As Paul goes on to imply, who can judge him as an apostle is a matter of jurisdiction. The reason he does not defend himself is that he speaks **in the sight of God** in Christ, his only true judge (cf. 5:10). Paul alludes thereby to his earlier statement in 2:17, that he speaks "in the presence of God," that is, before the divine throne of glory, just as Moses did. In light of the other allusions to Moses in the foregoing context (2:14–16; 3:1), Paul obviously has Exodus 32:11 in mind when he writes 2:17 and 12:19, especially in light of the *merkabah* experience described in 12:2–4. There is thus a unique, heavenly dimension to Paul's apostolic role that sets him well apart from his opponents, who merely peddle the word of God for profit. In this way Paul shows that he is sufficient as a revelatory mediator because, like Moses, he speaks "in the presence of God." As a revelatory mediator, Paul ultimately has no need of defending himself. He speaks on behalf of God and Christ (cf. 5:20).

Far from seeking merely to defend himself and to promote his own cause, Paul's purpose in everything he does is for the Corinthians' **strengthening,** or "edification" *(oikodomē)*. Indeed, the purpose for which the Lord gave the apostle his authority is "building up" *(oikodomē)* and not for tearing down, to use another phrase that is repeated in this letter (cf. 10:8; 13:10). Even when Paul defends his apostleship, it is for the benefit of the Corinthians, so that they will heed his warnings, correct their ways, and live more completely in light of the new covenant situation. This will necessarily include disassociation from the intruders (cf. 5:11–12; 6:14–7:1).

12:20 / Paul further explains (**For,** *gar*) his apostolic ministry with respect to the Corinthians, particularly in view of his imminent third visit (**when I come,** cf. 12:14). While the fundamental purpose of Paul's apostolic ministry is "building up" (v. 19), there can be another side to it. If, when he comes to Corinth, the Corinthians are not as he would like them to be, Paul fears he will be forced to deal with them severely (**you may not find me as you want me to be**). Whereas previously Paul had been quite "timid" when dealing with the Corinthians (cf. 10:1), this time he will act more decisively, if necessary. He does not spell out exactly what he might do at this point (see on 13:2; also 1 Cor. 4:21). While Paul hopes for the best, he fears the worst. Everything is contingent on the Corinthians' response.

In verse 20b, a vice catalogue follows, in which the apostle lists the sins of faction and sedition he fears may be characteristic of the Corinthian church when he comes. This vice list gives an important insight as to the nature of the situation in Corinth from Paul's perspective. Interestingly enough, all of these sins apply equally to Korah's rebellion in Numbers 16–17, which, as we have seen, is consistent with Paul's portrayal of himself as a Moses figure who confronts a Korah-like rebellion in Corinth. Hence, the situation that Paul fears when he comes is that the opponents will have entrenched their position within the congregation and will have formed a strong alliance against him, fueled by pride and malice.

The first sin is **quarreling** or "strife, discord, contention." The same word appears in other lists of vices (cf. Rom. 1:29; 1 *Clem.* 46:5), sometimes along with **jealousy** *(zēlos),* the second sin in our list (see the vice lists in Rom. 13:13; 1 Cor. 3:3; Gal. 5:20). Korah and his followers became contentious precisely because they were jealous of Moses and Aaron (cf. Josephus, *Ant.* 4.14; Ps. 106:16–18; Sir. 45:18; 1 *Clem.* 4:12; *b. Sanh.* 110a). The third sin is **outbursts of anger** *(thymoi).* According to Sirach 45:18, "Outsiders *(allotrioi)* conspired against him [sc. Aaron], and envied *(ezēlōsan)* him in the wilderness, Dathan and Abiram and their followers and the company of Korah, in wrath and anger *(en thymō kai orgē).*" The fourth sin is **factions.** The same word is found in the list of vices in Galatians 5:20. According to BAGD (p. 309), the term is found before NT times only in Aristotle, where it denotes a self-seeking pursuit of political office by unfair means (cf. F. Büchsel, *TDNT,* vol. 2, pp. 660–661). This would fit well with the ambitions of Korah and his followers, who wanted to usurp the authority of Moses and Aaron for themselves (cf. Josephus, *Ant.* 4.17). In the process, they also formed factions. The fifth sin is **slander.** Slander was a major part of Korah's campaign against Moses and Aaron (e.g., Num. 16:3, 13–14; Josephus, *Ant.* 4.15). According to Jewish tradition, Korah cast aspersion on Moses' claim to being a revelatory mediator (cf. Philo, *On the Life of Moses* 2.176–177, 278; *b. B.Meṣiʿa* 75b). The sixth sin is **gossip** *(psithyrismos),* another term found only here in the NT. The word is closely associated with **slander** in several vice lists (cf. BAGD, pp. 892–93). A cognate noun *(psithyristēs)* occurs in another vice list (cf. Rom. 1:29). The seventh sin is **arrogance** or "conceit" *(physiōsis)*, another hapax legomenon in the NT. The verb form of the word *(physiousthai)* occurs several times in 1 Corinthians (4:6, 18, 19; 5:2; 8:1; 13:4). Pride is Korah's fundamental fault. Although God had given him one prestigious position, he was prideful enough to seek the priesthood as well (cf. Num. 16:8–11; cf. Josephus, *Ant.* 4.14–19, 23). The final sin is **disorder** or "tumult," a term that was used earlier in a tribulation catalogue (2 Cor. 6:5). This term occurs elsewhere with reference to insurrection and social anarchy (cf. 1 Cor. 14:33 [opposite "peace"]; Luke 21:9 [with "wars"]).

12:21 / If Paul arrives in Corinth to find the church still in a state of open rebellion (v. 20b), he worries about what might happen to himself and to the congregation. Paul has already stated in 2:1 that he had decided not to make another painful visit to Corinth (lit., "not to **come again** to you in sorrow"). Thus, the theme of "coming again" in these verses draws the whole letter together and gives evidence to its fundamental unity (see similarly on 2:17 and 12:19–21). The last time that Paul visited Corinth he was severely offended by a member of the church; he was left in the lurch by the congregation, and he had to retreat in humiliation (2:1–11). It was to spare the Corinthians that Paul did not come again to Corinth (1:23). Instead, the apostle wrote a tearful letter in order to give them a chance to repent, so that when he did come again he might not suffer pain (2:3–4). Now, as he prepares for his third visit, Paul fears a repeat performance of the second, painful visit. He fears that he will be **grieved** by those who are still unrepentant, because then he will have to use his God-given apostolic authority for judging the congregation (cf. 10:8; 13:10). While part of the church (i.e., the "majority" in 2:6) has already shown encouraging signs of repentance, Paul still needs to send 2 Corinthians in order to bring even this group fully on board. Others in the church, however, remain quite factious (cf. 12:20b) and guilty even of the vile perversions, including **impurity, sexual sin,** and **debauchery.** From the apostle's dualistic perspective, there are only two kinds of people: those who stand on the side of Christ and the people of God, and those who stand on the side of Satan/Belial and his ilk (cf. 2:15–16a; 6:14b–16b). All evil is associated with the latter group, including lawlessness, darkness, and idolatry. In the present passage, the list of vices serves to vilify Paul's opponents in the Corinthian church even further, putting them in the camp of unbelievers, who are opposed to Christ and righteousness (cf. 13:2, which lumps together all unrepentant sinners in Corinth). In essence, the offenders are guilty of some of the same sins as the wilderness generation was (cf. 1 Cor. 10:6–10).

13:1–10 / Based on the feared condition of the Corinthian church (12:20b–21), the apostle threatens to take punitive action when he comes (13:1–4) and hence urges the church to repent beforehand (vv. 5–10).

13:1 / The first part of this verse basically repeats the announcement of Paul's third visit from 12:14 (lit., "This is the third time I am coming to you"). Nevertheless, we must not overlook that the very act of "coming" to a missionary territory like Corinth constitutes a divinely given apostolic prerogative, which the apostle fiercely defends against the intrusion of the "false apostles" (cf. 10:12–18; 11:4; 12:20). As we have seen, these interlopers who have "come" (cf. 11:4) to Corinth are attempting to deny Paul's apostolic authority and to usurp his apostolic territory. This is one of the main points of contention that the apostle will handle in a decisive way when he comes to Corinth for the third time.

The second part of 13:1 cites Deuteronomy 19:15 in abbreviated form (cf., similarly, Matt. 18:16). It is difficult to see how the two parts of the verse cohere. Is the citation about **three** witnesses intended to give the legal basis for Paul's **third** visit? What **matter** is being established—something about Paul's apostolic authority or something about the Corinthians' sin? And who are the two or three **witnesses** whom the apostle will use to establish this matter? Does Paul mean that his three visits to Corinth count as separate **witnesses** either against the opponents or against the Corinthians?

The answers to these questions are neither simple nor straightforward, and we must perhaps reckon with the possibility that Paul cites the Deuteronomy text in some general way that would make these questions superfluous.

Nevertheless, several cursory observations can be made: (1) It seems probable that Paul's coming to Corinth for the **third** time has nothing to do per se with the **three witnesses** of Deuteronomy 19:15, despite what appears at first to be a clear textual link between the two numbers. For otherwise, Paul himself would be the witness in every case, whereas the Deuteronomy text clearly requires a minimum of two separate witnesses (cf., however, CD 9.16–23, which seems to interpret Deut. 19:15 as allowing the use of the cumulative testimony of a single witness to successive commissions of the same crime, provided that the offense was duly recorded; L. H. Schiffman). Moreover, it is unlikely that the apostle would adduce his founding visit to Corinth as one of the witnesses, since that visit took place before any of the trouble had erupted between Paul and the Corinthians. (2) Given the apologetic nature of the letter, it seems more likely that the **matter** that needs to be **established** is Paul's own apostleship, rather than the Corinthians' sin. The latter seems relatively clear, whereas the issue of Paul's apostleship remains contentious in Corinth. When Paul comes into his apostolic territory this next time (see on 13:1a), then the Corinthians will be judged, if they fail to accept his apostolic authority (cf. v. 2). As the text goes on to state (v. 3), the Corinthians seek proof that Christ is speaking in Paul. The issue of Paul's apostolic authority and prerogative is very much in the foreground of these opening verses of chapter 13. (3) We must reckon with the possibility that the two (or three) witnesses to whom the apostle appeals may be none other than himself and God (and Christ). All along in the letter, Paul has appealed to himself (e.g., 1:12) and to God as witnesses (e.g., 1:23). We may compare Jesus' defense of his own sending as given in John 8:12–20. When the Pharisees claimed that Jesus was bearing witness to himself and that, therefore, his testimony was invalid (v. 13), Jesus defended himself by appealing to Deuteronomy 19:15, claiming that the joint witness of the Father and the Son fulfills the requirement of **two** witnesses: "In your law it is written that the testimony of two men is true; I bear witness to myself, and the Father who sent me bears witness to me" (vv. 17–18). A revelatory mediator like Jesus who has been sent by God finds himself in the awkward position of having to testify to his own legitimacy in the name of God. Josephus records that Moses also appealed to God as witness to vindicate himself during Korah's rebellion (*Ant.* 4.46). According to the text in Numbers 16:28–29, the miraculous judgment of the rebels would function as a sign from God of Moses' divine sending. As we shall see, this is precisely the point that Paul wants to make about himself in Corinth. As an apostle who speaks on behalf of God and Christ (cf. 2 Cor. 5:20), Paul is concerned to establish his claim to true apostleship in Corinth.

13:2 / Having announced his imminent apostolic visit to Corinth (v. 1), Paul again warns the Corinthians of the impending judgment. Already during the second, painful visit to Corinth, Paul had warned the church that when he came again he would not **spare** *(pheidesthai)* the unrepentant sinners among them, that is, anyone who still opposed Paul or his gospel. During the painful visit, someone in the congregation had evidently severely offended Paul as an apostle, while the rest of the church did nothing to intervene. Thus, according to 1:23, the apostle calls upon God as witness, asserting that "it was in order to spare *(pheidomenos)* you that I did not return to Corinth." The whole church could have been subjected at that time to divine judgment, but Paul opted for a period of grace. Paul made up his mind not to make another painful visit (2:1). The purpose of his absence was to give the church a chance to repent, which it had now done in part (cf. 7:9–11). Even now, the apostle does not want to have to judge the congregation, so in 2 Corinthians he repeats his original warning that he will not **spare** unrepentant sinners when he returns (cf. 12:21; cf. 1 Cor. 4:21).

We do not know with certainty what kind of punishment Paul has in mind. Perhaps it was to be similar to the punishment incurred by the man who offended Paul during the painful visit (see above on 2:6). On the analogy of Korah's rebellion we may suspect that the intended punishment was quite severe (cf. 13:10). This is reinforced by the verb *(pheidesthai)*. Elsewhere Paul uses this term in the sense of God's not sparing his own Son but giving him up to death (Rom. 8:32).

13:3 / Paul explains the reason he will not spare the unrepentant Corinthians when he comes. Paul claims to speak in the authority of Christ. He presents himself as an "apostle of Christ Jesus" (1:1), an "ambassador for Christ" through whom God himself speaks (5:20; cf. Rom. 15:18), and one who speaks "in Christ in the presence of God" (2 Cor. 2:17; 12:19). As we have seen, this puts Paul on a level with Moses as a mediator of divine revelation. Indeed, Paul calls himself a "minister of the new covenant" in conscious contrast to the ministry of Moses (3:6). Paul's claims are susceptible to the same challenge as Moses received from his opponents. The Corinthians are **demanding proof that Christ is speaking** through Paul. The issue is the legitimacy of Paul's apostleship, that is, whether he has really been sent by God. Under the influence of the interlopers, some

Corinthians had come to regard the apostle as a weak fraud who is vociferous only at a safe distance by letter (cf. 5:12, 16; 10:1, 10). According to Numbers 16:28–29, Moses responded to a similar challenge against his authority during Korah's rebellion by giving proof of his sending in the form of a miraculous divine judgment that obliterated the opposition in the congregation (see above on 13:1). Likewise, Paul threatens not to spare the unrepentant rebels in the Corinthian church, for the Christ who speaks through him and whose power rests on him (cf. 12:9) is not **weak** in dealing with the Corinthians but is **powerful** among them. Paul may be **weak**, but the Christ whom he represents is not, and ultimately Christ is the one whose authority they are challenging. The impending judgment will be proof positive that Paul is a genuine apostle of Jesus Christ.

13:4 / An explanation of Christ's **weakness** and **power** follows. The parallel between Christ and Paul here shows that the latter's apparent physical **weakness** cannot be used as an argument against Paul's apostleship. Paul shares both in the sufferings and death of Christ (1:5; 4:10) and in the resurrection life of Christ (cf. 1:9; Phil. 3:10–11). Moreover, Christ's **power** is made perfect in Paul's weakness (cf. 2 Cor. 12:9–10). The opponents completely misperceive the apostle when they evaluate him according to the flesh as weak. Unlike his opponents, Paul no longer knows anyone according to physical criteria (5:12, 16a). He admits that, as a Pharisee, he once evaluated Christ according to the flesh, that is, he saw Christ as a justly crucified messianic pretender. However, now that he has encountered the resurrected Christ on the way to Damascus, Paul no longer evaluates him by such criteria. Implicitly, the opponents make the same mistake in evaluating Paul according to the flesh as Paul once did when evaluating the crucified Christ. Just as Christ was set as Son of God in power by his resurrection from the dead (cf. Rom. 1:4; Phil. 2:9–11) and enthroned at the right hand of God (1 Cor. 15:25; Rom. 8:34), so also Paul has **power**, and that power will be manifested to the Corinthians when he returns to Corinth. Paul will be vindicated in his claim to true apostleship.

13:5–10 / Having warned the church that he will punish the unrepentant rebels when he comes (13:1–4), the apostle goes on to exhort the Corinthians to examine themselves and to repent in time, for Paul does not want to have to exercise his apostolic authority by judging them.

13:5 / As in 1 Corinthians, where Paul exhorts the Corinthians to **examine** themselves in order to partake of the Lord's Supper in a worthy manner (1 Cor. 11:28), he does so here again. At stake is whether Paul is a true apostle of Christ Jesus, that is, whether Christ is really speaking through Paul (v. 3). If so, then the Corinthians must believe Paul and his message in order to be **in the faith.** This recalls the whole discussion in 5:16–6:2, where Paul urges the Corinthians to quit seeing him as a suffering and dying apostolic pretender and to acknowledge him instead as the divinely appointed representative of Jesus Christ on earth and the minister of reconciliation that he really is, or else risk forfeiting the eschatological salvation of the Lord. Paul wants to make it clear that the controversy surrounding his apostleship amounts to more than a personal power struggle; the very salvation of the congregation hangs in the balance. Hence, when Paul exhorts the Corinthians to **examine yourselves** and to **test yourselves,** he effectively turns away from a defense of himself (cf. 12:19!) and forces the Corinthians to defend (or change) their own position. Really, the Corinthians are on trial (compare the testing of the wilderness generation in 1 Cor. 10:6–13), and the apostle's defense to this point has been an effort to help the congregation repent of its attitude toward him.

Although Paul urges the Corinthians to examine themselves to see whether they are in the faith (13:5a), he assumes that they are believers: **Do you not realize that Christ Jesus is in you?** (v. 5b). Similarly in 6:1, Paul urges the Corinthians not to receive God's grace in vain. This assumes that the Corinthians have indeed received the message of reconciliation which the apostle originally delivered to them, and therefore that they have received the grace of God. Or, as Paul puts it here, "Christ Jesus is in you." But there is a thinly veiled threat in 13:5b, for the apostle immediately qualifies this statement with the words, **unless, of course, you fail the test.** Again, the point is the same as in 6:1–2: If the Corinthians (particularly, the unrepentant among them) continue on their course of denying the legitimacy of Paul's apostleship, then they will have undermined their own faith and salvation, for the message of reconciliation and thus the grace of God itself came through Paul (cf. 5:18–20). Paul's ministry of reconciliation is inseparable from God's reconciliation of the world. The tacit argument that Paul employs here is much the same as the one that we have already seen several times in the letter: Ultimately, the Corinthians cannot deny Paul's original message to them and his mediatory role without at the same time rejecting the gospel and denying their own Christian existence (cf. 1:19; 3:1–6). It is impossible to reject Paul without also rejecting the gospel.

13:6 / Paul hopes that the Corinthians will come to the right conclusion about his apostleship. Whereas in the previous context he had been using the first person singular ("I"), here Paul begins to use the apostolic plural again **(we)**. As we have seen, this alternation of pronouns is typical of 2 Corinthians as a whole. Paul is convinced that he is a genuine apostle of Jesus Christ—a mediator of divine revelation who has been given a particular apostolic territory by God himself. Hence, Paul hopes that when he comes to visit the Corinthians will "know" (**discover,** *gnōsesthe*) that he is a genuine apostle **(that we have not failed the test).** The test for the Corinthians is whether they will recognize Paul as a genuine apostle (v. 5). Since Paul's apostolic sufficiency and competence come from God (cf. 2:16; 3:4–6; 12:9), Paul cannot be said to have failed the test of apostleship. Yet, if the Corinthians—the seal of his apostleship (1 Cor. 9:1–3)— end up rejecting him altogether, then they will have failed to support Paul in the face of opposition and to be tangible evidence of Paul's apostleship (cf. 3:1–6). In that case, Paul will have failed to substantiate his claim to being a genuine apostle and a mediator of the Spirit of the new covenant. Hence, the Corinthians are in a position to unravel Paul's whole mission in the east (to say nothing of the lost prospects for the west), if they consider that he has failed the test of apostleship. In the process, their own faith will be nullified.

13:7 / In this dire situation, in which the legitimacy of Paul's apostleship depends on the Corinthians' reaction to him, Paul resorts to prayer. This prayer **to God** actually conceals an exhortation to the Corinthians, that they should **do what is right** in the matter of recognizing Paul as a genuine apostle and accepting his message. This includes obeying his exhortations to repent and reform, especially as given in 6:14–7:1; for the Corinthians must simultaneously adhere to Paul and separate from the interlopers.

Paul claims to be concerned less about his own reputation in this matter than about the welfare of the Corinthians. They must be kept in the faith at all costs, even if it means sacrificing his own reputation by appearing weak or foolish. As we have seen, however, to reject Paul's apostleship has disastrous consequences for the congregation. Practically speaking, therefore, Paul's reputation goes hand-in-hand with the Corinthians' own welfare, and the distinction that Paul makes here seems difficult to maintain. Nevertheless, Paul emphasizes how selflessly he has given of himself for the benefit of the Corinthians (cf. 12:15, 19).

13:8 / Paul explains the reason (**For,** *gar*) he is more concerned about the welfare of the Corinthians than about his own reputation. As a true apostle of Jesus Christ and a true believer, Paul stands on the side of **the truth,** just as he stands on the side of righteousness, light, Christ, etc. (cf. 6:14b–16a). Hence, he claims that the "truth of Christ is in me" (11:10), and he upholds "the truth of the gospel" when it is violated (cf. Gal. 2:5, 14). He cannot do otherwise, for he is compelled by God to preach the gospel (cf. 1 Cor. 9:16). Throughout 2 Corinthians the apostle emphasizes that he speaks **the truth** on various matters (cf., e.g., 4:2; 6:7; 7:14; 12:6). Indirectly, Paul may be getting in yet another charge against his opponents, whom he characterizes as "false apostles" and "deceitful workmen" (cf. 11:13) who subvert **the truth** with a "different gospel" (11:4).

13:9 / Paul gives another reason (*gar,* untranslated NIV) he is concerned more about the welfare of the Corinthians than about his own reputation. This verse is part of Paul's paradoxical theme of "strength-in-weakness" in context (cf. 12:9, 10; 13:3, 4). Paul is **weak,** but that does not prevent the power of God and the resurrection life of Christ from displaying itself in and through the apostle to serve the Corinthians (cf. 13:4). Moreover, Paul's weakness and suffering redound to the benefit of the Corinthians (cf. 1:6–7; 4:12), and he selflessly expends himself for the congregation (cf. 12:15). Paul is actually **glad** (lit. "we rejoice") when this happens. Though Paul could be sorrowful based on his weakness and sufferings, yet he is always rejoicing, perhaps especially when he sees the fruit of his apostolic labor flourish (cf. 6:10).

Paul gives the content of his prayer for the Corinthians in a word: *tēn hymōn katartisin* (NIV: **your perfection;** NRSV: "that you may become perfect"). This leaves open what he may actually mean, for the noun *katartisis* occurs only here in the NT, and that without a full sentence in which to ascertain its usage. Perhaps it means "your restoration" (so Martin, Furnish). The cognate verb *(katartizein)* is used just two verses later (v. 11), where

Paul exhorts the Corinthians to concord. Since, as we shall see, 13:11 expresses the main purpose for the writing of 2 Corinthians, Paul's prayer in verse 9 may already look forward to that statement and thus express his desire that the rebellious factions in Corinth (cf. 12:20) be brought into harmony with him.

13:10 / The apostle concludes this hortatory subsection (vv. 5–10) with a summary of the purpose for which he has written chapters 10–13. The contrast between being **absent** and being **present** is familiar from the previous context (cf. 10:1, 11; 13:2). Paul introduced himself in 10:1 as the one who was allegedly " 'timid' when face to face with you, but 'bold' when away." In 10:11, however, he goes on to warn that people who take this position (cf. 10:10) should realize that "what we are in our letters when we are absent, we will be in our actions when we are present." Paul spells this out concretely in 13:2: "I already gave you a warning when I was with you the second time. I now repeat it while absent: On my return I will not spare those who sinned earlier or any of the others." Hence, when Paul states in 13:10 that he writes **these things** while **absent** so that when he is "present" he will not have to be harsh, clearly **these things** refers primarily to what he has written in chapters 10–13. In fact, by reiterating the opening words to chapters 10–13, the reference to **these things** and the "present-absent" contrast draws the whole last section of the letter together. The Corinthians are being given one last chance to repent while the apostle is still away. When he is present, he will be compelled to use his apostolic authority and deal harshly with any who are still unrepentant in the congregation.

Paul hopes and prays that he will not to have to **be harsh** (lit., "act harshly") when he comes. This is the reason he warns them in advance by letter of the impending judgment. Nevertheless, he does have apostolic **authority**, and he can prove that Christ is speaking through him (cf. 10:8, 11; 12:19–13:4). Of course, as the apostle has already stated (cf. 10:4, 8), the purpose for which Christ gave him apostolic **authority** was **for building you up** and not **for tearing you down.** So, if there is any way to avoid a purge in Corinth, he will work toward that end.

Additional Notes §13

12:14 / The expression **the third time** (lit., *this third [triton touto]*) goes back to a Hebrew expression (cf. Num. 22:28, 32, 33; 24:10; Judg. 16:15; John 21:14).

For examples of the use of **children** *(tekna)* without regard to age, see Exod. 20:5; 34:7; Num. 14:18; 16:27; Deut. 24:16; 29:29; 32:5. Sometimes the term is clearly used in the sense of progeny who survive their parents: cf. Lev. 25:46 ("for your children after you"). Toward the end of his life Moses pronounced the following blessing: "[Most] blessed be Asher of the children," i.e., the other children of Israel (Deut. 33:24).

The Aramaic word for corban *(qwrbn)* means "treasury." This is perhaps relevant for the verb used in our text *(thesaurizein,* meaning "store up [treasure]"), which the NIV translates **save up.** Furthermore, according to Josephus, corban belongs to the regulations that Moses ordered after Korah's rebellion (cf. Josephus, *Ant.* 4.73, 76). If, as we have seen, Paul compares the opposition in Corinth to Korah's rebellion, then a regulation stemming from that occasion may have come to mind.

Cf. also Robert Banks, *Paul's Idea of Community* (rev. ed., Peabody, Mass.: Hendrickson, 1994).

12:16–18 / We may note that, according to Josephus, Moses was quite concerned to vindicate himself during Korah's rebellion of the charge of extortion in connection with Aaron's appointment to the priesthood (*Ant.* 4.46; cf. Num. 16:15).

Whereas in v. 16 it seems that Paul was charged with being **crafty** *(panourgos)* in financial matters, in 4:2 the apostle denies that he uses "deception" *(panourgia)* with respect to his ministry of the gospel. In 11:3, the noun is used of the serpent who deceived Eve by his cunning.

It is sometimes argued that, when Paul asks the Corinthians whether Titus or any other of his emissaries had ever exploited them (vv. 17–18), this presupposes that chs. 10–13 were written after 8:6, 16–24 and 9:3–5, where Paul tells his readers he is about to send Titus. However, 8:6 shows that Titus had been sent on an earlier trip to Corinth in connection with the collection, and it is probably to this trip that 12:17–18 alludes.

Strangely, however, Paul does not mention Timothy as an example of someone who has never exploited the Corinthians, even though the latter had been sent to Corinth (cf. 1 Cor. 4:17; 16:10–11). Perhaps this is because Titus had been in Corinth more recently than Timothy, and he was also about to return. On the other hand, it is possible that Timothy has come under fire in the Corinthian church, possibly for cooperating with Paul in lording it over the Corinthians (see on 2 Cor. 1:24). If so, then Paul mentions Timothy with himself at several key points in the letter, including the superscription (1:1), in order to rehabilitate him in the eyes of the Corinthians.

Paul would not have been the first one to be accused of a confidence game involving gifts for Jerusalem. Josephus (*Ant.* 18.81–84) explains the expulsion of the Jews from Rome in A.D. 19 as the direct result of a scoundrel who enlisted the help of three accomplices in order to persuade a woman of high rank who had become a Jewish proselyte to give her purple and gold to the Jerusalem temple. When the four embezzled the gifts, which was their intention from the start, Emperor Tiberius learned of the deed and banished the whole Jewish community from Rome.

12:19 / By repeating his assertion that "we speak in Christ in the presence of God" (2:17; 12:19), the apostle provides a key indication of the fundamental, structural unity of the letter. It cannot be coincidental that this unity is supported by a repeated statement that expresses the cornerstone of Paul's apostolic claim and hence a major concern of the whole letter, that is, his encounter(s) with the *merkabah*.

12:20 / For other vice catalogues, cf., e.g., Rom. 1:29–31; 13:13; 1 Cor. 5:10–11; 6:9–10; Gal. 5:19–21; Eph. 4:31; 5:3–5; Col. 3:5–8; 1 Tim. 1:9–10; 6:4–5; 2 Tim. 3:2–4; Tit. 1:7; 3:3. See further Colin G. Kruse, "Virtues and Vices," *DPL*, pp. 962–63; John T. Fitzgerald, "Virtue/Vice Lists," *ABD*, vol. 6, pp. 857–59.

It could be argued that the list of vices in v. 20b fits better with the time of Paul's tearful letter (cf. 2:4) than with the time after Paul had heard the report from Titus that the church at Corinth had repented, and has now expressed complete confidence in the church (cf. 7:5–16). As we have seen, however, even after the good news from Titus about the repentance of the majority in Corinth, the situation is still tense; Paul is still in a position of having to defend himself. His statement in 7:16 is clearly an exaggeration, designed more to effect a positive response than to compliment the church for already having one.

12:21 / Scholars have debated whether the vice lists in v. 21b (**impurity, sexual sin and debauchery**) and v. 20b ("quarreling, jealousy, outbursts of anger, factions, slander, gossip, arrogance, and disorder") reflect two different factions within the Corinthian church. In the light of 2 Cor. 6:14–7:1, however, such a sharp distinction may not be necessary, for Paul sees all of these sins as part of same sphere of darkness and anti-Christ.

13:1 / Cf. Lawrence H. Schiffman, *Sectarian Law in the Dead Sea Scrolls: Courts, Testimony and the Penal Code* (BJS 33; Chico, Calif.: Scholars Press, 1983), pp. 73–88. On the sending of Jesus in John's Gospel see Colin G. Kruse, "Apostle," *DJG*, pp. 27–33 (here p. 30).

It may seem strange that Paul would cite the law (Deut. 19:15) in order to support the necessity of his third visit. This illustrates the apostle's highly complex view of the law. On the one hand, the law kills, and no one should seek to be "under the law." On the other hand, the law is holy, just, and good, and Paul appeals to it as an authoritative source of regulations for conducting one's life, including the lives of the apostles (e.g., 1 Cor. 9:8–10, citing Deut. 25:4). See further Peter J. Tomson,

Paul and the Jewish Law: Halakha in the Letters of the Apostle to the Gentiles (CRINT 3.1; Assen: Van Gorcum, 1990).

13:3 / On the comparison between Korah's rebellion against Moses and the Corinthians' opposition to Paul, see Philip E. Hughes, *Paul's Second Epistle to the Corinthians* (NICNT; Grand Rapids: Eerdmans, 1962), pp. 477–78; Martin, *2 Corinthians*, p. 474.

13:5 / Cf. Judith M. Gundry Volf, *Paul and Perseverance: Staying In and Falling Away* (WUNT 2/37; Tübingen: Mohr Siebeck, 1990), pp. 217–25. Second Timothy 3:8 uses the same word translated here **fail the test** *(adokimoi)* to compare those who are *adokimoi* concerning the faith with Jannes and Jambres, who opposed Moses, because they "opposed the truth."

Paul's exhortation to "examine yourselves to see whether you are **in the faith**" recalls 1:24, where Paul affirms that they stand firm "in the faith."

13:8 / On Paul's concept of **truth**, see L. Morris, "Truth," *DPL*, pp. 954–55.

13:9 / If *katartisis* is used here in the sense of **perfection**, we may note that the apostle speaks of "perfecting holiness" in 7:1, in a passage (6:14–7:1) that exhorts the addressees to live in light of the new covenant situation by separating themselves from his opponents. On the sense of "restoration," cf. Martin, *2 Corinthians*, p. 484; Furnish, *II Corinthians*, p. 573.

§14 Closing (2 Cor. 13:11–14)

These last four verses close Paul's second canonical letter to the Corinthians. Pauline letter closings are carefully constructed units, shaped and adapted in such a way that they relate directly to—sometimes, in fact, even summarize—the major concerns and themes taken up in the bodies of their respective letters (cf. J. A. D. Weima). Consequently, in important ways the letter closings aid our understanding of Paul's purpose, arguments, and exhortation. Moreover, if, as L. A. Jervis argues, "The opening and closing sections are where Paul (re)establishes his relationship with his readers and where the function of each of his letters is most evident," then we must pay special attention to 2 Corinthians 13:11–13, for then we may gain a clue not only about the major thrust of Paul's letter but also about its unity (or lack thereof).

Pauline closings typically contain an exhortation section, a peace benediction, greetings, and a grace benediction. These elements are also found in the closing to 2 Corinthians (in vv. 11a; 11b; 12–13; and 14 respectively). In the closing, Paul lays aside the harsh threats and bitter irony that characterized chapters 10–13, returning instead to the conciliatory tone and message that were more characteristic of the first nine chapters of the letter.

13:11 / Paul closes the letter (**finally,** *loipon*) with an appeal for concord. After four chapters of hard-hitting polemic and invective, Paul returns to a conciliatory tone that is more in keeping with his ultimate purpose of admonition, rather than condemnation. Hence, Paul again addresses the Corinthians as **brothers,** just as he did in the first part of the letter (cf. 1:8; 8:1). Earlier, Paul had emphasized the mutuality between himself and the Corinthians. Now he returns to that theme and reinforces it as his parting shot.

After addressing the Corinthians as **brothers,** Paul goes on to give (four or) five exhortations in rapid succession. Compared to other Pauline letter closings, 2 Corinthians has a fuller section of exhortation. First, Paul exhorts the Corinthians to "rejoice" (*chairete*). The NIV translates the verb as **good-by** (NRSV: "farewell"). Here, however, the verb can and probably should be taken to mean "rejoice," as it is throughout the letter (cf. 2:3; 6:10; 7:7, 9, 13, 16) and also in the immediate context (cf. 13:9; cf. also 1 Thess. 5:16). We may also compare the very similar wording of Philippians 3:1: "Finally [*to loipon*], my brothers [*adelphoi mou*], rejoice [*chairete*] in the Lord." Paul desperately wants the Corinthians to be a cause of his own rejoicing (cf. 2:3; 7:9, 16; 13:9). If the Corinthians repent of their attitude toward the apostle before he arrives, then they have reason for rejoicing—in the Lord, with each other, and with Paul (cf. Phil. 2:18; 4:4). Rejoicing thus becomes an expression of unity in the congregation, and unity seems to be the main thrust of the imperatives in 2 Corinthians 13:11.

Second, Paul exhorts the Corinthians to **aim for perfection** (*katartizesthe*). This verb is a cognate of the noun *katartisis*, which is used in 13:9, but, as we have seen, the interpretation of the noun is uncertain there. The problem is compounded by the fact that in verse 11 *katartizesthe* can be taken as either a middle or a passive verb. In light of the other imperatives in our verse, we may suppose that Paul is calling the Corinthians to positive action in order to remedy the perilous situation in the congregation, perhaps "aim at restoration" (so Martin, *2 Corinthians*, pp. 498–99). The thrust of verse 11 seems to be an appeal for concord.

Third, Paul exhorts the addressees either to **listen to my appeal** or possibly to "encourage one another," depending on whether the verb [*parakaleisthe*] is understood as passive or as middle. Here again the verb form is equivocal. Paul's usage of the verb allows for either possibility. Martin argues: "Since Paul is hoping that the Corinthians will again live in harmony, we take the verb to be construed as the middle voice" (p. 499). This does not exclude the possibility, however, that Paul is solemnly underscoring his appeal in verse 11.

Fourth, the apostle exhorts the Corinthians to **be of one mind** (*to auto phroneite*; lit., "think the same thing"). Unlike the first three imperatives, this verb is unequivocal in meaning. The idiom is used elsewhere in the sense of "be in agreement, live in harmony" (cf. Herodotus 1.60.2; Dio Chrysostom 34.20; Phil. 2:2; [3:16]; 4:2; Rom. 12:16; 15:5). Just as the Corinthians are being transformed into "the same image," that is, the image of the resurrected Lord (cf. 2 Cor. 3:18), so also they are to reflect this image by "thinking the same thing." As we have seen, the Corinthian church is wracked with dissension among factions (cf. 2 Cor. 12:20; 1 Cor. 1:10), much like the situation of Korah's rebellion (Num. 16–17). Therefore, Paul calls the congregation back to harmony both with himself and with each other in order to avoid divine judgment. The exhortation in 13:11 indicates that 2 Corinthians should be seen as an appeal for concord, a sub-category of discourse that seeks to calm the outbreak of faction by dissuading from strife *(stasis)* and exhorting to concord *(homonoia)*. This is not just harmony for harmony's sake, but unity in the truth as Paul understands it. In 6:15 Paul gives a reason the Corinthians must not be allied with "unbelievers" (especially the interlopers) by asking the rhetorical question, "What harmony is there between Christ and Belial?" Hence, while the congregation must separate completely from the false apostles, who are regarded as servants of Satan (cf. 11:14), they must also be of one accord with Paul. The apostle frequently emphasizes the mutuality between himself and the Corinthians (cf., e.g., 1:1–2, 3–11, 14, 18–22, 24; 2:2; 3:18; 4:12, 14; 6:11–13; 7:2; 8:1, 16–17; 9:11; 12:14–15; 13:11). Moreover, Paul has the "ministry of reconciliation" with a corresponding "message of reconciliation" (cf. 5:18–19), which the Corinthians have already accepted but are now in danger of forfeiting by their attitude toward him (cf. 6:1–2).

Finally, the apostle exhorts the addressees to **live in peace** *(eirēneuete)*. This is closely related to the foregoing exhortation, for thinking the same thing is the basis for living in peace. Some forty years after the writing of 2 Corinthians (ca. A.D. 96), Clement of Rome wrote a letter to the Corinthians *(1 Clement)*, which, as the closing explicitly states (63:2; cf. 65:1), was designed as an "appeal" *(enteuxis)* to "peace" *(eirēnē)* and "concord" *(homonoia)* in the congregation. The similarity to Paul's appeal to concord and peace in the closing of 2 Corinthians (13:11) is obvious, but it extends even further than the closing. For, as *1 Clement* makes clear, certain rebels in the congregation, consumed with jealousy and pride, had revolted against the presbyters' legitimate authority, founded on the tradition of the apostles and comparable to the Aaronic priesthood. The revolt caused the church to split over the issue of legitimate leadership. Therefore Clement calls the rebels to repentance, using Korah's rebellion against Moses and Aaron (Num. 16–17) as an example to warn the "leaders of rebellion and dissension" *(archēgoi staseōs kai dichostasias)* that schism due to jealousy has dire consequences (*1 Clem.* 51:1–4; cf. also 4:12). This shows that the Corinthian rebellion that Clement faced in the mid 90s was similar to the one Paul faced in the mid 50s, and that it necessitated a similar missive in order to restore concord and peace (note the conscious recollection of the earlier Corinthian correspondence in 1 *Clem.* 47:1–7). The peace of which Paul speaks in 2 Corinthians 13:11 is not just a cessation from strife, but rather a state of mutual harmony based on genuine agreement in the truth of Paul's apostolic gospel (cf. v. 8). Elsewhere Paul exhorts believers to "live peaceably with all people," insofar as it depends on them (Rom. 12:18; cf. also 1 Thess. 5:13).

Immediately following the exhortation to live in peace Paul adds a peace benediction: **And the God of love and peace will be with you** (cf. Rom. 15:33; 16:20; Phil. 4:9; 1 Thess. 5:23; 2 Thess. 3:16; Gal. 6:16). As a comparison of Pauline benedictions reveals (see the synoptic table in Weima, "Pauline Letter Closings," p. 9), the apostle sometimes varies the wording his peace benedictions in order to emphasize a particular element. Here, for example, instead of referring simply to "the God of peace" (cf. *T. Dan.* 5:2), Paul refers to **the God of love and peace,** that is, God is the source of **love and peace.** If the **And** *(kai)* that begins the benediction introduces a result ("and then"), the logic of the passage seems exactly the opposite of what we observed in 2 Corinthians 6:16–17. Whereas there obedience is a consequence of the promise of God's presence among his covenant people, here the promise of God's presence among his people seems contingent on their obedience (cf., similarly, Phil. 4:9b). Our text possibly presupposes an interdependent relationship between human responsibility and divine bestowment (cf. Phil. 2:12–13). Perhaps, however, we should understand our moralistic-sounding text merely as a prelude to the real conclusion and climax of the letter (see on 13:14).

13:12–13 / After the exhortations and the peace benediction (v. 11), Paul moves next to the greetings. First, he exhorts his readers to greet one another **with a holy kiss.** Three other Pauline letters contain similar exhortations in their closing sections (1 Thess. 5:26; 1 Cor. 16:20; Rom. 16:16). Paul was apparently the first person in the Greco-Roman world to have instructed members of a mixed social group to greet one another with a kiss, although it is found in another letter closing in the NT (cf. 1 Pet. 5:14: "Greet one another with a kiss of love"). There is no evidence in the NT that the practice was specifically connected with the liturgy. If the believers at Philippi and elsewhere are to be greeted as "holy ones" or "saints" (Phil. 4:21), the "holy kiss" is probably the kiss that "holy ones" give each other when they meet. On the analogy of the situation reflected in the greetings of Romans 16 (vv. 5, 10, 11, 14, 15), perhaps we can imagine in Corinth separate house churches sending greetings back and forth to one another by delegated representatives. If the Corinthian house churches provided a sociological context that encouraged the formation of factions, then this gesture of mutual goodwill and brotherly love would do much to overcome the natural schismatic tendency.

In the context of 2 Corinthians Paul's exhortation to greet one another with a holy kiss reinforces and underscores his prior admonitions to be of one mind and to live in peace (13:11). Like the rejoicing that Paul advocates in verse 11, this kiss may have been encouraged to demonstrate and strengthen the concord already achieved. Perhaps, too, the apostle hoped that the kiss would play a role in actually effecting the restoration still needed in the congregation.

Second, Paul conveys greetings from the believers **(all the saints)** in whose company he is writing the letter (v. 13). Just as the Corinthians are "holy ones" or **saints** (cf. 1:1), so also other believers in other localities are called **saints.** This presupposes that all believers are members of one universal church (cf. 1 Cor. 12:28)—the worldwide family of God (cf. 2 Cor. 6:18). Paul regularly conveys greetings from those who are with him when he writes his letters (cf. Rom. 16:3–23; 1 Cor. 16:19–20; Phil. 4:21; Col. 4:10–15; Phlm. 23). One of his goals in doing so was undoubtedly to promote self-identity, reciprocity, and unity within the church.

13:14 / The letter ends with a grace benediction. Usually Paul closes his letters with the simple formula, "[May] the grace of our Lord Jesus Christ be/is with you/your spirit" (cf. Rom. 16:20; 1 Cor. 16:23; Gal. 6:18; Phil. 4:23; 1 Thess. 5:28; Phlm. 25). Here, however, he employs a much more elaborate benediction that, in parallel structure, lists both the three persons of what we now call the Trinity and their main gifts to the church. Since the word **may** is not present in the Greek text, the verb to be supplied in translation could just as well be "are" (cf., similarly, 2 Cor. 1:3). In that case, Paul is expressing not a pious wish, but rather a confident matter of fact: "The grace of the Lord Jesus Christ, and the love of God, and the fellowship of the Holy Spirit *are* with you all." This statement concludes the letter on a very positive note, for Paul's confidence in the renegade Corinthians (cf. 7:4, 16) is based ultimately on God and his presence in their midst (cf. 13:11). After all, the Corinthians reveal that they are a letter of *Christ* written by the *Spirit* of the living *God* (3:3). Paul apparently expects them to pass the test after all (cf. 13:5).

The first gift listed in the benediction is **the grace of the Lord Jesus Christ** (cf. 8:9; 12:9). We might have expected the order Father-Son-Spirit as in the trinitarian formula of the later creeds. Instead, we have Christ-God-Spirit. Several explanations for this primary position of "Christ" are possible. Either Paul began with his ordinary benediction (see above) and then expanded it, or the last two gifts are understood as results of the gracious work of Christ on the cross. The second gift is **the love of God.** This probably means that God loves believers or that God is the source of love (cf. 13:11), rather than that God is loved by believers. God shows his **love** for believers by sending his Son to die for them (Rom. 5:8). Nothing can separate believers from "the love of God in Christ Jesus" (Rom. 8:39). The final gift is **the fellowship of the Holy Spirit.** In parallel with the first two gifts in the grace benediction, Paul probably speaks here of the fellowship created and given by the Holy Spirit, rather than of participation in or fellowship with the Spirit per se (cf. Phil. 2:1). The thrust of Paul's letter is to promote concord in the strife-ridden church at Corinth (see on 2 Cor. 13:11); therefore, Paul emphasizes the fellowship or solidarity that the Spirit creates. By putting into practicing the implications of the new covenant for their sanctification, the Corinthians will effectively open their Spirit-filled hearts to the apostle and thus affirm the solidarity of believers in the sphere of Christ (cf. 6:11–7:2).

Paul affirms that these three gifts are **with you all.** This is an amazing statement in view of the dissension and strife in the church at Corinth. Paul does not normally include the word **all** in this part of the closing grace benediction; therefore, its inclusion here is probably highly significant. Paul is saying that, despite the current factions and rebellion, his affirmation of trinitarian blessings applies to the whole Corinthian congregation. The apostle thereby expresses confidence about the ultimate outcome of the situation in the church (cf. 1:13–15; 2:3; 7:14, where Paul boasted to Titus about the Corinthians even before the delivery of the tearful letter). This confidence is rooted in Paul's "trinitarian" conviction expressed earlier in the letter: The *God* who is faithful and who vouches for Paul's word in the face of accusations has given the apostle a message of the *Son of God, Jesus Christ;* he has established Paul with the Corinthians in Christ; and he has given his *Spirit* in their hearts as a guarantee (cf. 1:18–22; also 1:15a; 3:3–4).

Additional Notes §14

13:11–14 / Cf. Jeffrey A. D. Weima, *Neglected Endings: The Significance of the Pauline Letter Closings* (JSNTSup 101; Sheffield: JSOT Press, 1994); idem, "The Pauline Letter Closings: Analysis and Hermeneutical Significance," *BBR* 5 (1995), pp. 1–22.

L. A. Jervis, *Purpose of Romans: A Comparative Letter Structure Investigation* (JSNTSup 55; Sheffield: JSOT Press, 1991), p. 42.

The difference in versification in this section between the Greek text and the English translation is due to the fact that the latter splits v. 12 into two verses.

13:11 / Paul frequently uses **brothers** as a form of address in his letters. In 1 Corinthians alone, it occurs twenty times. Sometimes he uses the term in exhortations toward the end of his letters (cf. Rom. 16:17; 1 Cor. 16:15; 1 Thess. 4:10; 5:14).

First Clement, a letter sent in the name of the apostolic father Clement from the church in Rome to Corinth late in the first century A.D., can also be classed as an appeal for concord. Cf. Laurence L. Welborn, "Clement, First Epistle of," *ABD,* vol. 1, pp. 1055–60 (esp. p. 1058). A number of examples of this genre have survived, several in the form of letters (e.g., Thrasymachus, *Peri Politeias;* Antiphon, *Peri Homonoias;* Isocrates, *Oratio* 4; *Epistulae* 3, 8, 9; Ps.-Plato, *Epistula* 7; Ps.-Demosthenes, *Epistula* 1; Socratic Epistles 30–32; Ps.-Sallust, *Epistula* 2; Dio Chrysostomus, *Orationes* 38–41; Aelius Aristides, *Orationes* 23–24; [Herodes Atticus,] *Peri Politeias;* Ps.-Julian, *Oratio* 35; see further Isocrates, 4.3; 5.16; *Epistula* 3.2; Cicero, *De Oratione* 1.56; Dio Cassius, 44.23.3; Philostratus, *Lives of the Sophists* 1.9.4; Iamblichus, *Life of Pythagoras* 9.45).

On the genre of 2 Corinthians, see, for example, John T. Fitzgerald, "Paul, the Ancient Epistolary Theorists, and 2 Corinthians 10–13: The Purpose and Literary Genre of a Pauline Letter," in *Greeks, Romans, and Christians: Festschrift for A. J. Malherbe* (ed. D. L. Balch, et al.; Minneapolis: Fortress, 1990), pp. 190–200.

13:12–13 / On the **holy kiss,** see William Klassen, "Kiss (NT)," *ABD,* vol. 4, pp. 89–92.

There is some evidence of house churches in Corinth. First Corinthians 16:19 mentions the church at the home of Aquila and Priscilla, and 1 Cor. 1:16 refers to the baptism of a household. Romans 16:23 implies that a number of smaller house churches existed in Corinth that met together as "the whole church" only occasionally (cf. 1 Cor. 14:23). On Pauline house churches, see Banks, *Paul's Idea of Community;* P. T. O'Brien, "Church," *DPL,* pp. 123–31 (here esp. p. 125).

13:14 / Paul also mentions the three persons of the Trinity in other letters (cf. 1 Cor. 12:4–6; 2 Cor. 1:18–22; Gal. 4:4–6; Rom. 5:1–11; 8:5–11; Eph. 4:4–6). A trinitarian substructure pervades the whole argument of 2 Cor. 2:14–4:6 (cf., e.g., 3:3). In our passage, Paul does not address the question of the ontological nature of the three persons of the Trinity; rather, he associates all three persons in the mutual activity of giving gifts to the Corinthians. We have seen evidence in 2 Corinthians that God and Jesus Christ share the divine throne-chariot, so that they work together or even interchangeably on the *merkabah* (see on 2:14; 5:10). By the same token, there is an intimate relationship, or perhaps even identity, between Christ and the Spirit (cf. 3:17).

On the interpretation of 2 Cor. 13:14 adopted here, see Martin Hengel, "Das Bekenntnis zum dreieinigen Gott (2. Kor 13,11–13)," *TBei* 16 (1985) 195–200.

For Further Reading

Banks, Robert. *Paul's Idea of Community*. Rev. ed. Peabody, Mass.: Hendrickson, 1994.
Barrett, C. K. *Paul: An Introduction to His Thought*. Louisville: Westminster John Knox, 1994.
_____. *The Second Epistle to the Corinthians*. Blacks New Testament Commentary 8. Peabody, Mass.: Hendrickson, 1993.
Belleville, Linda L. *Reflections of Glory: Paul's Polemical Use of the Moses–Doxa Tradition in 2 Corinthians 3,1–18*. JSNTS 52. Sheffield: JSOT, 1991.
Betz, Hans Dieter. *2 Corinthians 8 and 9: A Commentary on Two Administrative Letters of the Apostle Paul*. Hermeneia. Philadelphia: Fortress, 1985.
Bieringer, R. and J. Lambrecht. *Studies on 2 Corinthians*. Bibliotheca ephemeridum theologicarum lovaniensium 112. Leuven: Leuven University Press, 1994.
Carson, Donald A. *From Triumphalism to Maturity: a New Exposition of 2 Corinthians 10–13*. Grand Rapids: Baker, 1984.
Chafin, Kenneth L. *1, 2 Corinthians*. The Communicator's Commentary: New Testament 7. Waco, Tex.: Word, 1985.
Danker, Frederick W. *II Corinthians*. Augsburg Commentary on the New Testament. Minneapolis: Augsburg, 1989.
Davies, W. D. *Jewish and Pauline Studies*. 4th ed. Philadelphia: Fortress, 1984.
Ellis, E. Earle. *Paul and His Interpreters*. Grand Rapids: Eerdmans, 1961.
Fee, Gordon D. *God's Empowering Presence: The Holy Spirit in the Letters of Paul*. Peabody, Mass.: Hendrickson, 1994.
Georgi, Dieter. *The Opponents of Paul in Second Corinthians*. Philadelphia: Fortress, 1986.
_____. *Remembering the Poor: The History of Paul's Collection for Jerusalem*. Nashville: Abingdon, 1992.
Goulder, Michael. *St. Paul versus St. Peter: A Tale of Two Missions*. Louisville: Westminster John Knox Press, 1994.

Hafemann, Scott J. *Paul, Moses, and the History of Israel: The Letter/ Spirit Contrast and the Argument from Scripture in 2 Corinthians 3.* WUNT 81. Tübingen: Mohr Siebeck, 1995.

———. *Suffering and the Spirit: An Exegetical Study of II Cor. 2:14–3:3 within the Context of the Corinthian Correspondence.* WUNT 2/19. Tübingen: Mohr Siebeck, 1986.

Hay, David M., ed. *Pauline Theology, Vol. II: 1 & 2 Corinthians.* Minneapolis: Fortress, 1993.

Hays, Richard B. *Echoes of Scripture in the Letters of Paul.* New Haven: Yale University Press, 1989.

Hengel, Martin. *Between Jesus and Paul.* Philadelphia: Fortress, 1983.

———. *The Pre-Christian Paul.* Philadelphia: Trinity Press International, 1991.

Hooker, M. D. and Wilson, S. G. *Paul and Paulinism: Essays in Honour of C. K. Barrett.* London: SPCK, 1982.

Hughes, Philip E. *Paul's Second Epistle to the Corinthians.* NICNT. Grand Rapids: Eerdmans, 1962.

Jervis, L. Ann and Peter Richardson, eds. *Gospel in Paul: Studies on Corinthians, Galatians and Romans for Richard N. Longenecker.* JSNTSup 108. Sheffield: Sheffield Academic Press, 1994.

Kruse, Colin. *The Second Epistle of Paul to the Corinthians: an Introduction and Commentary.* Tyndale New Testament Commentary 8. Leicester: InterVarsity, 1987.

Luedemann, Gerd. *Opposition to Paul in Jewish Christianity.* Trans. M. Eugene Boring. Minneapolis: Fortress, 1989.

Marshall, Peter. *Enmity at Corinth: Social Conventions in Paul's Relations with the Corinthians.* WUNT 2/23. Tübingen: Mohr Siebeck, 1987.

Martin, Ralph P. *2 Corinthians.* Word Biblical Commentary 40. Waco, Tex.: Word, 1986.

Merritt, Wayne. *In Word and Deed: Moral Integrity in Paul.* Emory Studies in Early Christianity 1. New York: Lang, 1993.

Murphy-O'Connor, Jerome. *St. Paul's Corinth: Texts and Archaeology.* GNS 6. Wilmington, Del.: Glazer, 1983.

———. *The Theology of the Second Letter to the Corinthians.* New Testament Theology. Cambridge: Cambridge University Press, 1991.

O'Brien, Peter. *Introductory Thanksgivings in the Letters of Paul.* NovTSup 49. Leiden: Brill, 1977.

Pate, C. Marvin. *Adam Christology as the Exegetical and Theological Substructure of 2 Corinthians 4:7–5:21.* Lanham, Md.: University Press of America, 1991.

Plank, Karl A. *Paul and the Irony of Affliction.* SBLSS. Atlanta: Scholars, 1987.
Sandnes, Karl O. *Paul—One of the Prophets? A Contribution to Paul's Self-Understanding.* WUNT 2/43. Tübingen: Mohr Siebeck, 1991.
Segal, Alan F. *Paul the Convert: The Apostolate and Apostasy of Saul the Pharisee.* New Haven: Yale, 1990.
Sumney, Jerry L. *Identifying Paul's Opponents: the Question of Method in 2 Corinthians.* JSNTS, 40. Sheffield: JSOT, 1990.
Thrall, Margaret E. *A Critical and Exegetical Commentary on the Second Epistle to the Corinthians, Vol. 1: Introduction and Commentary on II Corinthians I-VII.* ICC. Edinburgh: T&T Clark, 1994.
Tomson, Peter J. *Paul and the Jewish Law: Halakha in the Letters of the Apostle to the Gentiles.* CRINT 3.1. Assen: Van Gorcum, 1990.
Webb, William J. *Returning Home: New Covenant and Second Exodus as the Context for 2 Corinthians 6:14–7:1.* JSNTSup 85. Sheffield: JSOT, 1993.
Weima, Jeffrey A. D. *Neglected Endings: The Significance of the Pauline Letter Closings.* JSNTSup 101. Sheffield: JSOT Press, 1994.
Witherington, Ben. *Conflict and Community in Corinth: A Social-Rhetorical Commentary on 1 and 2 Corinthians.* Grand Rapids: Eerdmans, 1995.
Young, Francis, and David F. Ford. *Meaning and Truth in 2 Corinthians.* Grand Rapids: Eerdmans, 1988.

Subject Index

a fortiori argument, 73, 74, 75, 195
Aaron, 4, 11, 19, 42, 43, 48, 56, 57, 92, 94, 97, 141, 145, 206, 209, 210, 237, 247, 257, 262
Abiram, 56, 57, 247
Abrahamic promise, 8, 214
Accusations, 5, 34, 44, 46, 49, 52, 53, 59, 87, 147, 159, 193, 194, 203, 206, 207, 213, 215, 265
Achaia, 7, 8, 10, 17, 19, 22, 52, 130, 173, 174, 184, 185, 186, 199, 209
Achaicus, 53
Adoption, 40, 41, 55, 99, 154
Ambassador, 22, 55, 140, 141, 146, 167, 171, 201, 251
Angel of light, 153, 204, 211
Anti-Pauline fragment, 160
Antitheses, 104, 125
Antithetical questions, 153, 192
Apology, 60, 89, 94, 144, 150, 155, 158, 159, 165, 245
Apostleship, 1, 5, 6, 13, 17, 18, 20, 24, 26, 36, 39, 41, 46, 47, 49, 51, 53, 59, 60, 63, 67, 68, 70, 76, 77, 78, 83, 85, 86, 88, 89, 90, 103, 107, 108, 110, 118, 119, 121, 123, 133, 139, 148, 149, 150, 151, 153, 155, 158, 159, 165, 169, 172, 178, 186, 193, 194, 199, 206, 207, 215, 220, 223, 227, 233, 242, 245, 246, 250, 251, 252, 253, 254, 255
Apostolic council, 9, 10, 12, 58, 173, 183, 198, 199
Appeal, 4, 5, 20, 35, 48, 51, 53, 60, 67, 68, 112, 121, 131, 133, 140, 142, 143, 146, 150, 155, 167, 171, 174, 179, 182, 193, 194, 203, 212, 260, 261, 262, 266
Arabia, 9, 220, 236
Aretas, 220, 236
Ascent, 63, 95, 111, 112, 120, 128, 195, 221, 224, 225, 226, 227, 228, 234, 237, 238
Asia, Asia Minor, 8, 9, 10, 23, 24, 25, 28, 29, 32, 45, 52, 104, 125, 173, 217
Atonement, 92, 123, 132

Authority, 1, 2, 3, 4, 6, 10, 11, 12, 15, 17, 18, 20, 21, 22, 34, 43, 49, 54, 56, 57, 59, 64, 76, 77, 84, 119, 124, 131, 140, 149, 151, 163, 168, 169, 173, 176, 179, 193, 194, 195, 196, 201, 205, 206, 207, 210, 211, 212, 213, 222, 223, 225, 226, 230, 231, 232, 237, 242, 246, 247, 248, 249, 250, 251, 252, 256, 262

Babylon, 155, 191
Barnabas, 18, 55, 125
Belial, 50, 51, 86, 153, 154, 161, 162, 204, 262
Beliar, 152, 154, 161, 248
Benediction, 260, 263, 264, 265
Boast, 12, 34, 35, 36, 93, 119, 120, 131, 148, 151, 160, 172, 184, 185, 200, 202, 203, 209, 212, 213, 214, 215, 216, 220, 221, 222, 228, 229, 230, 231, 237
Boldness, 76, 77, 97, 194, 197, 201
Brothers, 5, 19, 28, 40, 115, 160, 175, 179, 183, 184, 185, 186, 191, 206, 208, 219, 245, 260, 261, 266

Chariot (see also *Merkabah* and *Throne*), 61, 62, 63, 64, 83, 86, 87, 89, 91, 92, 102, 109, 118, 138, 223, 267
Chebar, river, 62, 83, 100
Children, 31, 32, 151, 161, 172, 243, 244, 257
Christology, 54, 55, 91, 97, 124, 126, 128, 129, 145
Claudius, 92, 191
Clement of Rome, 262
Collection, 3, 4, 5, 6, 9, 34, 35, 37, 38, 46, 51, 53, 58, 159, 170, 172, 173, 174, 175, 176, 177, 178, 179, 180, 181, 182, 183, 184, 185, 186, 187, 188, 189, 190, 192, 193, 195, 196, 200, 243, 245, 257
Comfort, 19, 23, 24, 25, 26, 27, 31, 32, 49, 144, 164, 165, 166, 170
Commission, 17, 22, 37, 59, 64, 65, 86, 103, 117, 118, 119, 138, 139, 140, 143, 153, 173, 199, 206, 222
Composite letter, 4, 6, 192

Concord, 4, 5, 51, 243, 256, 260, 261, 262, 264, 265, 266
Confidence, 5, 6, 13, 29, 32, 34, 44, 69, 70, 76, 104, 105, 106, 114, 115, 159, 160, 164, 165, 171, 172, 174, 184, 193, 258, 265
Conscience, 35, 53, 67, 84, 118, 119, 131, 147, 148, 157, 209
Consummation, 42, 78, 85, 107, 108, 109, 112, 114, 115, 129, 155, 181, 188
Corinth, 1, 2, 3, 5, 6, 7, 8, 10, 11, 12, 13, 15, 17, 18, 19, 20, 21, 22, 23, 24, 30, 32, 34, 35, 37, 38, 39, 42, 43, 44, 45, 46, 47, 52, 53, 54, 56, 57, 58, 59, 63, 68, 79, 82, 85, 86, 89, 95, 120, 126, 130, 140, 146, 153, 158, 160, 165, 166, 167, 168, 170, 171, 172, 174, 175, 176, 178, 181, 182, 183, 184, 185, 186, 190, 191, 193, 194, 195, 196, 197, 198, 199, 200, 201, 202, 203, 205, 206, 207, 208, 209, 210, 211, 212, 213, 216, 219, 220, 225, 228, 233, 234, 235, 242, 243, 244, 245, 246, 247, 248, 249, 251, 252, 256, 257, 258, 264, 265, 266, 267
Corporal punishment, 217
Covenant, 22, 54, 56, 75, 76, 78, 79, 96, 98, 99, 131, 136, 137, 146, 150, 151, 156, 162, 191, 263
Covenant formula, 155, 162, 163
Creation, 88, 101, 107, 112, 113, 135, 136, 137, 139, 144, 163
Credentials, 13, 140, 238
Crispus, 10

Damascus, 18, 58, 80, 83, 86, 87, 88, 96, 100, 101, 134, 135, 138, 142, 220, 221, 223, 236, 252
Dathan, 56, 57, 247
Daughters, 157
Day of the Lord, 36, 48, 54, 116, 119, 160
Death, 12, 27, 29, 30, 31, 32, 33, 43, 48, 49, 61, 64, 65, 72, 73, 74, 75, 77, 82, 84, 85, 88, 90, 92, 104, 105, 106, 108, 110, 111, 112, 114, 116, 123, 124, 125, 129, 135, 137, 139, 140, 141, 142, 149, 168, 211, 217, 237, 240, 251, 252
Defense, 5, 6, 17, 18, 23, 34, 41, 53, 59, 60, 62, 64, 66, 68, 69, 72, 79, 82, 84, 86, 89, 102, 103, 117, 119, 123, 133, 140, 146, 148, 150, 151, 153, 155, 158, 159, 165, 169, 173, 174, 193, 209, 245, 250, 253

Deliverance, 23, 24, 25, 26, 27, 28, 29, 30, 31, 32, 33, 106
Delusion, 87
Diaspora, 8, 10, 77, 98, 192, 235

Egypt, 9, 56, 65, 99, 113, 130, 135, 136, 157, 163, 235, 236
Embezzlement, 183, 192
Emissaries, 10, 15, 181, 182, 183, 184, 205, 210, 257
Endurance, 27, 31, 32, 235
Envoys, 146, 185, 201, 206
Ephesus, 2, 3, 28, 32, 37, 38, 52, 216
Epistolary aorist, 182, 192
Erastus, 8
Eulogy, 24, 25, 30, 31
Europe, 9, 10, 173, 175
Eve, 204, 211, 212, 257
Evil impulse, 126
Exile(s), 28, 69, 70, 71, 72, 78, 80, 81, 95, 98, 114, 116, 124, 125, 129, 130, 136, 145, 155, 156, 162, 164, 190, 191, 235, 237
Exodus, exodus typology, 56, 136, 156, 157, 162, 163
Exploitation, 208, 245
Ezra, 78, 97, 98, 112, 118, 180, 182, 183, 190, 224, 240, 245

Face, 5, 30, 42, 49, 64, 65, 73, 74, 76, 77, 86, 87, 88, 93, 97, 99, 100, 102, 103, 109, 112, 115, 120, 121, 122, 128, 131, 133, 147, 148, 151, 168, 194, 196, 203, 207, 231, 254, 256, 265
Faction(s), 2, 4, 11, 47, 170, 242, 243, 247, 256, 258, 262, 264, 265
Faith, 18, 20, 21, 40, 43, 49, 66, 68, 69, 80, 106, 115, 116, 128, 135, 141, 146, 147, 179, 199, 226, 242, 253, 254, 259
False apostles, 2, 3, 12, 20, 44, 66, 153, 203, 204, 210, 216, 219, 243, 249, 255, 262
False brothers, 210, 216, 218, 219
Famines, 191
Father, 5, 21, 24, 27, 31, 55, 64, 98, 137, 157, 163, 250, 265, 266
Fear of the Lord, 118, 119, 122, 123, 130, 131
Field (see also *Territory* and *Jurisdiction*), 15, 57, 113, 161, 198, 241
Financial support, 13, 66, 207, 208, 233, 243

Subject Index

Flesh, 14, 38, 47, 94, 95, 123, 126, 133, 134, 135, 136, 141, 165, 195, 210, 212, 228, 240, 252
Fool, foolishness, 203, 204, 212, 214, 215, 220, 226, 231
Fool's Speech, 34, 122, 203, 208, 213, 216, 219, 221, 225, 231, 232
Forgiveness, 50, 228
Fortunatus, 53
Foundation, 10, 231
Founding visit, 2, 37, 39, 59, 68, 243, 250
Four living creatures, 62
Fourteen, 238
Fraud, 13, 30, 87, 112, 117, 120, 122, 133, 159, 203, 221, 252

Gallio, 10, 130
Geography, 8, 9, 32
Gessius Florus, 218
Gift, 21, 37, 63, 69, 130, 173, 174, 178, 179, 183, 186, 188, 189, 202, 265
Glory, 9, 22, 27, 30, 41, 51, 59, 64, 72, 73, 74, 75, 76, 77, 78, 80, 81, 82, 83, 86, 87, 88, 91, 95, 96, 97, 99, 100, 102, 103, 104, 105, 107, 108, 109, 110, 112, 113, 115, 116, 120, 122, 124, 125, 126, 128, 129, 134, 148, 174, 182, 183, 194, 211, 224, 231
God of this age, 51, 85, 101
God-fearers, 10–11, 131
Golden calf, 50, 62, 73, 74, 75, 77, 78, 93, 97, 138
Gospel, 4, 8, 10, 11, 12, 17, 19, 20, 21, 23, 26, 27, 39, 40, 51, 52, 53, 55, 66, 70, 76, 77, 79, 83, 84, 86, 87, 88, 118, 119, 124, 138, 139, 140, 143, 147, 153, 163, 167, 173, 175, 182, 199, 203, 205, 208, 210, 214, 216, 217, 221, 232, 233, 234, 251, 254, 255, 257, 263; Paul integrally linked with, 20
Grace, 17, 18, 21, 23, 30, 36, 37, 65, 133, 142, 143, 146, 150, 153, 167, 173, 175, 178, 179, 188, 189, 199, 216, 229, 230, 251, 253, 260, 264, 265

Harmony, 4, 256, 261, 262, 263
Heart, 2, 5, 20, 32, 35, 36, 68, 69, 71, 78, 79, 80, 81, 83, 84, 88, 94, 95, 100, 106, 107, 108, 120, 121, 123, 126, 129, 133, 145, 149, 150, 151, 156, 158, 159, 164, 167, 168, 174, 176, 179, 180, 182, 186, 187, 194, 196, 228, 239, 244

Heaven, 50, 63, 64, 91, 97, 98, 102, 109, 110, 111, 112, 114, 120, 128, 129, 161, 188, 201, 221, 224, 227, 228, 237, 239
Hekhalot, 78, 89, 93, 95, 96, 112, 121, 122, 196, 224, 227, 229, 240
Holiness, 54, 118, 130, 142, 157, 163, 209, 259
Holy kiss, 263, 264, 266
Holy Spirit, 35, 41, 44, 55, 68, 110, 121, 148, 149, 170, 264, 265
House churches, 3, 13, 242, 264, 266, 267
Hyperbole, 14, 28, 32, 215, 216, 222, 227

Image, 4, 5, 19, 41, 50, 60, 61, 62, 63, 68, 82, 83, 86, 88, 92, 99, 101, 115, 126, 158, 261
Inclusio, 24, 150
Interlopers (see also *Intruders*), 11, 12, 13, 195, 199, 201, 204, 210, 228, 232, 242, 249, 251, 254, 262
Intruders, 7, 11, 12, 13, 15, 199, 201, 202, 205, 215, 219, 232, 242, 246
Irony, 34, 219, 233, 260
Israel, 9, 25, 32, 48, 56, 63, 69, 70, 71, 72, 73, 74, 75, 76, 77, 78, 79, 80, 81, 83, 84, 85, 88, 92, 93, 95, 96, 97, 98, 99, 100, 124, 128, 130, 134, 135, 136, 137, 141, 143, 144, 145, 146, 152, 155, 156, 157, 161, 162, 163, 164, 174, 180, 181, 188, 190, 191, 192, 201, 202, 204, 214, 218, 235, 236, 241, 257

Jannes and Jambres, 259
Japheth, 9, 10
Japhethites, 10, 12, 173
Jealousy, 204, 234, 247, 258, 262
Jerusalem, 2, 4, 5, 9, 10, 12, 13, 15, 19, 32, 34, 35, 37, 53, 55, 57, 68, 110, 111, 127, 128, 159, 161, 173, 174, 175, 176, 177, 178, 179, 180, 181, 182, 187, 188, 189, 190, 191, 192, 195, 199, 201, 205, 206, 210, 216, 219, 225, 235, 238, 239, 243, 245, 258
Jerusalem church, 55, 189, 216
Judaism, 11, 32, 55, 58, 69, 72, 92, 97, 125, 127, 131, 136, 144, 191, 214, 217, 225, 236, 239, 240
Judgment, 4, 6, 7, 20, 35, 36, 42, 43, 44, 45, 46, 47, 48, 49, 54, 56, 57, 69, 73, 74, 77, 80, 85, 92, 97, 103, 113, 116, 117, 118, 119, 121, 130, 139, 146, 167,

168, 191, 195, 200, 209, 233, 242, 245, 250, 251, 252, 256, 262
Judgment seat of Christ, 35
Julius Caesar, 8
Jupiter, 61
Jurisdiction (see also *Territory* and *Field*), 10, 12, 15, 193, 198, 199, 200, 201, 246

Korah, 4, 7, 11, 17, 19, 22, 34, 42, 43, 46, 48, 49, 56, 57, 58, 59, 66, 70, 73, 74, 79, 82, 87, 92, 96, 149, 158, 162, 163, 169, 198, 201, 202, 205, 206, 209, 210, 212, 218, 237, 241, 242, 247, 250, 251, 252, 257, 259, 262
Korah's rebellion, 4, 11, 17, 43, 46, 48, 49, 56, 57, 59, 66, 70, 73, 74, 79, 87, 149, 163, 201, 205, 206, 218, 237, 241, 242, 247, 250, 251, 252, 257, 259, 262

Labors, apostolic, 117, 213, 214, 215, 216, 219, 244
Law, 35, 69, 70, 71, 72, 73, 74, 75, 78, 79, 80, 95, 96, 99, 157, 161, 205, 236, 258, 259
Legitimacy, apostolic, 2, 5, 6, 17, 18, 35, 47, 51, 53, 59, 60, 66, 67, 68, 69, 76, 77, 83, 89, 102, 103, 117, 119, 121, 123, 133, 143, 146, 149, 150, 153, 158, 159, 165, 193, 232, 242, 245, 250, 251, 253, 254
Love, 31, 44, 45, 49, 123, 133, 147, 148, 149, 151, 178, 179, 184, 189, 194, 208, 209, 244, 263, 264, 265

Macedonia, 2, 3, 8, 34, 37, 38, 52, 53, 59, 60, 165, 166, 173, 175, 176, 178, 191, 208
Macedonians, 35, 37, 174, 175, 176, 177, 178, 179, 180, 182, 185, 186, 207, 234
Majority, of the Corinthian congregation, 3, 7, 36, 47, 57, 58, 78, 169, 170, 174, 194, 245, 248, 258
Malefactor, 46, 47, 48, 49, 50, 169, 243
Manna, 181, 192
Mediator (see also *Revelatory mediator*), 7, 26, 27, 60, 63, 65, 66, 67, 70, 76, 96, 121, 205, 230, 240, 246, 251, 254
Merkabah, 7, 62, 63, 64, 65, 67, 70, 76, 82, 83, 86, 87, 88, 91, 92, 93, 95, 96, 99, 100, 102, 108, 111, 113, 117, 121, 122, 134, 138, 139, 145, 195, 196, 197, 211, 221, 223, 225, 227, 228, 229, 237, 238, 239, 240, 246, 258, 267
Messiah, 55, 90, 91, 110, 134, 139, 141, 144, 147, 157, 162, 191, 204
Metaphor, 52, 55, 61, 62, 63, 68, 103, 110, 111, 125, 128, 129, 138, 152, 210, 228, 243
Metonymy, 78, 79, 84, 131
Minister, 59, 64, 67, 69, 70, 71, 72, 74, 77, 78, 96, 133, 137, 139, 142, 155, 183, 234, 235, 251, 253
Ministry, 8, 12, 19, 25, 26, 30, 37, 42, 59, 60, 65, 66, 68, 69, 70, 71, 72, 73, 74, 75, 76, 77, 78, 80, 83, 84, 87, 89, 94, 95, 96, 97, 102, 104, 105, 113, 117, 122, 123, 124, 125, 131, 133, 137, 138, 139, 140, 143, 146, 147, 148, 149, 150, 155, 177, 182, 189, 197, 208, 211, 212, 217, 223, 229, 242, 246, 251, 253, 257, 262
Minority, of the Corinthian congregation, 5, 7, 11, 36, 172, 195, 196
Mission, 10, 11, 12, 15, 23, 41, 53, 106, 113, 166, 170, 173, 181, 183, 190, 198, 199, 200, 205, 233, 241, 254
Missionary strategy, 7, 8, 191
Money, 13, 177, 180, 209, 243
Monotheism, 31
Mortal body, 2, 102, 103, 104, 105, 110, 116, 117, 121, 123, 127, 134, 135, 230
Moses, 4, 11, 18, 19, 22, 35, 39, 42, 43, 45, 46, 48, 49, 50, 56, 57, 59, 60, 63, 64, 65, 66, 69, 70, 71, 72, 73, 74, 75, 76, 77, 78, 79, 80, 81, 82, 83, 85, 86, 87, 88, 92, 93, 94, 95, 96, 97, 98, 99, 100, 102, 109, 112, 120, 124, 128, 131, 133, 137, 145, 146, 149, 155, 158, 161, 162, 163, 169, 176, 177, 195, 197, 198, 201, 205, 206, 207, 208, 209, 210, 212, 218, 223, 225, 230, 232, 233, 235, 237, 239, 241, 243, 246, 247, 250, 251, 257, 259, 262
Mutuality, 5, 43, 82, 189, 260, 262

Nakedness, 109, 113, 129
Nations, 8, 9, 10, 20, 39, 49, 81, 85, 86, 114, 124, 138, 139, 143, 157, 163, 173, 174, 180, 181, 183, 188, 189, 190, 191, 199, 202, 217, 220, 236, 241
New covenant, 20, 57, 59, 60, 64, 67, 69, 70, 71, 72, 74, 75, 76, 77, 78, 80, 81, 83, 84, 85, 94, 96, 121, 126, 137,

146, 150, 151, 155, 156, 158, 162, 163, 164, 237, 246, 251, 254, 259, 265
New exodus (see also *Exodus, exodus typology*), 72

Oath, 39, 42, 53, 209, 219, 220
Obduracy, 77, 78, 79, 80, 84
Offender, 3, 14, 45, 46, 47, 48, 49, 50, 51, 57, 166, 196, 241
Offering, 119, 123, 142, 174, 175, 176, 177, 180, 182, 183, 185, 186, 187, 190
Opening, letter, 17, 23, 30, 43, 66, 84, 97, 152, 155, 164, 260
Opponents, 5, 6, 11, 12, 13, 15, 17, 18, 22, 24, 26, 30, 35, 44, 46, 57, 60, 63, 64, 65, 66, 67, 79, 84, 85, 86, 89, 95, 96, 102, 103, 107, 109, 112, 115, 117, 120, 121, 122, 123, 129, 131, 133, 134, 135, 140, 148, 149, 150, 151, 152, 153, 156, 158, 159, 162, 163, 166, 193, 194, 195, 196, 197, 198, 199, 200, 201, 202, 203, 204, 205, 206, 207, 208, 209, 210, 211, 212, 213, 214, 215, 217, 219, 221, 222, 224, 225, 226, 227, 230, 231, 232, 233, 234, 235, 237, 243, 245, 246, 247, 248, 249, 251, 252, 255, 259

Painful visit, 4, 7, 12, 37, 38, 43, 44, 57, 89, 90, 167, 169, 220, 243, 245, 248, 251
Paradise, 64, 109, 224, 238, 239
Paraenesis, 154, 155, 157, 159, 163
Paronomasia, 68, 154, 244
Parousia, 27, 36, 37, 102, 106, 107, 108, 109, 110, 111, 112, 114, 115, 127, 204
Pax Romana, 138, 140, 145
Peace, 4, 17, 21, 22, 31, 51, 53, 137, 145, 164, 165, 248, 260, 262, 263, 264
Physical appearance, 194, 197, 211
Pilgrimage of the nations, 174, 188, 191, 230
Plural: apostolic (or literary), 19, 31, 60, 83, 87, 94, 109, 137, 254
Poor, 9, 81, 128, 149, 173, 176, 179, 187, 188, 190, 191, 208, 234
Poverty, 174, 175, 176, 180, 191, 208, 234
Power, 6, 26, 27, 29, 32, 33, 42, 57, 71, 85, 86, 103, 104, 105, 117, 123, 124, 125, 134, 148, 168, 193, 194, 195, 196, 201, 206, 226, 230, 231, 233, 234, 241, 242, 252, 253, 255
Praise of God, 30, 189

Prayer, 48, 57, 90, 128, 135, 191, 229, 231, 254, 255
Presence, 19, 45, 49, 50, 57, 58, 65, 67, 70, 72, 73, 80, 81, 82, 84, 86, 93, 99, 102, 106, 109, 114, 116, 120, 128, 130, 162, 171, 197, 230, 237, 246, 251, 258, 263, 265
Pride, 248
Priesthood, 56, 128, 209, 248, 257, 262
Profit, 65, 66, 246
Promises, 26, 27, 40, 41, 42, 55, 59, 69, 70, 114, 152, 155, 156, 157, 163, 198, 214, 241
Prophet, 22, 27, 57, 66, 81, 93, 97, 99, 117, 122, 134, 245

Qal wahomer (see also *a fortiori* argument), 73
Quadriga, 61, 62, 92
Qumran fragment, 96, 160

Rebellion, 7, 19, 34, 42, 46, 56, 59, 78, 84, 85, 89, 141, 172, 242, 247, 248, 257, 262, 265
Rebels, 4, 22, 64, 163, 201, 242, 243, 250, 252, 262
Recommendation, self-recommendation, 12, 67, 68, 70, 94, 119, 131, 160, 181, 183, 198, 200, 206, 232, 235
Reconciliation, 3, 22, 34, 42, 44, 53, 133, 136, 137, 138, 139, 140, 141, 142, 143, 144, 145, 147, 153, 158, 167, 177, 179, 193, 253, 262
Redemption, 41, 95, 96, 111, 113, 114, 136, 142, 156, 157
Repentance, 3, 5, 44, 59, 60, 75, 80, 100, 166, 167, 168, 169, 171, 172, 178, 245, 248, 258, 262
Res Gestae, 235
Restoration, 9, 22, 69, 71, 72, 75, 80, 88, 95, 96, 123, 124, 136, 143, 144, 145, 154, 157, 160, 162, 163, 173, 180, 181, 188, 190, 255, 261, 264
Resurrection, 26, 27, 29, 30, 32, 33, 41, 64, 72, 85, 104, 105, 106, 107, 108, 110, 111, 112, 113, 114, 115, 125, 128, 129, 134, 135, 142, 181, 230, 252, 255
Revelation(s) (see also *Visions*), 7, 12, 60, 63, 64, 65, 66, 67, 68, 70, 76, 78, 80, 82, 84, 87, 88, 96, 103, 105, 109, 146, 162, 203, 206, 213, 221, 222, 225, 226, 227, 230, 231, 237, 240, 251, 254

Revelatory mediator (see also *Mediator*), 26, 35, 41, 49, 55, 59, 60, 64, 65, 66, 70, 71, 88, 95, 162, 169, 223, 225, 229, 230, 246, 247, 250
Rhetorical questions, 38, 67, 151
Roman colony, 8, 10
Roman province, 8, 10, 19, 25, 28, 32, 184

Salvation, 26, 27, 30, 40, 54, 76, 79, 81, 86, 124, 131, 133, 143, 144, 153, 166, 168, 172, 181, 193, 242, 253
Sanctification, 20, 131, 154, 156, 157, 158, 265
Satan, 3, 13, 14, 18, 47, 50, 51, 54, 58, 65, 83, 85, 86, 153, 154, 204, 209, 211, 215, 228, 229, 234, 235, 248, 262
Second exodus (see also *Exodus, exodus typology*), 136, 156, 157
Second missionary journey, 55
Second visit, 5, 12, 34, 37, 44, 45, 51, 52, 168, 169, 233, 242
Sedition, 247
Self-commendation (see also *Commendation*), 66, 70, 90, 103, 119, 148, 203
Selflessness, 233
Self-recommendation, 12, 67
Serpent, 204, 257
Service, 22, 94, 105, 116, 173, 174, 177, 181, 182, 184, 189, 213, 214, 234
Shipwrecked, 218
Signs and wonders, 241
Silas, 39, 53, 54, 55, 217
Sinai, 50, 62, 63, 65, 75, 78, 80, 82, 92, 93, 95, 97, 99, 124, 237
Sinaitic covenant, 60, 70, 71, 72, 74, 75, 78, 79, 85, 156
Sinlessness, 141
Slander, 50, 247, 258
Son of God, 19, 24, 39, 40, 54, 107, 128, 134, 138, 145, 252, 266
Son of man, 132, 223, 237
Sons, 5, 9, 19, 40, 41, 57, 73, 85, 99, 107, 128, 154, 157, 241
Sorrow, 44, 48, 50, 166, 167, 168, 169, 236, 248
Spain, 10, 20, 53, 173, 198, 199
Spirit, 2, 29, 31, 35, 41, 55, 59, 64, 66, 68, 69, 70, 71, 72, 73, 74, 75, 77, 78, 79, 80, 81, 82, 83, 84, 91, 92, 93, 94, 95, 96, 99, 100, 105, 110, 112, 113, 114, 124, 126, 128, 131, 133, 146, 148, 149, 151, 156, 157, 158, 160, 172, 177, 179, 182, 186, 190, 201, 205, 226, 230, 233, 242, 254, 265, 266, 267
Stephanas, 53
Stoning, 216, 217, 218, 235, 236
Strife, 4, 13, 247, 262, 263, 265
Stumbling block, 134, 147, 149, 226
Substitution, 142
Suffering, 1, 2, 23, 26, 27, 28, 30, 32, 33, 45, 53, 61, 89, 90, 102, 103, 104, 105, 106, 107, 108, 112, 113, 124, 133, 135, 140, 148, 165, 194, 214, 215, 219, 220, 226, 227, 228, 229, 231, 244, 253, 255
Suffering Servant, 132, 135, 137, 141, 142, 144
Sufferings, 2, 23, 24, 25, 26, 27, 29, 32, 33, 104, 105, 107, 117, 134, 135, 140, 148, 191, 194, 203, 213, 214, 215, 221, 230, 231, 235, 236, 252, 255
Sufficiency, 65, 66, 69, 70, 83, 93, 104, 187, 197, 229, 239, 241, 254
Super-apostles, 12, 205, 206, 207, 214, 215, 221, 232, 234
Synagogue, 10, 11, 78, 79, 91, 98, 118, 217, 235

Tabernacle, 110, 127, 128, 174, 175, 176, 178, 180, 181, 183, 186, 187, 230
Table of nations, 8, 9
Tablets, 67, 69, 94, 95, 97
Tearful letter, 2, 6, 34, 36, 38, 42, 44, 45, 47, 49, 51, 52, 58, 60, 89, 90, 165, 167, 169, 170, 171, 172, 178, 186, 194, 197, 219, 245, 248, 258, 265
Temple, 110, 112, 127, 128, 154, 158, 162
Temple tax, 192
Tenor (see also *Metaphor*), 7, 61, 62, 138
Tent, 108, 110, 127, 129, 230
Tent of meeting, 80, 81, 82, 97
Territoriality, apostolic, 8, 10, 198, 201
Territory (see also *Field* and *Jurisdiction*), 10, 12, 15, 32, 198, 199, 205, 206, 209, 232, 249, 250, 254
Testimony, 22, 33, 35, 119, 217, 219, 250
Thanksgiving, 23, 24, 30, 31, 34, 43, 45, 53, 60, 61, 63, 105, 106, 144, 166, 188, 189, 228
Third heaven (see also *Paradise*), 97, 109, 111, 224
Third time, 24, 168, 184, 185, 196, 198, 243, 249, 257
Third visit, 3, 5, 34, 44, 171, 174, 186, 193, 197, 200, 203, 242, 243, 246, 248, 249, 258

Subject Index

Thorn in the flesh, 29, 33, 35, 102, 120, 197, 221, 226, 227, 228, 229, 230, 231, 239, 240
Threats, 260
Throne (see also *Chariot* and *Merkabah*), 21, 50, 62, 63, 64, 76, 82, 83, 84, 86, 87, 89, 91, 92, 93, 95, 102, 109, 117, 122, 130, 134, 138, 211, 223, 228, 238
Throne-chariot, 54, 117, 222, 223, 225
Timothy, 17, 18, 19, 39, 43, 53, 54, 94, 257
Titus, 3, 34, 38, 43, 44, 45, 48, 49, 52, 53, 58, 59, 60, 160, 165, 166, 167, 170, 171, 172, 173, 175, 178, 181, 182, 183, 186, 219, 245, 257, 258, 265
To this day, 78, 79, 83, 98
Torah, 63, 64, 74, 78, 93, 94, 95, 96, 103, 161, 201, 205, 236
Transformation, 5, 82, 83, 95, 97, 99, 100, 107, 108, 109, 112, 113, 114, 121, 128, 136, 145, 210, 234
Travel plans, Paul's, 2, 3, 4, 5, 14, 34, 36, 37, 38, 39, 40, 42, 44, 46, 52, 54, 59, 171, 195, 212, 233
Travelogue, 53, 59, 60, 89, 165
Tribulation catalogue, 215, 219, 220, 227, 229, 231, 248
Trinity, 144, 163, 236, 264, 267
Triumphal procession, 60, 61, 62, 63, 64, 90, 91, 92, 138, 223, 224
Troas, 3, 28, 38, 52, 53, 165
Troublemaker, 168, 169
Truth, 4, 35, 39, 42, 43, 84, 86, 119, 128, 131, 145, 153, 171, 172, 185, 209, 255, 259, 262, 263

Typology (see also *Exodus* and *Second exodus*), 73, 74, 99, 156, 157, 201, 210

Unbelievers, 51, 85, 86, 151, 152, 153, 154, 155, 249, 262
Unity of 2 Corinthians, 6, 7, 14, 30, 47, 65, 66, 140, 146, 167, 192, 194, 199, 200, 223, 238, 245, 248, 258, 260, 261, 262, 264
Usurpers, 199

Vehicle (see also *Metaphor*), 61, 62, 75, 138
Veil, 57, 72, 73, 74, 75, 77, 78, 79, 80, 81, 82, 84, 97, 102, 120
Visions (see also *Revelation[s]*), 12, 62, 63, 66, 91, 96, 100, 101, 112, 221, 222, 223, 224, 225, 237, 238

Weakness, 1, 2, 3, 24, 27, 35, 61, 113, 194, 213, 214, 215, 220, 221, 225, 226, 227, 228, 229, 230, 231, 233, 235, 237, 241, 252, 255
Wilderness (see also *Exodus, exodus typology*), 11, 22, 56, 72, 79, 110, 181, 207, 233, 247, 249, 253
Witness(es), 27, 35, 39, 42, 51, 53, 55, 56, 58, 68, 91, 118, 209, 220, 232, 249, 251
World, 8, 9, 10, 20, 22, 64, 76, 84, 85, 86, 90, 103, 124, 136, 138, 139, 140, 141, 143, 145, 149, 152, 168, 175, 187, 195, 202, 226, 239, 253, 263

Yoke, 152, 154, 161

Scripture Index

OLD TESTAMENT

Genesis **1:3–4**, 88, 136; **1:26–27**, 100; **1:26–28**, 126; **1:27**, 89, 100; **2:7**, 103, 107; **3:1–7**, 204; **3:13**, 204; **3:19**, 103, 107; **3:21**, 129; **3:24–25**, 129; **10**, 8; **10:2–5**, 9; **10:5**, 235; **10:6–20**, 9; **10:20**, 235; **10:21–31**, 9; **10:31**, 235; **12:1–3**, 214; **12:3**, 8; **12:7**, 214; **13:15–17**, 214; **14:20**, 31; **15:2–18**, 201; **15:18**, 214; **16:13**, 130; **17:7–10**, 214; **17:19**, 214; **18:18**, 8; **28:17**, 130; **31:44–55**, 56; **32:30**, 130; **47:26**, 98

Exodus **2:23b–24**, 113; **3:1–15:21**, 230; **4:10**, 65, 70, 92; **4:10ff.**, 96; **4:14**, 19; **4:21**, 86; **6:3**, 130; **6:5–6**, 113; **6:7**, 162; **6:20**, 19; **7:3**, 86, 232; **7:13**, 86; **9:12**, 86; **9:35**, 86; **12:4**, 241; **14:4**, 86; **14:8**, 86; **14:31**, 130; **15:16**, 171; **16:1–30**, 181; **16:7**, 99; **16:8**, 57; **16:10**, 99; **16:18**, 187, 192; **17:4**, 218; **18:10**, 31; **19:3–6**, 20; **19:6**, 22, 96, 163, 237; **19:9**, 57, 65; **19:21**, 130; **20:5**, 257; **20:12**, 244; **20:18**, 130; **20:19**, 65; **21:17**, 244; **24:1–2**, 65; **24:9–16**, 81; **24:10–11**, 91, 130; **24:12**, 94; **24:16**, 99; **24:17**, 99; **25:1–9**, 174, 176, 181; **25:2**, 176, 187; **25:8**, 230; **28:1**, 19; **29:45**, 20, 237; **31:13**, 157; **32–34**, 73; **32:9**, 77, 98; **32:11**, 50, 93, 246; **32:11–13**, 138; **32:27–29**, 73; **32:32**, 57, 93; **32:35**, 73; **33:3**, 73; **33:5**, 73; **33:11**, 93; **33:18**, 82; **33:18–23**, 73, 130; **34:6**, 29; **34:29**, 82; **34:29–30**, 99; **34:29–35**, 72, 76, 81, 97; **34:30**, 73; **34:30–32**, 73; **34:34**, 80, 82; **34:34–35**, 73; **34:34a**, 79; **35:4–29**, 174, 176, 181; **35:5**, 176, 187; **35:21**, 180; **35:23–24**, 180; **36:2–7**, 181; **36:3–7**, 174; **36:5**, 176; **36:5–7**, 177; **40:34**, 99; **40:34–35**, 110; **40:35**, 99

Leviticus **1:4**, 123; **4:21**, 142; **4:24**, 142; **5:12**, 142; **6:16**, 56; **6:18**, 142; **6:26**, 56; **9:6**, 99; **9:23**, 99; **11:44–45**, 20, 157; **17:11**, 123; **19:2**, 20, 157; **19:19**, 161; **20:2**, 218; **20:7–8**, 157; **20:24–26**, 157; **20:27**, 218; **22:32–33**, 157; **24:14**, 218; **24:16**, 218; **24:23**, 218; **25:46**, 257; **26:6**, 21; **26:11–12**, 155; **26:12**, 162; **26:14–38**, 75; **26:14–39**, 72

Numbers **12:7–8**, 93; **12:8**, 82, 100, 115; **14:10**, 99, 218; **14:18**, 257; **14:21**, 99; **15:16**, 209; **15:35–36**, 218; **15:40–41**, 157; **16**, 242; **16–17**, 4, 11, 22, 42, 59, 74, 206, 247, 262; **16:3**, 22, 43, 46, 66, 82, 87, 96, 162, 163, 208, 209, 237, 247; **16:5**, 56; **16:8–11**, 248; **16:11**, 40, 56, 206; **16:13**, 43, 46, 87, 247; **16:14**, 149; **16:15**, 158, 208, 209, 257; **16:19**, 73, 99; **16:20–22**, 46; **16:22**, 56; **16:26**, 20, 46, 163; **16:27**, 257; **16:28**, 18, 70, 206, 207; **16:28–29**, 46, 250, 252; **16:30**, 48, 206; **16:31–33**, 212; **16:31–35**, 209; **16:32**, 48; **16:34**, 48; **16:38**, 241; **16:40**, 205; **16:41**, 56, 92; **16:41–50**, 48, 243; **16:42**, 73, 99; **16:48**, 92; **17:13**, 85; **18:8**, 56; **18:28**, 56; **20:6**, 99; **21:5–6**, 65; **22:7**, 66; **22:28**, 257; **22:32**, 257; **22:33**, 257; **24:10**, 257; **25:1–13**, 204; **25:5**, 161; **26:9**, 56; **26:59**, 19; **27:3**, 56; **27:12–13**, 19; **33:55**, 228

Deuteronomy **2:25**, 171; **2:30**, 86; **3:14**, 98; **3:23–26**, 241; **3:26**, 239; **4:25–31**, 98; **4:34**, 232; **5:29**, 131; **6:2**, 131; **6:4**, 31; **6:22**, 232; **7:6**, 20, 237; **7:9**, 39; **7:19**, 232; **10:12**, 131; **10:20**, 131; **11:6**, 56; **11:25**, 171; **11:26–28**, 75; **13:1–2**, 232, 241; **13:10–11**, 218; **14:2**, 21, 20, 237; **17:2–7**, 218; **19:15**, 35, 249, 258; **21:21**, 218; **21:22–23**, 134; **21:23**, 134, 141, 142; **22:10**,

161; **22:21**, 218; **22:24**, 218; **24:16**, 257; **25:1–3**, 217; **25:4**, 258; **26:8**, 232; **26:19**, 20, 237; **27:14–26**, 75; **28:9**, 20, 237; **28:15–68**, 72, 75, 191; **28:46**, 232; **29**, 257; **29:3**, 232; **29:3–4**, 78; **29:4**, 77, 98; **29:12**, 162; **29:20–29**, 191; **29:28**, 98; **30:15**, 39, 64, 92; **30:15–20**, 72, 75; **31:16–32:47**, 75; **30:19**, 39, 64, 92; **32:1b–4**, 39; **32:5**, 257; **32:50**, 19; **33:24**, 257; **34:10**, 93; **34:11**, 232

Joshua **2:15**, 221; **6:25**, 98; **7:25**, 218; **7:26**, 98; **22:17**, 98; **23:8**, 98

Judges **1:21**, 98; **3:10**, 99; **6:22–23**, 130; **6:34**, 99; **10:4**, 98; **11:29**, 99; **13:22**, 130; **13:25**, 99; **14:6**, 99; **14:19**, 99; **15:14**, 99; **16:15**, 257; **18:12**, 98

Ruth **1:20**, 70

1 Samuel **6:19**, 130; **10:6**, 99; **12:1–25**, 56; **16:7**, 135; **16:13**, 41, 99; **16:14**, 99; **20:23**, 56; **21:10**, 218

2 Samuel **5–7**, 110; **7:2**, 110; **7:14**, 40, 55, 156, 157, 163; **7:24**, 162; **18:28**, 31

1 Kings **2:33**, 21; **7:31**, 111; **8:4**, 128; **8:11**, 99; **8:39**, 133; **9:13**, 98; **10:9**, 31; **12:19**, 98; **17:20**, 56; **18:4–18**, 230; **18:12**, 99; **18:39**, 130; **19:10**, 163; **19:13**, 130; **21:8**, 55; **22:19**, 91; **22:24**, 99

2 Kings **2:16**, 99; **2:22**, 98; **8:22**, 98; **9:11**, 122; **10:27**, 98; **17:7–41**, 131; **17:23**, 98; **21:15**, 98

1 Chronicles **4:23**, 103; **5:26**, 98; **6:3**, 19; **6:17**, 110; **9:23**, 110, 230; **17:22**, 162; **23:13**, 19; **28:18**, 91; **29:10**, 31; **29:16–22**, 187

2 Chronicles **5:5**, 128; **7:1**, 99; **7:2**, 99; **7:3**, 99; **18:23**, 99; **20:14**, 99; **24:19**, 80; **29:5–7**, 128; **29:9**, 98

Ezra **7:1–8:34**, 190; **7:15–16**, 180; **7:15–23**, 190; **7:22**, 180; **8:24–30**, 183, 245; **9:7**, 78, 98

Nehemiah **9**, 96; **9:6–37**, 135; **9:10**, 232

Esther **2:11**, 126; **3:4**, 126; **8:8–10**, 55

Job **1:6–12**, 228; **2:1–8**, 228; **4:8**, 186; **4:12–16**, 130; **5:20**, 29; **10:9**, 103; **16:20**, 56; **17:16**, 103; **21:15**, 70; **21:26**, 103; **28:28**, 131; **31**, 228; **31:2**, 70; **33:2**, 150; **33:30**, 29; **34:15**, 103; **37:1**, 130; **37:24**, 130; **40:2**, 70

Psalms **2:2–3**, 152, 161; **2:7**, 161; **2:8**, 138; **2:11**, 171; **8:5–6**, 126; **8:5–7**, 89, 99, 100; **15:4**, 131; **19:7**, 39; **19:10**, 131; **22**, 33; **22:24**, 131; **22:26**, 131; **23:4–6**, 32; **25:14**, 131; **26:9**, 104; **28:6**, 30; **29:11**, 21; **31:20**, 131; **31:21**, 30; **32:1–2**, 228; **32:2**, 139; **32:4**, 33, 228, 240; **33:8**, 130; **33:18**, 131; **33:19**, 29; **34:8**, 131; **34:10**, 131; **36:25**, 104; **36:28**, 104; **36:33**, 104; **37:22**, 104; **38:21**, 50; **55:5**, 171; **55:17**, 229; **56:13**, 29; **60:6**, 131; **65:6–9**, 130; **66:16**, 131; **66:20**, 31; **68:17–18**, 62; **68:18**, 62; **68:18–19**, 62, 63; **68:19**, 63, 82, 92, 99, 201, 237, 238; **70:9**, 104; **70:18**, 104; **71:1**, 32; **71:5**, 32; **71:13**, 50; **71:14**, 32; **71:20**, 32; **71:20–24**, 32; **71:22–24**, 32; **72**, 191; **72:8**, 139; **74:7**, 128; **76**, 130; **78:43**, 232; **85:8**, 21; **85:10**, 131; **86:1–2**, 32; **86:7**, 32; **86:12**, 32; **86:12–17**, 32; **86:13**, 32; **94:16–22**, 32; **94:17**, 32; **94:22**, 32; **103:11**, 131; **103:13**, 131; **103:14**, 103; **103:17**, 131; **103:31**, 99; **104:27**, 145; **104:29**, 103; **105:27**, 232; **106:16–18**, 56, 247; **106:28–31**, 204; **110:1**, 54, 80, 87, 91, 92, 100, 138; **111:5**, 131; **111:9**, 187; **111:10**, 131; **112**, 188; **112:9**, 192; **115:1**, 105; **115:5**, 72; **116:8**, 29; **116:10**, 105, 106; **117:18**, 240; **118:8**, 104; **119:74**, 131; **119:79**, 131; **124:6**, 31; **125:5**, 186; **135:9**, 232; **137:5**, 99; **139:9**, 104; **145:13**, 39; **145:19**, 131; **147:11**, 131

Proverbs **1:7**, 131; **1:29**, 131; **2:5**, 131; **3:3**, 95; **4:3**, 49; **7:3**, 95; **9:10**, 131; **10:2**, 29; **11:24**, 187; **15:33**, 131; **16:8**, 187; **21:22**, 195, 201, 237; **22:8**,

186, 187; **23:14**, 29; **24:12**, 133; **24:21**, 131; **30:8**, 187

Ecclesiastes **3:14**, 131; **3:20**, 103; **5:14–15**, 113

Isaiah **2:2–4**, 191; **2:2–5**, 181; **6:1**, 238; **6:1–5**, 117; **6:1–13**, 91; **6:3**, 92; **6:5**, 130; **6:9–10**, 78, 85, 98; **8:18**, 232; **9:1**, 88; **11:2**, 99; **11:10**, 181; **14:12**, 15, 211; **14:12–15**, 211; **14:13–14**, 211; **19:16**, 171; **20:3**, 232; **24–27**, 80; **24:1–23**, 81; **25:3**, 130; **25:6–8**, 81; **25:6–10**, 181; **25:7–8a**, 114; **26:12**, 21; **29:10**, 98; **29:16**, 103; **32:15–17**, 75; **35:2**, 99; **40–55**, 145; **40–66**, 191; **40:1**, 28; **40:2**, 48; **40:5**, 99; **41:5**, 130; **41:25**, 103; **42:22**, 180; **43:1–7**, 157; **43:6**, 156, 157; **43:10**, 55; **43:12**, 55; **43:18–19**, 136, 145; **45:1**, 58; **45:9**, 103; **45:22**, 180; **49**, 166; **49:1**, 22, 166; **49:1ff.**, 143; **49:6**, 86, 88, 143; **49:9**, 143, 166; **49:13**, 166; **49:18**, 204; **50:1–2**, 204; **51**, 32; **51:3**, 136; **52:2–10**, 81; **52:7**, 139, 163; **52:9**, 32; **52:11**, 20, 155, 156, 157, 163; **53:1**, 139; **53:4–5**, 132, 135; **53:5**, 137; **53:6**, 142; **53:9**, 141; **53:10**, 142; **53:11–12**, 132, 135; **53:12**, 142, 180; **54:1–8**, 204; **55:1**, 180; **55:1–13**, 188; **55:5**, 191; **55:10**, 174, 188; **56:6–8**, 191; **58:8**, 99; **58:12**, 192; **59:21**, 75; **60:1**, 99; **60:3–16**, 180; **60:5–7**, 191; **61:1**, 81, 99; **61:1–2**, 41, 81, 190; **61:6–7**, 180; **62:5**, 204; **63:17**, 86; **65:17–19**, 88, 136, 143; **66:12**, 180; **66:18–20**, 8, 9; **66:18–21**, 174, 183, 191; **66:19**, 241; **66:19–20**, 241; **66:20**, 190; **66:22**, 88; **66:22–23**, 136

Jeremiah **1:2**, 93; **1:5**, 22; **5:22**, 130; **5:24**, 130; **7:15**, 72; **7:23**, 162; **7:25–26**, 77; **8:3**, 72; **9:19**, 93; **9:23–24**, 200, 202; **9:24**, 93; **10:7**, 130; **11:4**, 162; **11:7–8**, 77; **12:13**, 186; **17:1**, 95; **17:12**, 91; **18:4**, 103; **18:6**, 103; **23:9–40**, 66; **24:7**, 163; **29:26**, 122; **30:18–22**, 163; **31:1**, 33, 163; **31:31**, 70; **31:31–34**, 69, 70, 71, 75, 76, 94; **31:33**, 69, 155, 163; **31:34**, 57, 96, 237; **32:20**, 232; **32:21**, 232; **32:38**, 163; **33:8**, 210; **36:23**, 55; **42:5**, 56; **52:25**, 49

Lamentations **2:2**, 195; **2:6–7**, 128; **4:2**, 103

Ezekiel **1**, 62, 82, 100; **1:1–28**, 91; **1:4**, 27, 83; **1:4–28**, 62; **1:26**, 82; **1:26–27**, 86, 88, 101; **1:28**, 82, 99, 118; **3:12**, 99, 112; **3:12–13**, 91; **3:14**, 112; **3:22–24**, 91; **3:23**, 99; **8:1–18**, 91; **8:3**, 112; **10:4**, 18, 99; **10:9–17**, 91; **11:1**, 112; **11:5**, 99; **11:19**, 67, 69, 71, 72, 94; **11:19–20**, 75, 95; **11:20**, 163; **11:22**, 95; **11:23**, 99; **11:24**, 112; **12:4–5**, 237; **12:7**, 237; **12:12**, 237; **13:1–16**, 66; **14:11**, 163; **16**, 204; **16:60**, 76; **18:32**, 168; **18:36**, 72; **20:12**, 157; **20:34**, 156, 157; **20:34–35**, 156; **28:24**, 228; **30:22**, 163; **33:22**, 150; **34:25**, 22; **36:24–29**, 75; **36:25–26**, 71; **36:26**, 67, 69, 72, 94, 126; **36:26–27**, 69, 71, 76, 155; **36:27**, 126; **36:28**, 163; **36:36**, 163; **37:1–14**, 72; **37:15–28**, 72; **37:23**, 163; **37:26**, 22, 76; **37:27**, 155, 162, 163, 230; **37:28**, 163; **38–39**, 9; **40–48**, 238; **43:3**, 100; **43:4**, 99; **43:5**, 99

Daniel **5:4**, 85; **7:9–10**, 82; **7:9–14**, 91; **7:13**, 122; **7:18**, 177; **7:21**, 177; **7:22**, 177; **7:25**, 177; **7:27**, 177; **9**, 96; **9:4–19**, 78, 98; **9:11–13**, 72; **10:8–9**, 130; **10:15–17**, 130; **10:16**, 150; **11**, 8; **12:4**, 240

Hosea **1–3**, 204; **1:9**, 162; **5:4**, 80; **6:1**, 80; **7:13**, 72; **9:7**, 122; **10:12**, 174, 188; **12:11**, 100; **13:14**, 33

Micah **1:1**, 225; **2:7**, 99; **3:5**, 66; **3:8**, 99; **4:2**, 191

Habakkuk **1:1**, 225; **2:14**, 99; **3:2**, 130; **3:8**, 62, 91

Zechariah **3:1**, 50, 228; **3:4**, 112; **3:5**, 112; **8:8**, 163; **9:5**, 130; **8:13**, 163; **12–14**, 54; **13:9**, 163

Malachi **3:5**, 56

New Testament

Matthew **5:9–13**, 31; **5:33–37**, 42; **5:46**, 127; **11:5**, 190; **11:28**, 170; **12:6**, 111; **13:41–42**, 149; **16:23**, 149; **18:7**, 149; **18:16**, 249; **21:13**, 111

Mark **2:10**, 223; **2:19**, 204; **2:28**, 223; **3:20–27**, 229; **3:21**, 121; **4:12**, 85; **7:8–13**, 244; **8:31**, 223; **8:38**, 223; **9:42**, 149; **10:44–45**, 87; **10:45**, 132; **11:17**, 111; **12:29**, 31; **12:41–44**, 180; **13:22**, 241; **14:32–41**, 229; **14:36**, 116, 229; **14:58**, 110, 111, 127, 128; **14:62**, 64, 87

Luke **1:32**, 54; **1:64**, 150; **1:68–79**, 31; **2:31–32**, 111; **3:22**, 41; **4:18**, 41; **4:23**, 233; **7:22**, 190; **11:2–4**, 31; **17:1**, 149; **19:46**, 111; **21:9**, 248; **22:38**, 241

John **1:14**, 128; **2:16**, 111; **2:19–21**, 111; **2:21**, 128; **4:24**, 81; **6:53**, 127; **8:12–20**, 250; **12:27**, 116; **14:2**, 110, 127; **21:14**, 257

Acts **1:8**, 10; **2:1–8:25**, 10; **2:19**, 232; **2:22**, 232; **2:43**, 232; **2:44–45**, 191; **3:15**, 106; **5:12**, 232; **7:47**, 111; **7:48**, 110; **7:49**, 111; **8:26–40**, 10; **9**, 220; **9:3**, 88; **9:12**, 237; **9:15**, 103; **9:20**, 39, 217; **9:23–25**, 236; **9:25**, 221; **10:36**, 87; **11:27–30**, 190; **13:5**, 217; **13:14**, 217; **13:47**, 10, 86; **14:1**, 217; **14:3**, 232; **14:5**, 236; **14:8–20**, 18; **14:10**, 241; **14:19**, 218; **14:19–20**, 104; **14:27**, 52; **15:12**, 232, 241; **15:21**, 79; **15:22**, 55; **15:24**, 15; **16:1**, 18; **16:2**, 18; **16:3**, 19; **16:8–10**, 52; **16:9**, 223; **16:9–10**, 237; **16:18**, 241; **16:22–23**, 217; **16:23–30**, 216; **16:37**, 218; **17:1–2**, 217; **17:10**, 217; **17:14–15**, 186; **17:17**, 217; **17:24**, 110; **17:34**, 22; **18:1–18**, 2, 11; **18:3**, 207; **18:4**, 118, 217; **18:5**, 39; **18:9**, 223; **18:9–10**, 237; **18:12**, 130; **18:14**, 150; **18:19**, 217; **18:26**, 217; **19:8**, 118, 217; **19:11–12**, 241; **19:23–20:1**, 28; **20:1–3**, 38; **20:4**, 19, 186; **20:7**, 52; **21:3**, 235; **21:19**, 189; **21:20**, 189; **21:27–30**, 174; **21:40–22**; **22**, 220; **22:6**, 88; **22:11**, 88; **22:17–18**, 223; **22:17–21**, 237; **22:19**, 217; **22:24**, 235; **22:25–29**, 218; **23:11**, 223, 237; **24:17–18**, 174; **26:12–23**, 220; **26:13**, 88; **26:24–25**, 131; **27:13–44**, 218; **27:23**, 223; **27:23–24**, 237; **28:3–6**, 241; **28:8**, 241; **28:23**, 118; **28:26–27**, 78

Romans **1:1**, 22, 235; **1:1–5**, 17; **1:2–4**, 40; **1:3–4**, 54; **1:4**, 29, 252; **1:5**, 49, 83, 229; **1:5–6**, 10; **1:7**, 21; **1:9**, 42, 58, 170; **1:13**, 51, 54; **1:16**, 217; **1:18–3:20**, 162; **1:29**, 247, 248; **1:29–31**, 258; **2:4**, 167; **2:6**, 16, 117; **2:9**, 25; **3:10–18**, 162; **3:25**, 123; **4:7–8**, 228; **4:13**, 42; **4:17**, 24, 26, 172; **4:24**, 106; **4:25**, 125, 132, 142; **5:1–10**, 137; **5:1–11**, 267; **5:3**, 25, 215; **5:6**, 142; **5:8**, 139, 142, 265; **5:9**, 123; **5:10**, 139; **5:10–11**, 137; **5:19**, 141; **6:2–11**, 124; **6:10**, 142; **6:19**, 162; **7:12**, 73; **7:14**, 123; **7:24**, 107; **8**, 99; **8:2–4**, 71; **8:3**, 141; **8:3–4**, 75; **8:4**, 156; **8:5–11**, 267; **8:9**, 81; **8:11**, 72, 99, 106, 114; **8:14**, 81; **8:14–16**, 81; **8:15**, 19, 31, 40, 41, 99, 229; **8:16**, 170; **8:17**, 27, 40, 42, 105, 107, 229; **8:17–18**, 32; **8:18–25**, 85; **8:19–22**, 136; **8:20**, 107; **8:21**, 81, 113; **8:22–27**, 112; **8:23**, 19, 41, 42, 72, 107, 111, 115; **8:24**, 27; **8:27**, 133, 177; **8:29**, 19, 24, 42, 115; **8:29–30**, 83; **8:32**, 42, 43, 251; **8:34**, 21, 54, 87, 117, 252; **8:35**, 25, 125; **8:39**, 265; **9–11**, 78, 84; **9:1**, 35, 39, 42, 209; **9:3**, 57, 93; **9:4**, 55, 19, 214; **9:6**, 93; **9:17**, 143; **9:32–33**, 147; **10:5**, 79; **10:9**, 106; **10:11**, 143; **10:12**, 87; **10:13**, 98; **10:14–17**, 139; **10:15**, 163; **10:19**, 79; **11:1**, 214; **11:1–2**, 88; **11:3**, 163; **11:8**, 78, 85, 98; **11:13**, 8, 20, 81, 139; **11:14**, 80; **11:15**, 181; **11:25**, 78; **11:25–26**, 80, 181; **12:1**, 116; **12:2**, 85, 116; **12:3**, 18, 229; **12:4–8**, 135; **12:12**, 25; **12:13**, 177; **12:16**, 261; **12:18**, 263; **13:4**, 148; **13:11–14**, 129; **13:12**, 51; **13:13**, 247, 258; **14:8**, 116; **14:10**, 21, 36, 116, 117, 129; **14:12**, 116; **14:13**, 147; **14:14**, 147; **14:15**, 147, 149; **14:18**, 116; **14:20**, 149; **14:20–21**, 147; **14:22–23**, 149; **15:5**, 24, 31, 261; **15:5–13**, 106; **15:8**, 55; **15:9–11**, 30, 189; **15:15**, 229; **15:15–16**, 18; **15:18**, 251; **15:19**, 173, 198, 199, 232;

15:19–20, 20; **15:20**, 10, 198, 199, 232; **15:22–24**, 28, 173; **15:23**, 20; **15:24**, 20, 199; **15:25**, 177; **15:26**, 173, 176, 177; **15:26–27**, 174; **15:27**, 181; **15:28**, 20, 173, 199; **15:30–31**, 30; **15:31**, 177, 189; **15:33**, 31, 263; **16:1**, 22; **16:1–2**, 67; **16:3–23**, 264; **16:5**, 264; **16:7**, 91, 217; **16:10**, 264; **16:11**, 264; **16:14**, 264; **16:15**, 264; **16:16**, 263; **16:17**, 149, 266; **16:20**, 50, 51, 263, 264; **16:23**, 266

1 Corinthians **1:1**, 22, 178; **1:2**, 229; **1:3**, 21; **1:4**, 135; **1:8**, 54, 130; **1:8–9**, 41; **1:9**, 39; **1:10**, 4, 262; **1:10–12**, 1, 13, 199; **1:10–4:21**, 213; **1:12**, 242; **1:16**, 20, 266; **1:17–2:5**, 197; **1:18**, 54, 92, 139; **1:22**, 233; **1:23**, 134, 147, 226; **1:23–24**, 226; **1:24**, 204; **1:30**, 142, 204; **1:31**, 36, 98, 200; **2:1–2**, 39; **2:1–4**, 226; **2:2**, 135; **2:3**, 171, 213; **2:3–4**, 1, 225, 226; **2:4**, 54; **2:4–5**, 68; **2:5**, 226; **2:6**, 85; **2:8**, 85; **2:11**, 81; **2:12**, 81; **2:12–15**, 130; **2:14**, 81; **3:3**, 247; **3:9**, 57, 139, 142; **3:10**, 229; **3:12–15**, 116; **3:13–15**, 117; **3:15**, 168; **3:16**, 81, 158; **3:16–17**, 128; **3:17**, 159; **3:18**, 85; **4:3–5**, 35, 117, 246; **4:4–5**, 35, 117, 118, 121, 130; **4:5**, 36; **4:6**, 248; **4:8–10**, 95; **4:8–13**, 178, 226; **4:8–17**, 1, 27; **4:9**, 29, 61, 90; **4:9–13**, 26; **4:10**, 213; **4:10–12**, 234; **4:10–13**, 125; **4:11–12**, 234; **4:11–13**, 104; **4:13**, 240; **4:14**, 151; **4:15**, 151; **4:17**, 19, 257; **4:18**, 248; **4:19**, 248; **4:21**, 43, 168, 247, 251; **5:1–13**, 47; **5:2**, 248; **5:5**, 48, 50, 54; **5:9**, 1, 36, 45; **5:10–11**, 258; **6:1–2**, 177; **6:2**, 177; **6:6**, 152; **6:11**, 81; **6:19**, 110; **6:19–20**, 128; **7:5**, 50, 51; **7:10**, 25, 54; **7:11**, 137; **7:12**, 179; **7:12–15**, 152; **7:22**, 135; **7:28**, 25; **7:34**, 157; **7:39**, 135; **7:40**, 81; **8:1**, 248; **8:7**, 147, 157; **8:9**, 147; **8:10**, 147; **8:11**, 149; **9:1**, 17, 86, 88, 134, 222, 223; **9:1–2**, 18; **9:1–3**, 254; **9:1–18**, 13, 233, 244; **9:2**, 59; **9:3**, 245; **9:8–10**, 258; **9:12**, 66; **9:13–14**, 56; **9:14**, 207; **9:15**, 66, 209, 234; **9:15–17**, 209; **9:15–18**, 34; **9:16**, 22, 119, 255; **9:18**, 66; **9:19**, 87; **9:19–20**, 80; **9:19–22**, 118; **9:20**, 217; **10:1–13**, 56, 156; **10:1–14**, 97; **10:6–10**, 249; **10:6–13**, 253; **10:9–10**, 64, 85; **10:10**, 56; **10:13**, 39; **10:25**, 35; **10:26**, 98; **10:27**, 35, 152; **10:29**, 35; **11:1**, 140, 179, 223; **11:11**, 135; **11:23**, 125; **11:25**, 71; **11:28**, 253; **11:30**, 43; **12:3**, 81; **12:4–6**, 267; **12:12–13**, 41; **12:12–31**, 135; **12:19–21**, 43; **12:28**, 264; **13:4**, 248; **13:12**, 36, 100, 115, 116, 118; **14:14**, 58; **14:16**, 41; **14:18**, 122; **14:22–24**, 152; **14:23**, 267; **14:33**, 248; **14:36**, 93; **15:1–5**, 132; **15:1–8**, 223; **15:1–11**, 86, 216; **15:3**, 142; **15:5–7**, 35; **15:8**, 222; **15:8–11**, 17; **15:9**, 36; **15:9–10**, 18, 65, 70, 83; **15:10**, 175, 216, 229; **15:12**, 95; **15:12–19**, 181; **15:20**, 106; **15:20–28**, 85; **15:20–58**, 129; **15:22**, 135; **15:23**, 52, 110; **15:25**, 21, 54, 87, 117, 252; **15:25–28**, 54; **15:27**, 100; **15:32**, 28; **15:33**, 159; **15:42–50**, 112; **15:43**, 108; **15:45**, 135; **15:50–55**, 128; **15:51–52**, 127; **15:51–54**, 112; **15:52**, 114; **15:53–54**, 113; **15:54**, 48, 114; **15:55**, 33; **15:58**, 135; **16:1–4**, 35, 46, 174, 177; **16:2**, 179; **16:3**, 37; **16:3–4**, 37, 181; **16:5**, 52; **16:5–7**, 14, 37, 38; **16:5–9**, 2, 4; **16:9**, 52; **16:10**, 18; **16:10–11**, 19, 67, 257; **16:15**, 20, 266; **16:17–18**, 53; **16:18**, 170; **16:19**, 266; **16:19–20**, 264; **16:20**, 263; **16:22**, 229; **16:23**, 264

2 Corinthians **1–9**, 7, 15, 47, 205, 242; **1:1**, 8, 17, 178; **1:1–2**, 189; **1:2**, 137; **1:3**, 31, 264; **1:3–7**, 106; **1:3–11**, 30, 31, 106, 189, 240; **1:4**, 46; **1:5**, 223; **1:8**, 19, 25, 160, 191; **1:8–11**, 104; **1:9–11**, 106; **1:12**, 93, 246; **1:13**, 5, 34; **1:13–15**, 265; **1:14**, 54, 189; **1:15–16**, 2, 14, 37; **1:17**, 38; **1:18**, 35, 38, 39, 118, 209; **1:18–22**, 42, 59, 266, 267; **1:19**, 18, 19, 43, 55; **1:20**, 114, 163; **1:23**, 2, 14, 168, 209; **1:24**, 18, 22, 176, 189, 206, 208, 257; **2:1**, 2, 37, 242; **2:1–5**, 236; **2:2**, 189; **2:3**, 2, 265; **2:3–4**, 1, 42; **2:4**, 2, 25, 94; **2:5**, 2, 12, 50; **2:5–11**, 3; **2:6**, 48, 251; **2:6–7**, 18, 46, 206; **2:7**, 209, 236, 241; **2:11**, 154; **2:12**, 135; **2:12–13**, 3, 89, 219; **2:14**, 54, 61, 62, 63, 64, 82, 84, 90, 99, 106, 117, 163, 223, 224, 238; **2:14–16**, 94, 246; **2:14–17**, 83, 223; **2:14–3:18**, 239; **2:14–4:6**, 88,

2 Corinthians

106, 124, 223, 267; **2:14–7:4**, 5, 59, 62; **2:15**, 18, 48, 206; **2:16**, 76, 89, 93, 229, 239, 241; **2:17**, 5, 93, 106, 115, 163, 206, 207, 223, 251; **3:1**, 12, 15, 94, 103, 181, 206, 246; **3:1–6**, 20, 131, 233; **3:1–18**, 12; **3:2**, 119, 150, 160; **3:3**, 18, 55, 71, 69, 81, 95, 205, 265; **3:5**, 65, 83, 241; **3:6**, 71, 72, 73, 78, 80, 82, 136, 205, 235, 241; **3:7**, 74, 86, 99, 102; **3:7–11**, 73; **3:7–18**, 108; **3:11**, 76, 78; **3:13**, 99, 102; **3:14**, 78, 79, 80, 85, 135, 136; **3:15**, 79, 85; **3:16**, 54; **3:17**, 81; **3:18**, 88, 96, 100, 106, 115, 162, 189, 261; **4:1–2**, 83; **4:1–6**, 83; **4:2**, 35, 93, 159; **4:4**, 51, 88, 99; **4:6**, 64, 103, 106, 134, 136; **4:7**, 117; **4:7–18**, 26; **4:7ff.**, 29; **4:8–9**, 28, 125; **4:8–12**, 231; **4:10**, 223; **4:10–11**, 61, 106; **4:10–12**, 26; **4:14**, 32, 51, 114; **4:15**, 30; **4:16**, 126; **4:17**, 25; **5:1**, 108, 111, 129, 162, 230; **5:1–2**, 128; **5:1–5**, 109; **5:1–10**, 127; **5:2**, 112; **5:3**, 14, 113, 117; **5:4**, 48, 129; **5:4–5**, 42; **5:6**, 235; **5:7**, 116; **5:8**, 110; **5:10**, 21, 35, 36, 118, 121, 139, 246; **5:10–12**, 146; **5:11**, 35, 42, 117, 138; **5:11–15**, 103; **5:12**, 5, 20, 102, 135, 210, 230; **5:13**, 131; **5:14**, 142; **5:15**, 135; **5:16**, 87, 141, 205; **5:16ff.**, 143; **5:17**, 14, 88, 107; **5:18**, 123, 136, 145, 172; **5:18–19**, 22, 262; **5:18–20**, 253; **5:18–21**, 137; **5:19**, 21, 64, 115, 117, 138, 140, 152; **5:20**, 22, 66, 82, 177, 201, 250; **5:21**, 123, 141; **6:1**, 21, 51, 139, 141, 159; **6:2**, 143, 166; **6:3**, 147; **6:3–13**, 147; **6:4**, 25, 51, 235; **6:4–10**, 26, 125, 231; **6:5**, 248; **6:6**, 51; **6:8**, 5, 134; **6:9**, 240; **6:10**, 236; **6:11**, 23, 244; **6:11–12**,159; 159; **6:11–13**, 189; **6:12–13**, 60; **6:13**, 243, 244; **6:14**, 86, 152, 153, 154, 161; **6:14–16**, 51, 65, 79; **6:14–7:1**, 20, 142, 151, 157, 163, 258, 259; **6:15**, 50, 86, 152, 154, 161, 262; **6:16**, 111, 127, 128, 156, 158, 230; **6:16–17**, 263; **6:16–18**, 22, 71, 155, 157, 162; **6:17**, 156, 163; **6:18**, 24, 40, 157, 161, 264; **7:1**, 20, 40, 55, 131, 157, 163; **7:2**, 158, 159, 189; **7:4**, 5, 265; **7:4–5**, 25; **7:5**, 3, 45; **7:5–16**, 258; **7:6**, 24, 166; **7:6–7**, 44; **7:7**, 261; **7:8ff.**, 42; **7:9**, 261; **7:9–10**, 174; **7:10**, 48, 167; **7:12**, 2, 12; **7:13**, 261; **7:14**, 265; **7:14–16**, 3; **7:16**, 5, 261, 265; 8, 174; **8–9**, 172, 188, 243, 245; **8–11**, 47, 236; **8:1**, 160, 262; **8:1–2**, 3; **8:1–24**, 174, 184; **8:2**, 25, 180; **8:3**, 180; **8:4**, 19, 37, 189; **8:5**, 179; **8:6**, 58, 257; **8:6–7**, 19, 37; **8:9**, 208, 265; **8:14**, 188; **8:16–17**, 189, 262; **8:16–24**, 257; **8:20–21**, 159; **8:22–24**, 67; **8:23**, 206; **9:1**, 189; **9:2**, 8, 172; **9:3–5**, 257; **9:5**, 38; **9:7**, 236; **9:8**, 175; **9:9–10**, 174; **9:12**, 189; **9:13**, 189; **10–13**, 7, 44, 89, 193, 200, 203, 242; **10:1**, 6; **10:1–2**, 214; **10:2**, 38; **10:4**, 2; **10:5–6**, 49; **10:8**, 43, 119; **10:10**, 76, 198; **10:12–18**, 8, 12, 15, 209; **10:13–15**, 2; **10:13–16**, 10, 20; **10:15**, 10, 199, 216; **10:17**, 36, 93, 98, 216; **11:1–4**, 12; **11:3**, 14, 159, 211; **11:3–4**, 51; **11:4**, 12, 13, 68, 210; **11:5**, 12, 13, 44, 235; **11:6**, 198; **11:7ff.**, 66; **11:7–8**, 159; **11:7–11**, 35; **11:8–9a**, 234; **11:9**, 234; **11:10**, 39, 234; **11:13**, 44, 216; **11:13–15**, 18, 79, 196; **11:14**, 50, 58; **11:15**, 12, 116; **11:16–17**, 119; **11:17**, 93; **11:20**, 13, 243; **11:21**, 119, 203; **11:21–23**, 231; **11:22**, 11; **11:22–23**, 12; **11:22–33**, 213; **11:23**, 13, 148, 210, 216, 235; **11:23–29**, 231; **11:23–33**, 28; **11:23b–29**, 130, 220, 237; **11:26**, 210; **11:26b**, 219; **11:28**, 45; **11:29**, 149; **11:30**, 63, 231; **11:31**, 35, 39, 209; **11:33**, 221; **12:1**, 12, 66, 231; **12:1ff.**, 62, 223, 225; **12:1–4**, 238; **12:1–10**, 89, 213, 221, 239; **12:2**, 115; **12:2–4**, 64, 111, 223, 224, 237, 238; **12:3**, 115; **12:5**, 63, 119; **12:7**, 29, 50, 51, 224, 228, 230, 239; **12:7–9**, 201; **12:9**, 33, 225, 228, 239, 252, 255, 265; **12:10**, 231, 252, 255; **12:11**, 15, 46, 206; **12:13–15**, 153; **12:13–18**, 159; **12:14–15**, 7, 262; **12:14–18**, 195; **12:15**, 255; **12:16–17**, 15; **12:17–18**, 257; **12:18**, 38; **12:19**, 84, 251; **12:19–21**, 49; **12:20**, 4, 7, 262; **12:20–21**, 243; **12:21**, 167, 168; **13:1**, 35, 243, 249; **13:1–2**, 44; **13:1–4**, 252; **13:2**, 256; **13:3**, 255; **13:4**, 26, 255; **13:5**, 146, 242, 265; **13:10**, 2, 242; **13:11**, 4, 31, 160, 256, 261, 262, 263, 264, 265; **13:11–13**, 260; **13:12**, 242; **13:13**, 31; **13:14**, 267

Galatians 1:1, 22, 106, 140, 172; 1:4, 85, 142; 1:6–9, 12, 205, 210; 1:8–9, 235; 1:10, 235; 1:12, 17, 140, 223; 1:13–16, 134; 1:14, 216; 1:15, 22, 229; 1:15–16, 17, 18, 39, 83, 143, 166; 1:16, 86, 88, 138, 223; 1:17, 220; 1:20, 39, 209; 1:22, 135; 2:1, 183, 238; 2:1–10, 12, 15, 173; 2:3, 58; 2:4, 210, 219; 2:5, 255; 2:6, 120; 2:6–7, 199; 2:7–9, 9; 2:9, 206, 229; 2:9–10, 178; 2:10, 9; 2:11–12, 205; 2:11–14, 10, 12, 15, 235; 2:12, 2; 2:14, 255; 2:17, 135; 2:19–20, 123; 2:20, 125, 172, 195; 3:1, 26, 105, 150; 3:1–5, 95; 3:1–14, 12; 3:8, 8, 214; 3:10, 72, 96; 3:10–14, 81; 3:13, 134, 141; 3:13–14, 179; 3:16, 55, 214; 3:21, 55; 3:26, 40, 135; 3:26–27, 128; 3:27, 135; 3:29, 40, 215; 4:1–7, 12, 40, 81, 128; 4:4, 144; 4:4–6, 41, 267; 4:6, 19, 31, 81; 4:9, 118; 4:12–20, 228, 240; 4:15, 240; 4:21–31, 81; 4:26–27, 111; 5:5, 129; 5:6, 135; 5:10, 135; 5:11, 147; 5:13, 210; 5:19–21, 258; 5:20, 247; 6:1, 48; 6:6–10, 192; 6:7–8, 186; 6:7–10, 129; 6:15, 136; 6:16, 263; 6:17, 26, 105; 6:18, 264

Ephesians 1:1, 22; 1:3–14, 24; 1:14, 41; 1:14–18, 137; 1:17, 31; 1:21, 85; 1:23, 135; 2:2, 51, 85; 2:7, 85; 2:14, 98; 3:16, 126; 4:4–6, 267; 4:4–16, 135; 4:8, 62; 4:22, 159; 4:31, 258; 5:3–5, 258; 5:22–33, 204; 5:23, 135; 6:5, 171; 6:10–18, 51; 6:11, 51; 6:14–17, 195

Philippians 1:1, 19; 1:6, 54; 1:8, 42; 1:17, 25; 1:19, 30, 81; 1:21–24, 116; 1:29, 108; 1:29–30, 175; 2:1, 265; 2:2, 261; 2:5–11, 179; 2:6, 89; 2:6–11, 131; 2:7, 87; 2:8, 141; 2:9, 21, 54; 2:9–11, 80, 252; 2:12, 131, 171; 2:12–13, 263; 2:12–18, 129; 2:16, 36, 54; 2:17, 244; 2:18, 261; 2:19–24, 19; 2:19–26, 29; 2:20–22, 19; 2:22, 49; 2:25, 183, 207, 210; 3:1, 261; 3:2, 210; 3:3, 29, 81; 3:5, 214; 3:5–11, 230; 3:7–11, 134; 3:10, 26; 3:10–11, 104, 135, 252; 3:16, 261; 3:17, 140; 3:19, 101; 3:20, 129; 3:20–21, 115, 129; 3:21, 99, 108; 4:2, 261; 4:3, 161; 4:4, 261; 4:9, 31, 263; 4:10–19, 176; 4:10–20, 207; 4:12, 125, 234; 4:13, 229; 4:14, 25; 4:15, 150; 4:16, 264; 4:17, 243; 4:18, 116; 4:19, 187; 4:21, 264

Colossians 1:1, 19, 22; 1:15, 89; 1:15–20, 101; 1:18, 135; 1:22–23, 147; 1:24, 135; 1:25, 93; 2:3, 124; 2:12, 172; 2:16–19, 135; 2:18, 227; 2:21, 163; 3:5–8, 258; 3:9–10, 107; 3:15, 135; 3:20, 116; 3:22, 131; 3:23–24, 131; 4:3, 52; 4:7–9, 67; 4:10, 67, 91, 217; 4:10–15, 264

1 Thessalonians 1:1, 19; 1:6, 25, 54, 140, 175, 179; 1:9, 80; 1:10, 39, 106; 2:5, 42; 2:9–12, 207; 2:10, 42; 2:12, 172; 2:13, 54; 2:14, 135, 175; 2:14–15, 175; 2:14–16, 77, 218, 236; 2:18, 50, 51, 54; 2:19, 36, 129, 160; 3:2, 19; 3:3, 25; 3:3–4, 175; 3:5, 51; 3:6, 19; 3:7, 25; 3:12–13, 229; 3:13, 129, 130; 4:8, 172; 4:9, 184; 4:10, 266; 4:13–18, 108, 127; 4:17, 115, 224; 5:1, 184; 5:2, 54; 5:5, 162; 5:8, 51, 195; 5:10, 116, 142; 5:12, 135; 5:13, 263; 5:14, 266; 5:16, 261; 5:18, 135; 5:23, 31, 130, 263; 5:24, 39; 5:25, 30; 5:26, 263; 5:28, 264

2 Thessalonians 1:4, 25; 1:6, 25; 2:9, 50; 3:16, 263

1 Timothy 1:9–10, 258; 1:17, 101; 1:20, 50; 4:5, 93; 5:15, 50; 5:18, 143; 6:4–5, 258

2 Timothy 2:14, 93; 2:19, 56; 2:25, 167; 3:2–4, 258; 3:8–9, 19

Titus 1:5, 58; 1:7, 258; 2:5, 93; 3:3, 258

Philemon 1, 19; 7, 170; 22, 30; 23, 91, 217, 264; 25, 264

1 Peter 5:14, 263

2 Peter 3:16, 36

1 John 2:1, 127

Jude 11, 56

Revelation 2:17, 192; 3:4–5, 112; 6:11, 112; 7:9, 112; 7:13, 112; 7:14, 112; 18:4, 155

Scripture Index

APOCRYPHA

Baruch **1:19–20**, 78, 98

Judith **2:28**, 171; **15:2**, 171

1 Maccabees **2:26**, 54, 204; **5:65**, 195; **8:10**, 175, 195

2 Maccabees **1:4**, 137; **4–5**, 164; **7:31**, 235; **7:33**, 137; **8:29**, 137; **14:24**, 49

4 Maccabees **7:11**, 92; **9:22**, 211

Sirach (Ecclesiasticus) **7:3**, 186; **13:2**, 153; **13:17–18**, 153; **14:11**, 180; **15:14–17**, 126; **33:10**, 103; **33:13**, 103; **35:8**, 187; **45:5**, 93; **45:18**, 57, 205, 247; **45:23–24**, 204; **49:8**, 89; **49:10**, 28; **51:25**, 150

Tobit **13:1–17**, 190; **13:6**, 80; **14:6**, 85

Wisdom of Solomon **1:6**, 56; **2:23–24**, 204; **6:4**, 148; **7:25–26**, 100; **9:15–16**, 127; **18:20–25**, 48; **18:22**, 48; **18:23**, 48; **18:25**, 48

PSEUDEPIGRAPHA

Apocalypse of Abraham **13:14**, 112; **16:1–4**, 118; **17:4–18:1**, 63; **23**, 204; **31:6–10**, 191

Apocalypse of Moses **31:1**, 129; **31:4**, 124; **32:4**, 129; **37:3–5**, 224; **37:5**, 224; **40:1**, 224

Ascension of Isaiah **1:8–9**, 161; **2:4**, 161; **3:11**, 161; **3:13**, 161; **4:2**, 161; **4:4**, 161; **4:14**, 161; **4:16**, 161; **4:18**, 161; **5:1**, 161; **7:25**, 120

2 Baruch **29:8**, 192; **48:6**, 110; **68:5**, 191; **72:2–6**, 191; **73:1–74:4**, 139

1 Enoch **14:8**, 239; **14:8–25**, 224; **30:12**, 129; **45:3–5**, 139; **45:4–5**, 136; **46:3**, 124; **60:2**, 71, 91; **62:15–16**, 112; **69:6**, 204; **71:11**, 118, 122; **71:11–12**, 63; **72:1**, 13; **90:20**, 91

2 Enoch **8:1–3**, 64, 224; **22:7–10**, 128; **22:8**, 129; **29:4–5**, 212; **31:6**, 204; **66:6**, 148

3 Enoch **22:11**, 9; **24:1**, 91

Ezekiel the Tragedian, *Exagoge* **7**, 235; **12**, 235; **35**, 235; **43**, 23; **107**, 235

4 Ezra **2:39**, 112; **2:45**, 112; **3:19**, 97; **3:31**, 97; **3:36–37**, 97; **10:29–30**, 118; **10:34**, 118; **14:4–6**, 240; **14:44–46**, 240

Joseph and Asenath **11:10**, 139

Jubilees **1:15**, 80; **1:17**, 110, 128; **1:20**, 86, 161; **1:22–24**, 71; **1:23**, 80; **1:24**, 55; **4:26**, 136; **15:33**, 161

Life of Adam and Eve **9**, 204; **9:1**, 211; **12–16**, 212

Lives of the Prophets **4:6**, 154

Psalms of Solomon **5:16–17**, 187; **17:30–35**, 191; **17:30**, 152; **17:31**, 190

Pseudo-Philo, *Biblical Antiquities* **16**, 205; **57:1–3**, 56; **59:2**, 120

Sibylline Oracles **3:63**, 161; **3:63–74**, 86; **3:73**, 161; **3:161**, 175; **3:172**, 175; **3:188–190**, 175; **3:290–294**, 180; **3:610**, 175; **3:741–762**, 139; **3:772–775**, 190; **3:785–795**, 139; **5:414–419**, 191; **5:420–425**, 110

Testament of Benjamin **9:2**, 191

Testament of Dan **5:1**, 161; **5:2**, 263; **5:10–11**, 161

Testament of Gad **5:7**, 172

Testament of Joseph **1:4**, 221; **20:2**, 161

Testament of Judah **24:3**, 55, 157

Testament of Levi **3:3**, 161; **3:4**, 111, 224; **8:2**, 128; **18:12**, 161; **19:1**, 161

Testament of Moses **1:14**, 65

Testament of Reuben **4:7**, 86; **4:11**, 86; **5:6**, 211

Testament of Zebulon **9:7**, 139; **9:8**, 191

RABBINIC LITERATURE

Mishnah: *Hagiga* **2:1**, 225; *Sanhedrin* **10:3**, 98

Babylonian Talmud: *Berakoth* **12b**, 161; **13a**, 161; **13b**, 161; **14b**, 161; **32a**, 94; **32b**, 98; **61a**, 126; **61b**, 161; *Megilla* **16b**, 238; **17a**, 238; *Sanhedrin* **80b**, 225; **94b**, 161; **106b**, 120; **110a**, 205, 247; **110b**, 98, 210; **111b**, 154; *Shabbath* **89a**, 50, 92; *Sotah* **16a**, 111; *Sukkah* **5b**, 111; **52a**, 94; **52b**, 126; *Ta'anit* **7a**, 103; *Yebamoth* **47b**, 161; **49b**, 100; **103b**, 204; *Yoma* **44a**, 111; **53a**, 111; **67b**, 111

Midrash Rabbah Deuteronomy **3:15**, 13; **6:14**, 94

Midrash Rabbah Ecclesiastes **1:9**, 192; **2:1**, 95; **9:24**, 94

Midrash Rabbah Exodus **2:6**, 238; **28:1**, 63; **42:3**, 72, 128; **42:9**, 77, 98; **43:2**, 138; **43:8**, 62; **46:4**, 126

Midrash Rabbah Genesis **3:9**, 125; **8:10**, 89, 100; **19:9**, 125; **20:12**, 129; **26:6**, 126; **35:3**, 238; **54:4**, 111; **67:7**, 161; **68:5**, 238; **68:11**, 238; **98:12**, 161; **98:15**, 238; **99:1**, 111

Midrash Rabbah Leviticus **1:14**, 100; **17:4**, 24; **29:3**, 130; **29:4**, 130; **29:6**, 130; **29:9**, 130; **29:10**, 130; **31:5**, 201; **34:16**, 19; **35:5**, 94, 95, 126

Midrash Rabbah Numbers **9:26**, 111; **9:32**, 111; **9:42**, 111; **10:24**, 111; **13:16**, 161; **14:6**, 161; **15:16**, 94; **18:1**, 94; **18:12**, 205; **18:20**, 210; **18:21**, 161; **19:26**, 161; **20:23**, 161; **22:7**, 202

Midrash Rabbah Ruth **3:1**, 126

Midrash Psalms **68:19**, 63, 195

Pesiqta de Rab Kahana **15:1:1**, 125, 145

Pesiqta Rabbati **10:6**, 99, 102

Pirqe Rabbi Eliezer **13:1**, 204

QUMRAN

CD **4.12–19**, 86; **4.13**, 162; **4.15**, 162; **5.8**, 162; **6.19**, 96; **8.21**, 96; **9.16–23**, 250; **14.18–19**, 141; **19.34**, 96; **20.12**, 96

1QH **1.15**, 103; **3.21**, 103; **3.23–25**, 124; **5.22**, 190; **10.14**, 31; **11.29**, 31; **12.5**, 99; **13.20–15.5**, 57; **13.20–22**, 90

1QpHab **5.8–12**, 57; **12.3**, 190

1QM **14.4–5**, 31

1QS **1.16–2.8**, 162; **1.17**, 162; **1.23–24**, 86, 162; **2.19**, 86; **4.20–22**, 75; **7.15–18**, 58; **7.24–25**, 58; **11.21–22**, 103

11QTemple **15.1**, 126; **17.12**, 126; **29.7–10**, 128; **29.8–10**, 110

JOSEPHUS

Against Apion **2.168–169**, 97; **2.171–178**, 96

Antiquities **1.166**, 97, 120; **3.104**, 176; **3.106**, 180; **3.107**, 176; **3.315**, 137, 138; **4.14–19**, 248; **4.14**, 198, 247; **4.15**, 247; **4.17**, 247; **4.22**, 218; **4.23**, 248; **4.41**, 56; **4.42**, 235; **4.46**, 56, 250, 257; **4.73**, 257; **4.76**, 257; **5.68**, 238; **7.120**, 201; **7.257**, 211; **8.107**, 111, 128; **8.117**, 120; **7.120**, 146; **8.114**, 128; **8.140**, 13; **7.186**, 120; **8.267**, 211; **10.114**, 122; **11.133**, 98; **12.165**, 146; **12.171**, 146; **13.35**, 120; **13.84**, 130; **13.85**, 120; **13.195**, 120; **13.260**, 146; **13.288**, 120; **14.8**, 120; **14.164**, 120; **14.198**, 146; **14.251**, 146; **14.378**, 191; **14.404**, 120; **15.81**, 120; **15.385–387**, 175; **16.267**, 120;

17.201, 130; **17.290,** 120; **18.81–84,** 258; **20.162,** 120

War **1.219,** 191; **2.122,** 191; **2.146–147,** 58; **2.308,** 218; **2.360,** 175; **2.365,** 175; **2.387,** 175; **7.56,** 120

PHILO

Embassy to Gaius **80,** 211; **210,** 96; **293,** 186; **346,** 211; **353,** 240

Life of Moses **1.258,** 146, 201; **2.70,** 97, 99, 102; **2.166,** 137; **2.176–177,** 278, 247; **2.271,** 77, 98; **2.284,** 56

On the Change of Names **268–269,** 186

On the Confusion of Tongues **21,** 186; **152,** 186

On Dreams **2.47,** 192; **2.76,** 186; **2.83,** 161

On Joseph 134–136, 175

On the Special Laws **4.149,** 96

Questions on Exodus **2.49,** 138

Questions on Genesis **1.24,** 12, 121

Who is the Heir? **24–29,** 201

CHURCH FATHERS

1 Clement **4:12,** 247, 262; **5:6,** 216, 235; **5:1,** 262; **46:5,** 247; **47:1–7,** 263; **51:1–4,** 262; **63:2,** 262

Eusebius, *Demonstration of the Gospel* **4:15:33,** 42, 91, 92; **5:3:9,** 92